MORETON BAY SCOTS

1841-59

John H.G. Mackenzie-Smith

This publication is supported through Brisbane City Council's Local History Grants Program

Church Archivists' Press

First published in 2000

© John Mackenzie-Smith 2000

All rights reserved. Apart from fair dealing for the purposes of private study, research or review as permitted by the Copyright Act, no part of this book may be reproduced or transmitted in any form or by any means without prior written permission from the publisher.

ISBN 1-876194-19-7

Cover design by Show-Ads Omega Pty Ltd

Published by Church Archivists' Press,
PO Box 130, Virginia, Q. 4014

Typeset & Printed by Toowoomba Education Centre,
January, 2000

CONTENTS

Foreword .... *v*

Preface .... *vii*

Acknowledgements .... *xiv*

Illustrations .... *xvi*

Chapter 1
Pioneer Scottish pastoralism 1841-48 1

Chapter 2
Pioneer urban Scots 1841-48 43

Chapter 3
Scots and the 'cultural desert' 1841-48 93

Chapter 4
The Lang factor 1849-59 135

Chapter 5
W.A. Duncan and material, moral Brisbane 1849-59 193

Chapter 6
The Scottish presence 1841-59 237

Bibliography 255

Table and maps 264

Index 269

FOREWORD

I am extremely pleased to write a Foreword to *Moreton Bay Scots 1841 – 59*. I have read the complete manuscript of this work, which was sent to me by the author prior to its publication.

When I commenced the reading, I knew that I would be interested in it, but 'interest' is too mild a word to reflect the grip which this book, written by John Mackenzie-Smith, has had upon me. It consists of a Preface, and six well-researched yet highly readable chapters, which closely examine and rationally analyse the involvement of Scots in the Moreton Bay district of the Colony of New South Wales from 1841, when the region was thrown open for free settlement and the first Scottish pastoralists came to occupy the land there, until Queensland became a separate colony itself in 1859.

The author claims to fill the void in Queensland history concerning the contributions to its development made by the Scots before 1860, and he does his job admirably with an intelligent and sympathetic approach, but with impartiality. It would be an understatement for me to say that the book fascinated me, another word too moderate and too often carelessly used these days to express the influence it has had on one's mind. As the author says, "A Scot is defined as a person who was born in Scotland or was born elsewhere to one Scottish parent".

Dr Mackenzie-Smith recounts the parts played by the Scottish migrants in the early days of the Moreton Bay district (the Northern District), and it would not do credit to his text were I to write of any specific occasions on which an individual group made any particular contribution to the growth of the Northern District.

Not only is the content of this book based on careful and intelligent research, but all the sources to which the author has had recourse are fully shown. The footnotes, as one would expect in a work such as this, are numerous, and illustrate the author's searching historical explorations which are there for readers and students of this significant period of early Queensland history to read, follow up and check. If the footnotes show an openness and a complete subservience to factual research, the immense bibliography is itself a true indication of the many sources to which the author has had reference.

In short, let me say that this is a publication which should be read by those who might claim to profess any knowledge of the development of Queensland. I have no doubt that all Queensland historians and students of Queensland history will read this work with considerable respect and approbation.

In the final chapter: "The Scottish Presence", the author comments without any show of partisanship, on the values and on the behaviour of the Scots who migrated to Queensland, concluding that the society at Moreton Bay was 'a prosperous and respectable one, largely attributed to (the) Scottish Protestant Ethic', and that the Scottish contribution to the establishment of a colony espousing democratic principles and practices was, considering their small number immeasurable. This persuasive and erudite work has convinced me of the truth of the above judgements, and I thoroughly commend this work to all, particularly to those who are genuinely interested in the history of the earlier years of European settlement in Australia.

Brisbane   [Sir] W. B. Campbell
1 November 1999

PREFACE

Having written a book and several journal articles on prominent pre-separation Scots, I became aware of the high representation of their compatriots in the administrative and economic power structure at Moreton Bay. In vain I searched for a regional study which outlined the apparent disproportionate influence of this small ethnic group upon colonial development. Like those who attempt to ascend unclimbed mountains, I undertook such a study because the data existed and it had not been done before.

This investigation is designed to fill the void which exists in the corpus of Queensland history concerning the contributions of distinguished Scots and their proletarian countrymen to development before 1860. It is neither advisable nor valid to extrapolate from data derived from elsewhere. Rather, this case-study of a discrete geographical area generates its own information which will permit comparisons to be made on the Scottish presence and influence in the British colonies.

In the process of explaining the alleged disproportionate Scottish influence on the broader Australian scene, historians have often attempted to define the elusive Scottish identity and the influences which shaped its formation. Focus on deriving psychic characteristics from a sample of prominent individuals has limited general application because of its skewed social and economic bias. Such methodology may well provide indications of the nature of Scottish leadership and enterprise, but does little to unravel the factors associated with the success of Scottish common folk.

To address this problem, statistical analysis was undertaken of records of assisted migrants who disembarked at Brisbane in that period when the southern goldfields held greater attraction. The collective profile derived in terms of age, marital status, place of origin, occupation, education and religion has complemented the scant biographical data available on common Scottish folk and has revealed definite regional influences operating among the Scots at Moreton Bay.

Unfortunately, the meagre corpus of Queensland research (or even Australian investigation for that matter) into distinguished northern Scots and the lack of work on the Scottish colonial proletariat sheds little light on this formidable problem connected with the Scottish identity. Impulsive categorisation in terms of inadmissable cultural stereotypes invariably overlooks the fact that mid-nineteenth century Scots encompassed the wide variety of personality types found at random in any nation. In fact, their diversity was a full mirror of Scottish society at that time.

Nevertheless, some historians have been willing to go out on a limb, attempting to explain the disproportionate Scottish success in Britain and its Empire in terms of steadiness, reliability, persistence, judgement, lack of deference, clannishness and adaptability.[1] These character traits are claimed to be the outcomes of a superior mass education system and Presbyterianism which Max Weber considered to be the purest form of Calvinism.[2] Others, who have discerned that colonists from other nations, such as the Roman Catholic Irish, demonstrated the same industry, perserverance and energy as the Scots, attribute successful colonisation to the acquisition of the techniques associated with urban capitalism.[3] Still, it should be remembered that Weber argued that Calvinism (and therefore Presbyterianism) was the counterpoint of Capitalism. As products of the Industrial Revolution and Calvinism, it is no coincidence that the predominantly Presbyterian Scots of all ranks were deemed to be 'on the make', concentrating on capital accumulation and eschewing the prospects of remaining employees. Thus many were inordinately successful in acquiring property, amassing profits and attaining the status of employers or managers. No wonder they supposedly made little impact on the ethos of the Australian working class.[4]

The complexity of the problem of unravelling the Scottish identity even challenged Robert Louis Stevenson. He pre-empted by over a century the current practice of describing Scottish characteristics in terms of regions and districts, such as the Gaelic-speaking Highlands, the Anglicised Lowlands, the North-East and the Borders. Stevenson avoided unbalanced centralist labels which were inappropriate for a deeply divided nation. Yet, he noted that such regional jealousies, religious differences and cultural rivalries were invariably cast aside when Scots met overseas, opting for unity based on national pride. He mused:

> Scotland is indefinable: it has no unity except upon the map. Two languages, many dialects, innumerable forms of piety, and countless local patriotisms and prejudices, part us among ourselves more widely than the east and west of that great continent of America. When I am at home, I feel a man from Glasgow to be something like a rival, a man from Barra to be more than half a foreigner. Yet let us meet in some far country ..., some ready-made affection joins us in an instant.[5]

* * *

The Moreton Bay District is defined as that area which comprised the Brisbane and Ipswich electoral areas and police districts in 1856. Geographical boundary markers are the Caboolture River and Glasshouses to the north; the Great Dividing Range in the south; the islands of Moreton Bay to the east and the Conondale Range to the west. The district, which is virtually the Brisbane River flood plain, is clearly marked in the accompanying adaption of Baker's map of 1846.[6]

The most straightforward method of distinguishing Scots from other settlers would be to demonstrate proof of Scottish birth. However, this would eliminate several pioneers who were born in England to Scottish parents, and were regarded as integral to the Scottish community in the colony. David McConnel of Manchester, educated in Edinburgh, married to a Scot and lay-founder of Brisbane's first Presbyterian church, contributed significantly to the Scottish ethnic group at Moreton Bay.[7] For the purposes of this thesis, the principle underlying current requirements for dual British-Australian nationality - descent from one British parent - has been adopted to define Scottish ethnicity. Accordingly a Scot is defined as a person who was born in Scotland or was born elsewhere to at least one Scottish parent.

This study merely aims to unearth the prominent Scots, give recognition to some of the more visible of their humble compatriots and document their contributions to the birth process of the infant colony of Queensland. There is no intention of setting up another 'state of origin' contest by attempting to demonstrate that the Scottish success story was disproportionate compared with the English, Irish, German or Chinese. Such a comparative study can be attempted later by someone with the inclination when the extent and nature of the Scottish contribution has been determined.

This investigation is set in that period between the arrival of the first Scottish squatters in the Moreton Bay District in 1841 and the separation of Queensland from New South Wales in 1859. During that time-frame, the wool industry was founded amidst adversity, the port of Brisbane was established not without opposition, the issue of transportation was finally put to rest and social engineering produced an urban middle class which successfully challenged squatter dominance. Finally, the long tussle for northern independence from the Sydney political and economic stranglehold was attained.

Brisbane's two newspapers, the *Sydney Morning Herald* and the reminiscences of pioneers indicate that 1849 was a watershed in the development of the Moreton Bay District. It was no accident that this date coincided with the direct arrival of John Dunmore Lang's urban and agriculturally-biased settlers of dissenting persuasion, many of whom were blooded in radical English agitation. It was also the period when direct government-assisted immigration commenced at Moreton Bay, after nearly a decade of squatter agitation, to fill the insatiable demands for pastoral labour. Logically the population exploded in accordance with the squatter's expectations. However, according to Lang's plans, the towns grew and consequently his designs for a flourishing Protestant and democratic society had every chance of success.

Lang's biographer, Donald Baker, has stressed the conscious intent to 'foster a social revolution in which increasing numbers of immigrants would throw down the mighty squatters from their seats'.[8] Being one of the few occasions when historians have agreed with Lang's assertions of self-importance, his catalytic claims upon mid-nineteenth century Moreton Bay society are not without foundation. William Coote, Henry Stuart Russell, David Macmillan and Ross Johnston all agree that pastoral domination received its first challenge during this period when the separation movement had gathered momentum and various strong demands to solve the 'immigration-labour issue' were initiated.[9] Allan Morrison echoed Lang's assessment: 'The democratic spirit of the townsmen and the farmers broke the hold the squatters had over the land and produced the democratic community of today'.[10]

For these reasons, the Scottish contribution to the development of Moreton Bay is explored in two eras, before and after 1849. In the 1841-48 period the squatters reigned supreme. During 1849-59 their power over most aspects of northern life was challenged and modified. Designedly, the indomitable John Dunmore Lang turned around the course plotted for Moreton Bay development which was heading inexorably towards oligarchy.

As well as Lang, this volume focuses on the contributions of two other disparate Scotsmen, Evan Mackenzie and William Augustine Duncan. Fortunately these men, particularly Lang and Duncan, have left behind voluminous letters, publications and newspaper articles detailing their thoughts, aspirations and actions. Data derived from these sources, supplemented by information from well raked-over primary sources of Ludwig Leichhardt, the Archers, the Leslies, Thomas Dowse and John Gregor enable valid reconstruction and evaluation of the efforts of prominent Moreton Bay Scots.

Further, this research has drawn heavily on two major sets of papers, one of which has not been utilised by other Queensland historians. Nancy Roberts drew my attention to a series of letters written by James Balfour, Edinburgh merchant and father of the brothers who formed Colinton. Corresponding with Sydney flour-miller Thomas Barker, Balfour outlined the meticulous planning which preceded Scottish forays into pastoralism and detailed the influential Edinburgh network which facilitated that drive. The collection throws fresh light on the Scottish motives leading to the occupation of the Brisbane River Valley in 1841. Moreton Bay's Scottish pioneer pastoralists certainly did not form their runs 50 miles outside Brisbane because the best land on the Darling Downs had been taken up.[11] In addition, the correspondence and diary of William Pettigrew, Lang's surveyor and prominent Brisbane saw-miller, not only provide valuable insights into Pettigrew's business planning and methods, but allow access to the narrow mind and behaviour of a rigidly committed Presbyterian Calvinist.

Identification, recording, categorising and gathering data on Moreton Bay Scots, prominent and humble, was an on-going process throughout the four years of this project. The most useful instruments for this purpose, apart from the passenger lists of direct British immigrants, were Marianne Eastgate's Pre-separation index for Moreton Bay and Rod Fisher's index on Moreton Bay people.[12] However, most of the references led to examination of two major newspapers, the *Moreton Bay Courier* and the *Sydney Morning Herald*. With the aid of these research tools and passenger lists at the Queensland State Archives a data bank of 1128 direct Scottish immigrants and 578 second stage immigrants to Moreton Bay (those who arrived from the south by steamer or overland 1841-59) was created.[13] This source proved useful in providing background information of those Scots encountered in this investigation and enabled the collective identity of the direct Scottish immigrants to be derived.[14]

***

In common with the experience of other colonists in other Australian settlements around the same time, the Moreton Bay Scots gained their livelihoods in communities divided by conflict and complexity. It is postulated that 'there were two structures being produced at the same time, which were not entirely compatible. One was the sharply polarised structure centred on the assignment system in the pastoral industry; the other, the much less polarised structure centred on mercantile capital and small production in towns and gradually extending as wage-labour relations in primary industries'.[15]

The pastoralists, as an integral part of the colonial ruling class at that time, were well developed in class consciousness in contrast to the other groups within society. This was based on their social exclusivity and economic power. While generally seeking to stay outside state control (except when seeking government funds for navigation and internal communication purposes), they attempted to exert hegemony over the districts in which they sought capital accumulation. Often referred to as the 'intelligence and enterprise' of their districts, they sought to entrench their control and maximise their profits through the *plantation system*. This was basically a two-tiered socio-economic structure of squatters and their dependent labour operating within the pastoral holdings with no challenge possible from an excluded third tier of assertive liberal bourgeoisie. It was the attempt to extend this system to the urban centres to maximise their dominance and the immoral ethos that arose from their influence that led to class conflict and the stirrings of democracy. Pastoral capitalism became incompatible with emergent urban capitalism. The attempts to obstruct attendant urban liberalism, while aggressively promoting pastoral hegemony, was at the source of the political struggles which occurred between the two capitalist clusters. These contests, which distinguished the period under consideration, 'were at a deeper level a clash between two orderings of colonial society'.[16]

Thus pastoralism created 'a polarised, patriarchal society in the countryside [and] a deep gulf of status and power separating the workers from the rulers'. Such a social rift was less severe within the towns where a free labour market and liberal individualism flourished, having been bolstered by assisted immigration, an expanding mercantile base, bourgeois assertiveness and responsible government. While the populist radicalism of the working class emerged lethargically as a third political force, plantation capitalism was on a collision course with urban, laissez-faire capitalism. It was inevitable that the commercial bourgeoisie would temporarily assume leadership over and fleetingly harness the raw power of the radical elements among the proletariat. Their anti-establishment radicalism, enshrining faith in democracy, was driven by resentment against class-driven, government-sanctioned oppression (such as the Masters and Servants Act). From this mass action, the stage was set for a vigorous political battle between the 'the people' and 'the monopolists' or squatters.[17] Such was also the nature of class conflict in the Moreton Bay District between 1841 and 1859.

Eminent or unheralded, Moreton Bay Scots between 1841 and 1859 played their parts in establishing the incipient colony on a sound economic, democratic and moral base - largely in cooperation with an identical range of settlers from other national groups. It may well be that the Scottish influence was disproportional and this could be established in another study - especially after the colonial Irish and English contributions have each been detailed. On this occasion, however, it is deemed sufficient just to unearth the magnitude of the Scottish presence and document its accomplishments; a record which undoubtedly stands alone on its own merits.

ENDNOTES

1. Sydney and Olive Checkland, *Industry and ethos: Scotland 1832-1914*, (London: Edward Arnold, 1984), p. 4.
2. Max Weber, *The Protestant ethic and the spirit of capitalism*, (London: Unwin University Books, 1930), p. 2.
3. Duncan Waterson, *Squatter, selector and storekeeper: a history of the Darling Downs 1859-93*, (Canberra: Australian National University Press, 1968), p. 4.
4. Russell Ward, *The Australian legend*, (Melbourne: Melbourne University Press. 1965), p. 43.
5. Ian Bell, *Dreams of exile: Robert Louis Stevenson, a biography*, (New York: Henry Holt, 1992), p. 4.
6. Selected features from Baker's map of Moreton Bay and part of the Darling Downs, Clarence Districts, showing the stations of the squatters in the Northern Districts of New South Wales 1846, Department of Natural Resources, Brisbane. See Appendix.
7. Monica Clough, Highland historian, defined a Scot as anyone who claims to be of that nationality and is accepted by the ethnic community as such. Interview with John Mackenzie-Smith, University of Queensland, 5 January 1995.
8. Donald W. A. Baker, *Days of wrath. A life of John Dunmore Lang*, (Melbourne: Melbourne University Press, 1985), p. 297.
9. W. Ross Johnston, *Brisbane: the first thirty years*, (Brisbane: Boolarong, 1988), p. 142. ; William Coote, *History of the colony of Queensland from 1770 to the close of the year 1881*, (Brisbane: Thorne, 1882); Henry Stuart Russell, *The genesis of Queensland: an account of the first exploration journals to and over the Darling Downs: the earliest days of occupation; the social life; station seeking; the course of discovery northward; and a resume of the causes which led to the separation from New South Wales*, (Sydney: Turner and Henderson, 1888); David S. Macmillan, *John Dunmore Lang*, (Melbourne: Oxford University Press, 1962).
10. Allan Morrison, 'Religion and politics in early Queensland (to 1881)', *Journal of the Royal Historical Society of Queensland*, 4 (1951), p. 459.
11. The Society of Australian Genealogists in Sydney permitted me the rare privilege of

photocopying most of Balfour's significant letters.

12   Marianne Eastgate, *A guide to the pre-separation population index to the Moreton Bay Region 1824-1859 together with a short history of the region*, (Brisbane: Queensland Family History Society, 1990); *A name directory of the Moreton Bay Region of New South Wales 1850-51, 1852-53, 1854-55*, (Brisbane: Queensland Family History Society, 1984,1985); Rod Fisher and John Schiavo, comp. *Moreton Bay in the news: a select newspaper subject index*, 1841-60, (St Lucia: Fryer Library, Queensland, 1999).

13   New South Wales Immigration Agent, Passenger lists, arrival at Moreton Bay 1848-59, micro Z 600, Queensland State Archives [QSA].

14   John Mackenzie-Smith, 'Scottish immigration to Moreton Bay 1848-59', in Rod Fisher and Jennifer Harrison ed., *Brisbane: Immigrants and industries*, Brisbane History Group [BHG] Papers No. 17, 2000 (in preparation).

15   R.W. Connel and T. H. Irving, *Class structure in Australian history*, (Melbourne: Longman Cheshire, 1980), p. 51.

16   Ibid.

17   Ibid, pp. 53, 120.

18   Map: Brisbane ca 1850's, adapted from David Parker, *Strange bedfellows: Rev Charles Stewart, Brisbane's first Baptist minister and the United Evangelical Church, Brisbane*, Research Paper, (Brisbane: Baptist Historical Society of Queensland, 1998), p. 37. Appendix.

19   Maps: Mid-nineteenth century Scotland, comprising selected features from Jennifer Harrison, *Guide to the microform collection of the State Library of Queensland*, (Brisbane: Library Board of Queensland, 1990), p. 146 and Malcolm D. Prentis, *The Scots in Australia*, (Sydney: Sydney University Press, 1983), p. 19 ; Moreton Bay District 1846 after Baker; Brisbane ca 1850's after Parker; Suggested boundary between New South Wales and Queensland,copied from the *Daily Mail*, 26 September 1925. Appendix.

ACKNOWLEDGEMENTS

The names of over 100 people who gave me valuable assistance are too numerous and overwhelming to mention here. Gareth Gillott shared her knowledge gained as a family historian on her ancestor Walter Grieve and the correspondence of another relative, Andrew Watherston, to provide further insight into the pastoral proletariat and the Balfour enterprise. In the same vein, two of my newly-discovered distant relatives Mary McCarthy and Joan Cooper provided me with family history information which added to my knowledge of the Black Isle contingent which accompanied Evan Mackenzie to Australia.

The librarians and archivists of local and Sydney repositories have provided research material with business-like professionalism. No publication which I required was too remote or rare for University of Queensland Reference Librarian Spencer Routh to locate. Ian Hill, Head of the West Search Room at the Scottish Record Office, made an exception and cheerfully conducted important research for me. He confirmed my firm belief that no Highland and Islands Emigration Society ships reached Moreton Bay. This contradicted the equally firm assertions to the contrary by several southern historians.

I am most grateful to Rev. Dr David Parker of the Baptist Historical Society of Queensland who gave permission to practise my creativity upon his informative map of Brisbane in the 1850s. By the addition of some other dominant features of the period, this map has been slightly adapted to suit the particular needs of this study.[18] The adept draftmanship of Damien Cassin of Schlencker Mapping, who created all of the maps found in the appendix, is apparent.[19] Many thanks also to the Library Board of Queensland, Queensland Newspapers, Brisbane Anglican Archives, Education Queensland, the Dixson Galleries, State Library of New South Wales, Rockhampton and Districts Historical Society for permission to reproduce photographs and other illustrations for which they hold the copyright. Further, the Brisbane History Group has kindly consented to my use of the map of Moreton Bay District 1846 after Baker. With similar generosity, the Royal Historical Society of Queensland has given permission for me to research the Pettigrew papers and to publish the results of that effort.

During a couple of periods of ill-health which delayed this project for a year, I received encouragement from many friends, especially from the History department of the University of Queensland then under Associate Professor Ross Johnston. The skills of Dr George D. Fielding, Dr George A. Fielding, Dr Roderick McLeod, Dr Robin Spork, Dr William Robinson, Dr Jeffrey Chick and Dr Tom Donohoe have ensured that I have been physically fit to undertake this demanding work. Also sustaining was the most welcome financial assistance from my University of Queensland Postgraduate Research Scholarship.

From afar, Professor Eric Richards of Flinders University, Highland historian, the late Monica Clough, and Black Isle stalwarts Alasdair and Jeannette Cameron have stuck with me through thick and thin. They have provided constant encouragement and demonstrated intense interest in my work. My wife Jenny has been most tolerant of the long hours spent away from her at libraries and at the computer. She has realised the importance of completing this work to me and even accords it greater significance in the historical world than I would claim. Her assistance in proof-reading has been invaluable. Dr Barry Shaw has always been in the background as a good-natured historical confidant, computer consultant and advisor on written expression. Shirley McCorkindale's proof reading skills have been invaluable.

Emeritus Professor John Laverty, has many valuable suggestions which I have take aboard, especially those regarding the development of early Brisbane. My writing has benefited from his many pertinent and detailed recommendations, particularly those related to points of style. Doctor Rod Fisher, who has already guided me through two theses and one book, has always been prepared to redirect my focus whenever I wandered from the topic. His initimate knowledge of the relevant sources and the scope of the thesis have contributed in no small measure to the final result. In addition, his detailed knowledge of Brisbane's history and constructive comments have been invaluable in shaping this work. I am grateful for his rigorous and unrelenting efforts on my behalf.

ILLUSTRATIONS

Sir Evan Mackenzie - front cover
Brisbane 1864 - back cover

Between pp. 81-92
Sir Thomas Brisbane
Sir Evan Mackenzie
Thomas Archer
Charles Archer
Patrick Leslie 1853
Alexander McDonald
Durundur Station 1844
Newstead House 1853
Captain J.C. Wickham
Rev. John Gregor
John 'Tinker' Campbell
James Davis (Duramboi)
David and Mary McConnel
Andrew Petrie
William Augustine Duncan
Hon. Louis Hope
First St John's Church of England Church
First Customs House 1873
St Stephen's Roman Catholic Church 1868

Between pp. 183-192
Rev. John Dunmore Lang
Ship *Fortitude*
James Swan
William Pettigrew
Rev. Thomas Mowbray
John Richardson
John Petrie
William Street 1856
Brisbane 1862
South Brisbane 1862
George Raff
Arthur Macalister
James Rendall
John Scott
Sir Robert Ramsay Mackenzie
United Evangelical Chapel 1872
Ann and Albert Streets corner 1862

CHAPTER 1

Pioneer Scottish pastoralism 1841-48

In 1957 L.J. Jay revealed in Britain the critical role played by Scottish squatters in opening the Darling Downs district in 1840. While reviewing the enterprise of the Aberdonian pioneers, Jay flung a passing salute to those Scots who formed the nucleus of the second wave of pastoral occupation in the Northern Districts one year later.[1] Ostensibly taking second best because the most desirable lands on the Downs had been already occupied, this vanguard, with a significant Edinburgh-driven component, formed runs on the upper reaches of the Brisbane River Valley across the Great Dividing Range. While some occupied this area of the Moreton Bay District outside the prescribed fifty miles limit from the penal settlement of Brisbane Town as consolation, the majority took up their runs by design.

In the main, they were drawn predominantly from the families of landed proprietors, businessmen, merchants and professionals who constituted the core of Scotland's ruling class. Putting designs of social and political ascendancy temporarily aside and enduring uncivilised conditions, they were driven by the urgency of accumulating capital through pastoralism for both their own benefit and the Scottish investors who were assured of quick return for their capital. James Balfour, Edinburgh merchant and father of two such aspirants at Moreton Bay, put it bluntly: these squatters aimed to 'acquire as much wealth as to make them comfortable in this life'.[2] Most expected their Australian experience to be short term before basking in the fruits of their labours in life-long security in Britain and in pleasure on the Continent. Hence, John Balfour rationalised his necessary isolation from society in terms of the ultimate prize: 'My heart is in the Bush & there it must stay till I shall be able to make an honourable exit with satisfaction to myself & all my well wishers'.[3]

In this quest for capital accumulation, the Scottish pastoralists exemplified the dominant characteristics attributed to those of their nationality and rank who sought their fortunes in other districts of greater New South Wales. Most enjoyed sound financial backing and invaluable assistance from various branches of British and Australian Scottish networks to provide them with a decided head-start over other pastoral aspirants. While confronting the same human, natural and fiscal problems in fostering the district's development, they demonstrated intra-national cooperation, temporary inter-class collaboration and the ability to work harmoniously with settlers from other nations. In common with other northerners, they were at the forefront of determined opposition to exploitation by the Sydney-based government and the Scottish-dominated mercantile establishment, the source of the movement for separation in the fifties. They possessed the ability to balance individualism with clannishness, probably influenced by their Calvinist upbringing which stressed personal responsibility for the conduct of daily life.

In the name of survival on the barbarous frontier, most temporarily cast aside the moral and religious precepts of their upbringing in favour of pragmatism and ruthlessness. Differences in regional approaches to obstacles were apparent, the Highlanders adopting a more confrontational approach than the Lowlanders. There was no united Scottish position. Within the social, political and economic turmoil in which Scottish squatters played dominant roles, Scots were antagonists, especially on issues related to class and humanitarianism. For example, the leader who planned the ascendancy of the squatters as well as those who thwarted his designs were prominent Scots. However, the attempt of the squatters to establish a squattocracy also demonstrated that profits were more important to them than the moral quality of the emergent Moreton Bay society. Although they polarised the northern community, the majority achieved that financial security which was the prime objective for temporarily enduring banishment to an hostile frontier.

James Balfour was sure his sons were seeking their independence in the right country and in the most profitable industry: ' I think sheep farming must be prosperous, the consumption of wools is encreasing in every part of the World, & will continue to encrease & the demand seems always to be keeping ahead of supply, and there is no Country that is suited as Australia to produce such useful wools'.[4] He was not only drawing on his own expert knowledge of world trade, but the advice of successful squatters such as his close friend Duncan Mackellar who had returned to Scotland to write best selling handbooks for aspiring Scottish pastoralists.[5] In fact, Mackellar laid down the blueprint followed by many Scottish squatters in establishing their runs in Australia. He considered it imperative that aspiring pastoralists attend to the careful selection of sheep and the importation of experienced Scottish shepherds to ensure their proper care.

To this end, most of these pioneer flockmasters enjoyed sound financial backing, access to the best British and Australian information as well as support from an extensive Scottish network. These well-connected and highly educated young capitalists were derived from a class which was renowned for its socio-political conservatism. Yet they also shared the entrepreneurial progressivism of their kith and kin who initiated the Scottish Enclosures, Clearances and Industrial Revolution.

Needless to say, their single-minded pursuit of pastoral profits scarcely left an unblemished record in the historical annals of northern Australia. In 1992 Ian Donnachie informed a large gathering of leading Scottish historians that the Scottish squatters in that region were equally as inhumane as those members of their caste who were responsible for the radical economic restructuring of agriculture and industrialism at home. He concluded, 'Certainly the brutality of the Highland clearances ... takes on a slightly different gloss when set against the ruthless treatment meted out by some Scottish settlers [and] pastoralists ... to the Australian Aborigines'. In addition, the callous treatment of European labour, free and penal, in the name of profits also attracted the condemnation of late twentieth century revisionists. Accordingly, it was asserted that Scottish capitalism, with great rewards for the same minority group, was as ruthless in Australia as in Scotland.[6]

The Darling Downs squatter Christopher Pemberton Hodgson was a rare contemporary critic of the dispossession process based on the doctrine of Terra Nullius. However, he was universal in his condemnation, being critical of both English and Scottish pastoralists alike. Nevertheless, he was impressed at the supportive Scottish network which operated in the interior. He related that the Scots 'stuck together like bricks' to surmount the succession of obstacles encountered in establishing pastoralism. In particular he was impressed with the industry and reliability of Scottish workers whom he regarded as the best in the Northern Districts.[7]

* * *

The selection of reliable and experienced labour, preferably from the Scottish Borders, was as important as purchasing the best stock according to ex-colonial authorities in Edinburgh such as Mackellar and David Waugh.[8] However, the overriding objective was to be first to acquire the best land in the newly opened districts. An extensive network, which emanated from Scotland and diffused throughout the colony, provided many of the aspiring pastoralists with access to the most reliable intelligence and influential facilitators to meet these preconditions. Most importantly, the home connection did not cease playing an important role once the pastoral enterprises were underway. Many Scottish ventures were 'orchestrated from Scotland and manipulated by Scots back home in banks [and] finance houses ... in Edinburgh, Leith, Glasgow, Dundee and Aberdeen'.[9] Bad luck and stupidity aside, it was to be expected that such well-connected and highly-advantaged Scottish squatters were high achievers in the colonies.

The colonial career of the Balfour brothers illustrates the invaluable assistance provided by those who were strategically placed in a Scottish colonial network. On reaching New South Wales the Balfours lodged in Sydney with wealthy flour-miller, Thomas Barker, before their initiation to pastoralism on one of his properties. When they were ready to form their runs, every assistance was offered at the highest levels. Colonial Secretary, Edward Deas Thomson, ensured they had the best possible start by providing them with a blank licence upon which they could record the boundaries of their selected property. Captain King of the Australian Agricultural Company permitted them the hitherto unknown privilege of selecting superior animals from among the company's flocks to stock their run. Finally, on reaching the New England District, George 'Humpy' McDonald, the Commissioner for Crown Lands, provided them with practical advice on selecting that run in the Liverpool Plains area.[10]

Scottish squatters had been prominent among those who beat the gun and established stations on the New England plateau before 1836. Their strong presence in this region ensured a chain of legendary Scottish support as the flocks and teams moved slowly northwards towards the recently surveyed Big River, subsequently known as the Clarence. Along this route, Glen Innes, Inverell, Armidale, Tenterfield and Guyra and other locations under Scottish occupancy were important stopping places as the frontiers were pushed northwards. Also, Falconer's Plains, leased by Donald McIntyre, became a convenient resting place for the drovers and their flocks. By January 1840, John 'Tinker' Campbell, who formerly conducted a cattle station on the Gwydir, occupied the northernmost station on the north bank of the Dumaresq, a sole ridge separating this basin from that of the Condamine.[11]

Advice from home and colonial experience emphasised not only the adage that first in is best dressed, but also the necessity of overcoming the tyranny of distance which made the marketing of wool unprofitable and arduous. Indeed, the major consideration of perspicacious Scottish squatters, such as the Leslies and Balfours, in locating their stations was proximity to the nearest entrepot. Hence Patrick Leslie emphatically stated, 'We care not whether we go NSE or West so be that we get good stock and not have too much land carriage'.[12]

In a progress report to his financial backer George Forbes in Edinburgh in 1840, John Balfour dropped the first hint that he would move to Moreton Bay to form his permanent station. In accordance with his father's exhortation to be 'the first in the field' to 'fix the best run', Balfour expressed the urgency of making an imminent start for the north. He was particularly optimistic that Brisbane was on the verge of developing into a port of international standing. With land carriage from his Liverpool Plains station to Maitland being an untenable 300 miles, the proximity of the new port to the first of the stations which could be established at the prescribed distance outside Brisbane made Moreton Bay a most attractive alternative.[13] In a letter which arrived at Sydney by the beginning of May 1841, James Balfour advised his indecisive sons to make all haste for Moreton Bay.[14]

During a lengthy conversation with James Balfour, Sir Thomas Brisbane, former Governor of New South Wales and President of the Royal Society of Edinburgh, had unequivocally advocated movement to Moreton Bay, thereby putting an end to procrastination. In one of his regular missives to Barker, dated 10 December 1840, James Balfour revealed Brisbane's critical input which resulted in the first free settlement outside the fifty miles limit of Brisbane Town:

> I am inclined to give Moreton Bay the preference ... I lately had a long conversation with Sir Thomas Brisbane who has been at Moreton Bay and he is of the opinion that not only will sheep, cattle & horses thrive in the mountainous part of the country in that neighbourhood but that the lower country will yield many tropical productions & there are many fine Rivers flowing from the interior of the country thereby opening up the resources of a vast portion of it. He was himself up one of the Rivers about 60 or 70 miles'.[15]

Movement to Brisbane Town and the subsequent selection of suitable land reflected the determined, vigilant and wise characteristics which arguably distinguished Scots. As well, it embodied the invaluable assistance rendered by the most experienced member of a Scottish network operating at the penal colony. To ensure they had the first pick of the best land within a short distance of Brisbane Town, John Balfour and his newly-arrived Highland friend Evan Mackenzie travelled ahead of their stock and other competitors by the fastest means available.[16] It was imperative that the Mackenzie-Balfour combination was first in the field to gain the upper hand and the freedom to forge their own destinies. Outwitting competitors was part and parcel of their operational mode, especially at the beginning of their ventures.[17]

This was never more evident than in the manner in which Balfour and Mackenzie arrived at Moreton Bay to select their runs in the company of the equally well-connected Francis Bigge. They applied independently to the Governor for permission to land their stores at Brisbane preparatory to selecting their stations, indicating collusion or probably advice from the same source.[18] Even the fact that the cutter *John*, which regularly plied between Sydney and the restricted port of Brisbane, was packed to the gunnels was no deterrent to Mackenzie. Following a second submission to the Governor, he was given permission to land eight of his servants and stores at Brisbane from a cutter he specially hired for the purpose. Highlighting his business acumen and knowledge of the shipping trade, Mackenzie was successful in gaining a government contract to take cargo to Sydney on the return trip.[19] Balfour, who delegated his Scottish servants to go with the rest of the Mackenzie party on the overland droving journey, apparently accompanied the elder Kilcoy on that cutter in the second week of May 1841.[20]

James Balfour stressed that thorough planning not only entailed arriving in an area to snap up the best land, but also stocking the run with the best wool-producing sheep - even if it meant importing them from Britain. Rather than follow Mackellar's advice to take out 'a few fine Saxon tups and ewes' to ensure the production of high quality wool, the Balfours imported Leicester rams to breed with the best quality colonial ewes.[21] These pampered animals, transported by dray to their Moreton Bay destination, were cossetted aboard the *Abberton* by experienced sheep man Walter Grieve of Roxburgh. Under his skilful supervision and care, Grieve ensured that the highest quality wool would be associated with Colinton station. With due gravity, John Balfour informed George Forbes that the good name of the stock (and therefore profits) 'is everything in this country'.[22]

On arrival, Balfour and Mackenzie immediately set about taking advantage of being the first in the district. After all, good stock needed plenty of the best quality, open grazing land, well-watered and interspersed with stony ridges to prevent foot-rot in wet weather. C.P Hodgson, with an eye to marketing the ensuing wool clip, advised that two other 'grand objects' after selection of land were proximity to a shipping port and a good road to that location.[23]

Among the small, free population at the transitory penal settlement at Brisbane, the advance party was indebted principally to Andrew Petrie for advice and active assistance in their quest.[24] Having gained invaluable knowledge of the surrounding country in his journeys as supervisor of works for the convict establishment and as an ardent explorer, Petrie directed his countrymen to the best locations to form their stations.[25]

Brought out to Australia as one of the celebrated Scotch mechanics on the *Stirling Castle* in 1831 by the Reverend John Dunmore Lang to construct his Australian College, Petrie was the epitome of the classical Calvinist skilled artisan. These rigid characteristics helped him forge a prosperous building firm in Brisbane.[26] In 1841, after four years habitation in the wound-down penal settlement, the shrewd Petrie was anticipating the urban business prospects which would follow in the wake of squatter occupation of the hinterland. He was only too willing to help Balfour and Mackenzie with whom he developed a warm relationship and whose plans he obviously approved. Remembered fondly for the warm hospitality provided at their home when Brisbane contained no hotels, Andrew and Mary Petrie became intimate friends of many of the Scottish squattocracy. These young men earned Petrie's approbation not only for the refinement, intelligence and bonhomie they brought to a basic, culture-starved Brisbane, but also for their pluck and enterprise.[27] Having demonstrated the legendary assistance shown by Scots one to another, Petrie put into practice the chauvinistic cliché which his clerical mentor was wont to utter: 'there's nae folk like our ain folk'.[28]

Having led the party which made the first European ascent on Mount Beerwah, the astute Petrie was in a prime position to identify station sites with the potential for direct communication with the future port of Brisbane.[29] As a result of his advice, the Mackenzies took up Kilcoy, the Balfours formed Colinton and the tardy Archers brothers were directed to nearby Durundur in the Brisbane River Valley. Balfour Snr proudly proclaimed to his London-based brother at Baring Brothers Bank, 'they took the pick of the district'.[30] John Archer, horse driver and storeman on the overland droving trek, agreed.[31] In a letter to his father soon after Durundur had been formed, Archer marvelled that the land and pasturage were better than he hitherto had seen in the colony.[32]

* * *

According to plan, Evan Mackenzie, and two of the Archer brothers, along with men and drays, blazed the Northern Road to Brisbane in the first few days of 1842. By their action they created the shortest possible land route available in the Northern Districts linking legally-formed pastoral stations with the entrepot.[33] The Archers later improved upon this direct line of communication by ingeniously constructing a substantial bridge across a significant creek that flowed near their station.[34] Less circuitous than the alternative route, which involved backtracking via Colinton, Mount Brisbane and Ipswich, this road gave the district's northernmost squatters a decided advantage over their colleagues in intercourse with the nascent entrepot.

Typical of the strategic thinking of prominent Scottish merchants who drove much of the northern pastoral invasion, Balfour Snr turned his attention to the entrepot's potential as an international port. He predicted the day when his sons might maximise their profits by shipping 'their wools in a vessel that will bring them home without sending them to Sydney'.[35] Running with this idea, and blending his own welfare with that of the district, Mackenzie took practical measures to control northern trade - a critical step in gaining northern independence from Sydney-based control. In arguing a case for financial support from Baring Brothers to establish direct trade with Britain, Mackenzie praised Moreton Bay District's potential, especially stressing the strength of the Scottish sector in the northern pastoral industry.[36] Knowing full well that many betrayed Scottish financiers were fed up with 'the airy and irresponsible guff produced to promote particular areas', Mackenzie appreciated that such a concentration of his single-minded countrymen would underline the veracity of his claims.[37] It was acknowledged in financial circles that Scottish capitalists were unlikely to waste time or money on an unprofitable district.

Mackenzie's report demonstrated that Scottish squatters were predominant in the Northern Districts. He revealed that Scottish pastoralists controlled 58% of the runs on the Darling Downs and 17 of 28 stations (or approximately 61%) in the Moreton Bay District.[38] Considering that the Scots made up only 12 % of the northern population by 1846, their representation among the group which claimed to reflect 'the wealth and intelligence of the district' was markedly disproportionate. By 1848, 67% of the runs were Scottish-owned in Moreton Bay, then comprising the counties of Stanley and Moreton. The most significant concentrations occurred on the upper Brisbane River Valley, the Logan and Boonah where the Scottish imprint on the landscape was evident by the names of the newly-formed runs. While place names principally reflect emotional ties to the squatters' places of origin, they also provide broad clues to unravel the relationships.[39]

The squatters in the Pine, Logan and Boonah areas, although having less impact on district development than the Brisbane River Valley group, were steadfast pioneers of their respective localities. They swelled the number of Scottish squatters at Moreton Bay while apparently solving some of the problems common to their northern peers in a less confrontational and more accommodating manner. Some were even exemplars of kindness.

Across the D'Aguilar Range on the main route from Brisbane to the northern stations, George, Francis and John Griffin, a seafaring father and son combination, set up Whiteside station on the Pine River in the middle of 1843. Mrs Janet Griffin, nee Taylor, a native of Stromness, was destined to be a formidable female squatter following the death of her husband in the early fifties.[40] Along with neighbouring female stockholder Isabella Joyner, she was the veritable founder of European settlement in the Pine Rivers district.[41] Further north, near the Caboolture River, the ill-fated Andrew Gregor, yet another Aberdonian and brother of the Anglican incumbent at Brisbane, established the Fogie run.[42]

The Logan River also boasted a nest of Scottish pioneer pastoralists, some established as early as 1842. These included Hugh Aikman who took up the first run at Bromelton, William Barker at Tamarookum and Sydney-based Robert Campbell tertius of Telamon and Melcolm. Donald Coutts, joined by his brother John, occupied Tambourine on the Albert tributary. In 1845, following a minor sub-division of Tambourine, Dugald Graham formed Tabragalba. Joseph Phelps Robinson of Quaker persuasion and partner of Benjamin Boyd, who was the largest and wealthiest squatter in New South Wales, put in Scottish managers at Beau Desert and Laidley.[43]

In the Boonah area, Scottish squatters were also present in significant numbers, occupying most of the eight runs. Although George Hunter and William Fyffe were first in the district, taking up Coochin Coochin in 1842, their stay was short. Both had left the area by 1845. The second station to be occupied in this vicinity was Rosebrook/Normanby in 1843, the founder being Donald MacLaughlin. Robert and William Wilson, formed Mount Flinders one year earlier, following brief settlement on the Downs. This was about the same time that Macquarie and C.L. Macdonald took on Dugandan. By 1845 the Cameron group 'occupied a virtual principality' of at least half of Boonah. John Cameron, originally from the Hunter Valley, was the first of his clan in the field, having taken up Fassifern in 1842 before other family members occupied Tarome, Moogerah and Dugandan.[44]

While the networks and the achievements of the Boonah Scots have been covered fully elsewhere, the backgrounds, connections and contributions of their more important Brisbane River Valley contemporaries to Moreton Bay development have received scant attention. The influence of this loose alliance within the district was far-reaching. Not only were the latter intimately linked with several of the Lockyer Valley squatters, but they also enjoyed close relationships with many like-minded, conservative Scots in Brisbane and Ipswich. In the style typical of colonial Scots they exploited those contacts to the full for both personal and regional gains. Significantly, this group contained within its ranks several prominent settlers such as Evan Mackenzie, John Balfour and David McConnel who either attempted to set the socio-economic agenda for the Northern Districts or were in the forefront of its major developments.

* * *

The majority of this set of squatters exemplified those characteristics which were common to leading Scottish pastoralists elsewhere in New South Wales. Most were privileged, enjoying influential contacts at home and in the colony, sound financial backing and support from specially imported Scottish labour in their hard-hearted implementation of pastoral capitalism. They also demonstrated strategic planning skills, the willingness to cooperate with their peers, regardless of nationality, and dogged resilience in facing a succession of seemingly insurmountable obstacles. Importantly, the majority appeared to be connected to varying degrees, either by direct friendship or through word-of-mouth peripheral relationships, with the Edinburgh-based planners of this pastoral incursion.

The seminal influence upon the Brisbane Valley network was James Balfour who had friendship or business ties with the families of nearly all the young men who sought their fortunes in the Brisbane River Valley. This network extended northward from Edinburgh to the Highlands and south to the Borders. In Edinburgh, they enjoyed close communication with Professor Graham and Lord Ivory. Balfour's life-long confidant, Sir Colin Mackenzie on the Black Isle, had formerly shared business interests, probably in Edinburgh. In the Borders region, Balfour was well acquainted with Alexander Scott, a prosperous proprietor and wool producer.[45] Another branch of the Scotts provided his sons' enterprise with their supervisor whose brother had close contact with the Archers' distant cousins. Less intimately, Balfour was acquainted with the maternal line of Bigges' family on the English side of the Tweed and had contacts with the Archers' maternal grand uncles and uncles in the capacity of leading British merchants.

The only Brisbane Valley pioneer who apparently had no ties, close or peripheral, with Balfour was Edinburgh-educated David McConnel of Manchester. As director of the Wine Company of Scotland, centred in Edinburgh with branches in Inverness and London, Balfour was an astute and progressive merchant. World trade fairly coursed through his veins, being born a British-Russian at Riga on the Baltic into a merchant family. Married to Mary Anderson, also a child of a merchant father with West Indian interests, Balfour was very much part of the Edinburgh business community.[46] Through his almost neurotic interest in his sons' affairs, wide reading and ready access to Scottish and colonial expertise, he became Edinburgh's resident expert on New South Wales.

Sir Colin Mackenzie, proprietor of the Highland estate of Kilcoy on the Black Isle was the father of Evan and Colin John Mackenzie who followed their Midlothian friends to Australia in November 1840. The Kilcoys and their retinue constituted the Highland branch of the Edinburgh-driven, pastoral thrust into the Moreton Bay District. Sir Colin, a powerful and popular Scottish laird, was Lord Lieutenant of the county, Colonel of the Ross-shire militia and a dominant shareholder in the Moray Firth and London Steam Packet Company.[47] He was as close to James Balfour as Barker.

In common with many other Scottish squatters, the Mackenzies enjoyed a decided head-start by possessing the financial wherewithal and having access to the influential contacts in their quest for pastoral profits. The outcome of an audience with Lord Glenelg, member for Inverness and Secretary of State for the Colonies was a warm letter of introduction to the Surveyor-General of New South Wales, Sir Thomas Mitchell.[48] Thereafter, Mitchell demonstrated interest in the

Mackenzies' colonial fortunes, continuing to be Evan's mentor until he left the colony. Further, Mackenzie was already known to the former Colonial Secretary Alexander Macleay from Ross-shire, a friend and neighbour of Thomas Barker. Having equal social standing, he also gained the patronage of the Governor, Sir George Gipps, during the initial stages of his colonial endeavour.[49]

Whereas the Balfours relied on taking into partnership prominent Edinburgh banker George Forbes for their financial backing, Sir Colin's generous patrimony of 8,000 pounds gave the Mackenzies a decided advantage over their less endowed and less independent friends.[50] Accordingly, the Mackenzie's run was named Kilcoy after their family estate on the Black Isle while the Balfours' choice of Colinton commemorated the former Forbes seat outside Edinburgh.[51]

To Moreton Bay the Mackenzies brought Highland traditions which ensured them of worker loyalty in a district later wracked by class conflict. Sir Colin was universally acknowledged as one of the few remaining Highland proprietors with feelings of warm paternalism towards his tenants. He exercised his particular style of benevolent management in the midst of a similar climate of class turmoil which emanated from agrarian relocation and the insatiable demands of the industrial south.[52] Evan, the elder of the Kilcoys, not only replicated his father's Highland paternalism towards his select band of Scottish workers, but also linked his profit drive with the welfare of the community in a similar manner. An ex-Etonian, former cavalry officer and magistrate, he was well qualified to assume leadership in the district's affairs. Colin John Mackenzie, nineteen years old and Edinburgh-educated, appeared to remain in his elder brother's shadow until 1846 when he had sole control over the Kilcoy venture. Thereafter he assumed a leadership role in the promotion of pastoral interests. Until Colin John left Australia in about 1857, he continued to enjoy a close association with John Balfour, based on a long personal friendship, family ties and identical aspirations.[53]

Although they were first in the district and prepared the infrastructure for their stations during June 1841, the Balfour and Mackenzie brothers were unable to take out the first licences in the new district. Regulations required them to await the arrival of their flocks before making application. Thus two months elapsed before they became official tenants of their stations.[54] Thereafter, their glowing reports of Moreton Bay country attracted the interest of family members who also decided to move northwards. Charles Balfour, who had been employed as a trainee manager on Matong, a Barker-controlled cattle station, formed an apparently unnamed cattle station with 'young Irvine' and assistance from Evan Mackenzie in 1842.[55] As 'chain migrants' from the West Indies, the Mackenzies' cousins Charles and Donald Cameron, sons of John Cameron fifteenth Chief of Glen Nevis, arrived at Moreton Bay in early 1845. Finding it necessary to settle outside the fully-occupied area, they founded Tarampa on the Lockyer in 1846.[56] Experienced Aberdonian squatter Donald Coutts, who probably was known to the fathers of Balfour and Mackenzie because of his family's pre-eminence in banking circles, established Rosewood on the Bremer.[57]

Other members of the Balfour-Mackenzie pioneering party, which was active in the district as early as June, were James Ivory and David Graham. They established Eskdale, named in honour of the former's birthplace. In 1840, they arrived at Sydney under Barker's care. The son of Scotland's solicitor-general, Ivory was an inseparable companion of Graham whose father held the chair of Professor of Botany at Edinburgh University. Dr Graham enjoyed national fame for his brilliant report on the role of emigration in alleviating Highland destitution.[58]

Gideon and Alexander Scott struck out alone to the south and took up Mount Esk, commemorating the Scottish district where their father was a large estate proprietor. The use of Esk in the name of two Brisbane River Valley runs points to a geographical relationship within the Esk River locality in Dumfries-shire. Mount Esk, taken up by Gideon and Alexander Scott, reflects the fact that these brothers were sons of Alexander Scott one of the four proprietors in the Knockhill parish of Dumfries. It is probably no coincidence that James Ivory, who formed a partnership with David Graham, was born nearby in the Esk River valley. Furthermore, Walter Scott, who accompanied the Balfours to Australia as overseer, aboard the *Abberton* and later took up Taromeo with his brother Simon, was born and bred at Langholm on the Esk, some five miles from Knockhill.[59]

The Scott and the Ivory families not only knew one another, but also were acquainted with James Balfour who was familiar with the proprietors and best sheepmen not only in Dumfries but also in Peebles, Roxburgh and Northumberland. There may have been some collaboration between this discrete group and the Bigge brothers who were Englishmen with a mother of possible Scottish descent and Edinburgh connections. They founded Mount Brisbane - a distinctly local name which provided no evidence of their Northumberland origins. Francis Edward Bigge (Little Bigge) and his brother Frederick Thomas (Big Bigge) were natives of Little Benton, Northhamptonshire. Nephews of Judge John Thomas Bigge whose report re-oriented Australia's direction from that which was plotted by Governor Lachlan Macquarie, the Bigges were the sons of Thomas Hanway Bigge, proprietor of Benton Hall, and his wife Charlotte Scott. Widowed by the time her sons embarked on their Australian venture, Mrs Bigge was well known to James Balfour as was her brother-in-law, William Ord, who was then MP for Newcastle in the county of Northumberland.[60] Later in the decade, the Bigges, especially Francis, played dominant roles in fostering northern development according to squatter designs.

After following the bent grass tracks formed by the drays of the first occupants of this lush valley, David, Thomas and John Archer founded Durundur as the most northern station in October 1841. Bearing the Aboriginal name for carpet snake, the Archers' station was located east of Kilcoy. Although their merchant uncle was well-known to Balfour Snr, the Archers were apparently not connected with the Balfour-Mackenzie group.[61]

The Archers, who arrived independently and last on the Brisbane River Valley scene, fitted easily into the Scottish network operating in that area. Unlike most of the Edinburgh-based group, they took up Durundur by default, their original plan to settle on the fully-occupied Darling Downs proving untenable because of a prolonged interruption to their journey in the south. These Norwegian-domiciled, Scottish brothers were relatives of Thomas Walker, nephew of the London-based merchant William Walker, who was well-known to James Balfour in Edinburgh.[62] However, there is no evidence in Balfour's correspondence, which usually contained reference to the colonial fortunes of Scots within his sphere of influence, that he was familiar with the Archer family.

There are signs of a tangential link between the Archers with the Brisbane River Valley Scots through a colonial association between another of their Walker relatives and Simon Scott. The latter had family links to the Balfour retinue through his brother Walter. James Walker, in command of his family's Australian pastoral empire centred at Wallerowang, provided David, Thomas and William Archer with colonial experience on that station. He also employed Scott on one of the Walker company's stations on the Castlereagh, having travelled out to Australia on the same ship as Walker some two years before the Balfour party arrived in Sydney.[63] When David Archer vacated his supervisory role at Wallerowang to form Durundur, he continued his close relationship with the grand-nephews of William Walker, taking aboard Edward Walker as a 'sleeping partner'.[64]

Independent of the majority of other Brisbane River Scottish squatters, David Canon McConnel took out the first licence for a sheep station in the upper valley of the Brisbane River at Cressbrook on 15 July 1841.[65] Son of a prosperous Scottish cotton manufacturer in Manchester, McConnel majored in chemistry at Edinburgh University under the supervision of the famous Francis Dalton. This led him to embark upon chemistry and calico printing as a career. Allegedly distressed by working conditions in the mills of Liverpool and excited by prospects as a squatter in Australia, McConnel took his large inheritance following the death of his father and unexpectedly set sail for New South Wales amidst pleas of protest from his ten siblings.[66]

On arriving in June 1840, McConnel considered several sites north and south of Sydney, eventually taking up a run in the New England District before the northward drive. Managing to find only an unsuitable run as one of the late-comers to the Darling Downs, the dissatisfied McConnel pushed on to the Brisbane River. Despite James Balfour's claims in extolling his sons' choice, McConnel took up the best land in the district in June 1841. He named this fertile river flat Cressbrook after the English property of one of his many brothers. In 1845, John and Frederic, two of those siblings, followed him to this Moreton Bay property. While Frederic's stay was short, John became the district's first real capitalist with lending capacity after taking over Crow's Nest from James Canning Pearce. Thereafter, the district's entrepreneurs benefited from John McConnel's share of the legacy derived from the family's cotton mill, several railway companies, banks and mines in and around Manchester.[67]

The financially-flush McConnels and Mackenzies were able to avoid the usual initial mortgage of their businesses to Sydney-based Scottish merchants such as

Gilchrist & Alexander, Donaldson & Dawes and William Walker & Co. Unlike may of their peers, they were able to keep their enterprises afloat until the proceeds of the first wool clip were realised. However, in common with their pastoral associates, they consolidated their business with one merchant in the name of efficiency and simplicity. Independent of the financial grip which their agents exerted over their livelihoods, squatters needed to employ southern agents to keep accounts, sell wool locally, consign shipments to London agencies, hire labour and forward supplies. The vice-like grip which the southern merchants had upon most Moreton Bay business enterprises and their vicious foreclosures during the financial depression of the early 1840s deepened the gulf between north and south. Their indecent profiteering, linked with exploitation of intra-colonial maritime trade, was ammunition for the separation movement.

The Balfours were scarcely independent agents, being accountable for their decisions to their financial backer George Forbes of the banking house, Sir William Forbes & Co in Edinburgh. Furthermore, in the initial stages, they were heavily reliant upon the Scottish merchant house of M.D. Hunter & Co in Sydney. Arising from the lax and indifferent manner in which the 'grasping' Hunter conducted his son's business affairs, the professedly 'poor' James Balfour found the financial wherewithal to allow them to be independent of a Sydney agent.[68] Thenceforth, they were only answerable to the canny Forbes until his son was old enough to be admitted to partnership. In the meantime, Forbes proved to be an unremitting, stern task-master, although operating from 13,000 miles away to the north.

Forbes closely followed and exerted a tight reign over the Balfours' plans and decision making. This strict surveillance was motivated primarily by the need to minimize risks to his capital investment. Such detailed supervision was indicative of the parsimonious business style of the Scottish financiers who made possible many an antipodean pastoral venture. There was no room even for family loyalty or assistance to friends when such actions could diminish profits - the antithesis of the strong Scottish supportive ethos practised in the colony.

Intervening emphatically when the Balfours' maternal uncles transmitted 2,000 pounds to their nephews to be invested in stock on thirds, Forbes objected and also raised grave doubts about including Graham and Ivory in the Liverpool Plains enterprise - regardless of their parents' status or the expressed wishes of Thomas Barker.[69] On the former problem he was stern in his direction: 'You should not undertake the management of Mr Andersons' sheep on any terms'. Rather than complicating their venture by becoming 'mixed up in other people's affairs' and expending time, energy and money on a relatively unremunerative project, Forbes advanced a further 1000 pounds at 5% to the Balfours for investment in additional stock.[70] The anxious John Balfour felt acutely the pressure and expectations emanating from Scotland, railing without reaction from his mentor about 'how much was expected from me from yourself'.[71]

Commentators in the Brisbane River Valley such as Thomas Archer were not exactly enamoured of the manner in which compatriots conducted their business transactions. Many succumbed to the diminished moral standards of frontier society. Henry Mort, staunch Anglican and supervisor of Cressbrook, regretted that the young pastoralists sold their souls to make money - their only thought. Even the doting James Balfour felt that his eldest son was trying to accumulate profits far too quickly, leading to increasing demands for additional capital from his patient financier.[72] According to Archer, probably referring to businessmen and merchants as much as squatters, the Scottish style was excessively canny, even bordering on dishonest. After nearly a decade in New South Wales, including five years in the Moreton Bay District, Thomas Archer concluded that the Scots 'in general did not have such a nice sense of honor as the generality of Englishmen; in fact, the specimens I have seen ... out here have not at all tended to raise my countrymen in my estimation. They are a great deal too canny'. After providing a long list of exceptions to this generalisation among the squatters, Archer implicated the ruthless business style of the Mackenzies and Balfours by omission.[73] However, the Durundur diary for 1843 and part of 1844 reveals only close cooperation and cordial relations among these northern-most neighbours and no signs of dissatisfaction, especially with the apparently supportive Mackenzies.[74] In fact the diary provides numerous instances, admired by Hodgson, of the mutual help rendered by the determined Scots as they confronted the numerous difficulties in opening up new land.

* * *

The squatters' satisfaction with the quality of the land they occupied was not matched by the conditions under which they had leased it. Their grip was insecure. Aboriginal resistance aside, government regulations and the prohibitive purchasing price of land caused much resentment among the pastoralists, with deleterious effects on the material and moral development of the frontier. James Balfour's fear that his sons would not be permitted to take up enough land to cater for natural increases in their flocks and that arising from a subsequent strategy to take sheep on thirds, appeared trivial to the land row that was brewing.[75] It fell to Evan Mackenzie, who had emerged as the leader of the northern squatters, to express forcefully his colleagues' objections to government policy in 1842. He was also required to convey their reactions to Gipps' highly unpopular Orders-in-Council of 2 April 1844, a set of rules that brought Australia's squatters to the brink of armed revolt.[76] The conflict further deepened northern anti-government sentiments, providing more ammunition for a separation movement.

In Edinburgh, James Balfour showed his sound grasp of the colonial land situation and the ramifications of restrictive regulations. While agreeing with Mackenzie's representative sentiments, he stressed the necessity of civilising the frontier by granting security of tenure. 'When they become proprietors of their stations, they would lay out this money more liberally in improvements & making themselves & the character of their people more comfortable dwellings &

establishments & improve the whole appearance of the country & the character and condition of the people'.[77]

After providing frank answers to a series of questions regarding the relative advantages of leasing or buying the runs at the 1844 inquiry into crown lands' grievances, Mackenzie opined that no problems would exist if the government dropped the purchase price of land from one pound an acre to two shillings and six pence. His reaction to the regulation requiring stockholders to purchase their homestead blocks, the most controversial aspect of the 1844 regulations, was also negative. Pre-empting part of the 1847 compromise adopted by Lord Stanley, Mackenzie informed the committee that 'he would prefer extending the lease of the option ...'.[78]

Under the leadership of Mackenzie, the first indignation meeting in the colony was held at Moreton Bay to protest against Gipps' regulations. The squatters' main concern was the compulsory purchase of 320 acres of their run at one pound per acre. This Moreton Bay Pastoral Association hoped to link up with the central body formed in Sydney under Ben Boyd, the largest stockholder in Australia, but its overtures were ignored.[79] Later, when Mackenzie paid them back for this insult in his own inimitable style, the parent body reacted with anger. After bringing Gipps to heel by exerting pressure even into the British parliament, this powerful body was unable to cope with being rebuffed by the northern squattocracy.[80] The squatter component of the Scottish network in New South Wales was definitely divided, a reflection of the widening gap which existed between the north and the south. Added to the despised government and exploitative mercantile establishment, the actions of the arrogant squattocracy exacerbated anti-southern sentiments.

Two prominent Scottish southerners, the Reverend John Dunmore Lang and William Augustine Duncan, who subsequently influenced the course of the Moreton Bay community, originally took up opposing positions on the contentious land regulations issue in 1844. Whereas Duncan championed Gipps' ideals, Lang was the Governor's mortal enemy. Ironically, they both possessed visions of Australia as a small farmer's paradise - the natural progression flowing from the Governor's actions. Although bitter foes based on differing religious ideals, they were united by the close of 1845 in opposition to the squatters' cause. Under the influence of fellow legislator Robert Lowe, Lang realised the issue was less centred on taxation without representation than preventing the socio-political designs of a privileged group which cared 'not a straw for public welfare or constitutional principle'.[81]

Like Duncan, Lang came to the conclusion that the squatters' ultimate demands for security of tenure would 'make it impossible for immigrants from the mother country to get homes of their own on Australian soil'. As a radical democrat, he realised that the elite plantation society would become a reality. By November 1845, when he visited Moreton Bay, Lang had been transformed into an implacable enemy of those who perpetuated 'the damnable doctrine of squatting'.[82]

With the appointment of Duncan to the position of Sub-Collector of Customs in the middle of 1846, the Moreton Bay District had been favoured over a two months period with the presence of two of the most fiercely committed anti-squatting agitators in the history of New South Wales. They were both accomplished manipulators of the major instruments of political protest - newspapers, mass rallies and petitions to the British government. Because of their rural roots, they shared a common passion to create a plural society based on opening up the pastoral land to small farmers whom they considered to hold the key to Australia's future. Both strongly believed that the prosperity, order and morality of the colony would be best advanced by tapping into the motives of independence and self-advancement of proletarian immigration which aspired to small-scale land ownership. Vast-scale, dispersed pastoral ownership not only deprived Australia of this yeoman input, but was regarded as 'a device of large landowners to preserve the interests of their caste'. The resulting plantation social structure, eschewing agriculture, promoted barbarism at the expense of civilisation.[83]

No matter how much they shared the same socio-political agenda, the Protestant Lang with his Chartist leanings and the Liberal Catholic Duncan remained opponents. Fresh from demolishing the claims of the Church of England to ascendancy, even challenging the legitimacy of Anglican orders, Duncan turned his guns onto the prejudiced Lang.[84] This dissenting zealot's religious bigotry, exemplified by his fierce opposition to Irish immigration and claims of Popish subversion, brought forth a belligerent defence from Duncan. So forcefully argued was Duncan's case that colonial authorities were induced to expunge deleterious references to Irish immigration from official communiques thenceforth.[85] Though Duncan may have been the master of most mortals in intellectual debate, the squatters possessed the political and economic muscle which proved to be more than a match for his widely circulated verbal aggression.

Duncan arrived in Moreton Bay from Sydney in 1846 a broken man. He had recently suffered the death of his only son, lost his radical newspaper (*Duncan's Weekly Register*) and was deeply in debt. As a consequence of being the only journalist in New South Wales who strongly, consistently and eloquently defended Gipps' regulations of 1844, his livelihood was systematically destroyed by the southern squatters. Hell-bent on preventing the squatters' designs to form a plantation economy with its attendant elitist social structure, Duncan bravely challenged the Australian Pastoral Association and its British parliamentary representative, Francis Scott. This resulted in his temporary ruin.[86] The ruthlessness of the Scottish-led southern squatters towards their fellow nationals indicated that there was no room for ethnic sentiment in removing obstacles to their socio-economic designs. This branch of the Scottish network based on pastoralism could be just as punitive to perceived antagonists as it could be helpful to sympathisers.

Defeated but not bowed, Duncan took up his position at Moreton Bay following Gipps' approaches on his behalf to the highest levels in England. Amid rabid accusations of nepotism from the squatters, he received the most loyal support from Australia's leading Scottish bureaucrat, Edward Deas Thomson.[87] By personal choice and by dint of his position as a civil servant, Duncan thenceforth attempted to divorce himself as much as possible from political agitation at Moreton Bay. Nevertheless, he continued as a fierce advocate of human rights, especially for the Aborigines. According to his biographer Margaret Payten, Duncan's efforts as a Sydney radical were not in vain - especially on the land issue: 'The beginning of the long struggle to open up the lands was here foreshadowed, and ... during the following decades, the seeds that Duncan had helped to sow were to bear some fruit'.[88] Although Eurocentric in approach, he predictably took the government line, showing little sympathy for those who were involved in wresting from the indigenes that land which would be basic to the fulfilment of his small-farmer vision for Australia.

* * *

The Scottish squatters may well have legitimately obtained the most prized land through a combination of Scottish acumen, assistance from their networks and fulfilling the requirements of British law, but this was no solace to the indigenous owners who were driven off their territory without consideration and compensation. It was all very well for John Balfour to report that he did not take up his land with hostile intent to the local clan, but arrogant dispossession in itself was an act of unpitying violence.[89] The formerly contented and self-sufficient traditional society fell victim to the alien policy of 'possessive individualism and progress; where the relationship of humans to objective nature was one of private exploitation for private ends and the creation of surplus for exchange, ... for the world market'.[90]

Naturally, the indigenes met this affront with hostile opposition. The ensuing battle for the land revealed the inhuman extremes of Scottish capitalism while demonstrating the strength of its frontier network. In this dangerous situation, regional variations in the severity of the Scottish response to aboriginal resistance were also discernible. This inter-racial conflict also revealed that the policies and actions of Scottish pastoralists towards Aboriginal eviction were fiercely opposed by humanitarians of their same nationality. There was no unanimous Scottish position on any issue at Moreton Bay, especially those centred on the racism and economic exploitation which were integral to Scottish pastoral capitalism. 'Although the Scots were in the front line in asserting settler superiority, they were also occasionally active in the defence of the rights of the native peoples'. [91]

Even within Scottish stations there was division. Henry Mort, English supervisor of Cressbrook, along with Frederic McConnel disagreed with David and John McConnel on the morality and severity of British colonisation of Australia. They considered it a heinous act that a powerful nation could wrest the native land from weak tribes by 'annihilating the unoffending and ... less avaricious savages'.[92]

Although Scottish humanitarians such as Lang, Duncan and the Archers supported the general policy of Australian colonisation based on this doctrine of Terra Nullius, they emphatically voiced their disapproval of the denial of human rights and the inhumanity shown towards the Aborigines. However, they expressed a minority opinion in the midst of the northern land grab. One educated young squatter, possibly a prominent northern Scottish flockmaster, in an altercation with Catholic primate Archbishop John Bede Polding, expressed the extremes of such injustice based on callous homicide. Convinced that there was nothing wrong in killing Aborigines who scattered his herds, he rationalised his actions by claiming 'it was preposterous to suppose they had souls'. Having been in a party which 'shot upward of a hundred', he considered that killing an Aborigine was similar to 'shooting a wild dog'.[93]

Whereas Duncan addressed the problem of abuse of aboriginal human rights and dignity predominantly within the urban environs, Lang focused on the seizure of sacred and hunting lands for runs on the frontier. He was particularly incensed that the indigenes were expelled from their native territory without compensation in any form.[94] Lang considered that uncontrolled extension of the squatting intrusion, with the immorality and disease which it left in its wake, would 'almost necessarily involve the speedy extinction of the Aborigines'.[95] In touch with Lang's sentiments, Kay Saunders has recently recorded that the excesses of Scottish-dominated pastoralism caused the Aborigines to lose 'their traditional mode of production as well as the cultural and spiritual foundations of their lives'.[96]

In the initial stages of Scottish occupation of Brisbane Valley runs, it appeared that it was the squatters and their workers who faced annihilation, so effective was aboriginal retaliation and the accompanying psychology of fear. While one such attack on Colinton in late 1841 elicited predictable support from the surrounding Scots, Balfour was unprepared for the unsympathetic approach in Sydney from Sir George Gipps. Reinforcements from Kilcoy may have delayed the temporary abandonment of Colinton and shelter may have been provided at Cressbrook, but in Sydney not even the formerly supportive Deas Thomson could save Balfour from Gipps' reprimand. Even the subsequent murder of a Colinton shepherd and woundings at Kilcoy and Cressbrook did not influence the intransigent English Governor to shift his stance on pastoral occupation based on peaceful coexistence.

The northern squatters learnt the salutary lessons that Scottish bureaucrats generally followed government policy to the letter; no favours were attendant to common nationality when vice-regal instructions and regulations were broken. Accepting the limitations of their influence, the settlers would have to rely thenceforth on their peers to deal expeditiously on the spot with the human problems arising from the establishment of their runs. In adopting this extreme stance towards a seemingly repressive government which showed a marked lack of empathy to the problems beyond the limits of location, the northerners were accommodating the northern antipathy which had its roots in the convict period.

Taking advantage of the communication problems caused by the significant distance separating the frontier from the Sydney government and press, the squatters resolved to solve the problems in their own manner. A conspiracy of silence involving all settlers regardless of nationality was organised in the north to keep southern authorities in ignorance. It also obviated the possibility of extreme legal repercussions such as those which Gipps had recently enforced in the wake of the Myall Creek massacre.[97] The rebellious Evan Mackenzie, adept at subterfuge and treachery, proved to be the foremost proponent of this facet of organised, anti-government stance which was ultimately adopted by the separationists.[98]

Duncan, who was one of those southern liberal editors kept ignorant of frontier developments, lauded Gipps' humane policies towards Aborigines in the *Australasian Chronicle*. He was in the vanguard of those who seized upon the smallest piece of evidence emanating from the north to attack the cruel aspects of dispossession. Accordingly, only mere snippets and innuendo related to the solution to the aboriginal problem were the sole forms of intelligence which trickled southward.

Probably the last hint of defensive strategies employed by squatters was contained in John Balfour's final complaint to Gipps about lack of government protection for settlers beyond the limits of location. Balfour proposed unsuccessfully that the numbers of the Moreton Bay Crown Lands Commissioner's police force be strengthened with paramilitary reinforcements from each of the stations.[99] This amalgamation of mounted, well-armed men formed the basis of European counter-attack in the bush before Balfour's attempt to seek their legitimacy. It probably continued to operate thereafter for defence and reprisals.

John Archer of Durundur asserted that the mode of interaction between station personnel and indigenes was the most important factor in maintaining harmonious relations. He asserted that the Aborigines' depredations were invariably the consequence of 'misconduct of the whites who seem to imagine that the blacks will allow themselves to be illused without attempting to take revenge'.[100] Not only was cruel dispossession at the base of this disharmony, but the extreme measures adopted to discourage any form of social intercourse irreparably widened the gap.

The Scottish squatters were among the most deliberate as well as the most casual around their stations in taking precautionary measures against aboriginal attack. Kilcoy earned infamy as a station exemplifying the most violent forms of aboriginal suppression.[101] If the hostile approach towards Aborigines at Colinton was the same as that at Kilcoy, it is little wonder that these two stations felt the brunt of the indigenes' anger - even as late as 1848 when one of Balfour's hutkeepers was killed. Evan Mackenzie informed the Select Committee into Immigration in July 1842 that it was impossible to communicate with the district's Aborigines without danger. Thus security was maintained by 'keeping them at a distance' - usually by gunfire or savage dogs.[102] On the Darling Downs, the Leslies were extreme in their caution. George Leslie confided to his parents, 'We never allow them to come about the station or hold any communication with them except it be with a gun or sword'.[103]

Nevertheless in that fearful environment, undermanned stations were laying themselves open to aboriginal aggression. Vigilance, exclusion and maintaining numbers constituted the first line of defence; those who ignored it suffered dire consequences for neglecting this basic frontier code. As the Scottish settlers were among the most conscientious and most lax adherents of this form of frontier pragmatism, they either survived or suffered accordingly. As a result of his disregard for safety precautions and his maltreatment of local indigenes, Andrew Gregor, along with his servant Mary Shannon, paid with his life north of the Pine in October 1846.[104]

On the basis of his experience with Aborigines in southern districts and in the Brisbane River Valley, F. Ludwig Leichhardt, the Prussian botanist and explorer, warned pastoral personnel that even Aborigines who were treated kindly had a propensity to turn treacherous.[105] The humane practices insisted by Scottish absentee Joseph Phelps Robinson towards Aborigines on the Beau Desert run were certainly not enough to save his station from assault. Dubbed 'Humanity" Robinson in Sydney, this important man on the greater colonial scene was a staunch Quaker and therefore oriented towards peace and non-violence. In accordance with such beliefs, the shepherds at Beau Desert were not permitted to carry firearms on the frontier out-stations. Further, Robinson was proud that 'the Blacks with us and about us have always been treated with the greatest of kindness'.[106] To Captain John Coley, a respected Brisbane resident since late 1842, this was a recipe for disaster. He confidently generalised to the Select Committee on the Native Police Force some nineteen years later that the Aborigines 'who were the most kindly treated committed the greatest depredations'.[107] Commissioner Simpson, while not agreeing with this sweeping statement, stressed in his report regarding an assault on Tertius Campbell's nearby station that a management policy which was 'too trusting' was a certain recipe for disaster.

Whereas the Scottish squatters were among the most repressive towards Aborigines, some were the most enlightened. Notwithstanding the arguably good record of racial relations fostered by McConnel at Cressbrook and the substantiated humanitarian policies of Robinson at Beau Desert, Christopher Pemberton Hodgson claimed that in the entire north he knew only of one exception to the squatters' contemptuous and aggressive approach to Aboriginal relations. Identifying the anomalous station owner as David Archer, Hodgson described him as 'a philanthropist imbued with generous principles who settled in an area near the seacoast where the blacks were most ferocious'. Although Hodgson claimed somewhat erroneously that Archer's station alone managed to escape unscathed 'when others were constantly in the alarm or actually were losing men and stock', inter-racial relations at Durundur were relatively harmonious.[108]

The Archers, who practised a less confrontative and more accommodating policy, noted the vast difference between the outcomes of the harsh system enforced at besieged Kilcoy and the more amicable situation at their station. Writing in 1845, Charles Archer outlined the Durundur approach: 'Davie considers the Black as the hereditary owner of the soil and that it is an act of injustice to drive him from his hunting grounds - at the same time punishing any case of sheep stealing when the culprit can be got hold of '.[109] By 'gentle and at the same time determined means', the Archers developed an excellent rapport with the Aborigines, employing some for token wages of consumables such as sweet corn or Indian potatoes. While allowing local clan members access to their station, they excluded outsiders. In this process, they were invariably assisted by trusted members of the favoured Durundur clan.[110]

Whereas most of the Scottish squatters fell within the broad average band on the inter-racial aggression scale, there were others who were located at either extreme. While the Archers and Robinson were foremost in attempting to foster peace and harmony, it was claimed that the Mackenzies of Kilcoy were the 'hammer of the Aborigines'. Captain John Coley, a respectable witness with inaccurate recall of sequence, asserted on information provided by Colin Mackenzie that hundreds of indigenes were killed at Kilcoy. The methods used to disperse threatening Aborigines who scattered flocks, and to exact revenge for the deaths of shepherds, included shooting or poisoning. However, it was the elder Mackenzie who had received an admonishing letter from Attorney-General James Plunkett, holding him responsible for Aboriginal deaths on his run and threatening prosecution if an official complaint was lodged.[111]

The disharmonious relations between the station personnel at Kilcoy and Aborigines may have been confined only to interaction with the plundering northern clans who descended from the Conondale Range rather than with the local indigenes. In 1845, just three years after a tragic conflict at Kilcoy involving Mary River indigenes, Charles and Donald Cameron, cousins of the Mackenzies, were welcomed by the local clan which performed a corroboree in their honour.[112] According to the Aboriginal code of honour, this singular privilege would hardly have been afforded to relatives of despised enemies.

Nevertheless it was at Kilcoy in late January 1842 that one of the most infamous and 'incredible crimes which disgrace [British] efforts at colonisation' occurred. On the outskirts of this run at the base of Mount Kilcoy, thirty to sixty Aborigines from the Wide Bay area died in agony from eating damper laced with strychnine, ostensibly provided by frightened, fleeing shepherds.[113] 'Acute anxiety was undoubtedly the sharpest and most insistent spur to [such] violence'.[114] Whatever the motive, this disgraceful incident 'helped to harden Aboriginal resistance throughout the south' and unleashed a cycle of bloody, revengeful and retaliative actions. The warfare commenced with the murder of two shepherds on the Kilcoy frontier within days of the massacre.[115]

Although the horrendous homicide occurred on a Scottish sheep run, recent research indicates that the Scottish component was probably innocent of the crime. Evan Mackenzie, commonly suspected for 150 years as the perpetrator merely because he owned the run, was in Sydney at the time of the outrage. Because of his absence, it is apparent that one of his management group made the fateful decision and prepared the lethal mixture which was distributed by two shepherds. Those hapless Sassenachs, one an assigned convict, the other a worker hired in Sydney, probably paid with their lives eventually. The Scottish members of the management team, comprising Colin John Mackenzie, John Macdonald and John Ker Wilson have hitherto been among the suspects, principal of whom was the formerly-untraceable first superintendent. During an interview with the Governor's secretary aboard the *Shamrock*, Wilson implicated this man. Supposedly evoking a negative reaction from the rest of the Kilcoy establishment, he recounted at an informal inquiry that the supervisor recommended that the troublesome Aborigines be given 'a dose'.[116]

With a second band of reticent Scottish workers about to arrive at Kilcoy, which was besieged by at least 100 hundred menacing Aborigines, and Evan Mackenzie off the run, the decision to administer poison was probably not the impulsive reaction of two terrified shepherds.[117] The station hierarchy was faced with the choice of getting rid of the large assemblage of Aborigines or losing by flight to Brisbane a valuable but apprehensive addition to the Scottish labour force. In his report on Aborigines for 1842, Commissioner Simpson confirmed that such a prospect was a real fear to pastoral employers. He underlined the tenuous hold such pastoralists had over labour, especially those who arrived harbouring fears of the indigenes. In 1842, it was 'almost impossible to obtain servants at any price ... and those who are already engaged take the earliest opportunity to leave their employers and will sooner put up with a scanty existence in the Settlement than expose themselves to the dangers of the bush'.[118]

After over 150 years of mystery, it is possible to unmask the prime suspect. Selected personally for the Kilcoys by James Balfour, who rated him 'an excellent man', this obviously well-connected overseer from Northumberland and Roxburgh, was the only Englishman in the Mackenzies' entourage.[119] On Evan Mackenzie's return, he suddenly disappeared into the Clarence district via the Darling Downs with his wife and five children.[120] With nothing to hide or else intent on 'brazening it out', Scottish members of the management stayed to face the music. Although this crime occurred on a Scottish run, it is conjectured that the infamous Kilcoy massacre, instigated by an Englishman and executed by colonial workers, was not a Scottish crime against humanity after all. Without doubt, Evan Mackenzie organised the conspiracy of silence to protect a man who may have had powerful connections, possibly in Northumberland or in the Borders. An aristocrat, Mackenzie was unlikely to go to such lengths to shield two colonial shepherds whom he regarded as 'mere labourers'. Ultimately, it was the indomitable Scottish cleric John Dunmore Lang who made the first breach in this wall. Sufficiently troubled with the prospect of being branded an informer if discovered, Lang surreptitiously brought an incriminating entry in the Rev. William Schmidt's missionary journal to the notice of the Governor.[121]

Although Kilcoy suffered the first retaliatory murders for this dastardly crime, there were few Scottish casualties. This probably reflects the protective attitude that the Scottish squatters afforded their sheepmen, many of whom were especially imported. The report which was issued by Captain John Clements Wickham, a native of Edinburgh and police magistrate, revealed that sixteen men were killed and nine wounded between 1841 and 1844.[122] None of the three killed at Kilcoy was of Scottish origin, re-affirming Rev. John Gregor's observation in 1843 that the Scots undertook work close to the head station.[123] James Robertson of Balfour's station was the second Scot killed in the district, the first being C. Campbell at Mocatta's station in October 1841. The last Scottish death reported by Wickham was G. Sinclair who lost his life at Graham & Ivory's Eskdale in June 1844.[124]

There is reason to suspect that the Glaswegian runaway convict James Davis (known as Duramboi to the indigenes), who was unearthed by Andrew Petrie's exploration party, may have been involved in Aboriginal retaliation at Kilcoy - if not a participant in the harassment of the frightened shepherds. Henry Russell, a member of Petrie's group clearly had his suspicions. An adopted member of the Giggabarah clan, which suffered severely from the poisonings, Davis was able to recount in chilling detail the death-throes of his clan brothers. In addition, his adopted father, Pamby Pamby, head of the clan, was in possession of the watch taken from one of the shepherds killed in revenge at Mount Kilcoy. Russell was convinced that Duramboi's role was more than vicarious, musing: 'Strange, I thought, that we should be first apprised of the white man's crime by a white man in the midst of their murderers'.[125] Probably sworn to silence to obstruct the course of justice, Davis returned to the settlement to forge a prosperous but taciturn life as blacksmith, retailer and interpreter.

A cycle of retaliatory actions from both sides was initiated, the most adverse reaction emanating from the Kilcoy run. The fact that Kilcoy was virtually a Highland enclave in the midst of a Lowland-dominated pastoral district may also account for the comparatively severe response towards Aboriginal resistance emerging from that station. After all, revenge and retaliation were as much a part of the Highlanders' psyche as the Aborigines'.

From January 1842, all the management and most of the workers at Kilcoy were Highlanders. They formed a close-knit community, united by region and even estate and family ties. Along with its closely protected proletariat, Kilcoy's distinctive Highland flavour was enriched by two pipers, an acknowledged Scottish dancer and a questionable reputation for illicit grog. While the management of other stations may have temporarily cast aside class distinction to form bonds with workers of the same ethnicity in the name of survival, Kilcoy was different in that the bonds had been formed in Scotland over a century of harmonious, laird-crofter relations and clinched in the close confines of the outward voyage.[126]

It has been suggested that the martial response at Kilcoy to these problems reflected the traditional Highland way of solving difficulties. Under the leadership of a former cavalry officer and deadly duellist, it was 'clan warfare ... transmitted to the bush'.[127] The Highland majority at Kilcoy subsequently united against the twin threats of aboriginal aggression and obstruction by colonial workers - formidable threats to the large Scottish investment.

* * *

While expecting to employ free workers, ticket-of-leave labour and assigned convicts, the Scottish squatters realised that management of the colonial component of the pastoral workforce would be fraught with problems. The stations were heavily dependent for progress and profits on the versatility and expertise of 'such immoral people', the free immigrants generally being 'too inexperienced to be of much use'. Leichhardt noted that such workers, who constituted the majority of the labour force operating in the Brisbane River Valley in 1843, were mainly transported convicts 'without a vestige of moral principle or feeling'.[128] As the colonial workers 'rarely identified their interests with those of their masters', the new squatters found it necessary to devise strategies to manage a class of worker about whom they were totally ignorant.[129]

This anticipated situation was swiftly despatched by the combined intelligence and experience of the Scottish network, tempered with the exercise of frontier expediency and pragmatism. Hence some Scottish squatters developed their runs with the assistance of a core of specially imported, loyal Scottish sheep specialists who were prized and protected. The colonial labour, predominantly of penal origin, was usually relegated to dangerous and peripheral tasks - shepherding on the dangerous outstations. Kept in line by the oppressive Masters and Servants regulations, these workers formed the violent interface between the Aborigines and European settlement. Predictably, the result was catastrophic for inter-racial harmony. 'Out of sight and out of mind' to their masters, they often became the casualties of aboriginal retaliation which they invariably brought upon themselves by their repertoire of amoral behaviour. Some unsparing Scottish squatters apparently deemed labour of convict origin as dispensible as it was cheap.

The fathers of the Balfours and Mackenzies made sure their sons were supplied with industrious, loyal and moral servants. However the Kilcoy Highland workers generally lacked expertise in managing sheep in comparison with the carefully selected Lowland group at Colinton. Acting on David Waugh's advice that agricultural workers could be easily converted to pastoral labour, Mackenzie reported that his hitherto untutored band took only the regulation three months of specialised training to master the unpopular, mindless and monotonous job of shepherding.[130] Once more Thomas Barker had obliged, making the facilities of one of his stations available to the Mackenzies and their retinue.

Whereas Kilcoy was established with the labour of five assigned convicts and the Balfours' work-force included six former convicts, both stations relied upon their Scottish 'new chums' to counteract the old hands 'well-documented propensity for subversion'.[131] Kilcoy possessed the advantage that its recruits were not only faithful and diligent workers drawn predominantly from the Mackenzie Highland estate, but they spoke Gaelic as well as English. This provided potential for creating a pro-pastoralist sub-group within the station based on cultural and linguistic exclusiveness. Early in the piece Mackenzie recognised the benefits of manipulating this distinguishing characteristic of the workforce to the detriment of the monolingual colonial labour and turned it to good advantage.

Already speaking four languages fluently, Mackenzie spent the voyage to Australia bonding with his servants in the process of learning their 'barbaric tongue'.[132] Nevertheless, Sir Colin and Evan Mackenzie had some difficulties persuading their recalcitrant tenants to leave the safety of their native shores for a dangerous life on the Australian frontier. Reports circulating in Inverness and on the Black Isle and letters published in the widely-read *Inverness Courier* painted Australia as a grim destination.[133] In particular, the immorality of the convicts and the ferocity of the Aborigines, not to mention heat, snakes and mosquitoes, rendered it necessary for the Mackenzies to strike a hard-wrought bargain.

On hearing of the Kilcoys' difficulties in recruiting workers, James Balfour demonstrated the typical contempt of a Lowlander businessman for the perceived northern, ignorant barbarians: 'They think the people in New South Wales are all Giants with large mouths and fiery tails so they may destroy and devour everything that comes in their way - so much for the superstition of the Highlander'.[134] When he was faced with similar difficulties in gaining recruits for Colinton, having returned from the Peebles hiring fair empty-handed, Balfour reflected that ignorance and prejudice were also attributes of the 'industrious poor' of the Lowlands. Despite reassurance from the Provost of Peebles, 'the same old bugbear of the drought, the danger of being killed by the Blacks & of being eaten by wild beasts and such like nonsense' was presented to Balfour as sufficient reason to stay home in the midst of a good harvest.[135]

In the final count, Evan Mackenzie reported that the foundation group of Kilcoy workers, mainly drawn from Sir Colin's Belmaduthy estate on the Black Isle, followed readily. With the Mackenzie brothers and their cousin John McDonald, they boarded the *Berkshire* which sailed from London in November 1840. It was later revealed by the elder of the Kilcoys that most of the six men and two married women were well-known to their masters and were regarded as friends - a rare situation in Australian master-servant relations. Apparently the Kilcoys made concessions unheard of in colonial circles to obtain this first invaluable core, including assistance for some to establish themselves in suitable urban occupations on the completion of a mere two years' service on their station. Under similar but less paternalistic contracts, seven single men, three married couples and two children which comprised the second intake of Black Isle immigrants to Kilcoy, arrived in Sydney ex *Anne Milne* on 17 January 1842.[136]

It was acknowledged throughout the colony that the Mackenzies had 'facilities greater than general in having labour sent out'.[137] Building on that reciprocal laird-tenant relationship which was disappearing rapidly in Scotland, and ensuring the numerical superiority of these Scottish free workers, the Mackenzies were guaranteed that Kilcoy would at least get off to a good start. Sir Colin was appreciated by his tenants for the love he showed them - and the feeling was mutual.[138] The children of those tenants entertained no doubt that this close tie would continue in the colony where they would need the traditional protection and assistance of the house of Kilcoy.

The strong presence of this Highland group with fealty to the Mackenzie family inhibited the growth of worker solidarity at Kilcoy. It would have been particularly resistant to any attempted subversion by the outsider shepherds. Assuredly, they would have demonstrated traditional deference which 'endorse[d] an order which legitimates their own political, material and social subordination' because they and their forebears had been well-served by and benefited from the rare brand of paternalism practised by the Kilcoy dynasty.[139] The wily Evan Mackenzie would have been well aware of this factor in formulating his plan for social engineering at Kilcoy station, based on the division between the Gaelic-speaking in-group and the marginalised colonial labour component.

The subsequent urban careers of this Black Isle group at Moreton Bay demonstrated that their deference, based on an harmonious relationship with the sons of their laird, was not transferred to other Scottish leaders apart from the humanitarian David McConnel. They possibly needed a highly respected, paternal figure after the Mackenzies departed. On emerging from Kilcoy to pursue their livelihoods, the Black Isle contingent asserted their rights, forming their own colonial network which provided support among themselves and their migrant relatives and friends who followed. Thereafter, many colonials, mighty and humble, learnt to their disadvantage that traditional demonstrations of respect and courtesy by this group of Highlanders should have never have been mistaken for subservience and docility.[140]

The majority of the workers who accompanied the Mackenzie brothers to Australia aboard the *Berkshire* were either related to each other or close friends. John and Alexander Smith were brothers. The latter was a farm servant working near Inverness while his elder sibling was an agriculturalist helping his father, a Chelsea Pensioner, manage his croft on the Rosehaugh estate. This tenancy adjoined the Mackenzie seat of Belmaduthy. Three months before embarking, John Smith married Isabella Davidson, a dairymaid, they knew by that stage they were bound for New South Wales.[141] John Matheson, shepherd, and barely nineteen, was a cousin of the Smiths and the youngest of the recruitees. One of the outsiders, who became a firm friend of the Smith's extended family at Moreton Bay was Alexander McIntyre, a carpenter from nearby Nairn. John Stewart, blacksmith, and future business colleague of McIntyre, was the only worker residing and toiling on the Belmaduthy estate. All were under the age of twenty-three, literate and adhered to the Presbyterian faith. This sample alone shows that the Mackenzies chose a nice mix of occupations relevant to founding a self-sufficient sheep run.[142]

Among those who were shipmates aboard the *Anne Milne*, some ten months later, was 25 years old Thomas Gray, apparently Jack of all trades. He listed his occupations as farm servant, shepherd, sawyer and bootmaker. John Davidson, future brother-in-law of Alexander Smith, also worked in the vicinity of Inverness as a farm servant. From the same area, farm servant John McDonald at 26 was the oldest of the Kilcoy imports.

Five women who were part of the foundation labour force at Kilcoy, were all wives and mostly designated as house servants. Isabella Smith, the exception as dairymaid, gave birth to yet another generation of Avochian John Smiths at Brisbane shortly after disembarkation from the cutter hired by Evan Mackenzie.[143] Thus, five children inhabited the dangerous Kilcoy property for the duration of their parents' contracts, the five offspring of the first supervisor having left early in 1842. Barbara Fraser (nee Mackenzie) whose forebears had served on the Kilcoy estates for over a century, accompanied her husband Thomas. Subsequently renowned in the district for his tuneful piping, Thomas Fraser was the only illiterate among the Mackenzie work-force - hardly a handicap to his subsequent urban security. Although more protected than their husbands, the Kilcoy mothers were expected to take on additional roles in the working life within the head-station confines such as cooking, gardening, housekeeping and duties in the dairy. Unlike their Colinton equivalents, they were apparently not required to act as shepherds, even close to the homestead.

On a visit to the Balfours' station, the Reverend John Gregor recorded the industry of a hutkeeper, a respectable widow with a large family to support. Touched by the tragedy of her life both in Scotland and the colony and impressed by her determination to rise above her misfortune, Gregor left Colinton 'with more real satisfaction than any one I have yet visited'.[144]

Since government immigration was not resumed until 1848, the squatters in the dangerous and unpopular Moreton Bay District were in dire straits because of the scarcity of labour arriving from the south. The newly-formed, squatter-oriented *Moreton Bay Courier*, amidst rumours that the immigration flow was about to resume, attributed the lack of British labourers independently seeking a better life in the colony to the explosion in railway construction throughout the nation rather than to popular misinformation alone.[145] Thus the supply of reliable labour was in inverse proportion to the increase in the flocks at that stage.

Reflecting the concerns attendant to a district-wide dilemma, Thomas Archer informed his father that Durundur was so short-handed that he and his brother Charles found it necessary to act as shepherds.[146] Having more labour than they needed, the Mackenzies allowed three servants to transfer to nearby Durundur to help the Archers out of this predicament - more indicative of Scottish cooperation than a dishonourable business style.[147] On the Downs, Walter Leslie reported to his parents that it was a free worker's market, the squatters being forced to pay high wages for diminished performance.[148] Although wages at that stage were too good for the squatters' liking, Moreton Bay never proved to be a popular destination for reliable, hard-working Scottish immigrants, especially the highly protected single women.

Until the labour problem was solved by the arrival of cheap, tractable labour, whatever the source, it was temporarily a worker's market in which the squatters contracted with variable results. There was no unanimity among the Scots on wage levels which reflected variations in worker assertion and degree of station security. In 1845, Kilcoy shepherds earned twenty-five pounds per year, those on Colinton twenty-one pounds and workers on Eskdale were paid twenty pounds. The discrepancy between those employees at Kilcoy and those on Graham & Ivory's run arose from Robert Graham's ability to hire workers in Sydney for his brother. The Mackenzies, who had no such close intermediary at that stage, found it necessary to inflate wages to entice workers to an infamous property.[149] By that time most of their especially imported Scottish servants had fulfilled their contracts and sought their fortunes in safer locations, mostly in urban occupations. Thereafter their former masters were forced into competition to strike less favourable agreements with dearer, less committed and more objectively-treated workers.

The Scottish network was prominent among those who aimed to turn the tide. Never one to succumb to adversity, Mackenzie suggested remedial strategies to overcome the shortage of labour as early as December 1843. In view of the exorbitant wages demanded and the inaction of the government in sending labourers to the north, he recommended that servants should be engaged by a Sydney-based agent such as the elder Graham and transmitted to Brisbane by the steamer.[150] This scheme was finally adopted in desperation in July 1846 with the foundation of the Moreton Bay Labour Fund which aimed to import at least 150 labourers into the Moreton Bay and Darling Downs districts. Although the scheme was open to persons employing labour in the neighbourhood of Brisbane, the majority of these were squatters who were required to subscribe in proportion to the size of their flocks. Of the 57 subscriptions forwarded to Brisbane's main Scottish storekeeper John Richardson, 19 came from squatters and 6 from businessmen who were all Scots. John 'Tinker' Campbell, who claimed to be dissatisfied with the quality and good faith of many of the tradesmen, was one of the three defaulters. Assisted by the fact that wages for shepherds and hutkeepers were the highest in the colony, Robert Graham persuaded 175 to immigrate with the prospect of twenty-six pounds per year and rations. For the time being, these workers satisfied the squatters' urgent need to tend flocks which had increased from an average of 700 in 1842 to 2,000 by the end of 1846.[151]

In the short term, the workers in the Moreton Bay district generally had the squatters 'over a barrel', but they got away with very little at Kilcoy and other Scottish-run stations. The *Moreton Bay Courier*, revealing its undisguised pastoralist bias, reported an outbreak in 'ungovernable insolence ..., unrestrained rapacity of demands and disgusting ingratitude to concession ... consequent upon the slender supply of labour'.[152] Whereas many employers were loath to diminish their work-force by pressing prosecution and 'tolerated impertinence', the Scottish squatters proved to be unrelenting in bringing their labourers to heel in accordance with the new Masters and Servants Act of 1846. During October 1846, Colin John Mackenzie and Alexander McDonald personally pursued a shepherd who absconded from hired service after losing forty-seven sheep and overdrawing his account, finally taking him into custody after disarming him in the vicinity of Cunningham's Gap. In an atmosphere of squatter intimidation, the *Courier* heaped praise on Mackenzie whose promptitude and resolution was seen as a lesson to other squatters.[153]

On the other hand, William Barker of the Logan was an example of an employer who did not subscribe to his caste's slogan of a fair day's wages for a fair day's work. His actions were a reflection of the worst of the Scottish business style which disappointed the Archers. However, Barker's prosecution was a tangible demonstration to the community that the Masters and Servants obligations cut both ways. Having been taken to the Police Court in February 1848 by an intinerant shepherd John Lane, Barker was successfully prosecuted for non-payment of wages due. Not only was he required to pay the outstanding wages and court costs, but also the expenses incurred by the defendant in bringing the matter to court. Alternatively, Barker had the option of fourteen days imprisonment in Sydney.[154]

Having reached desperation point with the shortage of labour, high wages, proletariat bargaining power and growing worker irreverence, the squatters were willing to seek station employees from any source. Although the stockholders had gained control of their leases in 1847 and their industry was booming, they well knew that such gains were worthless without labour. The *Moreton Bay Courier*, reflecting the dire state of the local economy, declared: 'An effort must be made to get labour, and that, without delay'. George Leslie confided in his parents that he did not care who they were or where they came from - free, convicts, starving paupers, vagabonds from Britain or Ireland - but labour he 'must have'.[155] Naturally the substitutes for the free European labour were required to be cheap, tractable and obedient.

The labour issue provided a chance for the Scottish-led squatters to establish a new society at Moreton Bay which was not only based on maximising profits and gaining wealth. It was also one more opportunity to set up a plantation economy and establish a squatter hegemony over the district. This was an opportunity to replicate the elitism of the Scottish, two-tiered rural social system in northern Australia. With a minimal middle class which was usually the source of dissension and protest, the bargaining power of a highly dependent working class would be severely diminished. A return to the halcyon days of cheap convict labour would also result in increasing the squatters' social control and profits. The upshot was a petition to Earl Grey, Secretary of State for the Colonies, from the employers of labour at Moreton Bay requesting annual intakes of at least 1000 male labourers, such as the Pentonville Exiles, to overcome the retardation being suffered by the pastoral industry.[156]

Charles Archer, one of the squatters without elitist aspirations, argued that the colony would be ruined whatever way the matter was settled. It was Hobson's choice. The respectable elements of labouring class and the minute middle class demanded that the moral tone of the colony should be preserved, even if that meant 'reigning in' squatters upon whom the economic survival and prosperity of the colony depended.[157]

At that time, despite their claims of financial insecurity, the squatters were riding the crest of the wave, having weathered drought, depression and deflated market prices in the foundation period. Patrick Leslie affirmed in April 1847, 'I do not think now there are six men in the two districts of Darling Downs & Moreton Bay who are in any sort of difficulty & no other part of N.S. Wales can say the same' - a tribute to Scottish know-how, perseverance and industry.[158] Nevertheless, without a steady supply of cheap labour, the pastoral interests would 'remain stationary' and the pastoralists would have 'to strictly curtail their flocks'. Despite the real threat to the progress of the wool industry and the well-being of the 'property. talent and ... intelligence' of the district, the labour problem stood in the way of their absolute social, economic and political control over the district.[159]

The Scottish squatters were at the forefront of experimenting with coloured labour in the name of pastoral progress and elitism. Philip Friell, fellow Etonian classmate of Evan Mackenzie, was reported to provide the model for the effective employment of Indian shepherds on his Tent Hill property. Furthermore, Scotsman and Etonian Gordon Sandeman had successfully founded his Burnett run with Coolie labour.[160] Colin Mackenzie (then a Darling Downs squatter at Warra Warra), John Balfour, Gideon Scott, John McConnel, Donald Coutts, Thomas and David Archer, along with an equal representation of English squatters, were sufficiently inspired to indicate their intentions to employ specially imported Indian workers at a meeting of stockholders and other employers in January 1848 at Brisbane. These Scots also formed the core of the committee of the Indian Labour Association, funded by local employers, to recruit and dispense this source of supposedly cheap, tractable form of labour.[161]

Back in Scotland, a highly prejudiced James Balfour, forever concerned about the minutiae of colonial economics, disapproved of his son's intention of employing Indian labour. He remarked in 1841 when the subject was first mooted, 'I am not quite sure of the advantage of your Coolie importation. They are neither beef eaters nor great consumers of articles of importation. I think all black devils are not to be trusted'.[162]

Yet, William Coote later recorded that the stockholders were so enthused with the prospects of finally solving their labour and financial problems that they virtually overlooked the arrival of twenty-three free immigrants from Sydney in April 1848, a result of the resumption of emigration from Britain and Ireland some eight months previously. Coote explained this enigma, recalling 'the residents were pondering over the best means of getting a cheaper variety'.[163] Unfortunately for the squatters but conveniently for the well-being of the Moreton Bay proletariat, the Legislative Council placed severe restrictions on the importation of Indian workers. The Indian Labour Association accordingly disbanded and thenceforth devoted their efforts to the stop-gap measure of importing Chinese workers from Amoy.[164]

The insensibility of the Scottish-dominated squatters as reflected in their attempt at social engineering in northern society knew no bounds. Temporary settlers in the main, they had tried to change radically the racial mix, moral standards and social composition, to delimit the economic status of Moreton Bay's proletariat society for their exploitative ends. When this tack proved fruitless, they looked to the expected influx of British immigrants to create a squatter-friendly labour market and quash the emergent working-class consciousness being whipped up by 'the violent language of some ... Sydney politicians'.[165]

Having attempted unsuccessfully to influence the local workers to act as lackeys of the local squattocracy, the *Moreton Bay Courier* under the new proprietorship of James Swan in 1847 attempted a more conciliatory approach. After he had fallen out with the first proprietor, Arthur Sydney Lyon, on the issue of transportation, this Scottish liberal and Lang follower tried appealing to the interrelatedness of capitalist and proletariat interests to achieve societal harmony. In particular, Swan emphasised the calamity that would assuredly ensue if both parties abrogated their necessitous, mutual dependence. This tried and true tactic, based on Calvinist doctrine, had been utilised consistently in Scotland to effectively dampen prospective working class awareness, resentment and agitation. Citing the pre-eminent pecuniary and mental resources which the squatters were investing for the good of the district but ridiculing the perception that they claimed inherent superiority, Swan argued that those who invested these means 'must be the most valuable members of the community'.[166]

The true attitude of capital towards Moreton Bay's assertive labour force, 'the fountain of all wealth', was embedded as a sting in the tail of Swan's otherwise pacifying article. Pushing the Calvinist line to its extreme, he threatened that workers who persevered in their selfish designs to ruin the capitalists by excessive wage demands, not only put their own well-being in jeopardy, but were 'traitors to the constitution of society'. With menacing tone, Swan assured the majority of workers who were undermining local prosperity that the surviving employers would never forget the ruin which would be wreaked upon some of their colleagues - the ultimate outcome of this 'misguided conduct'. Finally, the impending arrival of British and Irish migrants on a regular basis at Moreton Bay provided the ultimate threat. When they eventually swelled the labour market, it was anticipated that 'men will be glad of any employment' and the tables would be reversed on those who had systematically opposed the employers by 'exorbitant demands ... and neglectful performance of ... contracts'.[167]

It would appear that the time of Moreton Bay's proletariat was indeed 'at hand', but the powerful pastoralists within the district did not reckon on the determination of the Reverend John Dunmore Lang to enact his own form of social engineering.

His plan was incubated while visiting Moreton Bay between November and December 1845, during which he consulted with the Archers, Griffins, Petries, Dr David Ballow and other Scottish residents. His ideas were promoted in his book *Cooksland: the future cotton field for the Empire* in London during early 1847, the beginning of his quest to recruit his variety of desirable immigrants.[168]

Under Lang's grand design for Moreton Bay, the ethical and religious tone of the district would be changed and the squatter hegemony challenged. Basically he planned to create Moreton Bay as a bastion of Protestantism to counteract the growing influence of Popery in the colony. By systematic immigration, Lang envisaged that the injection of sufficient numbers of industrious Scottish Presbyterian farmers and 'mere labourers' into the district would not only raise the moral tone of society, but would combat squatter pretensions to social, economic and political ascendancy. In other words, the squatters' designs to create a two-class plantation economy would be stymied by the importation of many respectable small capitalists. These bulwarks of respectability, augmented by supporting teachers, lawyers, doctors and artisans would swell and fortify the existing numerically deficient but politically aware middle class of the district.[169] Lang believed that 'the whole framework of European society could be reproduced in the northern territory of Cooksland'.[170]

In the last month of 1848 when the resumption of immigration became a reality, the squatters felt that their fortunes had changed for the better and the workers would henceforth eat humble pie. Close on the heels of the *Nimrod* which unloaded fifty-six Chinese labourers, followed the *Artemesia*, the first ship to bring British and Irish working-class immigrants direct to Brisbane.[171] Regardless of national origin, the 200 immigrants were immediately swallowed into the work-force, the majority serving in the interior. With the prospects of a continuous flow of immigrants to solve the district's labour problems, the advent of 1849 augured well for squatter plans to consolidate and improve their prosperity and hegemonic prospects.

Ominously, Lang's recruitment drive in Britain over the previous two years was about to bear fruit when the first batch of nearly 600 personally selected God-fearing immigrants arrived on the 20 January of that critical year.[172] With a mixture of arrogance and ignorance towards this Protestant influx, the squatters initially appeared unaware of the potential threat that the markedly different Langites posed to their aspirations for untrammelled superiority.

* * *

By the unrelenting practice of pastoral capitalism, the Scottish squatters were well advanced in achieving their economic and social goals by 1848. They had made remarkable progress, making the best of the head-start they received as a result of their membership of a Scottish privileged caste and its networks. Overcoming all obstacles they encountered through their tenacity, courage and intellect, they had established a flourishing pastoral industry which secured a solid but undiversified revenue base for the Moreton Bay District. However, the opposition they encountered to their socio-economic pretensions by the bourgeois urbanites centred in Brisbane was destined to be more formidable.

Under Mackenzie's brief period of Highland paternalism from 1841 to mid 1845, northern society was united in meeting the threat of Aboriginal resistance, seeking a diversified economy, resisting the exploitation of southern merchants and confronting the inertia and disinterest of the government. Concomitant with the renewal of government activity from 1846, the squatters' hegemonic plans, their rejection of Brisbane, rebuff to wide-scale agriculture and designs for cheaper labour combined to destroy the social cohesion arising from Mackenzie's visionary leadership. This imminent threat to respectable immigration and the emergence of democracy heralded a massive downward impact on the living standards and work opportunities of the infant working class. Sensing the stultification of a new order based on middle-class morality and access to property, the incompatible figures of Lang and Duncan independently emerged as robust and vociferous opponents of the squatters. They determinedly resisted retrogade attempts to perpetuate Scottish class distinction and social injustice towards Europeans while denying human rights to Aborigines.

With the aid of the sympathetic *Moreton Bay Courier*, Lang advised the untried, northern liberals from Sydney as they tackled the thorny issues associated with the proposed plantation economy and antipathy towards the southern political and mercantile establishments. This antagonism, expressed in Brisbane bush rivalry, was destined to form the core of Moreton Bay's political agenda until 1859. Starting with Moreton Bay, Lang harboured a grand plan to build a better Australia by loosening the stranglehold of pastoralism and promoting agriculture. He aimed to redress the social and political imbalance of the anti-squatter sector by selective population increase and initiating the separation movement. This common cause against the universally-despised government temporarily overcame district factionalism and reunited the northern antagonists after cheap labour designs were finally rebuffed. Although prickly factionalism prevailed throughout, the visions of Scottish leaders set the northern agenda in this first period marked by aboriginal resistance, squatter dominance, free enterprise foundations, resurgent government control and the urban backlash.

The Scottish squatters had enjoyed decided advantages in their homeland and Australia in founding their runs, some answerable to their financial backers for some time thereafter. However, they were virtually on their own in dealing with the human problems arising from their forceful land acquisition and need for a tractable labour force. Courageous, single-minded and resilient as befitted the tradition of the Scottish ruling class, this privileged minority ran headlong into a indigenous and European majority with interests which clashed with their relentless pursuit of capital accumulation and social superiority. The result was racial and class conflict which was to occupy the stage of northern development for the rest of the nineteenth century.

ENDNOTES

1. L.J. Jay, 'Pioneer settlement on the Darling Downs', *Scottish Geographical Journal*, 73 (1957), pp. 36-44.
2. James Balfour to Thomas Barker, 23 February 1841, Balfour-Barker correspondence, 4/2215, Society of Australian Genealogists, Sydney.
3. John Balfour to Thomas Barker, 19 October 1840, Balfour-Barker correspondence.
4. James Balfour to Thomas Barker, 15 December 1841, Balfour-Barker correspondence.
5. Duncan Mackellar, *The Australian emigrant's guide manual, or a few practical observations and directions for the guidance of emigrants proceeding to that part of the colony*, 2nd edition, (Edinburgh: John Fletcher, 1839).
6. Donnachie, 'The making of Scots on the make', pp. 140, 150.
7. Hodgson, *Reminiscences of Australia*, p. 118.
8. David L. Waugh, *Three years of practical experience as a settler in New South Wales from 1834 to 1837*, Fourth edition with a map, (Edinburgh: John Johnston, 1838).
9. Donnachie, 'The making of Scots on the make', p. 141.
10. John Balfour to George Forbes, 19 October 1840, Balfour-Barker correspondence.
11. Syd H. Ware, Tamworth Historical Group, letter to John Mackenzie-Smith, 26 September 1994, with enclosure; J.S. Ryan, *Australian place names*, pp. 59-62.
12. Patrick Leslie to his parents, 10 October 1839; George Leslie to Thomas Leslie, 13 April 1839, Leslie family letters, OM 71-31, JOL.
13. John Balfour to George Forbes, 19 October 1840, Balfour-Barker correspondence.
14. James Balfour to Thomas Barker, 10 December 1840, Balfour-Barker correspondence.
15. Ibid. Sir Thomas Brisbane had obviously forgotten that the river in question bore his name.
16. James Balfour to Thomas Barker, 17 November 1842, Balfour-Barker correspondence.
17. Mackenzie-Smith, *Brisbane's forgotten founder*, pp. 106-24; John Balfour to George Forbes, 19 October 1840, Balfour-Barker correspondence.
18. Colonial Secretary to Commandant, Moreton Bay, 7 May 1841, 41/4580, 41/4613, Moreton Bay letter book, JOL.
19. Evan Mackenzie to Colonial Secretary, 6 May 1841, 7 May 1841, 41/4549, 41/4613, Colonial Secretary's correspondence, in-letters from Moreton Bay, JOL.
20. In Scotland and among the Scottish squatters, the Mackenzies would have been referred to and distinguished by their branch name, ie Mackenzies of Kilcoy abbreviated to Kilcoys.
21. Mackenzie, *The Australian emigrant's manual*, p. 65.
22. James Balfour to Thomas Barker, 10 June 1841; John Balfour to George Forbes, 19 October 1840, Balfour-Barker correspondence.
23. Hodgson, *Reminiscences*, p. 95.

24 John Campbell, *The early settlement of Queensland and other articles*, (Ipswich: *Ipswich Observer*, 1875), p. 6.
25 Hodgson, *Reminiscences*, p. 95.
26 Dimity Dornan and Denis Cryle, *The Petrie family: building colonial Brisbane*, (St Lucia: University of Queensland Press, 1992), pp. 1-21.
27 Henry Stuart Russell, *The genesis of Queensland*, (Sydney: Turner and Henderson, 1888), p. 211; Archer, *Recollections*, pp. 62-4.
28 Hewitson, *Far off in sunlit places*, p. 151.
29 *Brisbane Courier*, 22 February 1872, p. 2.; Constance Campbell Petrie, *Tom Petrie's reminiscences of early Queensland*, (Sydney: Angus and Robertson, 1932 ed.), p.223.
30 James Balfour to Charles Balfour, 28 March 1843, Baring Brothers and Company records relating to Australia, H.C. 6.4, Guildhall Library, London.
31 Archer, *Recollections*, p. 44.
32 John Archer to William Archer, 14 June 1842, in John Mackenzie-Smith, comp. *Brisbane River Valley 1841-50: pioneer observations and reminiscences*,[*Brisbane River Valley*], Brisbane History Group Sources No. 5, (Brisbane: Brisbane History Group, 1991), p. 14.
33 Archer, *Recollections*, pp. 74-6.
34 John Archer to William Archer, 14 June 1843, in *Brisbane River Valley*, p. 14.
35 James Balfour to Thomas Barker, 10 December 1840, Balfour-Barker correspondence.
36 Evan Mackenzie, enclosure, James Balfour to Charles Balfour, 28 May 1843, Baring correspondence.
37 Hewitson, *Far off in sunlit places*, p. 121.
38 James Balfour to Charles Balfour, 28 March 1843, Baring Brothers' correspondence.
39 Claims to leases of Crown Land, 1848, supplement to the *New South Wales Government Gazette* [*NSWGG*], 9 May 1848, pp. 6-14.
40 Lawrence S. Smith, ed., *Tracks and times: a history of the Pine Rivers Shire*, (Brisbane: Pine Rivers Shire Council, 1988), pp. 65-6. Francis Griffin was formerly the master of the HRSNCo. steamer *James Watt* which plied between Sydney and Brisbane. George and Janet Griffin knew Lang in Sydney.
41 Erica Long, 'Early white settlement on the Pine River', *RHSQJ*, 16 (1997), p. 195.
42 Ibid, p. 202.
43 Kathleen Nothling, *Then and now: the story of Beaudesert 1874-1974*, (Beaudesert: 1974), p. 3; Joan Starr, *Logan ... the man, the river and the city*, (Tenterfield: Southern Cross, 1988), pp. 6-8.
44 Angela Collyer, The process of settlement, land occupation and usage in Boonah 1842-1870s, MA thesis, University of Queensland, 1991.
45 See map, Mid-nineteenth century Scotland after Harrison and Prentis, Appendix, p. 225.

46 James Balfour, 14 Maitland Street, Edinburgh, Census 1851, District 715, Book 54, Schedule 29, Scottish Record Office [SRO], Edinburgh; James Balfour, death certificate, 28 October 1859, Register 685/1, St George, Edinburgh, Entry 690, SRO; James Balfour, Inventory, 3 February 1860, SCO/1/103/475, SRO; Mary Balfour, death certificate, 15 January 1872, 1872 Register 685/1, Edinburgh, Entry 96, SRO.
47 Mackenzie-Smith, *Brisbane's forgotten founder*, pp. 10-18.
48 Lord Glenelg to Sir Thomas Mitchell, 19 September 2840, Sir Thomas Mitchell papers, vol. 14, CY 244, A. 167-9, Mitchell Library, Sydney.
49 Evan Mackenzie to Colonial Secretary, 6 May 1841.
50 Sir Colin Mackenzie, Codocil to the will, 17 October 1840, Sheriff Court of Ross and Cromarty, Dingwall inventories, Vol. 741, fol. 496, SRO.
51 See map: Moreton Bay District 1846 after Baker, Appendix, p. 226.
52 Alex Sinclair, Ferintosh, statement, 1893, typescript, Alasdair Cameron, Wellhouse, Black Isle.
53 Mackenzie-Smith, *Brisbane's forgotten founder*, p. 30.
54 Although boundaries with neighbouring squatters may have been arranged and buildings erected, the pastoralists were not eligible to apply for squatting licences until their stock had been driven onto the property. Having travelled ahead of their stock by cutter in mid-May 1841, John Balfour and Evan Mackenzie were unable legally to claim their runs until the overland droving party arrived.
55 James Balfour to Thomas Barker, 27 June 1840, Balfour-Barker correspondence.
56 Kerr, *Confidence and tradition*, p. 11.
57 John Edwards, 'Kangaroo Creek', in *A history of Coutts Crossing and Nymboida Districts*, p. 131, enclosure in personal correspondence with Syd. Ware, December 1994. Thomas and Donald Coutts were connected by family ties to the banking house of John Coutts & Co. which operated in London and Edinburgh. Sir William Forbes, grandfather of George Forbes took over the Edinburgh enterprise before its union with the Bank of Scotland in 1831: Bettina McConnochie, Coutts' descendant, letter to John Mackenzie-Smith, 23 March 1996.
58 Roderick Balfour, Emigration from the Western Highlands and Western Isles of Scotland to Australia during the nineteenth century, M.Litt. thesis, University of Edinburgh, 1973, pp. 77-8; *Australian Dictionary of Biography* [*ADB*], Douglas Pike, ed. vol. 1, 1851-1890, (Melbourne: Melbourne University Press, 1966), pp. 12-15.
59 McConnel papers: notes on the Scotts and Ivory, 89/205, Fryer Library, University of Queensland; Archer, *Recollections*, p. 55; Kerr, *Confidence and tradition*, pp. 4-10.
60 *ADB*, 1851-90, pp. 464-5; Betty Iggo, historical researcher, Edinburgh, to John Mackenzie-Smith, 11 November 1996; James Balfour to Thomas Barker, 1 September 1843, Balfour-Barker correspondence; Michael Stendon, ed. *Who's who of British Members of Parliament*, vol. 1, 1832-85, (London: Harvester Press, 1976), p. 295.

61 Archer, *Recollections*, pp. 55-6.
62 James Balfour to Thomas Barker, 15 March 1841, Balfour-Barker correspondence.
63 McConnel papers, Note on Walter Scott.
64 Archer, *Recollections*, p. 36.
65 Nehemiah Bartley, *Australian pioneers and reminiscences 1849-1894*, (Brisbane: Gordon & Gotch, 1896), p. 203; 'The first years on the upper Brisbane River', typescript, undated, unpaginated, Cressbrook, 1991.
66 *ADB*, 1888-1850, pp. 153-4; Bartley, *Australian pioneers*, pp. 202-5; Kerr, *Confidence and tradition*, pp. 10-11; Mary Macleod Banks, *Memories of pioneer days in Queensland*, (London: Heath Cranton, 1933), pp. 17-18.
67 Banks, *Memories*, pp. 17-18; Pasturage Licences, *NSWGG*, 1840, p. 1194; *NSWGG*, 1841, p. 1483; Bill Thorpe, *Colonial Queensland: perspectives of a colonial society*, (St Lucia: University of Queensland Press, 1996), p. 142.
68 James Balfour to Thomas Barker, 17 November 1842, 28 March 1843, Balfour-Barker correspondence.
69 Before deciding to head for Moreton Bay, the Balfours formed their station on the Liverpool Plains. Taking sheep on thirds: Having agreed to add a speculator's flock to a station's complement, the proprietor received in return for agistment and care one third of the increase in stock and one third of the wool produced from that flock.
70 George Forbes to John Balfour, 6 July 1840, Balfour-Barker correspondence.
71 John Balfour to George Forbes, 19 October 1840, Balfour-Barker correspondence.
72 James Balfour to Thomas Barker, 20 May 1840, Balfour-Barker correspondence.
73 Thomas Archer to William Archer, 22 March 1846, in *Brisbane River Valley*, pp. 61-2.
74 Archer brothers, Durundur diary 1843-44, OM 79-111, JOL.
75 James Balfour to Thomas Barker, 15 March 1841, Balfour-Barker correspondence.
76 Evan Mackenzie, Evidence taken before the Immigration committee, 21 July 1842, *Votes and proceedings of the Legislative Council of New South Wales* [*NSWVP*], 1841, pp. 45-8; Evan Mackenzie, Reply to circular, The select committee on crown lands grievances, *NSWVP*, 1844, p. 248.
77 James Balfour to Thomas Barker, 28 March 1843, Balfour-Barker correspondence.
78 Mackenzie, Evidence, 1842, p. 47.
79 Stephen Henry Roberts, *The squatting age in Australia*, (Melbourne: Melbourne University Press, 1964), pp. 211, 236-59.
80 *Sydney Morning Herald* [*SMH*], 7 May 1845, p. 2; 17 May 1845, p. 3.
81 Baker, *Days of wrath*, pp. 215-18.
82 Ibid.
83 Margaret Payten, William Augustine Duncan 1811-85, MA thesis, University of New South Wales, 1965, pp. 104-111.
84 Baker, *Days of wrath*, p. 238; Payten, Duncan thesis, pp. 52-64.
85 Payten, Duncan thesis, p. 71.
86 William Augustine Duncan, undated, unpaginated, in William Augustine Duncan, papers, A2876-A2879, Mitchell Library, Sydney; Payten, Duncan thesis, pp. 129-33.

87 W.A. Duncan to Edward Deas Thomson, 21 September 1847, Deas Thomson papers, CY 721, Mitchell Library Sydney.
88 Payten, Duncan thesis, p. 133.
89 John Balfour to Commandant, Moreton Bay, 6 October 1841, Colonial Secretary's in-letters, micro A 12, 121, JOL.
90 Thorpe, *Colonial Queensland*, p. 53.
91 Hewitson, *Far off in sunlit places*, p. 273.
92 Mort, letter, 28 January 1844.
93 Archbishop John Bede Polding, evidence, Select Committee on Aborigines, 10 September 1845, *NSWVP*, 1845, p. 952.
94 John Dunmore Lang, *Cooksland in north-eastern Australia: the future cotton field of Great Britain*, (London: Longmans, Brown, Green & Longmans, 1847), pp. 268-9.
95 Lang, *Cooksland*, p. 268.
96 Kay Saunders, *Workers in bondage: the origins and bases of unfree labour in Queensland, 1824-1916*, (St Lucia: University of Queensland Press, 1982), p. 11.
97 *Sydney Gazette*, 20 December 1838, p. 2.
98 Mackenzie-Smith, *Brisbane's forgotten founder*, p. 78.
99 Balfour to Dr Stephen Simpson, Commissioner for Crown Lands, 8 August 1842, Colonial Secretary, in-letters, Moreton Bay.
100 John Archer to William Archer, 8 November 1841, Archer letters.
101 Captain John Coley, Evidence to the Select Committee on Native Police, 1861, V*otes and proceedings of the Queensland Legislative Assembly* [*QVP*], 1861, p. 20.
102 Mackenzie, Evidence, Emigration Committee, *NSWVP*, 1842, p. 46; Charles Archer to William Archer, 29 April 1845, Archer letters.
103 George Leslie to his parents, 24 June 1841, Leslie letters.
104 *Moreton Bay Courier* [*MBC*], 24 October, 1846, p. 3.
105 F.W. Leichhardt to his mother, 27 August 1843, in *Brisbane River Valley*, p. 71.
106 J.P. Robinson to Colonial Secretary, 10 June 1845, 44/8248, Archives Office of New South Wales. [AONSW].
107 Coley, Evidence, *QVP*, 1861, p. 21.
108 Hodgson, *Reminiscences*, pp. 81-2.
109 Charles Archer to William Archer, 28 April 1845, in *Brisbane River Valley*, p. 74.
110 David Archer to William Archer, 10 September 1843, Archer letters.
111 Coley, Evidence, pp. 19, 21.
112 Donald Charles Cameron, Journal, 11 February 1845, in *Brisbane River Valley*, p.72.
113 William Coote, *History of the colony of Queensland from 1770 to the close of the year 1881 in two volumes*. Volume 1, (Brisbane: Thorne, 1882), p. 45.
114 Henry Reynolds and Noel Loos, 'Aboriginal resistance in Queensland,' *Australian Journal of Politics and History*, 22 (1976), p. 225.
115 Raymond Evans, Kay Saunders, Kathryn Cronin, *Race relations in colonial Queensland: exclusion, exploitation and extermination*, (St Lucia: University of Queensland Press, 1988), p. 45.

116 John Ker Wilson, evidence, Select Committee on the Native Police Force, *QVP*, 1861, p. 85.

117 William Fraser, one of the second group of Mackenzie's imports recounted to Archibald Meston that he arrived at Kilcoy on the day following the poisonings. The diary of the German Mission at Nundah recorded the overnight stay of this group on 31 January 1842. *Daily Mail*, 25 August 1923, Meston cuttings, OM 72-82/84, JOL; Extracts from the diary of the German Mission to the Aborigines at Moreton Bay from 25 December 1841 to 13 May 1842, ML 2240, CY 479, Mitchell Library.

118 John Balfour to Commissioner of Crown Lands, 8 August 1842, enclosed in Commissioner of Crown Lands, Moreton Bay to Colonial Secretary, 14 September 1842, 42/6111, Colonial Secretary, in-correspondence from Moreton Bay, AONSW; Gipps' despatch No. 245, 41/1842 in Raphael Cilento, 'The life and residences of the Hon. Stephen Simpson', *RHSQJ*, 8 (1965-66), p.21.

119 James Balfour to Thomas Barker, 27 June 1840. Entitlement certificates, *Berkshire*, 4/4862, micro. 320, AONSW.

120 Bawden lectures, p. 126; Criminal Crown Solicitor to Colonial Secretary, 3 May 1848, SANSW.

121 *Colonial Observer*, 3 December 1842, p. 651.

122 Police Magistrate, Moreton Bay, to Colonial Secretary 19 October 1844, enclosing undated letter of F.W. Bigge, 44/7954, AONSW; Police Magistrate to Colonial Secretary, 'enclosing return of' white men that have been killed and wounded by the Aborigines in the District of Moreton Bay from the year 1841 to 1844 inclusive', 44/8349, AONSW.

123 John Gregor, *The church in Australia, part 11, two journals of missionary tours in the districts of Maneroo and Moreton Bay, New South Wales in 1843*, (London: Society for the Propagation of the Gospel, 1846) in *Brisbane River Valley*, p. 37.

124 Return on white men killed and wounded by Aborigines at Moreton Bay 1841-44.

125 Russell, *The genesis of Queensland*, p. 281.

126 Kay Saunders, *Workers in bondage*, p. 5; John Mackenzie-Smith, 'Moreton Bay Scots, 1841-96: a Black Isle contingent ', *RHSQJ*, 16 (1998), p. 194.

127 Hewitson, *Far off in sunlit places*, p. 176.

128 Lang, *Cooksland*, p. 271; F.W. Leichhardt to his mother, 27 August 1843 in F.W. Leichhardt, *The letters of F. Ludwig Leichhardt*, trans. M. Aurousseau (Cambridge: Cambridge University Press, 1968), p. 672

129 Frank K. Crowley, Working class conditions in Australia 1788-1851, PhD thesis, University of Melbourne, 1949, p. 201.

130 Ibid.

131 *NSWGG*, 15 June 1841, p. 820; Run No. 30, Liverpool Plains, 1841 census, AONSW.

132 Wenowah Greig, Kilcoy, Kilcoy Castle, typescript, undated, p. 6.

133 *Inverness Courier*, 4 November 1840, p.3; 2 December 1840, p. 3.

134 James Balfour to Thomas Barker, 27 June 1840, Balfour-Barker correspondence.

135 James Balfour to Thomas Barker, 6 March 1841, Balfour-Barker correspondence.
136 Entitlement certificates, *Berkshire*, March 1841; Evan Mackenzie, Evidence, 1842, p. 48.
137 Entitlement certificates, *Anne Milne*, January 1842, AONSW micro. 1341; Mackenzie, Evidence, p. 48
138 Statement by Alex Sinclair, farmer, Ferintosh, 1892; Evan Mackenzie, Evidence, 1842, p. 46.
139 MacLaren, 'Class and culture among farm servants in the North-East', p. 103.
140 Mackenzie-Smith, 'Moreton Bay Scots: a Black Isle contingent', pp. 502-8.
141 Marriage of John Smith to Isabella Davidson, 3 September 1840, extract from parochial register of Avoch, New Register House, Edinburgh.
142 Entitlement certificate, *Berkshire*; John H.G. Smith, From Avoch to Brisbane, 1984, typescript, unpublished.
143 Entitlement certificate, *Berkshire* and *Anne Milne*; John Smith, baptism certificate, 11 July 1841, born 23 June 1841, Parish of Moreton Bay. 2156, Vol. 25A, Registrar-General, New South Wales.
144 Gregor, Journal, in Brisbane River Valley, pp. 40-1.
145 *MBC*, 4 July 1846, p. 2.
146 Thomas Archer to William Archer, 14 October 1845, Archer letters.
147 Mackenzie-Smith, 'Moreton Bay Scots: a Black Isle contingent', p. 500.
148 Walter Leslie to his parents, 8 November 1841, Leslie family letters.
149 Robert Graham, evidence, Legislative Council Immigration Committee, 28 August 1845, *NSWVP*, 1845, p. 619.
150 *SMH*, 4 December 1843, p. 3.
151 *MBC*, 21 December 1846, p. 1.
152 *MBC*, 14 August 1847, p. 3.
153 *MBC*, 17 October 1846, p. 2; Depositions before Magistrates, 6 February 1846-20 October 1846, p. 35, CPS/AT, QSA.
154 *MBC*, 19 February 1848, p 3; .*MBC*, 4 July 1847, p. 3
155 George Leslie to his parents, 10 May 1847, Leslie family letters.
156 Ibid.
157 Charles Archer to William Archer, 10 April 1847, in *Brisbane River Valley*, p. 32.
158 Patrick Leslie to William Leslie, 23 April 1847, Leslie family letters.
159 *MBC*, 27 March 1847, p.2; Valerie V. Donovan, From Queensland squatter to English squire: Arthur Hodgson and the colonial gentry, 1840-70, MA thesis, University of Queensland, 1993.
160 *MBC*, 19 December 1846, p. 2.
161 *MBC*, 22 January 1848, p.2.
162 James Balfour to Thomas Barker, 15 December, 1841, Balfour-Barker correspondence.
163 Coote, *History of Queensland*, p. 80.
164 *MBC*, 22 April 1848, p. 2.
165 *MBC*, 28 September, 1848, p 2.

166 Ibid.
167 *MBC*, 28 September 1848, p. 2.
168 Lang, *Cooksland*, pp. 119-121, 143, 162-175.
169 Lang, *Cooksland*, p. 252.
170 Baker, *Days of wrath*, pp. 222-4, 236, 247; *Cooksland*, pp. 223-33.
171 *MBC*, 2 December 1848, p.3; *MBC*, 6 December 1848, p. 3.
172 Lang's articles, *British Banner*, 1 March 1848 to 24 January 1849; *MBC*, 21 January 1849, p. 2.

CHAPTER 2

Pioneer urban Scots 1841-48

Just as Scottish initiative, capital, enterprise and loyal labour ensured that the pastoral industry of the Moreton Bay District was placed on a sound footing, so a small but potent concentration of Scots determined the prosperity and development of Brisbane and Ipswich. Although predominantly composed of a more varied social mix than the two-tiered strata in the interior, the urban Scottish were driven as much by their nationally-derived, socio-economic agendas. In fact, a substantial number of those who were especially imported from Scottish estates to pioneer the district's sheep runs for their lairds' sons found their way to Brisbane and Ipswich to establish their own profitable businesses. The advantages of being 'first in the field', as outlined by James Balfour in writing to Thomas Barker, applied equally to humble artisans and labourers in the entrepot as much as it did to well-connected squatters in the hinterland.[1] However, Brisbane's proletariat slowly came to realise that the designs of the Scottish squatters were antithetical to their colonial aspirations.[2]

Between 1841 and 1845, Brisbane and Ipswich were fighting for their very survival along with the beleaguered pastoral industry. Most of the community demonstrated unity in the face of diversity, uniting to overcome the various obstacles which inhibited the sound economic development of the district. In this period, Brisbane in particular was bedevilled by uncertainty to the detriment of business investment.[3] Even before free settlement was permitted in early 1842, Deputy Surveyor-General F.A. Perry cast doubts over Brisbane's future as the entrepot for the Northern Districts.[4] Impermanence, inaccessibility, disunity and disarray were conspicuous; the wharves were in disrepair, government buildings were dilapidated and the business and shipping centres were located inconveniently on opposite banks of the wide Brisbane River. International shipping would never entertain Brisbane as a port of call until Moreton Bay was charted, the bar at the mouth of the Brisbane River was removed and the flats which impeded the twenty-five miles meandering trip to the settlement were dredged.[5]

Economically it appeared that Brisbane was too reliant upon the pastoral industry, virtually becoming a business disaster zone outside of the wool season or the rare recreational visits by squatters. It was evident that there was urgent need to diversify the local economy. Meanwhile the Sydney-based government rationalised its apathy and neglect towards Brisbane, conspicuously failing to connect this port to the interior by an adequate system of roads and bridges. In addition, Brisbane and its surrounds were under the tight grip of the southern mercantile octopus. Between them, the Scottish merchants in Sydney and the Hunter River Steam Navigation Company [HRSNCo.] reaped a fiscal harvest in high interest rates, foreclosed mortgages, excessive freight charges and fares.[6] Naturally the cupidity, parsimony and disinterest of the southern controlling bodies aroused resentment among those northerners who were struggling to establish themselves in a district which was severely at risk.

The message to the north was loud and clear: survival and ultimately prosperity depended on local co-operation, individual capitalist entrepreneurial activity, diversification of the economy and attainment of self-sufficiency. The ascendant leader Evan Mackenzie urged the settlers to have 'more dependence on our own resources and less on the stores of the merchant'.[7] In short, the inactive southern government and exploitive mercantile forces drove the northern settlers to take advantage of distance and disinterest to adopt an anti-Sydney stance.

The first half of the 1841 to 1848 period was distinguished by its reliance on free-enterprise and local initiative.[8] During this phase, squatter attempts to influence the district's entrepot were tolerated as it was widely accepted that the very survival of the region was dependent upon pastoral prosperity which was being threatened by depression, drought, high wool prices and Aboriginal resistance. At that stage, town and bush were in the same boat. While pressing this point as well as the mutual dependence of capital and labour, Scottish leadership united town and hinterland in the battle for survival.

Eventually it was Scottish initiative, enterprise and capital which saved the pastoral industry and placed Brisbane on a firm footing as the district's port. As the squatters inextricably linked their own prosperity with that of Brisbane, they plotted, planned and laboured for more ambitious objectives than mere survival.[9] The remorselessness and disregard which accompanied some of the major initiatives implemented in Brisbane and elsewhere in colonial Queensland has led Scottish historian Ian Donnachie to conclude: 'Scottish capitalism was just as ruthless in the colonies as it was at home'.[10]

Although the pragmatic and unpredictable tactics of Scottish laissez-faire capitalism laid the foundations of northern development in the first four years of free settlement, continued development was inexorably and less spectacularly achieved by re-invigorated government action between 1847 and 1848. The southern establishment, which lost much of its control over this northern district in the pre-1846 period, recovered ascendancy thereafter. Not only had the colonial treasury regained solvency, but local initiatives had borne fruit. The significant volume of exports demonstrated that the district was established on a firm footing.[11] Sydney interests had regained their absolute control over the district's economy.

Whereas progress prior to 1847 was determined by rebellious free-enterprise led by Scottish minor aristocrat Evan Mackenzie, agents of change thereafter were necessarily more compliant. District improvements were determined more conventionally by government decision, the outcome of a process involving public meetings, application, support from the local bureaucracy, parliamentary debate and availability of funds.[12] Rebellious deception and subterfuge, which had formerly attracted government and mercantile opposition to many northern demands, had noticeably receded with the ambitious Mackenzie's departure.[13]

Even though Captain J.C. Wickham continued unspectacularly in his role as Police Magistrate, the most influential government official of the later period was former radical journalist William Augustine Duncan. With every reason to be a rabid foe of the squatters, Duncan arrived in mid 1846 as Sub-Collector of Customs.[14] Unlike the actions taken by Mackenzie, Duncan's decisions threw doubts on Brisbane's future as the district's shipping port while concurrently exacerbating intra-urban rivalry. Armed with a formidable intellect, intransigent opinions, full government backing and a passionate belief in human rights, Duncan further divided the urban community. Although Brisbane learnt to live warily with this untouchable, iconoclastic public servant, the Scottish squatters attempted to ostracise him, redoubling their efforts to promote a rival port.[15]

The ultimate losers were the remaining Scottish squatters who lost control of the district's shipping port to an unlikely combination of emergent radical Brisbane citizenry and the southern Scottish-dominated political and mercantile establishment. Consequently Ipswich became the pastoralists' urban base and concerted efforts were made to eliminate Brisbane by developing port facilities at Cleveland Point.[16] Buoyed by their success in establishing a viable pastoral industry, the squatters' agenda for the district became patently evident. Not only did they wish to select a port which they could control, but their on-going parallel battle to obtain cheap, tractable labour (convict or coloured) indicated to the citizenry that the pastoralists would stop at nothing short of establishing a plantation economy. Indeed, the very factor that set colonial Queensland apart from its southern counterparts was the 'more pronounced plantation economy' which the predominantly Scottish 'quasi aristocracy' established on the Darling Downs, Brisbane River Valley and Logan.[17]

Contrary to the co-operative climate between the Scottish squatters and the proletariat which was evident before 1846, there were definite signs that the interests of both groups no longer coincided. Class conflict was inevitable as such a repressive and elitist system was in many aspects similar to that enshrined on most Scottish estates - one which many of the Scottish proletariat hoped they had left behind. While some fled either willingly or unwillingly from the exploitative and repressive representations of the estate system, a sizeable number were willing colonial exemplars of the more liberal variety.[18]

Opposition to the monopoly of social, political and economic power enjoyed by the landed proprietors formed the basis of radical agitation throughout Scotland and the rest of Britain. It also lay at the heart of the anti-squatter campaign at the Moreton Bay in the late 1840s and 1850s. Squatter aspirations to gain such group privilege within Australia also welded the disparate elements of the 'productive class' throughout the colony into a formidable opposition. For those immigrant Scots who enjoyed the same traditional patronage on the Moreton Bay frontier as at home, the mutual relationship which existed between master and man was their source of security. When this was removed, usually because of their master's return to Scotland, the formerly pampered Scots found reason to identify with the disaffected. Abandoned to the ruthless forces of colonial capitalism, this group eventually experienced the same exploitation which their less fortunate and less well-connected peers endured. On identifying common issues with other groups within the productive sector, they joined their like-minded fellow colonists to discover class consciousness.

With the northern visit of the Reverend John Dunmore Lang in late 1845 and the arrival of long-standing squatter antagonists such as James Swan and William Augustine Duncan, the 1846 to 1848 period reflected the hardening of urban resistance to pastoral hegemony. The ensuing trickle of influential middle-class and working-class settlers, many of whom were either exposed to British or southern radicalism, rallied to the democratic cause. Planter economy, land monopoly, class oligarchy and attendant expropriation of free labour had no place in the socio-economic plans of such converging forces which promoted Moreton Bay as the small man's frontier. The emergence of a Scottish ancien régime in the colony was incompatible with the ideals of social justice, equality of opportunity and economic independence promised by Lang's 'petty bourgeois utopia'.[19]

* * *

By 1848 the stage was set in Moreton Bay for a clash between pastoral capital and free European labour led by aspiring bourgeois capitalists over the form which the new society should take. Although the Scots lacked significant numbers within the pre-1850 Moreton Bay population, they more than compensated for this by the inordinate influence they wielded as either protagonists or foes in determining the nature of the district's development.

Due to lack of information on nationality in the census data, it is impossible to estimate the Scottish component among the 45 free men and 22 free women who inhabited the penal settlement of Brisbane along with 138 male convicts and their military guard in 1841. However, the large number of 42 professing membership of the Church of Scotland indicates a substantial proportion of 'double-distilled' Scottish convicts, widely acknowledged as the worst of the lot.[20] By 1846, the free population of Brisbane had increased to 829. Of this number, 483 lived at North Brisbane and the remaining 346 dwelt at South Brisbane, including Kangaroo Point. Thirty miles westward, the population of Ipswich, reflecting squatter designs for a limited service town as well as Brisbane's prominence, was a diminutive 100. Comprising 10.3% of the district's population, the Scottish component was equal to its proportion within Britain and the British immigrant intake to New South Wales.[21]

Within this Scottish component, many men played dominant, even formative roles in the day-to-day social and business life of the emerging urban centres of

Brisbane and Ipswich. Within all the class gradations existing in Moreton Bay's urban society, the Scots were not only highly visible, but were disproportionately successful. The 1848 Moreton Bay electoral roll, based on meeting considerable property qualifications, as an index of prosperity in that community, confirms this observation, revealing an incommensurate proportion of successful Scots. Over 30% of Brisbane and Ipswich householders and freeholders originated from 'the land o' cakes'.[22] Across the social spectrum, the Scottish dream of colonial prosperity through emigration in the face of a bleak future at home had become a reality.

In mid-1846 the Reverend John Gregor, Brisbane's first Church of England incumbent in the free phase and former tutor of the Leslie brothers in Aberdeenshire, provided a sweeping overview of the socio-economic composition and activities of Brisbane's population to the Society for the Propagation of the Gospel in Foreign Parts:

> With the exception of the Government functionaries, 6 professional men (three attornies and three surgeons), the inhabitants of the towns consist of traders, innkeepers, artisans and domestic servants. The traders furnish the settlers in the interior with such goods as are required for consumption on their establishments. The innkeepers sell wines, porter, beer and ardent spirits to all, but chiefly to the labouring population. The artisans are employed chiefly in the erection of houses. A few labourers are supported by sawing timber, of which a portion is exported to Sydney.[23]

The social structure in this early phase of settlement as broadly sketched by Gregor reflected the squatters' ascendant motives and Brisbane's function as the entrepot for the wool-producing hinterland. Accordingly Brisbane's middle class was small, a result of the settlement's role as the shipping, servicing and occasional recreational centre for the squattocracy. 'The only significant group separating the ruling class from the working class was a small group of petty bourgeois traders...'.[24]

This can be demonstrated by applying to Brisbane society Bill Thorpe's recently-compiled taxonomy which hierarchically delineates the classes operating within the political economy framework of colonial capitalism. By this instrument it is possible to classify members of Brisbane's Scottish population according to class membership and functions.[25] Reflecting the reality of mid-nineteenth century gradations within Brisbane society, Thorpe has proposed the following classification: predominantly working class, predominantly petty bourgeoisie, managerial/professional and colonial ruling class.

At the pinnacle of Brisbane's society was the colonial ruling class with 'major control over the apparatus of production, the entire supervisory hierarchy and sufficient stock to ensure influence on investments and accumulation'.[26] This small elite was composed of the higher government officials, the merchants and the pastoralists who had business or lived for periods in Brisbane.

The heads of the government bureaucracy were nearly all Scots. Wickham served as Police Magistrate, Duncan held the post of Sub-collector of Customs, Dr David Ballow was Government Medical Officer and James Burnett occupied the position of Surveyor in Charge. Among the first civilian magistrates appointed were Evan Mackenzie and John Balfour. Other Scots such as David McConnel, Dr William Mactaggart Dorsey, Ballow and Colin Mackenzie were subsequently gazetted to fill necessary positions arising from an increase both in population and in master and servant disputes throughout the district.

Apart from the legal power specific to such officers of government, capital and land were the major determinants of social position for the remainder of the population. According to William Archer, 'born to rule' squires and self-made proprietors predominated among those who fulfilled the criteria for entry to elitism.[27]

Those who could lay claim to membership of Brisbane's squirearchy, normally the epitome of breeding, wealth and property, were John, David and Frederic McConnel, squatters with extensive land holdings at New Farm. Also in this select company was Patrick Leslie, another squatter with short-lived intentions of urban residency. Possessing the necessary birth, but short on financial acumen, Leslie was domiciled only for a short period at his newly built cottage at Newstead from 1846.

Until mid 1845 Evan Mackenzie, heir to the Baronetcy of Kilcoy, combined the roles of squatter, merchant, industrialist and shipping agent, while exerting substantial influence over all three of Brisbane's rival localities. He was dominant among the few who possessed aristocratic or gentlemanly qualifications. Regardless of nationality, he was also the most dynamic merchant. In Brisbane Mackenzie bought Moutry's imposing, two-storied, brick complex at the southern end of Queen Street in 1843. With Englishman Edward Lord as his manager, Mackenzie received the squatters' wool, sold supplies and equipment while plotting to control Brisbane's trade. Having a foot in each of Brisbane's three rival localities, as well as within the business and dray areas in Ipswich, Mackenzie was set to carve out a profitable colonial career. In late 1842 Mackenzie erected the first licensed hotel in Brisbane opposite John William's de facto establishment in Russell Street on the south side. Replicating his strategy at Brisbane, he built another at Little Ipswich soon after. In addition, Mackenzie was credited with building the first new house in Ipswich following the initial land sales in 1843, presumably on his strategically-situated, river-bank allotment.[28]

Mackenzie arrived in Moreton Bay possessing superior funds, intelligence and a knowledge of business management learnt at his father's knee. His outgoing personality, family connections and undoubted promise as a colonial entrepreneur ensured that he tapped into the relevant sectors of both the powerful Scottish network and a critical part of its proletarian off-shoot to maximise his chances of success.[29]

One who straddled the managerial and merchant class in this period was highly-connected Robert Graham, former Sydney merchant and brother of the Brisbane

Valley squatter. He was also Mackenzie's agent until they fell out over the latter's attempt to sabotage the southern merchant establishment. Following Mackenzie's resignation as northern agent for the HRSNCo., Graham managed the company's activities from the new premises at South Brisbane. He formed the merchant company of Montefiore & Graham with the southern broker Jacob Montefiore, providing finance to aspiring and troubled pastoralists.[30] His northern career came to an abrupt halt when his import-export business failed along with the squatters' Cleveland Point project.

Although not in the same social class, Andrew Petrie, who was accorded patriarchal status, could be counted among this select group. His residence may have been of humble appearance, but Petrie's well-maintained property at the Bight exuded permanence, prosperity, industry and self-sufficiency.[31] The Petries were Brisbane's foremost builders, being involved in the construction of houses, bridges, renovation of decaying government structures and the repair of dilapidated wharves. While Andrew Petrie was well established at the northern extremity of Queen Street, his son John started his equally successful career from Kangaroo Point. Fortunate enough to command the services of an excellent foreman, David McNaught, the Petrie firm's prosperity grew in tandem with Brisbane's development, particularly between 1846 and 1848.[32]

Prominent among the proprietorial group of Scots was James Swan. He assumed sole ownership of the fledgling *Moreton Bay Courier* in 1847 after serving as foundation printer and foreman for the first year. Ex-squatters James Canning Pearce and Thomas Coutts, along with former punt operators John Boyland and James Reid, were pioneer proprietors of steamships which plied the river route between Ipswich and Brisbane from 1846.[33] In that same year John Campbell established his own state-of-the-art boiling-down works at Kangaroo Point after serving as manager at Mackenzie's establishment on the other side of the Point from 1843 to 1845. This industry in Brisbane's emerging industrialisation phase created employment for many anonymous butchers, tallow chandlers, coopers, carters and labourers; there were sure to be Scots among this predominantly immigrant labour from Sydney.[34]

The second highest group in the class structure was that composed of managers, who possessed the authority to administer businesses, and professionals who provided services based on their learned education. Whereas Scottish representation among the managerial sector appears to be small, its presence within the professional group is noteworthy. In addition to David Ballow, Ipswich-based William McTaggart Dorsey practised medicine. In matters religious, the Presbyterian community was provided with its first but transitory chance to worship during the short stay of the Reverend R. Taylor at Brisbane in late 1846. By the following year, an invalided Reverend. Thomas Mowbray, recognised as Brisbane's first resident Presbyterian minister, had settled at his substantial upper Kangaroo Point property.[35] From early 1843 the hapless John Gregor was the district's first Church of England incumbent and early teacher, with a brief to cover the whole of the Northern Districts.[36]

Philanthropist and storekeeper George Little assisted Gregor in providing the Anglican brand of education by conducting a Sunday school for those who could not afford private schooling.[37] Other pioneers in the educational field were William Halcro Robertson and David Scott who established much needed private schools in Brisbane during 1846 to 1847. The latter's establishment, located above Zillman's store, provided both day and evening classes.[38]

Although there was no Scottish representation in the legal profession, they had an ally in English solicitor Thomas Adams. In 1843 Mackenzie persuaded Adams, one of his fellow travellers aboard the *Berkshire* to foresake his budding career as a Darling Downs pastoralist to resume his legal career in Brisbane. No doubt Adams was attracted by the conveyancing business arising from the proliferation of land sales and the increasing volume of local mortgages. In addition, a lucrative legal practice would be assured just by the large volume of briefs which arose from the newly established Courts of Petty Sessions and Requests and a Court of Quarter Sessions in the offing - further results of Mackenzie's northern agitation.[39] With these legal institutions in place, Mackenzie subsequently made maximum use of their services to recoup local debts.[40]

The next class, the petite bourgeoisie, was composed of the self-employed, owners of small businesses and storekeepers. They are readily identified, principally the publicans, through their strong presence in the advertisement sections of the local newspaper. The Scots, obviously cognisant with the key role which watering holes played in the development of estate towns and other embryonic settlements in their homeland, were also predominant among Brisbane publicans. David Bow followed hot on the heels of Mackenzie in erecting the imposing Victoria in Queen Street. Alexander Wright, former supervisor for the Leslies, gained the licence for the Caledonian in George Street. Although Bow's bawdy inn possessed a much-used billiards table, many of the squatters preferred staying at the Caledonian or George McAdam's Sovereign because of their tranquil atmosphere.[41]

On the south bank in the vicinity of the Brisbane hotel, John McCabe took out the licence for the Commercial in 1846. At Grey Street Andrew Graham offered free accommodation at his Harp of Erin to John Dunmore Lang who endured squatter highjinks in the saloon in late 1845. Further downstream, yet another John Campbell presided. Tragically he died in harness while his Highlander's Arms was in the course of erection at Kangaroo Point in 1848.[42] Nearby, Brisbane's sole Scottish horticulturalist, Richard Cannan, tended his fertile two acre allotment, producing fruit, vegetables and flowers of prize-winning quality.[43]

Among Brisbane butchers and bakers, John Orr, George Edmonstone and William Cairncross reigned supreme among the Scots as well as within Brisbane. The latter, brother-in-law of Edmonstone, whose butchery was one of the early shops in the Queen Street, enjoyed a local reputation for his bread, biscuits and confectionery made on the premises.[44] Orr, in the company of his father Ebenezer and brothers, virtually monopolised meat retailing in South Brisbane.[45]

Among the first traders or storekeepers, those who were permitted to lease premises in the former Prisoners' Barracks in 1842, were John Richardson and George Little.[46] Richardson, the son of a Scottish clergyman from Ayr and a follower of John Dunmore Lang, set up a drapery store. A future merchant and competent legislator, Richardson was one of the few urban Scots who wavered in his support of the squatters in the early stage of Brisbane's development.[47] James Sutherland's ironmongery was also founded in Queen Street on the Edward Street corner. Across the river at Kangaroo Point, Robert Davidson was willing to pay the ferry fares for customers who spent a minimum of at least ten shillings at his general store.[48]

At the bottom of the social pile, were the working class composed of labourers, domestic servants and other unskilled employees 'who lived solely or predominantly on the sale of their labour and had no or minimal control over the labour of others'.[49] In the main, these were the 'invisible' or 'anonymous' settlers because they generally left no records of their existence or valuable labour. These were the 'mere labourers' whom Mackenzie considered ineligible to own land, amass capital and employ labour, the bases of upward social mobility in the colony.[50]

Because of Mackenzie's patronage towards both artisans and labourers within his entourage, it is possible to gain an indication of the fortunes of the otherwise anonymous proletariat at Moreton Bay. He ensured that his servants, particularly the first intake, were provided with a head start, making the most of the advantages afforded to those on the ground floor of the district's urban development. It appears that Mackenzie either assisted his servants in recognition of loyal service in establishing his run to establish small businesses or placed them in secure jobs through the wider Scottish connection. The strong network among the Black Isle contingent and its connections with prominent pro-Mackenzie colonials created advantageous employment opportunities for kinfolk who followed them to the antipodes.

While the grandiose plans of many aspiring British businessmen were dashed during this period, such humble members of the Scottish proletariat laid the foundations of their future prosperity in the district, thereby achieving their goals of colonial self-fulfilment. In such a fluid society which lacked the social polarisation of the pastoral interior and where socio-economic mobility was possible, there was but a small gap to leap between mechanic and employer. Eventually even 'mere labourers' found it possible to transform imperceptibly from self-employed contractors to small businessmen. Following this elevation, the possession of an urban allotment with a humble residence was a logical consequence. Mackenzie provided his Black Isle workers with decided advantages at the beginning of this process in which most were successful.

The Black Isle contingent, present from the beginning, prospered along with Brisbane within the principal business area of the township. In Brisbane's first decade John Stewart, Alexander McIntyre and Lachlan McLean, an independent immigrant from the Mackenzie town of Munlochy, were the leading blacksmiths/ wheelwrights. They dominated this sector of the servicing industry on both sides of the Brisbane River. McLean founded his business in Albert Street in 1843 while the other two operated at South Brisbane after commencing business from the stables area of Mackenzie's Brisbane hotel six months earlier.[51] Also from the Black Isle was Thomas Gray who established his prosperous bootmaking enterprise and emporium one year later in George Street after a short period as a stockman in Wide Bay.[52] Another member of this distinctive Scottish group was John Davidson who helped John Williams with the construction of his Captain Piper hotel at South Brisbane before establishing himself as a substantial property owner in that area.[53] Unconnected with the Mackenzie group, was James Davis, the former runaway who made a fresh start as an indifferent blacksmith at Kangaroo Point near Daniel McNicol's cooperage.[54]

Another Kilcoy pioneer, Thomas Fraser along with his brother William, laid the foundation of his future comfortable life by hard manual labour. Renowned throughout the district for their tuneful piping, Thomas worked as a sawyer and William joined David McKay as a member of the pilot's whaleboat crew.[55] The brothers Fraser, who were irreverent towards colonial law, came to Brisbane via service at Durundur, evidently receiving minimal help from Mackenzie.

Others who followed on the coat-tails of Mackenzie's activity in Ipswich also thrived. Following the strategy he adopted in Brisbane, Mackenzie established himself as the leading entrepreneur within the settlement's businesss heart and at the outer dray terminus at Little Ipswich. In the vicinity of Little Ipswich, adjoining another Mackenzie hotel, Alexander Smith established his carrier business. Having worked for a short period as a drayman for the Petries in Brisbane, Smith gained sufficient experience to benefit from trade emanating from the Darling Downs, the Brisbane River Valley and the Burnett. By 1845 he became a landowner in that outer-Ipswich area after the sale of Mackenzie's land. Possibly a cousin of Smith, Donald Davidson was appointed to manage the pound for straying animals within Ipswich before entering the hotel trade at the Red Cow.[56]

The Black Isle contingent took every advantage of the opportunities offered them to gain capital, property and employer status - the means of upward social mobility for plebeian settlers. Exhibiting the qualities traditionally attributed to Scots, such as thrift, industry, perseverance and devotion to calling, they demonstrated signs of prosperity as early as 1847. Having served on the frontier under pragmatic Mackenzie and in the absence of the restraining influence of the Kirk, they probably added a liberal dash of ruthlessness to their behavioural repertoire. By 1848 Gray, McIntyre and Thomas Fraser (the only illiterate among the Kilcoy workers) had gained the highly selective franchise, the most reliable indicator of their colonial success. Other members of the group followed in the 1850s, having gained the substantial property qualifications.[57]

The Black Isle network by no means fitted the stereotypical description of inert and subservient Highlanders as described by Somers following his visits to famine ravaged estates in 1848.[58] Because of contiguity to Inverness and constant interchange with Aberdeen, the population of this peninsula possessed many dominant Lowland characteristics, especially assertiveness, resourcefulness and ambition. Unconcerned with colonial radical politics, at least until Mackenzie departed, this group had few reasons to adopt either an anti-landlord stance or its colonial equivalent. However, subsequent attempts by the colonial establishment to treat them as simple inferiors demonstrated that they considered themselves to be the equal of any individual. Egged on by Mackenzie, McIntyre took delight in being the thorn in the side of the HRSNCo; John Smith put a leading squatter's wife in her place on receiving complaints about his lowly clientele; Alex Smith took a prominent pastoralist to court when he felt he had been defrauded and Thomas Gray demanded and obtained police protection for his relatives and friends who were pioneering a new district outside the metropolis at Bald Hills.[59] They closely followed the direction which the new society was developing and located their businesses accordingly. Apart from McIntyre's involvement, there is no evidence that this close-knit group became embroiled in the intrigue which dictated the alignment of local political and economic forces.

* * *

This band was fortunate to have connections with the three Scottish businessmen to whom Brisbane's ascendancy was largely attributed. In his study of early Brisbane, Ross Johnston gives credit to Evan Mackenzie, Andrew Petrie and John 'Tinker' Campbell for much of the settlement's development to a solidly-based entrepot which transmitted the produce of its hinterland southward and overseas.[60] Through their planning and initiative, these close friends were to the fore in a resentful community committed to filling the void caused by government disinterest. On the American frontier, such innovators were known as boosters - upstart businessmen who founded upstart urban centres.

American sociologist Daniel Boorstin noted that such entrepreneurs intermingled personal and public prosperity while fusing their destiny with that of the community. His colleague Howard P. Chudacoff explained that this involvement transcended 'greedy self-interest'. Such resourceful businessmen were able to evoke public spirit, discovered profitable opportunities and provided much-needed community leadership.[61] Noted for their fearless and visionary approach, these pioneers provided direction and growth, welded community unity and achieved commitment to well-publicised strategic development plans. They enunciated and operationalised 'concrete growth strategies linked with specific description of economic patterns'.[62]

This triumvirate of Mackenzie, Petrie and Campbell was the tip of the iceberg of the strong Scottish network among Brisbane's leading citizens who boosted the district's development. Whereas Petrie provided the advice and Campbell contributed his colonial skills, a financially-flush Mackenzie assumed leadership.

Their actions, which often diminished or destroyed the expectations of other settlers, created as many enemies as allies. Thomas Archer, who was obviously among those who had adverse dealings with his fellow Scots, considered the business style of such entrepreneurs to be just too shrewd, lacking the Englishman's sense of honour.[63]

Yet Mackenzie's positive contribution cannot be underestimated. He nurtured and brought to prominence an embryonic Scottish support system. His initial backing among the powerful Scots embraced the Edinburgh mercantile establishment, the Secretary of State for the Colonies, the Surveyor-General of New South Wales, the northern squatters and most of the government officials in Brisbane. This support even extended into the Scottish middle class who hoped to benefit from his initiative and drive and the humble workers with whom he enjoyed a warm relationship. As the consummate risk-taker, Mackenzie's colonial career was distinguished by a series of spectacular successes culminating in one large failure. Whereas this bruised his ego, it did not materially affect his subsequent privileged life. For those who risked their all, hoping to prosper in his wake, it was a different kettle of fish. While he finally alienated many within his external Scottish support system, especially the Sydney-based establishment, most of the unaffected Moreton Bay group remained loyal. On the whole, through his contentious leadership and despite the human casualties, he left Brisbane and the Moreton Bay District in a much better condition than he found it.

It should not be assumed that Mackenzie operated alone. Although he took the limelight as local leader, there is scattered evidence that the Scots-dominated squatters were also deeply involved in the on-going process of formulating the district's strategic plan. Tom Dowse in his regular Moreton Bay report in the *Sydney Morning Herald* cited several instances before the foundation of the Mackenzie-led Moreton Bay Pastoral Association of squatter assemblies convened to make critical decisions on urban development - especially around race-meeting day. Perhaps the most important of these was in 1843 when the stockholders gave support for Mackenzie's proposal to introduce the boiling-down of excess stock at his factory at Kangaroo Point after weeks of considering Cleveland's possibilities for the curing of beef on a large scale.[64]

Whereas Petrie and Campbell contributed their detailed knowledge of the district and acknowledged expertise in their respective fields to this equation, Mackenzie as leader of the squatters, motivator of Brisbanites and tormentor of the Sydney expropriators was obviously Brisbane's booster par excellence. He coldly calculated the district's needs, formulated pragmatic strategies, moulded district consciousness and fearlessly implemented remedial action. In the process, he identified the southern mercantile forces as the major obstacles to the district's survival and ultimate prosperity.

As Mackenzie saw the wider picture, he was not content merely to take advantage of local opportunities as were Petrie and Campbell. He was playing for higher stakes. To achieve Moreton Bay's independence he took the battle to the south by subterfuge in the north. Determined to promote Brisbane as an international port, he even activated a powerful Scottish mercantile network operating in London for the necessary substantial financial support to realise his plans.[65] Although he came very close to success, it was the resistance of the powerful colonial forces rather than lack of northern support which led to his undoing. If contemporary Scottish historians such as Donnachie profess to be just as interested in Scottish entrepreneurial failure as in its success, they need look no further than the development of Moreton Bay in the mid 1840s with particular focus on Mackenzie and those who speculated on his plans. Moreton Bay of this period was replete with 'Scots on the make'.[66]

Such were Mackenzie's charisma and achievements in the north, that many years passed before another leader emerged with the ability to unite urban and rural forces for the common good. Obviously ignoring those episodes of manic excess and perfidy that ultimately contributed to his downfall, two contemporaries with their fingers firmly on the pulse of Moreton Bay society emphasised the restorative and formative influences this enigmatic Scotsman exerted during adversity. Perhaps Thomas Dowse was a little too effusive when he considered that the name of Evan Mackenzie should be venerated in the annals of Moreton Bay, given Mackenzie's devilish side. Nevertheless his fellow settlers were overjoyed that he saved the squatters and the district from ruin by establishing the boiling down works under the management of John Campbell.[67]

Accolades also came from a most unexpected source, given the uncompromising role this enterprising Scot was to play in diminishing squatter power over Brisbane. Never one to heap praise upon exponents of 'the damned doctrine of squatting' and an advocate of colonial adaptation rather than emotive Scottish transference, Lang stated in 1847 that he was proud to acknowledge Mackenzie as a fellow Scot. While not approving of Mackenzie's promotion of Kangaroo Point to the detriment of Brisbane unity, Lang described him as one of those rare longheaded (perspicacious) people who occasionally found their way to the colony.[68] Obviously Lang formed this assessment on the basis of his widespread consultations with Scottish settlers during his visit to the north in late 1845. Six months previously Mackenzie left the district to live in Sydney before taking over the management of his late father's Kilcoy estates.

It is evident that Mackenzie had the 'common touch'. He enjoyed wide-spread support which transcended nationality. For a person who had just attained his twenty-fifth birthday upon his arrival in the north, he possessed business acumen far in advance of his tender years. Although proud of his Scottish heritage and eager to celebrate it on appropriate occasions, Mackenzie was largely free of 'that bastard [ethnic] sentimentalism' which Lang felt was out of place in an already unnecessarily divided colonist society.[69] While eschewing a narrow Scottish-oriented agenda, Mackenzie managed to tap the self-acknowledged clannishness of his fellow Scottish settlers, distributing or witholding favours in the typical style of a Highland laird. In his personal relations he applied his sophisticated brand of Europeanisation and Britishness to win over settlers from other countries and develop a regional consciousness for the benefit of the wider community.

Perhaps the most notable feature of the early urban experience was the readiness with which dominant Scots cooperated and collaborated with their English counterparts. No inward-looking Scottish policy or exclusivity is discernible as the professionals and petty bourgeois tradespeople combined with the squatters in the drive for district unity and ultimately communal survival. This phenomenon was but an extension of the relationship which had existed between professional, proprietorial and mercantile Scots and their English counterparts for centuries.[70] The frontier situation threw together people of differing nationalities regardless of their wider experience. There they learnt to put national differences aside and cooperate, if only to survive. While this may have been a steep learning curve for formerly isolated Highlanders, the Scottish elite as represented in Moreton Bay by Mackenzie would have few problems of adaption.

Ultimately all workers at Moreton Bay benefited from Mackenzie's go-ahead style of leadership and brand of benevolent capitalism which had their origins on the Kilcoy estates. In a period of northern development when capital and labour were truly dependent and laissez-faire capitalism ensured that business and population were strictly curtailed, Brisbane's proletariat weathered the latter stages of the financial depression that gripped every part of the colony. As Dowse commented in early 1845, 'the Brisbane folk ... have escaped want in any shape and the working classes have generally found full employment and a wide field of laying out their little savings to good advantage'.[71]

Nevertheless there was a strong Scottish Highland flavour to the plan to establish Brisbane as the squatter-controlled port and the attempt to solve the problems which were preventing the emergence of such a facility. The campaign to diminish the power of the southern Scottish-dominated merchant monopoly in the north resulted from district-sanctioned strategies such as those based on the self-sufficiency principle and the personal subterfuge of Mackenzie with the aid of his Edinburgh contact.

Generally the Scottish financial backers of the Moreton Bay squatters showed little interest in encouraging their young squatting proteges to establish themselves in the former penal settlement. Although Sir Thomas Brisbane was enthusiastic about the occupation of the Brisbane River Valley hinterland, he apparently made no significant recommendations to James Balfour about establishing a squatter presence in the future port of Brisbane.[72] Yet, Balfour, while constantly urging his sons to be 'first in the field', requested that they consider the purchase of the best town blocks for speculative reasons. This was reinforced by George Forbes who allocated additional funds for the purchase of such key property or investment in more sheep. Forbes' instructions left no doubt that Scottish financiers were very much in touch with and exercised firm control over their colonial investments. The Balfour brothers were informed, 'I have desired Messrs M.D. Hunter & Co. to hold that additional sum at your disposal and I authorise you either to invest the whole of it in additional stock, or to the extent 3 or 400 [pounds] in the purchase of allotments at Moreton Bay'.[73] The Balfours evidently chose the former option as there is no evidence that they had substantial land holdings in Brisbane, let alone being involved in the township's affairs. As for their Scottish colleagues, they were too busy establishing their runs in the midst of drought, financial stringency and Aboriginal resistance, besides having extra time, energy or money to devote to founding a township experiencing its own set of teething problems.

The financially flush and energetic Mackenzie had arrived in the north with well-formulated plans for his involvement in urban affairs. With the benefit of hindsight, it appears that he attempted to replicate his father's successful career as proprietor, merchant, shipping executive and entrepreneur at Moreton Bay. Uppermost in his mind was the prosperity and status which he and his caste could accrue from applying Sir Colin's benevolent style of estate management to the unsettled socio-economic environment in the northern pioneering community. In such a scheme, it was imperative that Brisbane should remain a squatter town, subservient to the stockholders' needs.

In Scotland, proprietorial control over estate towns was common. Such settlements usually contained a mill to process the grain produced on the estates, an hotel owned by the landowner and a limited number of rent-paying artisans and mechanics for service purposes. Furthermore the staff of the estate church and school were selected by the proprietor if the town was large enough. A storekeeper, a tailor and a bootmaker provided for the material needs of the inhabitants and the crofters who leased nearby small farms. Often such settlements contained rented accommodation for day labourers who worked on the estates. 'Step by step, man by man the organisation of the community proceeds'.[74] Some of these towns, such as the Mackenzie-owned Munlochy, were also on shipping routes which enabled the produce of the estate, such as timber and barley, to be shipped south to London or Liverpool markets to help satisfy the needs generated by the Industrial Revolution. After all, many of the progressive proprietors, including Sir Colin Mackenzie of Kilcoy, were also involved in shipping and mercantile pursuits in addition to property management and local politics.[75]

Although these centres were firmly under landowner control, the number and character of inhabitants was strictly limited to those who had contractual connections with the laird. Outsiders, especially the politically aware artisans from urban areas, were excluded as they were wont to incite discontent among a compliant peasantry and hence weaken landlord power. There was every reason to prevent such agitation, as anti-landlordism was the common cause which inflamed the virulent forms of Scottish radicalism in the 1840s. As peasant proprietorship was virtually non-existent in Scotland, there was no threat posed to landlordism from yeoman farmers who were in the thick of revolutionary foment elsewhere in Britain and France.[76]

In many respects, the formative phase in the history of the Moreton Bay District may be interpreted as an attempt by the squattocracy to replicate the carefully controlled estate system in the antipodes. Having established complete control of their socially polarised runs, virtually locked up the land and obstructed the emergence of agriculture, the squatters then set about establishing a similar stranglehold over Brisbane. Accepting that the urban population would be under the administration of a small coterie of government officials and served by an similar number of sympathetic professionals, the squatters planned to restrict the social composition of the remainder of the population of their proposed port.

As the function of such settlements was predominantly related to the provision of service facilities for pastoralist exporters, a curtailed number of shops and hotels was necessary along with a core of specially selected artisans. They were to be kept subservient by conditional pastoral patronage. As Dowse painfully recorded, the long intervals between the squatters' spasmodic visits to the township limited business to bare necessity. Demographically this restrained population growth and truncated the aspiring and restless middle class. This ensured that Brisbane could not function independently of squatter custom. Thorpe's observation that only a scant middle class prevented the bipolarisation of Brisbane society reflects the success of this strategy before 1846.[77]

Brisbane was indeed a town controlled by and dependent on the predominant Scottish squatters who apparently patronised the businesses of their humbler compatriots. Few financially troubled Scots are cited within the pages of the Dowse diary which constantly attributed local business difficulties not only to the massive problems which the squatters faced in the interior, but to the scarcity of their money circulating within Brisbane. Dowse, the pessimistic diarist who recorded the demise of a succession of ruined Brisbane businessmen as they spiralled towards insolvency, reflected the squatters' cash flow problems in that period as well as the selective nature of their custom. The favoured Scottish artisans and retailers were not only 'first in the field', but some were strategically placed in 'a miserable place where all [were in] pursuit of Mammon'.[78]

Mackenzie's manoeuvres kept Brisbane in a state of confusion. To the chagrin of the township's early land purchasers, he variously indicated preferences for South Brisbane and Cleveland over North Brisbane as the district's preferred shipping location before settling on Kangaroo Point. Eventually his machinations at Kangaroo Point in 1844 led Andrew Petrie to take a backward step from what appeared to be a joint effort to set up a commanding position in Brisbane. As Mackenzie cut a swathe through Brisbane's mercantile and shipping interests, his subterfuge also evoked adversarial reactions not only from thwarted Brisbanites and local officials, but also the southern merchants, the powerful HRNSCo. and the bureaucracy in Sydney. Some of the powerful Scots within these sectors had been involved in assisting the Mackenzies and Balfours establish their colonial careers. The underhand method by which Mackenzie duped the newly arrived police magistrate to grant him a building licence was not appreciated. Having been rebuked by the Governor for his liberality in granting building licences, Wickham attempted to withdraw from sale the land which Mackenzie had virtually earmarked for purchase. Only the intervention of Surveyor-General Thomas Mitchell, one of Mackenzie's last supporters in the colonial bureaucracy, thwarted Wickham's remedial action. Undoubtedly this last minute attempt to obstruct the Kangaroo Point strategy was partly motivated by revenge.[79]

Perusal of the list of purchasers of Kangaroo Point land at the two sales in 1843 and 1844 provides an indication of the significant support which Mackenzie's controversial venture received from the Scottish sector at North Brisbane. Predictably John Petrie was to the fore. Between them, Petrie and Mackenzie owned the six best waterside allotments on the western side of the Point opposite Andrew Petrie's establishment and contingent to the proposed ferry to the north. Upstream, Thomas Adams had bought residential blocks for Mackenzie's managers, Edward Lord and John 'Tinker' Campbell. In between lay the properties of Richard Cannan, who continued his horticultural activities, and James Warner whose surveying skills resulted in the subdivision of land he held in joint ownership with Mackenzie. Along with his allies, Mackenzie had taken up virtually all the western side. The only outsider was Irish cooper Philip O'Reilly whose industry, vital to the boiling-down process, was located on the western division of the actual point.[80]

The land on the eastern side, made available at the second sale, was also snapped up by a Scottish majority. Prominent among these was Wickham himself. Rather than level charges of hypocrisy against him, there are signs he 'buried the hatchet' with Mackenzie and followed his practice of acting in the best interests of the district. Furthermore, Brisbane's Scots were quick to recognise profitable investments, regardless of affinity. In addition to the squatters Andrew Gregor and William Wilson, the government medical officer Dr David Ballow also sought to prosper in Mackenzie's wake. Also John Campbell and Edward Lord purchased valuable properties opposite the Mackenzie-Petrie concentration.[81] After Mackenzie's departure from Brisbane, Campbell built Brisbane's second, short-lived boiling-down establishment on this site. The heavy mortgages taken out on his property on the Point and in the eastern suburbs to finance this enterprise were ultimately foreclosed by Thomas Sutcliffe Mort, leading to insolvency.[82] Subsequently the buildings housed Robert Douglas' soap and candle manufactory.

The rest of Brisbane was probably content that the first malodorous boiling-down establishment was confined to the relatively isolated Kangaroo Point, despite its district-saving reputation. However, they were less than happy that Mackenzie directed steamer traffic to that location in his capacity as northern agent for the HRSNCo. First, he created a price war between the powerful company and the schooners, to the latter's advantage.[83] Further, when the aggrieved company decided to foresake Kangaroo Point for South Brisbane, Mackenzie enlisted the aid of McIntyre to deprive it of the land with the best waterside frontage.[84] There seems to have been a large element of Highland revenge and retaliation involved in this subterfuge.

As he was assured of two-thirds of the Northern District's wool clip for 1844, Mackenzie could have severely curbed the power of the HRSNCo in Brisbane if he had been successful in cutting it out of northern trade. However, his plan to establish a direct sea route between Brisbane and Britain received only moral support from the squatters because of lethargy or their heavy financial commitments to the southern merchants.[85] Through his Edinburgh connection he achieved access to and aroused the interest of powerful financial circles in Britain, within which Scottish bankers and merchants were dominant.

Mackenzie's proposal was forwarded by James Balfour to his brother Charles, a senior official within Baring Brothers Bank.[86] Unfortunately the bargaining process eventually ground to a halt because of Mackenzie's lack of disposable cash, his money being tied up in stock.[87] With the death of Sir Colin during negotiations and the subsequent refusal of Kilcoy's trustees to supply bridging funds, Mackenzie's financial backing, and thus his colonial power, dissipated.[88] His colonial ambitions thwarted and having no intentions of using his substantial personal legacy for colonial purposes, Mackenzie returned to Scotland to assume the Baronetcy of Kilcoy.

His secret dealings with Baring Brothers also ensured that he terminally incurred the enmity of the Sydney-based, Scottish financial establishment when they were eventually revealed. A direct threat to the Scottish merchant monopoly in Sydney such actions were viewed as extravagant and rash by his erstwhile mentor Thomas Barker and undoubtedly others of his ilk.[89] After all, Mackenzie was fully aware of the repercussions of his subterfuge when it was revealed. He admitted that the southern Scottish-controlled establishment 'would not allow 30 or 40,000 tons of wool to go through another channel (besides other produce) without making an effort to finger it nor will the Steam Co submit to losing 5 or 6000 [pounds] of freight without a struggle'.[90]

The ire of Sydney's Scottish merchants towards Mackenzie was severe as it was swift. Even his erstwhile friend turned on him. On being apprised of the threat to his colleagues, Robert Graham, Mackenzie's Sydney-based agent, demonstrated where his ultimate loyalty lay. To Mackenzie's dismay, Graham demanded that he remove his business as their interests no longer coincided.[91] Mackenzie left many and varied destroyed relationships in his ruthless path to personal power.

While the Scottish-led government bureaucrats Edward Deas Thomson and Campbell Riddell were having their doubts by 1844, it was inevitable that he would fall foul of another main component of the southern establishment - the squatters led by Ben Boyd.[92] However, Mackenzie was more than a match for their arrogance towards him and his peers. The Pastoral Association, formed by southern squatters with Boyd at the helm to fight Gipps' contentious land regulations of 1844, made the mistake of ignoring the overtures of the Mackenzie-led Moreton Bay Pastoral Association [MBPA] which was identical in purpose.

Although the MBPA was dominated by Scots, this was irrelevant to their southern compatriots when power and profits were involved. Regardless of nationality, the Moreton Bay inhabitants had a track record of antagonism towards apathetic southern forces which tried to 'screw [them]of their last farthing'.[93] The southern Scottish power-base was unprepared for the opposition they received from a neglected community led by a rebellious member of their caste who identified not only with its struggle but also with its resentment. Accordingly, Boyd's demand for the funds which the MBPA allocated to fight Gipps and his regulations was given short shrift.

Despite the outcry of perfidy in the editorial in the *Sydney Morning Herald* of 7 May 1845, Mackenzie delivered his parting shot against his southern counterparts. In the process Robert Graham, the man who contributed most to his colonial demise, felt his wrath.[94] On relinquishing his leadership of the MBPA on the previous day, Mackenzie ensured that the contentious funds were ear-marked for local development purposes. Having fulfilled its functions, the MBPA was transformed into the Moreton Bay District Association which was in need of such funds. The committee of the new association under Patrick Leslie's leadership, a combination of squatter and pro-pastoralist Brisbanites, intended to foster the district's progress and address retarding factors, especially the long-standing communication and labour needs.[95]

Mackenzie's commitment to the development of Brisbane as an international port was reflected in his insistence that the contentious funds should be appropriated for improved navigation of Moreton Bay. This decision, taken in conjunction with the vision he articulated in his correspondence with Baring Brothers, revealed that he was no mere speculator. Like his father, he had the ability to combine the profit motive with commitment to the community's welfare. In August 1844, he related his hopes for Brisbane as a centre for 'steam communication' as well as his designs. Mackenzie envisaged an international port attracting Pacific whalers, Asian trade via an overland route from Port Essington (hence his substantial support for the Prussian explorer Leichhardt), direct shipment to Britain and southern shipping arriving via the safer northern passage around Moreton Island. His aim was to be Brisbane's leading merchant and shipping agent. He had broadened his vision of Brisbane as a duplicated Scottish estate toun.

In Mackenzie's opinion the only impediments to Brisbane's attainment of an international reputation were the attitudes of the squatters towards Brisbane, the lack of involvement of British capital and the unfounded negative perception of the shipping capabilities of Moreton Bay. He was positive that 'with a little fostering care from home and a little energy on the part of the squatters we have every prospect of becoming a flourishing place'.[96]

The physical problems were quite soluble. The sandbars at the mouth of the river could be quickly annihilated 'as the Yankees say' by a 'dredging machine', as would the flats along the river. In common with other Moreton Bay businessmen, Mackenzie was fully aware that the publication of sailing directions to permit access by international shipping was dependent on the success of local initiative to chart the Bay.[97] With these obstacles overcome, it was expected that the proclamation of Brisbane's free-warehousing status would be a mere formality.

To these ends, Mackenzie marshalled local Scottish maritime and surveying talent - in the same manner as he harnessed local Scottish expertise to start Brisbane's first industry at Kangaroo Point. Captain J.C. Wickham was the obvious choice.

Having gained world-wide recognition for his navigation and charting skills, accrued from his long service as junior officer and master on HMS *Beagle*, Wickham willingly gave of his talents for the well-being of the Moreton Bay community. In addition, the services of Andrew Petrie were highly valued. He possessed an unsurpassed knowledge, gained during his period of convict supervision, of the Brisbane River and the bay into which it emptied. Consequently Wickham, Petrie and Mackenzie started the survey from a whaleboat in the free-enterprise period when government funding was either not available or not offered. In a letter to James Balfour dated 19 October 1844, Mackenzie revealed that he was about to join a party to survey the bay.[98] This group included the recently appointed assistant-surveyor James C. Burnett, late of Aberdeen.

After this preliminary work, the government stepped in. Burnett was ordered to survey the northern channel while Wickham assisted Lieutenant Yule in HMS *Bramble* with other navigation surveys, the basis of formulating sailing directions to safely traverse the Bay. Mackenzie's passion for this process, which was basic to Brisbane's maritime status, was apparent when he made the special trip from Sydney in March 1846 to entertain Yule and his crew to acknowledge their critical role in laying the foundations for Brisbane's independence. The dinner was celebrated at David Bow's Victoria Hotel where Mackenzie, Burnett and Campbell stayed late into the night playing billiards before retiring to Alexander Wright's less boisterous Caledonian.[99] The culmination of Mackenzie's hopes and Wickham's efforts occurred when the brig *Eliza Kincaird* loaded wool bound direct for London six months after the former left Moreton Bay for Sydney.[100] This was a high point at the end of the period dominated by the objectives of independent Scottish entrepreneurial capitalism.

* * *

With Moreton Bay thereafter under close government surveillance, the days of rebellious, free-enterprise were over. Enterprising capitalists had established Brisbane's prosperity after it had been abandoned by the government at its time of greatest need. Having awaited dispassionately for the outcome of the battle for survival while merely collecting revenue, the Sydney-based government decided that the time was finally propitious to take over. From 1846 Moreton Bay's power-base and development drive shifted from independent Scottish entrepreneurs to Scottish bureaucrats who were accountable to a more responsive Sydney-based government.

The change-over period was marked by a tragedy which could have been avoided if the lessons of the free-enterprise period had been heeded by the profit-driven Sydney merchants and their mercantile allies. Unfortunately it took the tragic loss of the *Sovereign* in March 1847 for southern authorities to take heed of Mackenzie's advice that the northern channel was a safer and more efficient route to the mouth of the Brisbane.[101] Shortly after this catastrophe, Wickham's sailing directions for the north channel were published and Captain Owen Stanley arrived in HMS *Rattlesnake* in October 1847 to complete the survey of the bay and report on the shipping capabilities of Cleveland Point. The expectations of those Scots such as John Balfour and Robert Graham, who had been leading a strong campaign for a township at Cleveland for well on a year, were high.[102]

Since early 1842 when Sir George Gipps experienced the levelling effects of bayside mud, Cleveland Point's prospects had been left in abeyance.[103] Following the failure of Mackenzie's personal campaign to establish a direct trade route to Britain from Brisbane, the squatters renewed their interest in forming a port on the bay. Led by Scots who had a historical record of invariably repaying affront, the squatters were not likely to forgive their original allies in Brisbane who had betrayed their cause.

By recourse to conventional means which could not alienate the southern power-brokers, a squatter-dominated settlement similar in function and composition to the typical Scottish estate town could be established from scratch. The search for an entrepot other than Brisbane began in earnest. Apparently, Andrew Petrie's 'half-hearted' promotion of Toorbul Point, in a direct line with Archers' Durundur, was swiftly despatched.[104] In his survey of the northern entrance, Burnett had rejected this option in his report of October 1845 for various cogent reasons. These included the lack of fresh water, distance from the Downs, extensive mud flats and general lack of deep water. For similar reasons, notably extensive flats exposed at low tide and lack of a road over the far-reaching marshes to Brisbane, Lieutenant Yule's tentative recommendation of Cabbage Tree Head as a customs site was also dismissed three years later.[105] After considering Burnett's report which arose from the expenditure of the Moreton Bay Pastoral Association's excess funds, the pastoralists decided on Cleveland which had long been their preferred option.[106]

The Ipswich-Cleveland threat to Brisbane's very existence emerged. Driven by revenge as well as sound economics, the Scottish-led squatters were bent on eliminating Brisbane in the same manner as South Brisbane was by-passed in Mackenzie's plan for a North Brisbane-Kangaroo Point connection. Following the construction of basic port facilities at Cleveland such as a long jetty, wharves and stores, overseas shipping could take on cargo and unload supplies.[107] Consequently the southern stranglehold could be broken and higher profits were assured.

Less than six months after Mackenzie's departure from the district in mid-1845, it was obvious that the first phase of the squatters' plan centred on the development of Ipswich, was well advanced. While Dowse noted in late 1845 that most teams from the interior left their wool at Ipswich for shipment by river to Brisbane, Dunmore Lang observed:

Indeed, the people of Brisbane are already somewhat jealous of the growing importance of Ipswich, and not without good reason; for in the event of a commercial port being established in the Bay; either at Toorbul or at Cleveland Point, the wool and other produce from the interior would unquestionably be all shipped direct for that port from Ipswich, without being landed at Brisbane at all.[108]

Frequent sightings of the Scottish pastoralists in Ipswich from mid-1846 and reports of rapid development in that settlement indicate that the Ipswich-Cleveland option had been adopted as preferred squatter policy. This was not unexpected as Wickham and Andrew Petrie, had surprisingly come out in favour of Cleveland over Brisbane for the preferred port for the northern region after Lang's visit in November 1845. At that stage, with no significant concentration of fellow Langites in Brisbane, Petrie was on excellent terms with the squatters. This decision would earn him a reputation for duplicity among the aggrieved Brisbanites among whom he lived and prospered. Wickham, although generally impartial and consistently professional, was inclined towards the squatter cause. He had family connections with the Leslies through his wife Anna Macarthur of 'The Vineyard' and conducted a small run on the Downs.

The most unexpected proponent of Cleveland, considering the vindictive treatment meted out to him by the squattocracy, was Duncan, the newly-appointed Sub-Collector of Customs. Settling in quickly to the impartial role of a government official at the Commissariat Store, he assessed: 'Cleveland Point is well situated for the convenience of most of the wool growers, a matter of no little weight'.[109] Thus with the backing of the most influential Scots in Brisbane and on the basis of the advice of the highest ranking government officers, it appeared as if the Ipswich-Cleveland connection would prevail. This was reflected by further increased activity in Ipswich where the inhabitants were 'in high spirits' with a linkage to Cleveland in the offing.[110]

* * *

In comparison with a stagnant Brisbane in the throes of a building slump, development in the 'remote village' of Ipswich was going ahead. Ipswich 'assumed many of the characteristics of an established town'.[111] The substantial Scottish presence exuding squatter sympathies indicated that this emerging urban centre at the head of navigation of the Brisbane River was shaping up to challenge Brisbane's ascendancy. It was widely acknowledged at home and abroad that Scots were continually 'on the make' and did not waste their time on ill-conceived projects.[112] Furthermore they could invariably be found at the embryonic stage of potentially successful projects.

Public demand for a lock-up, a court house, schools and Protestant clergy as well as the auction of suburban land were indicative of Ipswich's growth and development.[113] Quick to discern lucrative openings for auctioneers and station agents, Aylmer Campbell and Walter Gray established their businesses between 1847 and 1848. While Dorsey and Gray carried out their magisterial duties consistently and faithfully, other Scotsmen such as Colin Mackenzie and John Balfour, were intermittent in their attendance at the bar.[114] By 1848 John Campbell's new complex at Long Pocket was one of the two boiling-down establishments which probably sounded the death knell of this type of industry in Brisbane which was then disadvantaged by distance.[115]

Campbell's defection to Ipswich to make a fresh start following insolvency was also an ominous sign of the danger which this 'remote village' posed to the town which he had formerly supported. Furthermore there were signs that his 'longheaded' entrepreneurial colleague who had given his all to the development of Brisbane had deserted the township by the beginning of 1845. It may have been more than mere coincidence that the promotion of the formerly insignificant Ipswich was associated with his apparent withdrawal from his urban protege. Probably living with his intended, Sarah Anna Philomena Parkes late of Londonderry and Sydney, Mackenzie was sighted on the verandah of George Thorne's Ipswich hotel.[116] Of greater significance, Thomas Dowse found it necessary to travel to Ipswich by the short-lived day coach to cash an order drawn on Mackenzie. He realised that Brisbane's prominent booster had permanently vacated the town in which he was no longer interested.[117] As Mackenzie's drive for revenge was strong, it is not beyond the realms of reason to conjecture that he may well have contributed to or masterminded squatter plans to promote Ipswich at Brisbane's expense. Periods of brilliant mania followed by recuperative phases of vengeful, depressive retreat were consistent features of Mackenzie's life script.[118]

With the benefit of hindsight, the principles and strategies associated with Mackenzie's initial urban strategy were consistent. Just as he formed a hotel and service facilities in the southern dray centre of Brisbane and established a store with direct wharf access on the north bank business section, so he provided similar facilities in Ipswich. From the house on his Bremer River property within Ipswich, Mackenzie conducted a substantial stock and station agency.[119] In the working-class area of Little Ipswich, with direct access to the interior, his drays provided provisions and equipment for the Darling Downs squatters and transported their bales of wool for conveyance by barge to Brisbane. Mackenzie's significant presence in the major districts within Brisbane and Ipswich gave him the potential to monopolise the trade emanating from the sheep stations of the entire region.

Despite the threat of the Ipswich-Cleveland connection, Brisbane maintained its position as the district's port by default. Meanwhile Ipswich assumed the role for many stockholders as the dray terminus. Since the road between Ipswich and Brisbane was a disgrace and as valuable time could be saved, Scottish entrepreneurs turned to being first in the field in river transport – navigational obstacles and tide problems notwithstanding.

As ship owners and agents, Moreton Bay Scots exercised a monopoly over river transport. From as early as July 1842, Andrew Petrie had unsuccessfully attempted to interest the HRSNCo. and promotors of sail in establishing a Brisbane to Ipswich river run. Having made the trip, Captain Chambers, master of the steamer *Sovereign*, was deterred by the narrow river and the hazardous outcrop of rock at the Seventeen Mile Rocks section.[120] Four years later, pioneer storekeeper James Canning Pearce enlisted the services of Captain Aylmer Campbell who successfully navigated the steamer *Experiment* to Ipswich where it was welcomed by the pipes of T. Wightman.[121]

Based at South Brisbane Robert Graham was northern representative for the HRSNCo. as well as agent for the *Experiment* until the beginning of 1848 when it sank off Kangaroo Point. After salvaging the ship, John Boyland and James Reid, also of South Brisbane, entered the steamer into short-lived Brisbane River service in the middle of that year. Having assumed the role of prominent river conveyors, they ensured their superior position by launching the *Hawk* at Winship's yards in November 1849. To maintain their dominant position it was necessary to fight off competition from Aberdonian Thomas Coutts. A former shipowner with family connections to a major British banking house, Coutts had introduced the steamer *Raven* to the river trade in the previous year. Loading and unloading cargo and passengers at South Brisbane and Kangaroo Point, the *Raven* plied the river course two hours faster than the *Experiment* and made the journey three times per week. Its Ipswich destination was the warehouse of Walter Gray who was also local agent for Montefiore & Graham.[122]

The Scots had also been prominent in pioneering the cheaper service of punt transport. Forever vigilant for new business ventures and consistently interested in the commercial potential of the river, John Petrie put behind him his earlier failure to establish a port at Redbank and ventured into the less remunerative alternative to steam by 1847.[123] Petrie's storage facilities were at Kangaroo Point on the southern steamer's route. This building, originally designed for his failed Redbank venture, was subsequently converted into Mackenzie's boiling-down works. Before concentrating on steam, South Brisbane ferry lessees, James Reid and John Boyland, provided competition for Petrie's *Jenny Lind*. In January 1847 they launched their punt *Mary Ann* with a carrying capacity of 100 bales. Nine months later they erected a large store in Ipswich to complement the facilities already operating at South Brisbane.[124]

With three steamers and three punts in operation, river trade at Ipswich was severely hampered by the want of wharfage. Following local outcry and public subscription, 'respectable Scotch tradesman' James Johnston took up the contract in June 1848 to provide Ipswich with a wharf 'equal to any in Sydney'.[125] Within less than two years, the river transport system had been securely established and well-serviced with a more than adequate infrastructure of stores and wharves at both termini. Thenceforth dray transport, inching along the 'apology of a road' which linked Brisbane to Ipswich, was regarded as a less desirable alternative.

Although there were business opportunities within the carrier industry between Ipswich and the Darling Downs and the lower sections of the Brisbane River Valley, it appeared that the Scots seem to have been neither numerous nor prominent among draymen. Apparently the long absences, isolation and dangers not only made the drayman's life unappealing, but posed ominous threats to the security of capital investment. In addition, the general scarcity of carriers operating into the interior was attributed to the lack of bridges and the inadequate state of the already defective roads which were totally impassable during wet weather. The possibility of being held up for long periods by swollen rivers during the wet and the threat of Aboriginal attack were also major disincentives to prospective draymen.[126] It was an accepted fact that the prosperity of the two major northern settlements depended not only upon good communication with the outside world but also with effective passage through to its productive hinterland.

Communication with the Downs had improved immeasurably after a good line of road had been blazed by Henry Alpin in March 1847.[127] Brisbane businessmen never gave up hope that a shorter and more remunerative road than the existing route to Ipswich would be constructed on the north bank of the river to terminate at their North Brisbane enterprises. One month before Alpin's achievement, their hopes had been dashed when the road from the upper Brisbane River to Brisbane via the D'Aguilar Range was finally judged unsuitable.[128] Although only a paltry 100 pounds was granted in 1848 for the repair of roads and bridges in the entire north, this gesture was enough to renew efforts to discover and form new dray roads. Particular attention was paid to the possibility of forming that north bank passage. Fuelled by inter-township rivalry, considerable activity was generated among Scottish opportunists to be the first to blaze such a road which would not only afford direct access to the Lockyer and Brisbane Valley stations but by-pass Ipswich.[129]

As proprietorship of a wayside inn had been a traditional Scottish occupation, the transport routes between Brisbane and the Downs via Ipswich opened up several opportunities for enterprising settlers with accumulated capital and a bent towards hospitality. While Scottish publicans were numerous in Brisbane, there was none within Ipswich and only one outside these settlements by early 1849. John Smith took over the lease of Woogaroo Hotel, in the vicinity of the headquarters of the Commissioner for Crown Lands, to seek a goodly share of trade generated by overland traffic between Brisbane and Ipswich. The *Moreton Bay Courier*, in welcoming the 'genial host', informed patrons that they would be assured of 'caed mille fatheagh' at this centrally located establishment.[130] There were definite signs that the urban infrastructure and facilities existing in North and South Brisbane were being replicated within and around Ipswich.

* * *

Despite its progress and improved trade facilities, the dominance of Ipswich in the region depended on the location of the entrepot which in turn was reliant upon bureaucratic opinion and decisions. In common with their style of involvement in other controversial Moreton Bay issues, the Scottish inhabitants aligned and agitated with the various local interest groups in that campaign. Eventually the government intended to make the choice on the basis of professional opinion in conjunction with the wishes of opposing pressure groups. William A. Duncan, was destined to play a pivotal role in this process. Given a colonial career devoted to literary brawling with the squattocracy, his pro-pastoralist judgements and insensitivity to the interests of the main urban groups were an enigma. Contrary to government intentions, it appears that he flew in the face of expert opinion and ignored the impact upon local power dynamics in formulating his pronouncements.

In his determination to be the 'new broom' of the north, within a month of his arrival Duncan created controversy by his over-zealous application of the regulations. With each of his early decisions, he appeared to drive a wedge between himself and established Brisbane interests. Robert Graham, representing the HRSNCo, even went to Sydney where he successfully lobbied Duncan's superior, Colonel Gibbes, to reverse one of the contentious decisions. Duncan undoubtedly had thought through his own conclusions, but they appeared iconoclastic and even insulting to individuals, groups and localities. In November 1846, within his submission recommending that the government should not hesitate to set up a township at Cleveland Point, he sneered that Brisbane could 'never be aught than a country village'. With its livelihood at stake, Brisbane's business community was not unreasonably incensed by this tactless jibe.[131]

Just when it was expected the Cleveland option would be contingent only on the construction of a substantial jetty, given the necessity of ships to anchor up to a half mile from land, the government decided that its final decision was dependent on the best location for the customs house. Duncan fuelled the squatters' expectations by persisting with Cleveland, thereby provoking a fierce counter-attack by Brisbane forces. Prominent among those inhabitants of North and South Brisbane who memorialised the government in November 1846 for a port and customs house at Brisbane were the urban Scots John Richardson, David Bow, Alex. McIntyre, Thomas Gray and Lachlan McLean. Although Duncan and Andrew Petrie were present at the meeting, their roles were unclear; possibly they provided advice and clarification.[132]

Increased in stature by the manner in which he handled Brisbane's defence, the merchant John Richardson emerged as the dominant figure within this Scottish ethnic group fighting for Brisbane's survival. Right from that meeting in November 1846, he stayed at the forefront of efforts to raise Brisbane's claims to district port status and customs house location above Cleveland's. He fought the Colonial Secretary's presumption that Brisbane's future as principal commercial town was destined to be short-lived. With others, he indicated to the Governor the detrimental effects such predications exerted upon the township's confidence and development and tactfully suggested that 'his Excellency would not suffer the inhabitants to be injured in the manner proposed'. Proof that the Scottish maxim of first in was best dressed appeared inappropriate on this occasion, Richardson noted that many businessmen had expended their entire savings in buying land, erecting buildings and effecting other improvements in the expectation that the government's earlier assurance of Brisbane's pre-eminence was inviolate.[133]

Petitions, counter-petitions, letters to the editor, renewed claims of government arrogance and protests arising from both the colonial secretary's and Duncan's autocratic and offensive treatment of northern inhabitants issued forth. The refusal of the government to grant free warehousing status to Moreton Bay as late as February 1848, after three years of agitation and petitioning, particularly raised local anger[134] Ultimately, the death knell to Cleveland's claims was sounded when Owen Stanley, captain and surveyor, proclaimed to the Colonial Secretary on 18 April 1848, 'I saw no place during my stay at Moreton Bay which, in my opinion, would form an eligible site for a customs house as the one in Brisbane'.[135]

With the site of the district's port apparently settled, Brisbane's three contending localities then engaged in battle for the site of the customs house. The hopes of those who had bought land in the vicinity of the Commissariat Store, Duncan's interim Customs House, were temporarily buoyed but doomed to be dashed. Duncan took great pride in the rigorous reasoning and research which he undertook to reach his decisions which he regarded as final and non-negotiable. Unmoved by the pressure put upon him by the claimants, Duncan arrived at yet another independent and unpopular decision.

In conveying his choice of North Brisbane, Duncan's insulting dismissal of South Brisbane as a mere swamp ensured his alienation from the inhabitants of that place. Further intra-settlement protest ensued when the government ultimately approved of his recommendation that the customs department would be built opposite Kangaroo Point. The proposed situation was most inconvenient, located a mile from the existing business centre at the southern end of Queen Street which had easy cross-river access to the south bank shipping centre. When it was revealed that the site was close to the allotment of land 'recently purchased by the Sub-Collector', the ensuing accusations of conflict of interest were deafening.[136] By one official decision, Duncan had virtually achieved that Petrie Bight-Kangaroo Point nexus which Mackenzie had unsuccessfully attempted over three years of subterfuge. Unfortunately the Point was a spent force by that time.

In May 1849, following yet another petition, the colonial secretary refused the request of the thirty-six signatories that the customs house be located opposite South Brisbane.[137] Finally the two senior Scottish officials united, Wickham stating, 'I have no hesitation in stating that the site proposed by the Sub-Collector of Customs is the most eligible'.[138] To conclude the affair, the Colonial Secretary Edward Deas Thomson informed North Brisbane businessman George Le Breton, organiser of the memorial, that the final decision was in accord with the recommendation of Duncan and Wickham.[139]

Brisbane's business interests quickly realigned. John Richardson, who was allocated one of three sufferance wharves on the basis of his substantial trading activity, established his warehouse and wharf in Eagle Street by 1852 to benefit from the new arrangements.[140] Also accepting the finality of Duncan's decision and not having a permanent commercial base like the entrenched interests at the south of Queen Street, George Raff quickly followed.

The last-minute ploy that the so-called Queen's Wharf, the ruinous government jetty adjoining the Commissariat Store, be accorded sufferance status received short shrift from Duncan. His comments ridiculed the claims by the unsuccessful petitioners that the long-standing Queen's Wharf had been removed elsewhere in an arbitrary manner. Duncan denied that this Ordinance Department landing place had ever been accorded the official standing as claimed. He indicated that it was mandatory that sufferance wharves were the responsibility of private individuals and pointed out that the proposed wharf, if repaired, was too far from the new customs house.[141]

The inexperienced Duncan's persistent selection of Cleveland despite the government's support of Captain Stanley's expert recommendation reflects his formidable self-righteousness, extreme confidence and intransigence. His previous experience in Scotland and in Sydney is replete with traumatic incidents, some debilitating and others triumphant, arising from his inflexible values and actions. Like Mackenzie before him, but for more humanitarian reasons, Duncan was unafraid to tackle the highest authorities in the land when he sought to rectify a perceived injustice. Those who affronted this unyielding and tactlessly independent man were treated to belligerent invective from his acid tongue and rapier pen. During his quixotic career he made many implacable foes, enjoyed various powerful associations and coldly rejected close relationships with the lower orders whom he formerly championed.[142] In sum, he was powerful and persuasive but unpopular.

Basking in the patronage, friendship and confidence of the government hierarchy and its bureaucracy, Duncan enjoyed at Moreton Bay his first taste of security. His confidence grew as he relished the official protection from those antagonistic urban and rural forces which had bedevilled him since his arrival in Australia in 1837. He disembarked at Brisbane in 1846, a marked man with a formidable reputation, cocooned from initial rumblings of local displeasure by that immunity which accompanies unqualified government support.[143] Brisbane had thrust into its midst a seasoned radical journalist who had campaigned for and made his mark in Sydney on many of the issues which were emerging in northern politico-economic life. However, he decided to remain aloof. Entering a new phase of his life and confident in the support of even W.E. Gladstone, Duncan no longer had anything more to prove. He was content to observe the 'uncivilised' northerners replay the campaigns that he had fought and won at cost. Shortly after taking up his duties, Duncan informed his friend Henry Parkes, 'I keep myself very little in the way of local information, except what is indispensable, to the discharge of my duties'.[144]

Commencing his colonial life in Sydney as editor of the Catholic-owned *Australasian Chronicle*, Duncan shifted his focus from the promotion of colonial Catholicism to other cogent issues which affronted his highly developed sense of social responsibility. Making maximum use of the power of the press, his acerbic writings reflect his abhorrence of oligarchy, pursuit of religious equality, affirmation of civil rights and support for the government's control of Crown land. As may be expected, he made powerful enemies among the colonial establishment - the Church of England hierarchy, the landowners and above all the squatters. Inevitably his uncompromising radical journalism in the *Australasian Chronicle* led to his removal as a mouthpiece of Catholicism in New South Wales.[145]

In contrast to the squatters, Duncan was an opponent of coloured immigration, re-introduction of transportation, depression of working-class wages and pastoralist pretensions of class dominance. As the only journalist who supported Gipps' land regulations of 1844, he made bitter enemies of the powerful squatters who ensured the speedy demise of his *Weekly Register*. On the brink of ruin, his loyalty to Gipps was repaid with his Moreton Bay appointment amid the accusations of nepotism in Sydney and by squatter forces in the north. Nevertheless, he had foreshadowed 'the long struggle to open up the land ... during the following decades', a process which ultimately severely diminished squatter power.[146]

Like Lang, Duncan placed great faith in the resurgence of civilising influences through agricultural expansion to obstruct the squatters' plan for a plantation society. He reasoned that as long as the land system favoured by the squatters impeded the immigrants' hopes of self-advancement and social mobility, there was little hope of forging an improved life over that which had been left behind in Scotland. Margaret Payten, Duncan's biographer, has underlined the strength of his stand for democracy in the face of fierce opposition from the squatters. He saw through and agitated against the pastoralists' anti-democratic attempt to tie up the land and manipulate immigration for their own ends - the nemesis of the respectable immigrants' quest for self-improvement. Having been in the thick of agitation for the 1832 Reform Act, which ostensibly was the first blow against proprietorial power in Scotland, he 'was simply transporting colonial landowners for aristocratic oligarchies at home'.[147]

Despite their irreconcilable differences, mainly related to Irish immigration and Roman Catholicism, Duncan and Lang had much in common as important southern radical leaders. Although they shared Chartist leanings, their influence on the political activities at Moreton Bay were diametrically different. Whereas the former had a pronounced effect on the challenge to squatter hegemony at Moreton Bay, the latter withdrew from the fray. Duncan may well have been subdued by his elevation to the ranks of impartial colonial officialdom and determined to stay clear of political involvement, but he never discarded his sense of social justice and his unyielding independence. The initial opposition he encountered within Brisbane and from the interior only served to strengthen his resolve to stay aloof from the less civilised opposition. Instead he sought out culture within his library and music room and confined social interaction to the bare minimum required by the dictates of duty and convention.[148] He was among a tiny minority of Scottish Catholics in the district and his pre-occupation with European history, ecclesiastical expositions and liturgical music set him further apart from the run-of-the-mill Scotsmen in Brisbane.[149] After probing a few of Moreton Bay's raw nerves in his initial period of service in the customs, Duncan ultimately became prominent for his leadership in transforming the quality of the district's religious, cultural and educational pursuits.

Possessing an intellectual and cultural refinement far in excess of any other settler at Moreton Bay, Duncan eschewed the leadership role vacated by Mackenzie and infused his liberalism with a distinct conservative flavour. Although he was credited in the south with the title of champion of the immigrants and operants as well as exerting a significant influence on the arousal of working-class political awareness, he had finally lost faith in the power of the people to effect socio-political change in the colony by the time he reached Brisbane. Hence Duncan's Moreton Bay phase was marked by an increasingly conservative outlook. Reflecting confidence in the newly-emergent, enlightened policies of the Colonial Office and the ability and achievements of the urban bourgeoisie, he left plebeian politics behind. 'One of the most significant middle class leaders of the new lower class political forces in the 1840s' merely watched its arrival in Brisbane while licking his wounds.[150]

With the departure of Evan Mackenzie, who had acted as a focal point for Brisbane's Scots, a leadership void existed in the Scottish community from 1846 to 1848. Conservative Duncan was hardly a rallying point for the Scottish middle-class and proletariat whose ethos of self-improvement was under dire threat from a re-invention of the repressive hierarchical social system.

This role was tenuously filled by John Richardson who was often found in the forefront of Brisbane's counter-defence against the Ipswich-Cleveland Point proposal. Following Lang's visit to Brisbane in 1845, which heralded the establishment of northern Presbyterianism, Richardson occupied a central role in the Scottish community. Influenced by Lang's writings and subsequently taken into his confidence, Richardson was nevertheless an astute businessman. He also accepted that Brisbane's prosperity at that stage was irrevocably linked with pastoralism. Similar to the stance adopted by Andrew Petrie, he made sure his lines of communication with the squatters were kept open during his advocacy for Brisbane's well-being. Possessing a commanding presence, an enormous voice, an austere manner and not being narrowly conservative, the energetic Richardson is reputed to have commanded esteem and affection.[151] He was destined to make his mark from 1851 through his loyal and competent representation of Moreton Bay in the legislature where he joined Lang to labour tirelessly for separation.

* * *

For the previous seven years, Richardson had experienced first hand the dominating influence of the Scottish squatting majority as it battled to save the pastoral industry, strengthen the district and impose its hegemony. In that campaign to form an united, self-sufficient district, Mackenzie's leadership had tapped as much into widespread anti-government feeling as the universal quest for capital accumulation. He not only wished to make the Moreton Bay District independent of Sydney, but planned to establish squatter control over Brisbane - a future international port. In attempting to fulfil his vision, he alienated a large section of the formerly loyal urban society as well as the bureaucratic and maritime interests in Sydney.

Having led the Scottish entrepreneurial activity in Brisbane in the free-enterprise period in the face of government disinterest, Mackenzie used his energy and capital to initiate many of the communication, navigational and mercantile innovations. Ultimately, it was the decisions of Scottish bureaucrats acting within the confines of the despised government which resulted in the fulfilment of these initiatives. In common with the actions of Mackenzie and other dominant Scots who strove for the betterment of the entire northern community, there was no pro-Scottish agenda basic to the objective judgements made by the Scottish-dominated bureaucracy. In fact, Duncan appeared to go out of his way to be unresponsive to all local pressure groups in his eccentric version of objectivity. Despite the attempts to foster unity among the various national groups, Mackenzie's demise and government resurgence resulted in general disunity throughout the district.

The battle lines had been well and truly drawn in the final stages of Moreton Bay's free-enterprise period in the late 1840s when the renewed government presence was more pronounced. While the 'wealth and intelligence' of the district stayed in the interior and favoured Ipswich, Brisbane became the insecure base of the aspiring urban middle and working classes. The squatters considered that these groups were dominated by 'the cupidity of a few individuals'.

Bereft of strong Scottish leadership and deserted by their former squatter patrons, the proletarian Scots were thrown upon their own resources, their ethnic insularity being weakened. In the process of coming to terms with the changed political-economic situation, they were forced to interact with the wider community, adapt to other attitudes and values, and diversify their relationships. Though the plebian section of this ethnic group was transformed from a nuclear, self-sufficient community to an open-ended type, their networks became more important as class consciousness emerged. With the physical and mental withdrawal of the battle-scarred Scottish bureaucrat who could have provided opposition to the real squatter threat, a leadership vacuum was created. As a consequence of John Dunmore Lang's machinations in Britain between 1847 and 1849, it was only a matter of time until this gap was filled and the Scottish-dominated squatters were 'forced onto the back foot' by his predominantly English, urban-oriented imports.

ENDNOTES

1. James Balfour to Thomas Barker, 10 December 1840, Balfour-Barker correspondence.
2. McMichael, *Settlers and the agrarian question*, p. 214; T.H. Irving, 'Some aspects of radical politics in New South Wales in 1856', *Bulletin of Australian Society for the study of Australian history*, 5 (1963), p. 21.
3. John R. Laverty, Development of the town of Brisbane, 1823-1859, BA thesis, University of Queensland, 1963, p. 21.
4. James Bonwick comp. Great Britain Public Record Office documents relative to Moreton Bay 1822-49, (Brisbane: 18—), Fryer Library, p. 416.
5. Ross Johnston, 'Not a capital idea: the birth of Brisbane', *Australian Journal of Politics and History*, 29 (1983), 27, pp. 243; Evan Mackenzie to Charles Balfour, 28 March 1844, Baring Brothers correspondence.
6. John Dunmore Lang, *A historical and statistical account of New South Wales*, vol. 1, (New Haven: Yale University Press, 1875), pp. 189, 286-7.
7. *SMH*, 4 December 1843 in John Mackenzie-Smith, comp. *Brisbane Town News in the Sydney Morning Herald 1842-6*, Brisbane History group, Sources No. 3, (Brisbane: Brisbane History Group, 1989) [*BTN*], p. 35.
8. Donald Charles Cameron, Journal, in *Scots in Queensland*, ed. Grant and Treena Cameron, (Brisbane: Society of St Andrew of Scotland [Queensland]), 1988), p. 9.
9. Johnston, *Brisbane*, p. 75.
10. Ian Donnachie, 'The making of "Scots on the make": Scottish settlement and enterprise in Australia, 1830-1900', in T.M. Devine, ed. *Scottish emigration and Scottish society*, (Edinburgh: John Donald, 1992), p. 150.
11. *SMH*, 10 September 1844, in *BTN*, p. 64.
12. Mackenzie-Smith, *Brisbane's forgotten founder*, pp. 151-85.
13. Ibid.
14. *MBC*, 20 June 1846, p. 3.
15. Margaret Payten, William Augustine Duncan 1811-85: a biography of a colonial reformer, MA thesis, University of New South Wales, 1965, pp. 236-51.
16. Johnston, *Brisbane*, p. 149; See map Moreton Bay District 1846 after Baker, Appendix, p. 226.
17. Thorpe, *Colonial Queensland*, p. 135.
18. Evan Mackenzie, Minutes of evidence, Immigration committee, *NSWVP*, 1842, p.46.
19. Payten, Duncan thesis, p. 135.
20. *SMH*, September 1841, p. 5.
21. *SMH*, 23 July 1846, in *BTN*, pp. 148-51.
22. *MBC*, 4 July 1846, p. 2.
23. John Gregor, Report to the Society for the Propagation of the Gospel in Foreign Parts, 22 May 1846, Anglican Archives, Brisbane.

24 Thorpe, *Colonial Queensland*, p. 136.
25 Ibid, pp. 141-9.
26 Ibid.
27 Ibid, p. 139.
28 Bill of sale between William Stuart Moutry and Evan Mackenzie and James Robert Balfour, 11 March 1843, Packet 1167, Queensland Titles Office, old system; Minutes of the evidence taken before the Select Committee of the declaration and qualification of Patrick Grant Esq., *NSWVP*, 807-10; *Town and Country Journal*, 23 February 1884, p. 351. The lone residence of George Thorne was already in existence when Ipswich was first surveyed.
29 Mackenzie-Smith, *Brisbane's forgotten founder*, p. 18.
30 *MBC*, 20 June 1846, p.1; *MBC*, 21 November 1846, p. 1; A.J. McConnel, Miscellaneous notes on early settlement in south-east Queensland, pioneer families etc., unpaginated, 89/205, Fryer Library.
31 John Mackenzie-Smith, 'Andrew Petrie: father of Brisbane', in *Colonial Brisbane*, in Rod Fisher and Jennifer Harrison, ed. Brisbane: *squatters, settlers and surveyors*, ed. Brisbane History Group Papers No. 16 (Brisbane: Brisbane History Group, 2000), in preparation.
32 Dornan and Cryle, *The Petrie family*, p. 111.
33 Margery Brier-Mills, *The romance of the Bremer*, (Ipswich: Historical Society of Ipswich, 1982), pp. 12-16.
34 Rod Fisher, 'Against all odds: early industrial enterprise at Brisbane 1840-60', *Journal of the Royal Australian Historical Society*, 76 (1990), p. 107.
35 *MBC*, 12 September 1846, p.3; Richard Bardon, *The centenary history of the Presbyterian Church of Queensland*, (Brisbane: The General Assembly of the Presbyterian Church of Queensland, 1949), pp. 26-7.
36 *MBC*, 26 January, 22 February 1843, in *BTN*, pp. 8,10; 'The Reverend John Gregor's missionary tour 1843', in *Brisbane River Valley*, pp. 35-45.
37 *MBC*, 26 December 1846, p. 3.
38 *MBC*, 4 July 1846, p. 3; 4 September 1849, p. 3.
39 *SMH*, 3 May 1844, in *BTN*, p. 50.
40 Bench of Magistrates, Brisbane: Register of cases tried in the court of Requests/ Petty Sessions for the recovery of small debts etc, 6 May 1844 - 3 February 1845, QSA.
41 Merle Norris, comp., *Brisbane hotels and publicans index*, Brisbane History Group Sources No. 6, (Brisbane: Brisbane History Group, 1993), pp. 3, 18, 20.
42 Ibid, 22, 23, 31.
43 *SMH*, 22 August 1843 in *BTN*, p.25; Mackenzie-Smith, *Brisbane's forgotten founder*, p. 142.
44 Dotti Kemp, 'The Cairncross family in Brisbane in the 1840s', *RHSQJ*, 15 (1994), pp. 429-3.
45 Eastgate, *Moreton Bay Directory*, 1850-51: a name directory of the Moreton Bay region.

46   Johnston, *Brisbane*, p. 89.
47   Stewart, 'Another of Brisbane's forgotten founders', pp. 121-2.
48   *MBC*, 23 October 1847, p. 3.
49   Thorpe, *Colonial Queensland*, p. 146.
50   Mackenzie, Evidence, 1842, *NSWVP*, p. 47.
51   Conveyance, Evan Mackenzie to Henry Hughes and Henry Isaacs, 29 August 1844, 343-7, Extract 15, Queensland Titles office, old system.
52   *Brisbane Courier*, 20 January, 1877.
53   Johnston, *Brisbane*, p. 91.
54   Dornan and Cryle, *The Petrie family*, p. 65.
55   Archibald Meston, 'Recollections of the Frasers', *Daily Mail*, 25 August 1923, in Newspaper cuttings from various papers both by and about Meston OM72-82/1, JOL; Eastgate, *Moreton Bay directory, 1850-51*, unpaginated.
56   *MBC*, 20 June 1846, p. 1; *MBC*, 21 September 1852, p. 2.
57   *MBC*, 17 April 1847, p. 3; *MBC*, 22 April 1848, p. 3.
58   Somers, *Letters from the Highlands*, pp. 170-71.
59   J.J. Knight, *In the early days: history and incident in pioneer Queensland*, (Brisbane: Sapsford, 1895), pp. 118-19; Mary McConnel, *Memories of days long gone by/by the wife of an Australian pioneer*, (Private printing, 1905), in *Brisbane River Valley*, p.90; Benjamin Brookes and Thomas Gray to the Government Resident, 19 October 1857, Government Resident, Moreton Bay, Miscellaneous in-letters, Res. A1, QSA.
60   Johnston, *Brisbane*, p. 75.
61   Daniel Boorstin, in *Cities in American history*, Kenneth T. Jackson and Stanley K. Schultz, ed. (New York: Alfred A. Knopf, 1972), p. 15; Howard P. Chudacoff, *The evolution of American urban society*, (New Jersey: Englewood-Cliffs, 1973), p. 36
62   Carl Abbott, *Boosters and businessmen: popular economic thought and urban growth in the antebellum west*, (Westport: Greenwood Press, 1981), p. 8.
63   Thomas Archer to William Archer, 22 March 1846, in *Brisbane River Valley*, p. 62.
64   *SMH*, 2 May 1843 in *BTN*, p. 17.
65   Correspondence of Mackenzie and James Balfour with Baring Brothers Ltd, 28 March 1844 - 28 April 1845.
66   Donnachie, 'The making of 'Scots on the make', pp. 135, 150.
67   *Brisbane Telegraph* cutting book, January 1872, and Thomas Dowse, Diary, recollections, and scrapbook, JOL MS OM/79-68; Campbell, *The early settlement of Queensland*, p. 17; *SMH*, 12 February 1844 in *BTN*, p. 43.
68   Lang, *Cooksland*, p. 104.
69   *British Banner*, 21 June 1848, p. 440.
70   Colley, *Britons*, p. 374; R.A. Houston, *Scottish Literacy and the Scottish identity*, (London: Cambridge University Press, 1985), p. 263.
71   *SMH*, 14 January 1845, in *BTN*, p. 77.

72   James Balfour to Thomas Barker, 10 December 1840, 23 February 1841, Balfour-Barker correspondence.
73   George Forbes to John Balfour c/- M.D. Hunter & Co., Sydney, 6 July 1841.
74   Rent lists, Kilcoy estate, 1832-40, Castle Fraser; Mowat, *Easter Ross*, pp. 7-43, 98-108, 149-52; 'Parish of Kilearnan', *New Statistical Account of Scotland*, pp. 63-72; Somers, *Letters from the Highlands*, p. 83.
75   *Inverness Courier*, 6 December 1837, 22 January 1845; *The Gentleman's Magazine*, February 1845, pp. 201-2.
76   Devine, *Scottish emigration and society*, p. 6, 54-7; Smout, *A century of the Scottish people*, pp. 2-9, 60, 260, 475, 485; Checklands, *The industry and ethos*, 56-59; Lord Henry Cockburn, *Journal of Henry Cockburn, 1831-54*, vol. 2, (Edinburgh: Edmonston and Douglas, 1874), pp. 169-170, 197, 205.
77   Thomas Dowse, Diary, 23 November 1844, OM/84/31, JOL; Thorpe, p. 136.
78   Dowse took possession of George Edmonstone's Queen Street store on 2 July 1846 following nine weeks' arrears in rent. John Campbell's household furniture was sold by Dowse on 28 September 1846 after he was declared insolvent.
79   Commissioner of Crown Lands to Colonial Secretary, 12 January 1843, 43/216, Colonial Secretary's in-letters, Moreton Bay, JOL, micro A213; Police Magistrate to Colonial Secretary, 19 December 1843, 43/9448, enclosed with 43/8021, AONSW.
80   *NSWGG*, 23 July 1844, p. 94; Return of land sales at Brisbane, Moreton Bay, 20 March 1844, Colonial Secretary's correspondence, in-letters, Moreton Bay, JOL, micro A2.14/72.
81   Ibid.
82   Campbell, *The early settlement of Queensland*, pp. 15-22; Mortgage John Campbell to Thomas Sutcliffe Mort, 9 March 1846, Extract 80, Queensland Titles office, old system.
83   *SMH*, 4 December 1843; 20 January 1844; 27 August 1844 in *BTN*, pp. 34, 41, 61.
84   *SMH*, 28 June 1845, in *BTN*, p. 103.
85   Mackenzie to Baring Brothers, 10 September 1844., Baring Brothers' correspondence.
86   James Balfour to Charles Balfour, 6 April 1844, Baring Brothers' correspondence.
87   Mackenzie to James Balfour, 10 September 1844, Baring Brothers' correspondence.
88   James Balfour to Charles Balfour, 5 April 1845, Baring Brothers' correspondence.
89   James Balfour to Thomas Barker, 28 March 1843, Baring Brothers' correspondence.
90   Mackenzie to Baring Brothers, 10 September 1844, Baring Brothers' correspondence.
91   Mackenzie to James Balfour, 25 August 1844, Baring Brothers' correspondence.

92 In March 1844, the revenue branch of the Treasury demanded a report on Mackenzie's landholdings in the colony. Revenue branch, Treasury, documents on land acquired by Evan Mackenzie, 29 March 1844, 44/7 Colonial Secretary, Land, 2/7922, AONSW, micro 1160.
93 Patrick Leslie to his parents, 1 December 1843, Leslie correspondence.
94 *SMH*, 7 May 1845, p. 2.
95 *SMH*, 7 May 1845, in *BTN* pp. 90-3.; *SMH*, 27 May 1845, pp. 96-7.
96 Mackenzie to Charles Balfour, 25 August 1844, Baring Brothers' correspondence.
97 Ibid.
98 Mackenzie to James Balfour, 19 October 1844, Baring Brothers' correspondence.
99 J. Sweatman, Journal of the voyage of the HMS *Bramble*, 1842-7, vol. 2, p. 140, State Library of New South Wales, ML A1725/2486.
100 *SMH*, 24 December 1845 in *BTN* p. 121; Hodgson, *Reminiscences*, p. 117.
101 Mackenzie to Baring Brothers, 10 September 1844, Baring Brothers' correspondence; *MBC*, 13 March 1847, p. 2; 20 March 1847, p. 3.
102 *MBC*, 19 June 1847, p. 2.; 11 September 1847, p. 3; 23 October 1847, p. 3.
103 Russell, *The genesis of Queensland*, p. 245.
104 *MBC*, 8 January 1848, p. 2.
105 *MBC*, 8 January 1848, p.2.
106 James C. Burnett to Surveyor-General, 15 October 1845, 45/86, Surveyor-General, letters received from surveyors 1822-55, micro 3054, AONSW.
107 *MBC*, 24 October 1846, p. 3.
108 *SMH*, 16 November 1845 in *BTN*, p. 118; Lang, *Cooksland*, p.113.
109 Duncan to Colonial Secretary, 9 September 1846, 46/6771, Colonial Secretary's in-letters, Moreton Bay, JOL (micro A2.16).
110 *MBC*, 3 July 1847, p. 2.
111 *MBC*, 2 October 1847, pp. 2-3; 13 May 1848, p. 3.
112 Devine, 'The making of 'Scots on the make', p. 150.
113 *MBC*, 8 August 1846, p. 2.
114 *MBC*, 2 October 1847, p. 2.
115 *MBC*, 24 July 1847, p. 3.
116 *MBC*, 17 July 1845, p. 2; Evan Mackenzie to Police Magistrate, 15 January 1845, Colonial Secretary's in-letters, Moreton Bay, JOL, A2.15/162-7.
117 Dowse diary, 28 and 29 March 1845.
118 Mackenzie-Smith, *Brisbane's forgotten founder*, pp. 217-21.
119 Ipswich Garden allotment documents of 14 and 16, package 3497 and Ipswich Garden allotment documents of 17 and 18 of section 2, package 5808, Queensland Titles Office, old system; Evidence, Patrick Grant qualifications, *NSWVP*, 1845, p. 808; *SMH*, 20 May 1844 in *BTN*, p. 53.
120 Commissioner of Crown Lands, Moreton Bay, to Colonial Secretary, 1 July 1842, 42/5059, Colonial Secretary's correspondence, AONSW.
121 *MBC*, 20 June 1846, p.1: Brier-Mills, *The romance of the Bremer*, p. 12.

122 *MBC*, 5 February 1848, p. 1; Brier-Mills, *The romance of the Bremer*, pp. 13, 15; *MBC*, 10 October 1848. p. 3.
123 *MBC*, 30 September 1848, p. 1.
124 *MBC*, 2 January 1847, p. 3; 2 October 1847, p. 1.
125 *MBC*, 24 June 1848, p. 2.
126 *MBC*, 16 December 1846, p.2; 25 March 1848, p.3; 30 September 1848, p. 2.
127 *MBC*, 10 April 1847, p. 2.
128 *MBC*, 6 March 1847, p. 3.
129 *MBC*, 7 October 1847, p.2; 11 March 1848, p. 3.
130 A Gaelic welcome. *MBC*, 10 March 1848, p. 2.
131 W.A. Duncan to Colonial Secretary, 9 September 1846, p. 4; *MBC*, 14 November 1846, p. 2.
132 *MBC*, 21 November, 1846, p. 2.
133 Ibid.
134 *MBC*, 5 February 1848, p. 2.
135 Captain Owen Stanley to Colonial Secretary, 11 April 1848, *NSWVP*, 1848, p. 1.
136 *MBC*, 30 December 1848, p. 3
137 George Le Breton, forwarding memorial from Brisbane residents respecting the site of the proposed Customs House, 14 March 1849, *NSWVP*, 1843, p. 7
138 Police Magistrate, Brisbane, to Colonial Secretary, 3 April 1849, *NSWVP*, 1849, p.8.
139 Colonial Secretary to G. Le Breton, 11 June 1849, *NSWVP*, 1849, p. 8.
140 Stewart, 'Another of Brisbane's forgotten founders', p. 123.
141 *MBC*, 2 March 1850, p. 2; See map Brisbane ca 1850s after Parker, p. 227.
142 Duncan, Autobiography, pp. 57-55; Payten, Duncan thesis, pp. 135, 156
143 Duncan to Colonial Secretary, 21 September 1847, Deas Thomson papers, CY reel 721, Mitchell Library.
144 Duncan to Parkes, 20 October 1846, vol. 11, Sir Henry Parkes correspondence, CY reel 33/235-6, Mitchell Library; Payten, Duncan thesis, p. 236.
145 Duncan, Autobiography, p.29-67; *The Advocate*, 9 January 1958, p. 13.
146 Payten, Duncan thesis, pp. 130-3.
147 Ibid, p. 150.
148 Duncan to Parkes, 20 October 1846, Sir Henry Parkes Correspondence, vol. 51, CY 73, Mitchell Library.
149 Duncan, Diary, 1856, micro CY 164, Mitchell Library; Duncan, Literary journal, 1845-48, 1852-53, CY 161, Mitchell Library.
150 Payten, Duncan thesis, p. vii.
151 Stewart, 'Another of Brisbane's forgotten founders', pp. 121-2.

Sir Thomas Brisbane
(John Oxley Library)

Sir Evan Mackenzie
(John Oxley Library)

Thomas Archer
(John Oxley Library)

Charles Archer
(Rockhampton & District History Society)

Patrick Leslie 1853
(John Oxley Library)

Alexander McDonald, Superintendent of Kilcoy Station from 1842
(John Oxley Library)

*Durundur Station 1844
(John Oxley Library)*

Newstead House 1853, by Lord Henry Douglas-Scott-Montagu (Dixson Galleries, State Library of New South Wales)

Captain J.C. Wickham
(John Oxley Library)

Rev. John Gregor
(Anglican Archives, Brisbane)

James Davis (Duramboi)
(John Oxley Library)

John 'Tinker' Campbell
(John Oxley Library)

David and Mary McConnel
(John Oxley Library)

Andrew Petrie
(John Oxley Library)

William Augustine Duncan
(John Oxley Library)

Hon. Louis Hope
(John Oxley Library)

First St John's Church of England church
(John Oxley Library)

St Stephen's Roman Catholic church 1868
(John Oxley Library)

First Customs House 1873 - Petrie Bight (John Oxley Library)

Chapter 3
Scots and the 'cultural desert' 1841-48

When William Augustine Duncan arrived in Brisbane in June 1846 to take up his post as Sub-collector of Customs, he was less than impressed with the poor moral tone of the settlement and attendant low standards in cultural refinement. He intimated to his close friend Henry Parkes that he had taken up residence among an uncivilised and lawless people who eked out their precarious existence in a cultural wilderness.[1] The state of affairs at Ipswich was not much better.[2] As Leichhardt observed, the situation in the interior with its predominance of immoral convict-origin workers was even worse.[3]

Duncan, as an editor of two major Sydney newspapers spanning some twenty years of southern colonial life, was well aware that the northern colony was virtually a closed society.[4] A conspiracy of silence, embracing the highest officials to the humblest shepherd, held sway. Even the police magistrate and other government officials, who knew the full extent of Aboriginal suppression, failed to act against white aggression unless directed by their southern superiors to do so. This universal code deprived the southern press of intelligence of unharmonious racial relations and other contentious issues of which the colonial government should have been apprised. Only mere snippets of non-incriminatory local news via Thomas Dowse's regular column in the *Sydney Morning Herald* filtered through to Sydney.[5] Coinciding with Duncan's arrival in the north, Brisbane's first newspaper, the *Moreton Bay Courier*, was established with a decidedly squatter bias and the potential to perpetuate the restricted frontier mentality of the Northern Districts.[6]

If Duncan understood culture to be a reflection of the quality of community life, including morality as well as adherence to the arts, he may well have concluded that the Moreton Bay District of 1846 was culturally moribund. With his eminent background in religion, music, literature, journalism and publishing, and having only recently left a culturally and morally reinvigorated Sydney, his subsequent withdrawal to his own library and music room for intellectual and aesthetic inspiration was quite understandable.[7]

However, the lack of community means for enjoying high culture was not as threatening to the moral fibre of the district as the rapacious mass culture which fed on ignorance and violence. While the middle culture embraced both forms, those who privately maintained their interest in books and the current variety of Christian morality were in a decided minority. General apathy towards religion, high levels of child illiteracy, lack of schools, disregard for authority, drunkenness and the ascendant crime rate indicated that frontier Moreton Bay would have difficulty attracting upright citizens until the situation was remedied. In fact, C.P. Hodgson went so far as to say that many an expectant mechanic or labourer was 'more or less disgusted on their arrival' with a society which was the antithesis of that promised in 'Dr Lang's manual'.[8]

Scottish skilled workers and those labourers who opted for respectability were characterised by exemplary lifestyles and moral attitudes based on thrift, cleanliness, drink, recreation, sexual behaviour and religion. Such persons were known for their self-discipline in systematically 'avoiding drunkenness, gambling, swearing and fighting ... paid their debts on time, and [presented] a clean and decent home to the neighbours'.[9] The rowdiness and disorder which characterised the settlements at Moreton Bay along with 'bawdiness and crudity of popular culture' exerted a repellant influence on highly moral Scottish farm labourers and servants, especially women, who preferred to remain in Sydney or Scotland.[10]

Thomas Archer, the northernmost Scottish squatter with a penchant for the trappings of urban civilisation, waxed lyrical on the rehabilitative effect married women and the ensuing arrival of a trickle of well-connected single girls exerted on the manners and conduct of males of his caste at Moreton Bay. He intimated that increasing numbers of women, along with the production of the first newspaper and the establishment of the first church, heralded the emergence of civilised life at Moreton Bay.[11] According to Archer's criteria, an indication of the district's level of respectability in 1846 can be determined from the statistical analysis of the married female component of its population. Considering the unfavourable comments of contemporary observers on the state of Moreton Bay society, it is not unexpected that only a mere seven single women over twenty-one years of age, mostly daughters of the well-to-do urban inhabitants, lived in the north at the beginning of that year.[12] It was an aggressive and vigorous male domain which lacked the most important element of the mid-Victorian code of behaviour - respectability.[13]

Unlike the British situation, the pursuit of wealth by the well-connected and established members of the colonial social elite was not accompanied by an upsurge in respectable behaviour. It was severely deficient, at least in terms of outward shows of decency, cleanliness, manners, refined speech and religious observance. In the Moreton Bay District, capitalism was practised in a lop-sided manner according to Calvinist-based evangelical philosophy. Philanthropy, salvation and sobriety were thrown to the wind as the settlers, urban and rural, became preoccupied with the pursuit of Mammon.[14] Pastoral prosperity, fundamental to the formation of a proposed plantation economy and a dependent entrepot, produced neither commensurate material improvements in the labourers' lot nor the district's moral tone.

* * *

Modern historical research has largely attributed the blame for societal degradation evident throughout Australia as much to the influence of the local squatters as to the debauched and directionless behaviour of many of the large, dependent working class.[15] Margaret Kiddle did not exonerate the Scottish pastoralists in Victoria who, despite their strict Calvinist background, largely ignored the moral precepts of their religion and the exhortations of their parents. Instead, they embraced hard-hearted, pragmatic frontier values and behaviours in their quest for quick profits. These young men cast aside polite conventions and adopted diametrically different principles from those which they had been taught in Scotland.

The harshness of frontier life, debasing influence of convictism and threats to the very existence of the squatters and their workers by the dispossessed Aborigines left little time or energy for the niceties of civilised life. Some squatters, such as the Archers, in fact returned to rather primitive modes of existence.[16] Emphasis was placed on work, defence, survival and profits. Formerly upholders of class distinction, many squatters temporarily abandoned displays of superiority towards their workers, especially those of similar ethnic origin, to ensure cooperative endeavour in the solid foundation of pastoral empires. In the absence of effective law-enforcement agencies, many masters and men demonstrated defiance towards government control and adopted attitudes and practices towards their fellow colonists which could only be described as underhand, manipulative and dishonourable.[17] Protected by the secrecy accompanying isolation, primitive justice was dealt out to quell Aboriginal resistance.

As elsewhere in Australia, the Moreton Bay Scots had the option of 'preserving intact distinctive [national] cultural elements in Australia' or 'contributing to the emerging Australian culture'. In that period before the establishment of the first Presbyterian church in the district in 1849 and the emergence of the first national associations in the 1860s as distinctive ethnic focal points, the Scottish settlers, mighty and humble, adopted the latter course.[18] Largely Anglicised and accustomed to cross-border interaction and enterprise in Britain, the adaptable Scots readily determined that their survival and prosperity on a violent frontier depended upon what they could selectively retain from the old world and assimilate from the new. In the absence of modifying religious and moral influences, many of the Scottish squatters cast aside temporarily the precepts which governed the lives of their parents. It is claimed that they unleashed a harsher form of capitalism to that which overwhelmed mid-Victorian Scotland and England.[19]

Of course, there were exceptions. Some Scottish squatters such as the McConnels and Archers managed to be exemplars of pastoral capitalism while retaining their humanity and morality. Thomas Archer, after a tirade about his countrymen's lack of honour to his father, suddenly pulled himself up, realising the dangers in generalising. Mindful that the Scottish group contained many of the highest models of morality as well as a minority of the greatest exponents of villainy (across all classes), he qualified his assessment stating, 'Of course there are exceptions to every general rule so to this also - some English are great rogues and some Scotch are very honest men'.[20]

The primary consideration was maximum capital accumulation. Apart from rendering assistance or facilitating advantage to compatriots, Scottishness was largely a secondary consideration until all obstacles to prosperity had been overcome and an independent living in Britain was assured. Regardless of nationality, it appeared that a large number of the squatters exercised double standards in moral and ethical behaviour - ruthless and amoral norms in the colony and those inculcated by the 'pillars of respectable society' at home. Roe concluded that these young men, who claimed to be the colonial aristocracy on the basis of their contribution to the economy and control over the land, 'lacked that sense of honour and obligation which ought to distinguish an elite'. In fact, they created social and cultural anarchy.[21]

Kiddle and Roe's assessments of southern pastoralists are equally applicable to those who formed the first runs on the Darling Downs and Moreton Bay. This is confirmed in the contemporary account of the life of the squatter as revealed by Hodgson. He maintained that most squatters were resigned to 'a few years of banishment, of self-denial and hardship' in the quest to establish their financial independence in Britain. Incurring the wrath of his peers, he noted that there were many who took advantage of the reality that 'they [were] out of reach of guardians, unkind relations, and at liberty to do as they like'.[22]

As one of a large family of Scottish squatters whose moral standing in the Moreton Bay District was beyond reproach, Thomas Archer's assessment of the gentlemanly demeanour of his predominantly Scottish peers demonstrates that the culture of the northern frontier exerted exactly the same debasing influence on honourable behaviour as that 1,000 miles to the south. Some of those who would have been acknowledged as gentlemen in Scotland were the antithesis of this standard in the colony. Unfortunately, their lowered standards became the behavioural model adopted by new arrivals. Archer attributed lowered standards to youth, inexperience, lack of supervision, dearth of wise counsel and desensitisation to commonplace frontier immorality:

> ... most of them come out here very young, before fixed principle of conduct is formed. They are generally cast adrift here ... to fight their own way, perhaps without a relative or a friend to look up to for guidance. They see roguery and villainy around them every day , which by degrees are divested of the ugliness they formerly possessed in their eyes ... and at last practise things which they could never have brought themselves to at home, and for which they would have been scouted out of society in almost any country but New South Wales.[23]

There were, however, those who went to great lengths to ensure that their offspring were thoroughly prepared for the irreligious and immoral society in which they were to seek their fortune, remote from church and family. In an extraordinarily lengthy espistle on morals and ethics, William Leslie emphatically informed his son, Patrick, of paternal expectations based on Calvinist-flavoured precepts and the complementary secular code of respectability. While stressing that the Leslie children had been raised in a respectable home environment, the Laird of Warthill exhorted Patrick to 'persevere steadily on the straight and narrow path and 'to resist the temptations to vice which you may <u>hereafter</u> be exposed'. In addition to being truthful and straightforward in all actions, thoughts and deeds, Patrick Leslie was admonished to be 'strictly just, honourable, and even liberal in ... intercourse with others'. As he was about to enter a society which was deficient in people of high religious and moral character, he was frequently implored to adhere to the code of respectability and never forget or neglect God's precepts. Consistent with the Calvinist tenet which stressed the all-pervading, supervisory influence of providence in everyday affairs, Leslie was reminded of the wrath of divine retribution as well as the blessing of divine intervention. According to his father's beliefs, the material success of his son's undertaking and his physical well-being were dependent on that assistance and protection which God could either provide to the deserving or withhold from the unworthy.[24] This missive emanating from the pen of an avid Episcopalian is indeed interesting as an example of how deeply evangelical thought was imbedded in the general religious and secular thinking of that era.

The counsel which James Balfour provided his sons at Colinton was mainly in the form of a wise economic strategy to increase profits. Although Balfour probably inflicted a shorter, oral version of the Leslie lecture upon John and Robert James before they left for the colony, he basically trusted that their up-bringing provided them with the moral fibre to withstand the temptations of the tainted society in which they would have to labour. While the barrage of letters which Leslie showered upon his sons is not extant, the surviving letters written to Thomas Barker from Edinburgh in the late thirties and early forties provide a reliable guide to the older generation's expectations - ethical as well as economic.

Hoping that Thomas Barker would be his sons' surrogate father in Australia with accompanying powers of supervision and admonition, James Balfour was quick to respond to his friend's report of infringements of acceptable behaviour - usually Barker's over-reactions to minor incidents and challenges to his demands for unquestioning deference. The worldly Balfour, who knew the strengths and weaknesses of his sons and encouraged them to be actively involved in rational decision-making, took strong exception to Barker's severe and heavy-handed disciplinary approach to relatively insignificant infringements.[25] Eventually this personality clash led to the complete alienation of both generations of Balfours from their brusque and petulant colonial mentor. On that occasion, surveillance arranged in the colonial situation was less effective than the filial trust that bridged distance and time.

Nevertheless, the sons relayed back to Scotland the kind of information their father and their financial backer wished to hear. George Forbes was informed by

John Balfour before he departed north for the Clarence that he would be attending church as that would be the last time he could do so in the foreseeable future.[26] When he settled at Moreton Bay, John Balfour was more noted for his practice of pragmatic and ruthless pastoral economics than for his support of the emergence of cultural and religious activity in the district. This success, forged in the face of vicissitude, reflected the more narrow economic bias contained within his father's many anxious letters.

Considering the brief references to aboriginal 'problems' at Moreton Bay and his derogatory comments about non-Europeans, it is arguable whether James Balfour would have been overtly concerned even if he had been apprised of fuller details by his sons - he was certainly fearful for their safety. The aim of ruthless Scottish capitalism was wool production and profit regardless of the cost to indigenes who were wasting a valuable economic resource. Even when Barker expressed his anger to Balfour about the Mackenzies' behaviour in Moreton Bay, it was not centred on the poisonings at Kilcoy, but on their excessive spending and rash risk-taking.[27] The reactions of William Leslie, who was the epitome of declining eighteenth century aristocratic higher values, to his sons' claims that they taught local blacks a lesson they would never forget is unknown.[28] However, it is evident from the large surviving volume of homeward letters that he never called upon them to justify these actions on moral grounds.

Patrick Leslie and John Balfour, well out of sight of their fathers and guided by voluminous, on-going written advice, achieved different personal results arising from variations in personality and maturity. Leslie, who was burdened with more detailed, moral injunctions than Balfour, may well have outshone him in regular religious observance, but was not nearly so successful in judicious capital accumulation. Although Leslie took a leadership role in the beleaguered Church of England affairs during his short sojourn in Brisbane and conducted religious services on his Darling Downs property, his initial record in financial management did not reflect the cautious dealing, straight-forwardness and concern for the interests of others demanded by his father. Certainly, his friendships indicated the mandatory respectable connections, but H.S. Russell has hinted that he may well have had problems 'regulating his conduct'.[29] William Leslie never wrote more prophetic words to his fiscally-careless son: 'Inconsiderate expenditure is ... a rock on which many a promising youth has made a shipwreck of his future fortune'.[30] Despite his obvious flaws in character, Leslie never descended to the depths reached by many of those who undertook the labouring jobs on the pastoral runs.

Leichhardt painted a most unflattering picture of European pastoral workers whom he designated as mainly unmarried, transported convicts 'without a vestige of moral principle or feeling'.[31] The Reverend John Gregor often came across similar types in the course of his peripatetic ministry acting as out-station shepherds and hut keepers. Among the hardened frontier shepherds who ignored his prayers and were unresponsive to his entreaties was one located at a frontier outpost at

Kilcoy. He was described as 'the most hardened creature in iniquity who has ever come under my observation ... totally insensible to every religious, virtuous and good impression'.[32] The experiences of Gregor and Leichhardt in the early 1840s with such bush labourers reinforces the *Moreton Bay Courier's* negative view near the end of the decade. The first journal in the north reported that these workers constituted 'an uneducated and unreflecting class without much sense of social and religious duties', prone to dissipation and wild, irrational extravagance.[33]

At Kilcoy, Gregor contrasted the evil demeanour of the 'old hands' with the respectability of the Scottish workers and their families who were accorded the privilege of working within protective distance of the head station. They were attentive, thankful and earnest in their devotions.[34] A similar, but less extreme dichotomy existed among the workers at Durundur and Colinton. One group of devout Scottish people at Colinton was judged by Gregor as remarkably 'respectable for their station in life'. At Graham and Ivory's station, where most of the workers were apparently Scottish, they were assessed as being attentive, devout and 'well bought up'.[35] According to Gregor's observations, the Scottish workers in the Brisbane River Valley were a well-educated group for the time and reflective on religion, forming a distinct, respectable sub-group among the largely immoral and hard-hearted pastoral work-force. Faithful and experienced sheepmen such as Walter Grieve at Colinton and Donald Davidson from Durundur ensured that their masters were given a head-start by neutralising colonial obstruction with ethnic cooperation. After all, both the Scottish squatters and workers in the initial stage of pastoralism were thrown together 'for the sole purpose of procuring ... comfort and respectability...' which was virtually unattainable in their native land.[36]

This two-tiered demographic structure of masters and servants, together with the squatters' resistance to the establishment of agriculture in the interior, contributed to the retardation of civilisation throughout the district.[37] Over 60% of the population of the Moreton Bay District earned their wages either by labouring in the settlements or by shepherding.[38] Although separated by an insignificant middle-class component of small capitalists, an approximation of this bipolarised structure also existed in the settlements and exerted similar degrading effects. In common with the even smaller ruling/professional class, many of the urban-based storekeepers and artisans aspired to socio-economic advancement and internalised the sober social discipline of respectability which arose from Evangelicalism.[39] However, their numbers were not large enough to exert any discernible ameliorative effect. The respectable Scottish pastoral workers who sought their fortunes in the settlements when their contracts expired augmented the numbers of the small besieged middle-class, but hardly swelled them.

* * *

Ultimately the ethical and cultural resurrection of Moreton Bay depended on increasing the size of its thin layer of morally upright middle-class and upwardly-mobile artisans to create a new culture and dilute the degenerative influences in the urban settlements. The interior, being the domain of the squatters until the government decided on a policy of close settlement, was temporarily a lost cause.

Much to their chagrin, the respectable sections of Brisbane's populace could only look on helplessly as the squatter-promoted robust masculine culture was periodically unleashed on an already troubled settlement.[40] This was the ultimate affront to their community and code of decency. The developing life in the towns, apart from their recreational and trading functions, held little interest to the disrespectful and irresponsible young squatting majority. According to Roe, the squatters as a class acted 'without grace or restraint or care for the public good'.[41]

In his campaign to ameliorate Sydney's reputation as the 'dunghill of the Empire', Lang felt he had demonstrated that the lawless and immoral products of convict culture could be successfully subverted by embourgeoisement of the community with specially selected Scottish middle-class artisans. In contrast to those colonials whose destiny was centred around an aimless, degenerative cycle of itinerant work, drinking and debauchery, these aspirants for socio-economic elevation based their futures on self-improvement, sobriety, industry, reliability and respect for God's word. A precedent had been set: one group of Lang's Scottish importees, who arrived aboard the *Stirling Castle* to build his Australian College, were arguably responsible for injecting new-found respectability into Sydney's society in 1831.[42]

Such a strategy had yet to be tried in Moreton Bay where the deleterious socio-economic and cultural effects of squatter policy were as powerful as the debasing influences of convictism. Although Lang preferred to swell the district's population with Presbyterians, whose religion offered a 'well-organised and integrated instrument for imposing a pattern of social, economic and moral behaviour...', he was not averse to recruiting within Britain and Germany from other Calvinist-based religious groups, such as Baptists, Wesleyans and Lutherans.[43] The increased cooperation between dissenting religious groups, which transcended national boundaries in mid-nineteenth century Britain and their leadership in anti-establishment political agitation, would assuredly be transferred to the northern colony.

The tone of mid-nineteenth century Moreton Bay society was antithetical to the democratic, moral and religious codes of British dissenters.[44] Lang argued that the establishment of nonconformist religion and education would bring respectability to Moreton Bay. Politically it would unleash forces, initially operating from the settlements, which would diminish squatter control over the district. Agriculture and close settlement around the pastoral runs, the precursors of civilisation and morality in the interior, would deliver the final blow.[45]

Modern research and contemporary observations identify squatter policy as a major cause of the depressed state of culture and morality in the Northern Districts.

However, it is unwise to assume that all northern Scottish pastoralists were cast in the mould outlined by Kiddle merely because of their numerical superiority among that group. Nor should it be assumed that those working-class Scots, who had embarked on the ascendant path to minor capitalism in the settlements, were tainted with the same immoral stigma as the aimless and short-sighted element among the labouring population. Leichhardt and the Archers saw vital differences between the actions of Moreton Bay squatters, particularly the better behaved Brisbane Valley Scots and their Darling Downs counterparts, which affected northern culture.[46]

The Scots did not seem to promote or impose their own national expressions of cultural identity aggressively in the settlements or in the bush. Instead, English lower class culture appeared to overwhelm Brisbane society, especially during festivals and special occasions. On their rare visits to Brisbane, the squatters were preoccupied with the English elite sporting culture. In common with their humbler countrymen, the Scots demonstrated that adaptability to colonial conditions for which their national group was renowned. Celebration of the distinctive features of Scottish culture was mainly confined to intimate gatherings of friends and other sub-groups within the settlements' ethnic community and to concentrations of compatriots on the stations.[47] Occasionally, the wider community enlisted the services of Highland pipers and even dancers to enliven the atmosphere at major sporting and social gatherings. Generally, however, there was not an effective rallying point for an organised dissemination of Scottish culture until the foundation of the national church.

As for Scottish contributions to the emergent Australian forms of cultural expression, the early pioneering nature of the district, the sparse, dispersed population and the scarcity of men and women educated in the refined arts precluded the formation of formal, specific interest associations. Even among the Scottish minority in the urban and rural populations, which possessed educational and artistic backgrounds as well as leisure time for creativity, both artistic and literary activity were forms of individual immersion. Once the primitive living phase of the foundation period of dirt floors, damper and mutton was over, the well-educated Scottish squatters privately continued their pursuit of literary, scientific and musical culture within their homesteads. However, they contributed minimally to the developing society beyond.

* * *

Nevertheless there were some isolated artistic and literary contributions from the pioneer Scottish squatters which formed a rough and ready genesis of the corpus which constitutes Queensland's cultural heritage. Their privileged upbringing and wide experience were immediately commented upon by newcomers and visitors to the district. Leichhardt was astounded that so many squatters had visited or studied in Germany and that some such as ex-Etonian Evan Mackenzie could converse with him in his native tongue.[48] While Thomas Archer was impressed with the urbane and learned Bigges, Charles Archer considered David Graham to be 'a very steady, sensible young fellow, much respected in the district'. Also listed by the Archers among the highly educated was University of Edinburgh graduate, David McConnel, who was acknowledged as widely read and 'in possession of a great deal of information'.[49] Gregor recorded that the Scott brothers of Mount Esk were 'of Scotia's gentlest blood'.[50] Unrecorded by local commentators were the educational credentials of Colin Mackenzie and the Balfours who received their secondary education at the prestigious Edinburgh Academy.[51] It is also worthy of note that the Scottish superintendents, such as John McDonald at Kilcoy and Donald McKenzie at Colinton, were often of the same social and educational standing as the proprietors.[52]

Donald Cameron's experience of an evening of talking, playing chess and reading in the Bigges' well-stocked library was apparently commonplace.[53] Spare time at Cressbrook could include serious debate of controversial social issues among the McConnels and their morally upright supervisor Henry Mort, a staunch and intelligent Anglican layman.[54] While Thomas Archer regaled trees with Shakespearian verse or wrote doggerel verse during stints of shepherding, brother David wrote long letters with religious overtones. Further, the talented Charles Archer carved chess pieces and produced at least one proficient painting which depicted life at Durundur. The latter also waxed lyrical in a letter home on the joys of reading Byron, Scott and Goldsmith while remembering fondly the plays he witnessed at the Haymarket.[55] Rugby-educated George Fairholme was also another early Scottish artist who provided a record of daily life on pastoral properties on the Downs and some of the earliest records of Brisbane's hamlets and its unspoiled river.[56] Consistent with the intellectual and cultural development of the Anglicised Scottish elite of the mid-nineteenth century, these young men appeared to be at ease not only with their English peers but also equally appreciative of their neighbours' artistic expression in its various forms.

Although Gregor remembered his quiet night at Kilcoy as a battle against pipe smoke, it would not be unreasonable to conjecture that on occasion the station became alive with Scottish strains of musical celebration. As the only Highland concentration in the district, boasting a majority of Gaelic speakers, two expert pipers and an acknowledged dancer, the stage was set for spontaneous expression of northern Scottish tradition.[57] Charles Archer excitedly related to his sister how Mackenzie's superintendent 'footed sundry national dances, such as the Highland Fling, Jacky Tar, the Sword Dance etc' to accordion music at Durundur in April 1847. John Balfour, 'considered to be a fine singer in England', touched the heartstrings of several Scottish squatters and their superintendents who gathered at Ivory's for Christmas 1845 with a nostalgic rendering of 'some old Scotch songs with great taste such as 'Ye Banks and Braes' [and] 'Dinna ask me gin I loe ye, Troth I darna tell'.[58]

In spite of the fact that Leichhardt felt that the warmly accommodating Scottish squatters were disinterested in his geological and botanical forays, they possessed substantial knowledge about their environment. Their personal, perceptive observations recorded in journals and letters not only attest to their thorough educational grounding in the natural sciences, but also constitute some of the original records of Moreton Bay flora and fauna.[59] In fact, David McConnel, of scientific bent and graduate qualifications, 'took more than common interest in [Leichhardt's] pursuits'. It was the cumulative knowledge and assistance rendered by all the Brisbane Valley squatters which enabled him to identify over 120 new trees and enjoy oysters with his 'friends' of the dreaded Ningy Ningy clan. They also helped him explore the Bunya Bunya Mountains and directed him to a spot in Cressbrook Creek where he could study *Castanospermum Australae* and the Moreton Bay chestnut.[60] This scientific information was not merely confined to the notebooks of amateur and professional gentlemen, but also had important practical applications.

Though Gregor's classical and theological training did not provide him with technical or scientific knowledge, he was capable of appreciating beauty in flowers and identifying the granite outcrops so familiar in the countryside of his native Aberdeen.[61] Just as Gregor recognised the potential of granite blocks as material for the font on his proposed church, Charles Archer was able to list the major trees in his vicinity along with their usefulness on the station. Bloodwood 'splits clean and freely', iron bark 'is used for shingles' and the useful stringy bark 'is generally used for making huts, fences, stockyards'. Taking every advantage of local, natural materials, even wheel barrows were fashioned from the common gum.[62]

In common with every visitor and settler in the district, Archer regarded the bunya bunya tree, confined to the mountain scrubs, as 'the wonder of the country'. He noted for his father's edification the ingenious manner in which the fruit was harvested and the central part it played triennially in the life of the local Aborigines: 'The seed is a favourite food of the Blacks and during the season of the year it is eatable, they live under the trees, gorging themselves and sleeping off their surfeit'.[63] Sadly the small clumps of bunya trees planted on many properties by Europeans became stark symbols of the vanished aboriginal clans which were driven from their spiritual and hunting territories.

The original, roughly built slab huts were gradually replaced by more substantial homesteads and out-buildings constructed from local timbers with which the squatters had become thoroughly familiar through their own experience and knowledge gleaned from aboriginal sources. During his visit to the Pine River area in 1845, Lang was bemused by the incompatibility of the elegant mahogany furniture which was housed within the Griffin's standard, primitive dwelling. Concluding that such a structure was temporary on the basis of the grace of the interior fittings, he provided a description of the typical squatter homestead which reflected colonial pragmatism devoid of any Scottish influence. It consisted 'of rough slabs fixed in sleepers below, and in a grooved wall-plate above, and roofed with large sheets of bark, supported by rough saplings for rafters'.[64]

David McConnel made maximum use of local red cedar in the interior of his shingle-roofed house at Cressbrook which was described in 1843 as 'neatly built of the wood of the iron-bark tree, a species of the genus Eucalyptus'. Designed in a similar but simpler style, John McConnel's adjoining cottage was a timber-framed construction with brick nogging, overslung with a deep verandah in the manner of the traditional, Australian colonial homestead. The large stockyard, the dairy and the numerous huts for servants not only reflected local opinion that Cressbrook was the finest cattle station in the district, but demonstrated pioneering ingenuity in the sensible exploitation of local resources.[65]

In accordance with the ideal of self-sufficiency, horticultural produce was designed purely for station consumption; the Scottish squatters were particularly aware of its health-promoting properties. While Leichhardt admired the industry of those squatters who grew vegetables to add nutritional value and variety to a monotonous fare of meat, damper and tea, Lang was also impressed with the range of crops grown by the Griffins in allocated agricultural and horticultural enclosures around their North Pine station. To Lang, Griffin's bountiful wheat fields, avenues of tropical fruit trees and furrowed vegetable gardens were not only vivid testimony to the suitability of the Moreton Bay climate and soil for agriculture, but also indicated that socio-economic change was possible. He determined that the district could readily support myriads of Scottish and English small farmers who would promote a more occupationally and socially diversified population.[66] The stage was set for the mid-century arrival of the squatters' wives, the long-awaited, harbingers of civilisation.

* * *

Apart from Mrs Griffin who played an effective role in the running of Whiteside, no Scottish squatter's wife lived permanently in the northern part of the Moreton Bay District until David McConnel brought his new bride Mary McLeod from Edinburgh to Cressbrook in 1850.[67] On the whole, the Scottish squatters sought their wives in the south or in Scotland. While Evan Mackenzie wooed his Irish bride in Sydney and John Balfour went back to Scotland to marry his intended, several of the squatters such as Colin Mackenzie and the Scott brothers remained life-long bachelors.[68]

J.O. Balfour confirmed to prospective Scottish capitalists the widely-held belief that respectable women exerted a perceptible influence of refinement in the settlements and the interior. He claimed that ' a traveller can always tell within a few hundred yards of a shepherd's hut whether a woman is there by the gardens, the general look of comfort, and the indescribable cleanliness and neatness ...'. Such a view is in accordance with the male-dominated, mid-Victorian Scottish idealisation of woman's domestic role as a morally superior, nurturing wife and mother - 'the very antithesis of the outside world and the market place'. Yet feminist-historian Elizabeth Windschuttle has argued that despite women's powerlessness and restricted opportunities from the narrow, romanticised wife-mother concept, they gained in status and self-esteem. Their active and equal participation with males as pioneers on the frontier diminished that patriachal subordination which was a feature of nineteenth century Scottish and colonial society.[69]

Within their families and colonial society, service on the sheep stations was indeed a liberating experience for the Scottish married women pioneers. Not only was the perceived role of women broadened by the increased variety of duties required, but the interdependence of husbands, wives and children in a hostile environment led to the formation of stronger family ties. Although the male protective role was heightened due to the hostile frontier experience, the strong Scottish tradition of patriarchy was loosened by an intensified economic partnership, close companionship, expanded skills and heightened awareness of personal aptitudes. In common with those of their gender who enjoyed higher social status at that time, the primary focus of married female pastoral workers was still centred upon being a good wife and mother.[70]

* * *

Without the refining and restraining influence of females of their own caste, the squatters' self-centred and insensitive behaviour during their periodic invasions of Brisbane for shipping and recreational purposes earned them a negative reputation. Although the majority of the squatters in the Moreton Bay District were of Scottish origin, caution should be exercised in attributing the immoral and lawless atmosphere in the settlements to young men of this nationality. If relief from privation and isolation were basic to such actions, the more distant Darling Downs squattocracy, containing a greater English component, surely had more reason to indulge in wild, intemperate behaviour in the town than the nearby Moreton Bay group. For most of the Brisbane River Scottish sector, the main settlement was only a matter of a comparatively short ride away. Ultimately, the only bases for laying blame for unrestrained, individual or group pastoralist behaviour within Brisbane are contemporary testimony and opinion.

Leichhardt, who was present in the district for the 1843-4 wool season, detailed the long drinking bouts and wild orgies of squatters and their men in Brisbane after a prolonged period of isolation, presumably on the Darling Downs. In August 1843 Thomas Dowse had occasion to request the squatters to act less like bullock drivers and more like gentlemen when they came to town to 'violate our little community'. Their 'drinking, whoring and folly by night' was getting beyond the pale.[71] Tying a billy-goat to the bell at St John's, dressing as females, switching shop signs, demonstrating horsemanship in a public house, deflating bagpipes in full drone with a knife outside Gray's bootshop were just a sample of the pranks usually associated with the 'madness of German students or English Oxfordmen'.[72]

Apart from Russell's cryptic comment concerning Patrick Leslie's 'puerile pranks', the identity of the wild jackaroos who let off steam in the settlements is not confirmed by the contemporary chroniclers.[73] Leichhardt, who recounted that only a minority was responsible for the pastoralists' poor reputation in Brisbane, unequivocally exonerated the Brisbane River Valley squatters. The non-involvement of these Scots, whom he considered to be 'sober, well educated men who would be a credit anywhere' is virtually supported by the observations of Thomas Archer whose brother David had signed the pledge.[74] The shy, pious David McConnel, the quiet, sensible David Graham and the Bigges who 'would be considered estimable ... gentlemen in any country' were singled out by Archer as men of exemplary conduct.[75] John Gregor, Brisbane's Scottish Anglican incumbent who was quick to pass judgement, similarly expressed the highest opinion of Ivory, the Scotts and especially the 'kind and gentlemanly' John Balfour.[76]

Dowse, foremost among the defenders of Brisbane's decorum against squatter assault, remembered Evan Mackenzie for his dignity, especially the urbane manner in which he presided over the dinner given to Leichhardt at Bow's hotel on the eve of his expedition to Port Essington in August 1844. Supported by John McConnel as croupier, Mackenzie held the party in the palm of his hand with his eloquence; his language was glowing as he expressed his faith in Leichhardt and proposed the toast wishing him health and success. Such was Leichhardt's gratitude for Mackenzie's moral and material support for this venture, he named the first substantial river that he encountered in his honour.[77] Constrained by his leadership ambitions, Mackenzie sought out the hospitality of the sober Andrew Petrie when he visited Brisbane. In Sydney, he resided at the exclusive Australian Club.

* * *

Yet Mackenzie was as much at home on the back of a galloping, finely-bred horse as taking a leading role in other male-dominated forms of colonial elitism such as testimonial dinners, exclusive clubs and pastoralists' associations. In common with the Bigges, the Leslies, 'Tinker' Campbell and Charles Balfour, the Mackenzies were renowned for the high quality of their stables which produced a large proportion of the winning horses at the annual racing carnivals of the Moreton Bay Racing Club between July 1843 and May 1848.[78]

Racing was the sporting extension of the squatter's socio-economic ascendancy. It permitted the pastoralists an opportunity to flaunt their superior riding skills, finely bred horses and wealth to a public which provided an appreciative audience. The Scottish squatters from the Brisbane Valley were significant mainstays of the colony's dominant sport which was traditionally a symbol both in England and the colony of affluence, power and elitism.[79] It was no coincidence that informal meetings of squatter policy-making bodies and the critical deliberations of the Moreton Bay District Association were scheduled concurrently with these highly-anticipated events in Brisbane's sporting calendar.[80] Indeed the development of horseracing in Brisbane during the first five years was a barometer of the rise in the squatters' hegemonic intentions and the settlement's declining prospects as the entrepot for the wool-producing hinterland.

Depressed economic conditions led to small numbers attending the first and second racing carnivals of the Moreton Bay Jockey Club at Cowper's Plains, but the informal, spur-of-the-moment steeple-chase challenges around the principal thoroughfares of North Brisbane attracted large crowds of mixed social status. Thomas Dowse recalled some twenty-five years later, 'We were occasionally gladdened by an extempore race, got up by some half-dozen squatters who, in coming to do business in the settlement, found time hang heavy on their hands'.[81]

Mackenzie's legendary farewell race around Brisbane streets symbolised a watershed in the development of town-country relations - a farewell to a popular order which united the district and the entry of a 'new broom' intent on making Brisbane know its dependent and subservient position.[82] From the 1846 annual meeting of the Moreton Bay Racing Club, Brisbane's citizenry found the new exclusive policy unpalatable. Non-subscribers to the club were precluded from entering any of the events and townspeople were ordered from the course. In his diary, Dowse noted the wedge that was driven between the squatters and the townspeople: 'Much dissatisfaction expressed by all inhabitants of Brisbane from the exclusive conduct of the Squattocracy'.[83] The respectable elements were also unamused by the squatters' antics in Queen Street after leaving the post-carnival dinner held habitually at Bow's Victoria - almost a symbolic departing insult to a subserviently-resistant Brisbane.[84]

An attempted compromise was struck for the 1847 meeting, enticing the squatters to return to competition, but continuing animosity ensured that 'attendance was more select than numerous'.[85] Although the Brisbane River Scottish squatters re-appeared, many from the Darling Downs and Ipswich decided to stay away, unresponsive to the plea that town and country had common interest in ensuring a successful carnival. Seen as one more instance of the squattocracy's attempt to dominate Brisbane and symbolic of the promotion of Cleveland's prospects, this on-going racing controversy ensured that the town-country rift was entrenched. Dowse once again reflected Brisbane's anger: ' 1st day of the races did not go out to see them, too exclusive the great Squatting gents of this district fancy themselves above the common herd'.[86]

Finally, with the imminent establishment of a 'back country' racing circuit, embracing Ipswich, Drayton and Warwick, the 1848 races at New Farm witnessed the last significant squatter participation in the Brisbane event. Disappointed that the races had not been wholly thrown open to the public and that the Jockey Club was determined to revert to exclusiveness, the inhabitants of Brisbane were adjusting to the distinct possibility that future race carnivals would be mainly an intra-settlement affair. This sparsely attended carnival ended in the abuse of stewards and the ultimate withdrawal of Brisbane's last body of pastoralist support, the Scottish squatters from the Brisbane River Valley. Their absence at the first Brisbane Races of 1849 was met with open-mouthed incredulity.[87]

**

After 1848 the principal reminders of the period when Scottish squatters dominated Brisbane life were the Victoria Hotel, Evan Mackenzie's brick store in Queen Street, the New Farm racecourse, an abandoned shed at Kangaroo Point and Patrick Leslie's Georgian cottage at Newstead. Whereas some Scots such as Kangaroo Point storekeeper Robert Davidson, Richard Cannan and John Gregor maintained their allegiance to the pastoralists throughout the turmoil, there were others such as Andrew Petrie who kept a foot firmly placed in both camps. Former recipients of squatter patronage, Alexander McIntyre and Thomas Gray, were on the verge of changing camps, having experienced increased aloofness and arrogance in business and social interaction. However, for the majority of respectable townspeople, especially the Scottish Calvinists and English dissenters, the dissolute environment arising from the bawdy, male-orientated, popular culture was far more threatening to the moral fibre of urban society than preserving or severing social ties with a basically reputable squattocracy.

In their account of the genesis of sport in Queensland, Max and Reet Howell indicated that popular recreational activities not only reflected the societal mores of the mass culture but with their emphasis on participation and interaction, 'served as social intergrational forces' - the antithesis of horseracing.[88] With its origins in English village life, 'popular leisure was public, boisterous and gregarious and ... allowed social restraints to be tossed aside ...'.[89] Hence the emphasis on physical strength rather than skill and the revelry that accompanied the celebration of colonial festivals such as Boxing Day, the Queen's birthday and Anniversary day (26 January) were valid reflections of the norms and values of the urban working-class society. It undoubtedly required supreme strength and fitness to crew a whaler over a course which started at the South Brisbane ferry and traversed a route to Kangaroo Point, upstream to Walmsley Point and finished by the boat moored at the starting point.[90]

This form of English sport adapted to colonial conditions was eagerly embraced by Brisbane's Scottish community as participants and as merry followers, given the national predisposition to tippling. Dowse was amazed at the drinking capacity of the Kangaroo Point spectators: 'The disciples of Father Mathew have been put to the blush in seeing such quantities of the raw material consumed at the Bush Inn on the Point'.[91] Although Scottish townspeople were indisputably capable of 'exhibiting a few Bacchanalian feats' as well as those representatives from other countries, their names were noticeably absent among the sorry and sore few who fronted the Police Magistrate's Court on the day following such celebrations.[92] Unlike the volatility which often emerged at the end of elitist racing carnivals, good fellowship among all classes was generally the hallmark of Brisbane's holiday regattas, drink-induced violence being rare. As in all facets of colonial life on this frontier, potentially divisive nationality was cast aside in favour of harmonious displays of assimilation and integration.

If these festivities brought forth any displays of Scottish loyalty, it was related to activity within the residential areas within the settlement. Different localities were responsible for providing the entertainment, victuals and regatta which were usually the components of the Christmas festivities. In 1846 Kangaroo Point organised public amusement for Boxing Day while both North and South Brisbane combined to make the New Year's day arrangements. Following the success of 'Tinker' Campbell's boat at the former location and T.H. Green's at the latter regatta, arrangements were made for them to contest the overall championship on Anniversary Day.[93]

Although the regattas were colourful events and attracted a large, enthusiastic following, competition in the large, cumbersome boats, manned by a cross-section of the local citizenry, precluded a Henley-on-Thames atmosphere. There were no sleek, polished, racing shells or blazer-clad spectators, giving the impression of elitism and privilege; rather whalers, gigs and dinghys were the order of the day. Indeed, the Brisbane Regatta, which featured 'a number of gay boats, their streamers waving in the wind' and 'a very large assemblage of spectators who seemed determined for once to make a holiday', had a distinct levelling effect. Result sheets showing the prominence of Scottish competitors Thomas Gray, John Campbell, Edward Orr, John and Walter Petrie in the regattas, along with Englishmen Thomas Dowse, Arthur Binstead and Dr Richard Cannan, reflect a spirit of overall community involvement and harmony. In fact the very appearance of the proficient Aboriginal oarsmen from Amity Point, who had been awarded the whaler *Pirate* for their role in rescuing survivors from the steamer *Sovereign*, and the game challenge thrown out by representatives of the less-experienced Brisbane clan, did much to foster inter-racial reconciliation within the township. In contrast to the annual racing carnival, the Brisbane Regatta was a healing and unifying initiative.[94]

The epitome of plebeian pleasure was held during the 1848 Christmas season at Ipswich and Kangaroo Point, both following the same format. At both localities impromptu working-class horse races took place in addition to 'good old English sports' which included climbing the greasy pole, jumping in sacks and hunting the pig with the greasy tail. While most of the competitors remain anonymous, the plight of unfortunate 'Scotchie the sawyer' who was treated successfully by Dr Dorsey in Ipswich after being 'run full tilt into a tree by his horse' was given prominence in the *Courier* report of the festivities.[95]

At Kangaroo Point and South Brisbane, where the Boxing Day sports of 1847 'passed off without accident or unpleasant occurrence of any kind', the enjoyment of the revellers was increased by foot-racing contests. Pedestrianism was very popular in the township as the result of interest generated in a challenge race and the antics of an eccentric athlete turned showman. Brisbane inhabitants vividly remembered the thrashing James Davis 'alias the Dorrum Boy' received from Kangaroo Point horsebreaker William Harrington in August over 300 yards.[96] This feat of pedestrianism prepared the way for William Francis King, the 'Ladies Walking Flying Pieman' who failed to perform as promised his bizarre sequence of pedestrian feats at Kangaroo Point. Instead, Ipswich citizens were treated to his performance which included running backwards for half a mile, taking fifty flying leaps and drawing a hefty woman in a gig.[97]

Brisbane had only seen such a display of aberrant athleticism on one previous occasion when the acrobatic troupe and unfunny clowns of George Croft performed at his specially constructed South Brisbane Amphitheatre. No doubt as a sop to the settlements' substantial concentration of Scottish inhabitants as well as the ultimate display of his balancing proficiency, Croft performed the Highland Fling on the tightrope 'in character'. Although it is unrecorded whether this dance was performed to the usual quick tempo of pipe music, it was noticed that 'A number of Aborigines [who] were admitted to the arena stared in stupid amazement at the proceedings'.[98]

* * *

Of course there was always a section of an audience which clamoured for less elevating entertainment such as Croft's rendition of obscene songs. The *Moreton Bay Courier* correspondent articulated the sense of insult felt by the respectable section of the audience.[99] This protest, accompanied by the demand for more refined entertainment, resulted in a widespread campaign by the middle class and their working-class adherents to eradicate the immoral influences within Brisbane's society. It was envisaged that respectability would be eventually attained by stricter law enforcement, more vociferous displays of public opinion and support for society's civilising influences. Among the means of achieving the former were agitation for more vigorous prosecution of disruptive elements, more stringent application of penalties by the various courts and greater accountability of publicans for the conduct of their establishments. In addition, the widespread dissemination of education and religion could only elevate the standards of propriety and foster more enlightened forms of behaviour.

With the gradual increase of urbanisation and the squatters' antagonistic attitudes towards Brisbane, there was concomitant demand to regulate the bawdy bush-inspired behaviour of the labouring sector - the basis of Brisbane's reputation as an uncivilised frontier town. For too long the settlement had been held to ransom by the aggressive and intemperate masculine culture which had been fostered by the hostile nature of the frontier society. It was also driven by a squattocracy which benefitted from temporarily prosperous bush workers with legendary drinking habits. Gregor, one of Brisbane's moral guardians, witnessed the culmination of this influence in 1846 declaring, 'There are in Brisbane too much radicalism, too much infidelity, too much drunkenness and immorality of every description ...'.[100]

Official attempts to curb lawlessness and unseemly behaviours had their beginnings in April 1843 when Evan Mackenzie petitioned the Governor to establish a Court of Quarter Sessions at Brisbane after noting the increase in offences of a serious character which accompanied 'the [periodic] influx of strangers of all descriptions from the interior'.[101] When Brisbane's labouring classes met up with bush workers at South Brisbane or Kangaroo Point, the result was often explosive. Writing anonymously to the Colonial Secretary, George Wise had warned in November 1842: 'As the season is now approaching when the Wool drays will be coming to the township, it is more necessary that an immediate stop be put to the selling of spirits, otherwise the scenes that will ensue amongst the Bullock Drivers and draymen will cause more serious disturbances and will very materially injure the respectability and welfare of the District'.[102]

While Chief Constable Fitzpatrick had been appointed as early as 1843 to 'curb some of the unruly spirits' in a more effective manner than his predecessor, it was acknowledged by the end of the year that he needed an offsider to protect persons and property on the unruly south side of the river. Subsequently his colleagues were often unsuitable, two being dismissed for dereliction of duty.[103] Because of 'the inefficient and low levels of policing', it was difficult to address let alone quell all instances of rowdiness and disorder in the towns, which were an affront to respectable standards of public morality.[104] The misconduct of Scottish constable James Macalister contributed significantly to this deficiency in the maintenance of law and order. After reproof from the police magistrate, he resigned from the constabulary. Taking advantage of his police experiences, he thereafter established Brisbane's first private security service as a freelance nightwatchman.[105]

Judgements passed at the Brisbane Police Office, where Captain J.C. Wickham presided, appeared to be fair and impartial. There, employers and employees were treated equally before the law. The cases which came before the police magistrate, often in company of the current officer commanding the 99th regiment, reflected the strain which existed between employers and labour in the settlement. Scottish employers such as John Stewart, George Edmonstone, Lachlan McLean and John Campbell were swift to use litigation to resolve matters which usually related to disobedience, neglect of duty or drunkenness on the job. Campbell's former squatter status and entrepreneurial importance within the township cut no ice at the police court, as illustrated by the several judgements against him for non-payment of wages.[106]

Although conditions were not propitious to establish temperance leagues, the Scottish tension between fondness for and abhorrence of alcohol was as strong at Moreton Bay as it was in Scotland. Perhaps the contrast between the sobriety and piety of the majority of the Mackenzie Black Isle contingent and the drinking habits of the roguish brothers Fraser best illustrates this paradox. William Fraser and brother Thomas, to a lesser degree, were frequently brought before the police magistrate to face drink-induced charges which ranged from driving a dray on the footpath to petty theft.[107] Having navigated a fine line between freedom and penal servitude, William Fraser's most significant attempt to establish his respectability was undone by his addiction. The Blue Bonnet store which he established with his Highlander wife Lexie lasted but a short time. Unfortunately for the Frasers, the general store was stocked with tempting ale, porter, brandy, rum, gin and port in addition to the ubiquitous supplies of starch, soap, candles and drapery.[108] Still, this foray into legitimate business was a step upwards from his former unsavoury employment which ranged from burying victims of shipwreck and aboriginal attack to retrieving the dismembered body of a murder victim at Kangaroo Point.

This murder case which occurred in 1847 was finally tried at Sydney following the preliminary proceedings in Brisbane. The unfortunate Scot, William Fyfe, paid the ultimate price on circumstantial evidence, being unable to afford the costs associated with bringing witnesses to the southern trial. Fyfe pleaded that one witness in particular could have accounted for his movements at the time when the murder took place. William Fraser asserted that Fyfe, a well bred Scottish ex-convict, went to his death because he refused to involve a woman with whom he spent the night - enough to ruin her reputation and disgrace her family. He was attended on the scaffold by the Reverend John McGarvie, leader of the Synod of Australia. After suffering the extreme penalty in a manner that sickened even persons habituated to executions, doubts were raised in Brisbane about the guilt of this hapless hotel cook who had always professed his innocence. Eventually, one guilt-wracked man allegedly confessed to the murder on his death bed, confirming suspicions that there was a grave miscarriage of justice.[109]

It was not this lone homicide which caused Brisbane's citizenry to reach the end of their tether regarding Brisbane's pervasive depravity, especially within the waterfront areas. Nor was the limited incidence of assault, robbery and theft the cause of serious concern. Also, the large number of cases relating to disputes under the Masters and Servants Act were regarded as perfunctory, demonstrating that the increasing use of litigation safeguarded the rights and obligations of both employees and workers. Far more serious was the epidemic of drunkenness, 151 cases being 'disposed of by the Brisbane Bench' from January 1847 to April 1848 - a mammoth number considering that the figures for twenty remaining categories of offences ranged between one and twenty-five and rarely reached five.[110]

As it was argued that there was a direct relationship between drink, crime, obscene language and blasphemy, regulations were promulgated to make publicans more accountable for upholding public decency. In this process, they were to be encouraged by increased police surveillance. Targeting hotels which tolerated offensive drunks who especially shocked respectable women, the *Moreton Bay Courier* noted that publicans were either unable or unwilling to 'interfere with the amusements of their customers'.[111]

Brisbane's thirsty 'pub culture' was particularly strong in 1847. The ratio of hotels to population was 1 to 70. This was indeed a generous allocation compared with the figures for Glasgow for 1843 which indicated that there was one inn for every 130 citizens. In 1841 Sydney imbibers had to contend with a relatively ungenerous ratio of 1 to 255.[112] The Scottish publicans who controlled five of the twelve hotels were David Bow and Alexander Wright at North Brisbane and John McCabe and Andrew Graham in South Brisbane while John Campbell presided for a short period at Kangaroo Point, before his premature death. While all appeared to be respectable houses on the surface, they were closely watched by a revitalised constabulary which responded appropriately to pressure exerted by the respectable community and surveillance by the local newspaper. By 1846, the respectable elements in Brisbane were determined that a vigilant eye would be kept on its pubs and publicans in the name of moral improvement.

Hospitality for visitors to Brisbane had undoubtedly improved from 1841 when the void was temporarily filled by the Petries, Lt Owen Gorman and his fellow regimental officers. From late 1842 the Scots were in the forefront of continuing this traditional warmth towards visitors by establishing the first licensed hotels. According to H.S. Russell and Thomas Archer, it was indeed a joyous day when Bow's hotel opened its doors as the first hotel on the north bank. 'Cooking, cleanliness and chambers', 'clean white table cloths, the plates, cups and saucers' along with 'fresh eggs, milk, butter and real bread...' were welcome substitutes for tin quarts, salty boiled beef, damper, tea and smoke - even though rough and ready service was provided by a 'mongrel waiter'.[113]

The establishment of Mackenzie's Brisbane Hotel in November 1842 had been effective in diminishing South Brisbane's flourishing, illicit liquor trade as well as providing civilised accommodation for masters and men. Arguing that a hotel in the interior could effect similar results, the *Courier* floated the idea some five years later that perhaps there was a need for such an establishment in the vicinity of Mount Esk or Cressbrook in view of the heavy traffic from the Burnett. Confronting tentative magisterial resistance to such a move, the *Courier* argued, ' ... public houses are not necessarily nuisances, and they only become so when the management of them is entrusted to improper persons'.[114] The respectable persons who followed up on this suggestion were John and Isabella Smith, formerly of Kilcoy station, who established the Wivenhoe Inn between Ipswich and Esk on the North's Brisbane River property in 1849.[115]

* * *

While respectable Brisbane could well do without bawdy counter-attractions such as Croft's Emporium, the nature and composition of the population was not suitable for the establishment of temperance societies and a variety of uplifting cultural associations. It was time to take stock of society's direction. Indeed, most of the initial attempts to inculcate culture and civilised behaviour into the inhabitants of the settlement were unsuccessful among those whose behavioural repertoire and intellectual horizons were limited by the immediate gratification provided by liquor. While the mass culture in the settlement at that time had no time for literature, there is evidence that many of the professionals, civil servants and petite bourgeoisie possessed refined literary tastes and substantial collections of books.

Admittedly from 1846 a reading room operated at South Brisbane, but its services were short-lived due to lack of subscribers. However, many settlers such as the Balfours probably received Scottish newspapers such as the *Edinburgh Courant* or the *Inverness Courier* from relatives and formed an unbreakable habit of subscribing to the *Sydney Morning Herald*, the *Australasian Chronicle* or the *Sydney Gazette* before and after the publication of the local paper in 1846. Such avid newspaper readers also possessed their own cache of books which they frequently augmented in accordance with the latest tastes and trends. Middle-class readers, in comparison with the large numbers of illiterate and unreflective labouring class, took responsibility for updating their own knowledge and keeping abreast of the latest literary tastes. While this small number probably could not provide enough support for public libraries and reading rooms, the majority was completely apathetic.

The private libraries of the Scottish squatters and the extent of their recreational reading cited by Gregor, Mort and Cameron vividly indicated that respectable townspeople also shared these cultural attitudes and avid reading habits.[116] When Lyon relinquished control of the *Moreton Bay Courier*, the prominently publicised auction of his paintings and book collection, including Adam Smith's *The wealth of nations*, William Cowper's works, Shakespeare's plays and 38 volumes of *British essayists* indicated that the leaders of the literati were in step with the best intellectual standards in Australia.[117] Similarly, following Gregor's death in early 1848, the auction of his personal effects included books which reflected the intellectual proclivities expected from a Scottish Master of Arts.[118]

Nevertheless, none could compete with Duncan, another Aberdonian intellectual, for the sheer volume and weight of his reading. Receiving books in crate-loads from Britain and Sydney, it was commponplace for Duncan to digest daily three or four books of the most challenging erudition. Whether the books were written in English, French, German, Spanish, Greek or Latin, Duncan never deviated from his daily literary regimen. His reading log for the 12 October 1847 comprised *Histoire du Lutheranism* 'par Louis Staimbourg', *Calvinisme* 'par la même', Butler's *Memoirs of English, Irish and Scottish Catholics* and two other biographies. From the twenty-nine volumes he read for leisure between 5 January to 12 May 1846, he considered Franklin's *Sophocoles* to be excellent, but Gibbon's *Decline of the Roman Empire* was 'Not history at all. Pompous trash mixed with some good articles'.[119] When not reading or gardening, Duncan privately played and arranged sacred music on his harmonium in a room specially allocated for this purpose. In contrast, the unbookish Frasers took their pipe music to the street to enliven public events and add colour to the rare ethnic celebrations.

Duncan's treatise on the *Culture of olive trees*, first published in serial form in the *Australasian Chronicle* in 1844, reflects another passion of the elite Scottish settlers in Moreton Bay. Lang was impressed with Ballow's substantial gardening knowledge and skills which produced 'healthy and vigorous' pilot crops of sugar and cotton'. This observation, pertaining to the Griffins' establishment at the Pine River, confirmed his theory that small farmers could successfully establish an alternative agricultural economy to pastoralism at Moreton Bay and strike a blow against slavery.[120] Across the river at Kangaroo Point, the orchards and gardens of culinary vegetables of Richard Cannan which adjoined the substantial horticultural estate of surveyor James Warner, produced prize-winning crops which were commercially profitable.[121]

Gardening skills were also to the fore on the opposite bank of the Brisbane. In their new cottage at Newstead, on the site of a convict garden, Police Magistrate Wickham and his wife Anna Macarthur not only entertained the district's privileged to Brisbane's best dinners and balls, but built upon the gardening skills of the former owners Patrick and Kate Leslie (nee Macarthur). In addition to orange, lemon, peach, nectarine, apricot, mulberry, guava, loquat, fig, quince, almond and olive trees, beds of peas, beans, cabbages and cauliflowers thrived. English flowering shrubs such as roses, jasmine, honey suckle and ivy also flourished in the fertile soil. In August 1846 Leslie described his prowess in cultivating the vine at Newstead to his father: ' I put a great many cuttings last year which came on beautifully many of them throwing out shoots 15 feet long and one grew to the immense length of 26 feet 9 inches. ... I will have an abundance of grapes this year'.[122] Perhaps, Newstead's gardens looked their best in the mid fifties when Anna Wickham employed Robert Lane to establish a new river-side garden and orchard using bullock team and plough. Mrs Wickham, sister of Kate Leslie and daughter of Hannibal Hawkins Macarthur of the Vineyard, was acknowledged as an enthusiastic and knowledgeable gardener who received plants and expert advice from her botanist uncle, William Macarthur of Camden.[123] Compared with the subservient role of many Scottish wives, Anna Wickham exercised considerable autonomy in horticultural and domestic matters at Newstead. Unlike her British counterparts who were house-bound and firmly under their husband's control, the Macarthur women and their restricted social circle 'experienced greater freedom, status, and in some cases power ... because of the isolated circumstances in which they lived'.[124]

In Scotland married women, despite their prominent and idealised domestic role in a male dominated society, were scarcely suppressed and passive. Being regarded among the most influential moral enforcers of society, they were usually the mainstays of their families while their accumulated actions prevented the whisky culture among their men-folk from getting totally out of control.[125] Indeed Gregor, while expounding his reasons for the drunkenness and immorality of Moreton Bay society in May 1846, placed great faith in the ameliorative effects which would follow when the young squatters decided to marry and a number of respectable married couples poured in following the promises of a re-invigorated government immigration scheme.

Only when they married and became heedful of the need to create a civilised society in the interests of their wives and children, would the squatters adopt and promote more respectable attitudes, values and behaviours both in the interior and the settlements. Henry Mort, who was in daily contact with the squattocracy and its labour force, predicted that the highly contaminated and grossly licentious society would be dependent upon, 'the softening ... influence which the other sex invariably exercised over the tastes and habits of all grades of men'.[126] Focusing on government policy rather than Mort's claims about the pastoralists' preoccupation with profit-making, the pro-squatter Gregor believed that squatter marital status and attendant socio-cultural improvements would not be possible until security of tenure over runs was granted.[127]

* * *

As they were very familiar with Reverend Thomas Chalmer's policy of systematically introducing religion and education to morally redeem the unrespectable industrial towns, Brisbane's Scots would naturally urge the establishment of familiar Presbyterianism. It would act as a wholesome moral influence within the unruly township. As in Scotland, dehumanising towns such as Brisbane were the products of greedy economic controllers and depraved elements within the citizenry. The distinctive social and moral flavour which generally pervaded Scottish society was achieved by the teaching of a church which directly influenced the behavioural standards of large numbers of its worshipping population.

According to respectable elements within the Scottish ethnic group and Rev. J.D. Lang, the first Presbyterian minister to visit the district, Brisbane and Ipswich were in need of a large dose of Calvinism. In his fact-finding tour in late 1845, Lang deplored the lack of Protestant influence apart from the 'purer moral atmosphere' of the German Mission to the Aborigines some six miles northward.[128] Having experienced first-hand squatter disregard for and disruption of the even tenor of life at South Brisbane, Lang remarked that such misbehaviour would not be tolerated in Sydney with its firm urban base and strong popular opinion. Thus he was not surprised at the low moral tone which prevailed given the lack of interest in religion shown by the majority of the population, the embryonic state of the Catholic church and the floundering Episcopal church. These churches nominally catered for the bulk of the 'humbler classes' - mostly expiree convicts. Inferring that the considerable number of Scottish Presbyterians was the mainstay of morality within the two major settlements, Lang expostulated that the existing churches were pernicious threats to 'the cause of civil and religious liberty, as well as education [and] morals'.[129] A fanatical advocate of voluntarianism, Lang subjectively argued that the Catholic church, bolstered by a large number of rebellious Irish immigrants, spread Popery. Just as insidious, the Anglicans, led by a despicable Presbyterian turn-coat, fostered Puseyism, clerical despotism and reliance on the public purse.[130]

As Lang undoubtedly preached to his flock 'which had never been present at divine service ... since they arrived in the Colony', it was no wonder that the moral guardianship at Moreton Bay was found wanting, given the nature of the established churches.[131] Accordingly, he ascertained the need for two Presbyterian clergymen and prepared the way for a promised influx of 'the right sort of people' to dilute squatter power. It was also expected that the introduction of such reputable settlers would numerically weaken and morally overwhelm the undesirable elements in Moreton Bay society. He anticipated that he might well have to organise respectable, Protestant emigration from Britain himself as it was difficult to arouse the interests of Scotland's leaders to ameliorate the lot of fellow nationals in the colonies, let alone improve the moral condition of the communities in which they toiled. Lang maintained that the Scottish establishment, often with colonial interests, worshipped exclusively the god of Mammon, demonstrating little interest in bettering the religious, educational and moral condition of the societies which they fiscally milked:

> If there is money to be made in a British Colony, however remote, however unhealthy, Scotsmen are sure to find their way to it in sufficient numbers; but as anything like an enlightened and vigorous effort, at all worthy of the intellect and enterprise of Scotland, for the welfare of her children in the Colonies, - as to any Scotsman of independent fortune emigrating to these infant empires, to secure to them the institutions of his glorious fatherland - the thing is unheard of and has never occurred.[132]

In his *Sydney Morning Herald* column Dowse reminded Lang that he had promised to send two Presbyterian clergymen from the seven who were expected to arrive in Sydney at the beginning of 1846.[133] Obviously intending to appoint one minister at Brisbane and the other at Ipswich, Lang found his task complicated by Brisbane's intense inter-regional rivalry. The competition between Scots of North and South Brisbane for the location of the church, and the predictable claims of the small populations within each of Brisbane's three major areas for its own cleric caused him much angst. However, this problem was temporarily pushed aside until 1849 as an active, permanently-based clergymen in whom such high expectations resided could not be found.[134]

In the meantime, the district's Presbyterians obviously carried on in their usual manner, either seeking the sacraments of baptism and marriage from Presbyterian ministers in Sydney, the Lutheran clergy at Zion's Hill or from their Episcopal equivalents in Brisbane.[135] However, there was a brief Presbyterian clerical presence in Brisbane between 1845 and the arrival of the first minister in 1847. The Reverend R. Taylor, who spent a few weeks in Brisbane in August 1846, seeking a warmer climate to restore his health, conducted divine worship in the Court House during his sojourn. Highly esteemed by the Protestant community, Taylor received a testimonial of over twenty-two pounds from Brisbane's loyal

Scottish Presbyterians, prominent among whom were members of the Mackenzie-connected, Black Isle group. The subscription list included: Mr and Mrs John Smith, Mr and Mrs Alex McIntyre, Mr and Mrs Thomas Gray, Mr and Mrs John McIntyre, Mr and Mrs Lachlan McLean, Mr and Mrs James Swan, Mr and Mrs John McCabe, Mr and Mrs George Edmonstone, John Stewart, George McAdam, Richard Cannan, William Stuart and John Boyland.[136] It was not until late 1847 when another sun-seeking invalid, the Reverend Thomas Mowbray MA, arrived in Brisbane that the Presbyterian community received its closest approximation to a permanently-based minister. Consistent with the Scottish Kirk-school connection, he also became one of the most highly esteemed colonial educators.[137]

At Ipswich in 1848, the correspondent to the *Moreton Bay Courier* complained vociferously about the irreverent manner in which the Sabbath was kept by all classes. He attributed this sacrilege to the lack of ministers of all denominations to conduct worship. With a population of 200 adults and 90 children, 'the churches of England, Scotland and Rome still remain supine and to the most essential of our wants'. Within nine months, the numerous Presbyterians within Ipswich were raising funds to erect a Kirk, but were restricted in achieving the final objective by the success of Lang's manoeuvres.[138]

Not as popular as Taylor or Mowbray within the Brisbane community was Brisbane's first Church of England incumbent of the free settlement period, the Reverend John Gregor MA, who arrived in Brisbane with the first Police Magistrate Captain John Clements Wickham in January 1843.[139] Formerly brought to Australia in 1837 by Lang as an ordained minister of the Church of Scotland, Gregor converted to the Church of England priesthood, following intense examination by Anglican primate Bishop W.G. Broughton.[140] This 'treachery' to obtain an assured government salary and his obsequity to Puseyism, according to the voluntaryist Lang, earned Gregor the undying enmity of that colonial leader of Presbyterianism and most of his Brisbane adherents.[141]

The majority of Gregor's nominal Episcopal flock was derived from those elements of the incorrigible labouring population who were 'hardened to iniquity and ungodliness'. Among his most powerful opponents were those most capable of hastening his demise. Gregor reported that his antagonists included the disaffected leaders within his flock and radically inclined, puritanical outsiders, the followers of Lang. Thus he was attacked from within and without his congregation by dissatisfied parishioners and unforgiving Presbyterians.[142]

In spite of the fact that Gregor was continuously supported by Wickham and his family, he endured ostracism and meetings of no confidence from his flock and personal attacks from Lang and his followers.[143] Despite a glowing start when his indefatigable energy was universally acclaimed, he was ultimately denigrated for his aloofness, unavailability, inflexibility and possibly the Calvinist flavour he injected into the more relaxed brand of Anglicanism.[144] It was often remarked that he was more suited to the demands of the refined atmosphere of an established Sydney parish than those of a frontier society which required the physical and personality attributes possessed in abundance by his Catholic colleague, the Reverend James J. Hanly.[145] Whereas Broughton found him 'one of the best qualified Scots ministers, ... his character [standing] high and irreproachable in every respect', the late twentieth century Anglican primate, Keith Rayner, deemed that Gregor 'lacked the qualities of leadership and determination so necessary for a [frontier] missionary'. Unlike Hanly, 'there was none of that mutual confidence that should mark a healthy relationship between priest and people'.[146]

Although Gregor nearly extinguished organised Anglicanism at Moreton Bay, it was a Scottish squatter Patrick Leslie who played the leading role in attempting to resurrect it. After assuming the lay leadership role in Anglican affairs during his brief period of residency at Newstead House, Leslie's presence amidst Gregor's scant congregation promoted church-going as a fashionable activity for the first time.[147] One of the popular Scottish squatters in the settlement, this former chairman of the Moreton Bay District Association organised fund-raising within Brisbane, the Brisbane Valley and the Darling Downs for 'the erection of a church, and also of a parsonage suitable for the decent support of the clergyman'.[148] While this campaign was apparently unsuccessful, Gregor was heartened enough fifteen months later, on the eve of his death, to commence another which bore fruit.[149]

Tragically, Gregor never saw the church of St John the Evangelist which was designed by diocesan architect Thomas Blackett of Parramatta.[150] Following Gregor's drowning in Kedron Brook in January 1848, Wickham, Ballow, Andrew Graham and Gideon Scott formed part of the Anglican contingent which laid their plans before the newly appointed Bishop of Newcastle, William Tyrrell, when he visited the north six months later.[151] Although Gregor left behind a less unified and less vibrant flock than that of the Roman Catholic faith, his dream of a stately Church of England church adjoining the Military Barracks was assured of fulfilment.

The flourishing Catholic congregation was ably led by the popular priest, the Reverend James Hanly, and formidable Scottish layman William Duncan. Standing head and shoulders in power, intellect and theology above any others within the Catholic community in Brisbane, which was mainly Irish, Duncan exerted a positive influence over the development of his faith in Brisbane. Members of the Catholic congregation included but a few Scots. In addition to the future substantial benefactor James Davis, were storekeeper George Le Breton, Constable William Fitzpatrick and three publicans - Robert Rowland, Michael Sheehan and David Buntin. With his rigorous Benedictine background, Duncan played an important role as Brisbane's leading Catholic layman, exhibiting talents in theological disputation, leading the choir and arranging liturgical music.[152] Together with Duncan, Fr Hanly established a strong Catholic community at Moreton Bay.

A child prodigy who was groomed for ministry in the Kirk, Duncan converted to Catholicism at the age of sixteen, and with aspirations for a Benedictine vocation was expelled from home accompanied by the curses of his mother. His arrogant pride in his exceptional intellectual prowess and superior educational accomplishments together with his inability to control his caustic tongue cost him his religious vocation.[153]

Following an ordinary publishing career in Aberdeen, Duncan was recruited by the Reverend Dr William Ullathorne for service as a teacher in New South Wales. On returning from West Maitland to Sydney in disgust with colonial teaching, he was offered the post of foundation editor of the *Australasian Chronicle*, the journal which Archbishop John Bede Polding established as the mouthpiece of colonial Catholicism.[154] From this position he fearlessly attacked the claims of the Church of England to supremacy and privilege, defended Irish immigration and declared Lang's anti-Catholic ravings to be humbug before losing his position because of his pre-occupation with radical political journalism.[155]

The mastermind of Polding's campaign to gain equal status with Broughton, Duncan distanced himself from the Benedictine prelate who gave him little support following the newspaper coup d'etat.[156] Thereafter he used his intellect and ability with the written word to pour scorn on the Benedictine Order which rejected him and on the administration of the archbishop who betrayed him.[157] Having taken on the Catholic, Anglican and Presbyterian hierarchy and enjoying the full support of an appreciative colonial government, there was no person in the north who could pose any real threat to him within or outside the undistinguished Irish-biased Catholic community when he arrived in June 1846.

* * *

The Catholic community and Brisbane were also fortunate in having Duncan in their midst because of his widespread reputation as a practitioner, theorist and advocate of the role of education as an antidote to colonial immorality. Testifying at the Select Committee on Education in 1844, Duncan demonstrated that he was fully conversant with current educational trends in Britain and Europe, practical teaching techniques, efficient forms of classroom organisation and the intricacies of the Irish or National system of education which he advocated. He emphatically stated that he was dissatisfied with the denominational system under which he laboured for a short period as a qualified Irish system pedagogue at Maitland before giving it up in disgust.

Duncan placed great faith in the National system which comprised four days of secular instruction and one set aside for religious instruction by clergymen. Education in common schools, he argued, would diminish internal religious rancour within communities and act as a unifying agent. Furthermore, widespread government provision of education throughout the colony would lead to a decrease in vice which he viewed as the companion of ignorance. Hence the assertion that universal, compulsory child education would amend the deleterious effects of convictism and the immorality of the mass of society could well be seized upon by the respectable elements in the north to improve the morality of the settlements.

The problem was not only to persuade the less reputable and uneducated parents to share this conviction, but also to dilute the all-pervading materialism fostered by the 'pastoral elite' and the inaction of the Anglican church.[158]

If Brisbane was dissatisfied with the paucity of education provision and the hordes of untutored children making nuisances of themselves in the streets, Duncan placed the blame for this situation on the lack of altruistic leaders; the lower orders really wanted their children to be literate, numerate and moral.[159] Such select men with the requisite educational qualifications, sense of mission, commitment to the colony and energy to fight for popular education were a rare commodity. Despite the gloomy picture painted by Ezra Wyeth in his overview of early education at Moreton Bay, there were such men - principally Scots.[160]

Despite the indefatigable efforts of these dedicated teachers to promote denominational education or their private teaching businesses, exactly the same complaints about ignorant children exposed to vice on the streets were as prominent in the local journal in 1848 as in the *Sydney Morning Herald* five years earlier.[161] Public forms of education were reaching only that respectable minority who valued it, leaving most untouched. According to the *Moreton Bay Courier*, the schools were there, albeit few in number, but the masses were not taking advantage of the opportunity available to better the moral condition of their children. Government intervention was needed in the form of fairer apportionment of public expenditure for education purposes. Backing its dramatic predictions with census statistics demonstrating a 25% illiteracy rate among the population under twenty-one years, and the imminent closure of a North Brisbane school because of poor teacher remuneration, the *Courier* stated :

> It is really distressing to think, that in the course of another year or two, the greater part of the population of this district will be composed of persons who can neither read nor write, whose ignorance will unfit them for anything beyond the mere drudgery of the passing hour. What can our rulers expect...but increasing crime, and depraved habits among the people ...'.[162]

Gregor, one of the *Courier's* scapegoats for this situation, shared these fears for the district's future. In a report to the Society for the Propagation of the Gospel in mid 1846, he emphasised the reticence of the inhabitants to send their children to schools. Among the rejected options available in Brisbane, Gregor listed fee-paying institutions run in private houses by near-impoverished schoolmasters or his Sunday School where instruction and books were offered at no charge. In agreement with editorial comments made in the *Moreton Bay Courier*, Gregor indicated that better educational provision relied on Colonial Treasury intervention, with particular reference to greater remuneration for teachers. Until that happened, he could not see the average attendance of the two denominational schools in Brisbane and the sole Ipswich institution under his superintendence exceeding the present number of sixteen. The bleak prospect of 'the great ignorance which must soon prevail in these districts' could only be reversed by better educational provision for the humbler and poorer classes of society'.[163]

The Protestant inhabitants in the fast growing town of Ipswich particularly felt the lack of a minister of religion and the slow progress in establishing a church and school. As in Brisbane, direction and financial assistance were requested of the government for the education of the 'poorer classes' to overcome the unwholesome atmosphere. In an immoral culture devoid of significant spiritual and intellectual influences, it was felt that Ipswich would need a gaol rather than a school unless determined steps were taken to introduce such. When most of the children were catered for by a day school conducted by a lay teacher (probably Mr Munro) in the following year, there were deeply held regrets that no clergymen were available to provide religious instruction to the children who represented the three main denominations.[164] In 1848 the Church of England adherents took steps to remedy that deficiency. Under the leadership of Scottish Episcopalians, Dr Dorsey and Walter Gray, the Ipswich citizenry raised the necessary funds to erect an Anglican denominational.[165]

The foundations of education may well have been securely laid by 1848, but provision for children in the bush remained a perennial problem. Duncan, who admitted to the select committee on education in 1844 that he did not have a firm answer to this problem, put forward the tentative suggestion of district boarding schools. He considered that it was impractical to compel 'every master to have a school on his farm'.[166] Nevertheless, along with the introduction of National education, the New South Wales government made provision for bush boarding schools in 1848.[167] The implementation of two of Duncan's major recommendations reflects the high regard in which Duncan's opinions on education were held in influential circles. In the absence of residential institutions in the north, perspicacious squatters such as George Leslie and David McConnel established schools for the children of their workers on their properties during the 1850s.

Men of Scottish origin also played prominent roles in the provision of education, Anglican and private, in Brisbane. Despite Gregor's remonstrances, he lacked that leadership in educational provision and in pastoral interaction required by Duncan and his bishop to entice mass participation. Initially he worked tirelessly to form a school and entice suitable teachers northward, but apparently these efforts decreased as his unpopularity grew and his period of residence in Brisbane became shorter.[168] However, it was the initiative of an individual Scottish layman, similar to that exercised by Leslie within church affairs in the early years of Gregor's incumbency, which established the Church of England Sunday School on a sound footing.

George Little, one of Brisbane's first storekeepers, had gained the esteem of the respectable members of the community by his tireless efforts to promote religious and moral principles among the youth of the settlement. Dismayed by the lack of supervision and immorality of the local children, Little attributed their moral decline to the scarcity of teachers in the district and readily filled a gap. The farewell function in December 1846 for this 'genuine philanthropist' was attended by sixty of his pupils and their parents. His four years of altruistic labour were rewarded by the presentation of a gold watch. Prominent among the twenty-seven subscribers were fourteen Scottish persons. Led by David McConnel and John Richardson, these respectable Scots also included four of the Black Isle group.[169]

Scottish pedagogues definitely provided the backbone of quality education in Brisbane before 1849. One month after Little's departure, another Scottish educator, Corporal Leslie of the 99th Regiment, was honoured with a published letter of appreciation by grateful parents whose children were permitted to attend the Military School at the Barracks during his two years' tour of duty.[170] Another of the rare educators, 'anxious to render himself useful to his fellow-creatures [by imparting] religious knowledge to the young' was David Scott. Recommended by Gregor and Ballow, Scott opened a day and evening school above Zillman's store for those who were willing to pay one shilling per week for day classes and ninepence for evening tuition.[171] With schoolrooms situated on both sides of the town, William Halcro Robertson survived by instructing students in subjects ranging from reading to trigonometry and navigation, in addition to conducting adult education classes in the evenings at moderate terms. Apparently there was little encouragement for H. Kilner, late second master of Sydney Grammar School, who was willing to 'instruct young persons and adults in the higher branches of Education' and even less response to the advertisement placed by Dr Dorsey's brother, the Reverend Alex. D'Orsey of the High School Glasgow. On the off-chance that Moreton Bay contained folk who really valued a Scottish education and would spare no expense to obtain it, D'Orsey was happy to receive in Glasgow colonial students wishing to be prepared for the English and Scottish universities.[172]

In the meantime, those such as Duncan who really appreciated the benefits of education beyond its power to inhibit 'barbarous ignorance and heathen darkness', and were financially able to do so, employed private tutors.[173] However, in mid 1848, Duncan was no doubt overjoyed to learn that his pet educational project of National schooling had become a reality with the formation of its board and publication of its regulations. Most important in relation to the quality and continuity of education provision was the regulation which guaranteed teachers a minimum salary of forty pounds a year to be supplemented by further income raised by local subscription.[174] As no Normal school was envisaged at that stage in either Brisbane and Ipswich, the teachers at the denominational schools at these centres were granted salaries for 1849 ranging from thirty-five pounds at the Ipswich Roman Catholic school to forty-five pounds at the Brisbane school of the same denomination for which Duncan had supervisory interests.[175]

By 1849 the school for Aboriginal children, operating since the late 1830s at the Lang-inspired German Mission at Zion's Hill, had been abandoned as futile. The Church of Scotland and its ministers of religion were not interested in Lang's missionary endeavour to civilise the Moreton Bay Aborigines and convert them to christianity. 'Unlike many of his contemporaries, Lang firmly believed that the Australian Aborigines were just as much human beings as were Europeans'.[176] Not to be daunted, Lang found the necessary clerical and lay missionaries among Lutherans trained at Gossner's training school in Berlin in 1837. After their frustrating experience of trying to change the 'deep-rooted customs and habits' of adult Aborigines, added to the necessity of having to work for or grow their food, the missionaries changed tack.[177]

* * *

Contemporary commentators demonstrated extreme racism based on ethnocentric interpretation of learning capacity. Gregor purported to articulate the attitude of the European population at Moreton Bay when he wrote: 'these untutored savages ... are essentially an inferior race of beings', with 'utter incapacity to discern spiritual things'. He obviously chose to ignore the first-hand experience of his Lutheran colleague, the Reverend William Schmidt, who considered the Aboriginal children who attended the mission to be 'intelligent, quick to learn and at least the intellectual equivalent of European children'.[178]

Gregor's shallow observations and uninformed racist comments represented that entrenched prejudice in the community which led to the marginalisation of Aborigines in Moreton Bay society. Such attitudes produced behaviours which hastened the Aborigines' degradation, legitimised their repression and dampened prospects for inter-racial harmony. There was no meaningful place even in the morally and culturally deficient settlements such as Brisbane for the Aborigines whose culture was viewed as inferior rather than different. Performing menial tasks within Brisbane such as chopping wood, fetching water and conveying messages, those members of the Turrbal clan who were based at York's Hollow and at Coorparoo across the river were treated with a mixture of ridicule and caution.[179]

Already harrassed by Brisbane police and exploited by its citizens, these generally peaceful, urban fringe-dwellers were in danger of suffering the 'rough justice' previously confined to the bush. The siege mentality within Brisbane, exacerbated by each nearby Aboriginal assault, led inexorably to the hardening of inter-racial relations. Generalised retribution upon the innocent was about to appear in the main settlement. In the interior, European revenge posses invariably concluded their attempts to apprehend Aboriginal offenders by 'indiscriminate attacks on any groups of blacks who came within rifle range'.[180] Within Brisbane, similar 'collective acts of white violence' were unleashed upon a group of local Aborigines in 1846 in the aftermath of Andrew Gregor's murder, north of the Pine.[181]

Secure within his cocoon of white supremacy, Gregor casually related, without the slightest hint of moral reproach, the rationale for the white vigilantism which followed Aboriginal transgressions:

> When the settlers find their property carried away and destroyed by the barbarians, they unite for the punishment of the depredators. The Europeans

have destroyed the Aborigines generally in expeditions undertaken for [this] purpose ..., the Government being unable or unwilling to chastise them for their breaches of laws of civilised men.[182]

The 'law was a dead letter' so far as punishment of white aggressors was concerned; 'no one heeded it' and there was insufficient force to impose it.[183] In common with practice in the Scottish-led interior, this ruthless and impulsive demonstration of rough white justice was tacitly approved by the Scottish-dominated officialdom. Moreover, Lyon's *Moreton Bay Courier* applauded such action, guaranteeing its unconditional support of the squattocracy and demonstrating that the district's only journal would be a 'mouthpiece of virulent racism and white supremacy'.[184]

As with other disputatious issues in the north, there was obdurate and powerful Scottish opposition to the flagrant denial of aboriginal human rights when it exploded in the settlement right under the nose of William Duncan. He wielded his powerful pen to vehemently oppose squatter barbarity and to passionately advocate the protection of aboriginal welfare. Duncan's war of words with the *Moreton Bay Courier* and his forceful letters to the southern press not only exposed the extremes of northern racism, but ensured that the Brisbane community lost its relative immunity from government scrutiny.[185] The days of the closed society in the north, the basis of aboriginal abuse, were numbered from the first day of Duncan's arrival.

Among the local Aborigines Duncan was affectionately known as 'Brother belong to Blackfellow'. Forging this close bond among the local clans while collecting their vocabulary in his leisure hours, Duncan enjoyed harmonious relations with his aboriginal friends.[186] With time on his hands in the north, Duncan befriended the Turrbal fringe-dwellers, recorded their customs and offered employment to their 'peaceable' elder, the Duke of York. It was the attack on this inoffensive man and his followers which provided the vehicle by which details of Brisbane's racial suppression were exposed to the world.

The questionable raid on the camp in search of a suspect following Andrew Gregor's murder, along with the deaths, casualties and traumas suffered by the Duke of York and his followers, was the stimulus for Duncan to renounce his resolve to avoid involvement in Moreton Bay's local affairs.[187] Attempting to bring to justice the constables responsible for this outrage and the members of the survey department who abducted native women, Duncan successfully protested against the first official inquiry conducted by a biased Wickham in 1847. After the charges had been dismissed, Wickham intimated angrily to Duncan that he would act in a similar way to Aborigines under the same circumstances. Thus he demonstrated that he was quite capable of partiality when the reputations of his squatter allies and officialdom were under threat.[188]

In the name of humanity, Duncan drove a wedge within Brisbane's coterie of Scottish government officials. Not only did he earn the enmity of Wickham, but deputy-surveyor James Burnett mounted a vigorous defence on behalf of his men.

Duncan enjoyed less powerful support, his principal allies being Fr James Hanly and James Macalister. The latter, a humble Scottish messenger in the customs department at that stage, had also showed kindness to the Turrbal elder.[189] Ultimately the Colonial Secretary had to accept Wickham's anti-Aboriginal verdict from the second inquiry which Duncan claimed was influenced by the evidence of bribed indigenes.[190]

Although Duncan had to bear the official judgement that his claims were exaggerated, he emerged as a moral victor. Both Wickham and Burnett received letters of reprimand from the Colonial Secretary for their lax control while Duncan was informed that 'the government did not disapprove of the steps [he] had taken in view of accomplishing so desirable an end'.[191] In the final count, Duncan may not have substantially altered the attitudes of Europeans towards Aborigines, but he was content in the knowledge that he 'had some effect in putting a stop to bloodshed, at least under the tacit approbation of the magistrate'.[192]

Disregarding the *Courier's* suggestion in 1847 that he be ostracised from society, Duncan continued to assume the role of Brisbane's watch-dog in matters of racial oppression and moral injustice. He went on successfully to prosecute a member of the survey department in February 1848 for assaulting an Aborigine and brought to public attention a similar case eight months later.[193] Labelling the white offender a drunken ruffian, the *Courier*, under different management and editorial policy, took a diametrically different stance. Proprietor James Swan warned in his weekly editorial that such cowardly actions were out of place in current Brisbane which was intent on changing the image 'so industriously circulated of the general inhumanity of the inhabitants'.[194] With his principal journalist William Charles Wilkes, Swan ensured that the major voice of the community was firmly in the hands of those intent on asserting Christian morality.

* * *

From mid 1848 the re-invigorated *Courier* intimated that the values of respectable, independent Brisbane were at odds with and intolerant towards those arising from the dehumanising influence of squatter pragmatism and insensitivity. Brisbane was intent on throwing off the morally debasing influences of convictism and pastoralism while attempting to establish a more enlightened social climate founded on religion, education, cultural enrichment and law and order. Lacking the numbers to make any significant dent in the squatter's armour, but strengthened by a sympathetic journal, the respectable elements of the township with new-found assertion eagerly awaited that influx of God-fearing, industrious and thrifty immigrants promised by Lang. After all, the weapons of successful dissenting radicalism and urban pressure groups were founded as much on numerical assertion in public meetings and petitions as on influence over a widely-read, literary mouthpiece.

The Scottish influence at Moreton Bay between 1841 and 1848 had unleashed potent forces, healthy and unhealthy. During the first phase, this was often negative as squatters, the majority of whom was Scottish, indirectly and directly promoted acts of immorality and reduced Brisbane to a cultural desert. Ironically it was the Scots who were also at the forefront in providing the catalyst to remedy this situation through the influence of such prominent urban compatriots as Duncan, Swan and Richardson. The frontier mentality which inhibited cultural development began slowly to recede; a turning point had been reached.

Although the Moreton Bay District was reliant on the Scottish-dominated pastoral industry in 1847 and squatter control was overriding in the interior, there were definite signs that resistance to this hegemony was festering in defiant Brisbane. Having survived attempts to bring the settlement under squatter control and thereafter the campaign to deprive it of its entrepot status, Brisbane appeared to be the optimum location from which to launch an organised campaign for moral and cultural resurgence.

The self-centred policies of the pastoralists and the influence of the frontier had created an immoral and uncivilised society in which respectability, religious observance and cultural activity were largely a matter of individual pursuit rather than the outcome of community-held values. As a result of squatter designs to create a two-tiered population of masters and labourers within a plantation economy society, the district sorely lacked solid middle-class leadership to turn the situation around. Educational provision was haphazard and inefficient, despite the valuable personal efforts of Scottish pedagogues. While the Church of England church suffered from the weak leadership of a Scottish cleric and nonconformism was without institutional form, the Catholic faith prospered under the partnership of a popular Irish priest and a Scottish intellectual. Thus the lower orders contained as many who were repelled as attracted by religious tenets. Although their presence among the district's criminals was scant, the Scots were as well represented among the habitual tipplers as the abstainers. In addition, they were as prominent among the persecutors of the Aborigines as their champions.

Brisbane in 1848 was on the brink of a cultural, moral, religious and educational renaissance, a significant breach having been made in the bureaucratically-sanctioned closed society which had hitherto denied social justice to the Aborigines and gave moral support to the squatters. Scottish urban leadership was about to revolutionise the composition and quality of the society moulded by the Scottish squattocracy. Lang intended to create Presbyterianism and a numerous, respectable middle-class; his ally James Swan largely supported his ideals and upheld the values of a humane, just society. Duncan continued to advocate for social justice for religion and education. A self-sufficient, moral Brisbane, with independent control over its port facilities and a strong domestic business base, would be the culmination of these endeavours. The squatter's control over Brisbane would be finally broken. Thenceforth the only issue which really united bush and town was the desire to be independent of the arrogant, Sydney-based government and merchant establishment.

ENDNOTES

1. W.A. Duncan to Henry Parkes, 20 October 1846, Sir Henry Parkes correspondence, vol. 11, A881, CY 33, pp. 233-6.
2. Elizabeth (Libby) L.A. Connors, The birth of the prison and the death of convictism: the operation of the law in Pre-Separation Queensland 1839 to 1859, PhD thesis, University of Queensland, 1990, p. 161.
3. F.W. Leichhardt to his mother, 27 August 1843, in *Brisbane River Valley*, p. 71.
4. Duncan was editor of the *Australasian Chronicle* 1839-43 and *Duncan's Weekly Register* 1843-45.
5. See *Brisbane Town News in the Sydney Morning Herald* [*BTN*] for the majority of Dowse's contributions 1842-46.
6. The first issue of the *Moreton Bay Courier* appeared on 20 June 1846. Denis Cryle, *The press in colonial Queensland: a social and political history 1845-1875*, (St Lucia: University of Queensland Press, 1989), pp. 6-7.
7. Bryan Doyle, 'Australia's first catholic newspaper editor', *The Advocate*, 9 January 1958, p. 13; Duncan to Parkes, 20 October 1846.
8. Hodgson, *Reminiscences*, p. 16.
9. Smout, *A century of the Scottish people*, pp. 89-90.
10. Libby Connors, 'Drinking, folly and whoring by night': Law and order in the 1840s', *RHSQJ*, (1995), p. 497-99.
11. Archer, *Recollections*, pp. 104-6.
12. Calculated from the Moreton Bay census 1846, *MBC*, 4 July 1846. Of the 244 females 21 years and over, 237 were married.
13. Connors, The birth of the prison, p. 160; Michael Sturma, *Vice in a vicious society: crime and convicts in mid-nineteenth century New South Wales*, (St Lucia: University of Queensland Press, 1983), p. 187.
14. Michael Roe, *Quest for authority in eastern Australia 1835-1851*, (Melbourne: Melbourne University Press, 1965), p.76; Kiddle, *Men of yesterday*, pp. 22, 115; Dowse, Diary, p. 26 January 1846; Mort, letter, p. 28 January 1844, *Brisbane River Valley*, p. 55.
15. Sturma, *Vice in a vicious society*, p. 148; Roe, *Quest for authority*, pp. 43, 61.
16. Thomas Archer to Frau Kate Jorgensen 14 July 1845, *Brisbane River Valley* p. 18.
17. Kiddle, *Men of yesterday*, pp. 103, 114, 117,131; Roe, *Quest for authority*, pp. 62,75.
18. Prentis, *The Scots in Australia*, p. 195.
19. Roe, *Quest for authority*, pp. 74 -5; Kiddle, *Men of yesterday*, p. 103.
20. Thomas Archer to William Archer, 22 March 1846, in *Brisbane River Valley*, p. 62.
21. Roe, *Quest for authority*, pp. 43, 73.
22. Hodgson, *Reminiscences*, p. 15.
23. Thomas Archer to his father, 22 March 1846; *Brisbane River Valley*, p. 61.
24. William Leslie to Patrick Leslie, 16 October 1834, Leslie family letters.

25　James Balfour to Thomas Barker, 15 April 1842, 20 October 1843, Balfour-Barker correspondence.
26　John Balfour to George Forbes, 19 October 1840, Balfour-Barker correspondence.
27　James Balfour to Thomas Barker, 28 March 1843, Balfour-Barker correspondence.
28　George Leslie to his parents, 7 November 1841, Leslie family letters.
29　Russell, *The genesis of Queensland*, p. 393.
30　William Leslie to Patrick Leslie, 16 October 1834, Leslie family letters.
31　F.W. Leichhardt to his mother, 27 August 1843, in *Brisbane River Valley*, p. 71.
32　Gregor, Missionary journal, *Brisbane River Valley*, p. 37.
33　*MBC*, 11 September 1847, p. 3.
34　Gregor, Journal, in *Brisbane River Valley*, p. 37.
35　Ibid, p. 42.
36　Anne Summers, *Damned whores and God's police: the colonisation of women in Australia*, (Ringwood: Penguin, 1975), p. 293.
37　R.W. Connell and T.H. Irving, *Class structure in Australian history: documents, narrative and argument*, (Melbourne: Longman Cheshire, 1992), p. 58
38　*MBC*, 4 July 1846, p. 2
39　Sturma, *Vice in a vicious society*, p. 287; G.M. Young, *Portrait of an age*, (London, Oxford University Press, 1969), p. 5
40　Connors, The birth of the prison, pp. 497-8.
41　Roe, The *quest for authority*, p. 61.
42　Baker, *Days of wrath*, pp. 83, 130.
43　A. Allan MacLaren, 'Presbyterianism and the working class in a mid-nineteenth century city', *Scottish Historical Research*, 46 (1967), p. 124.
44　Callum G. Brown, 'Protest in the pews: interpreting Presbyterianism and society in fracture during the Scottish economic revolution', in T.M. Devine, ed. *Conflict and stability in Scottish society 1700-1850*, (Edinburgh: John Donald, 1990), pp. 88-9.
45　Lang, *Cooksland*, pp. 225-6; Baker, *Days of wrath*, pp. 218, 264
46　F.W. Leichhardt to William Nicholson, 6 February 1844, in *Brisbane River Valley*, p. 50; Thomas Archer to William Archer, 22 March 1846, in B*risbane River Valley*, p.61.
47　Charles Archer to Kate Jorgensen, 21 December 1845, in *Brisbane River Valley*, 57-8; Charles Archer to Julia Archer, 25 December 1846, in *Brisbane River Valley*, p. 60.
48　F.W. Leichhardt to R. Lynd, 19 October 1843, in *Brisbane River Valley*, 79.
49　Thomas Archer to William Archer, 22 March 1846, in *Brisbane River Valley*, p. 62; Charles Archer to William Archer, 1 March 1846, in *Brisbane River Valley*, p. 31.
50　Gregor, *Missionary journal*, p. 38.
51　Edinburgh Academy Register, Mr Ferguson's class, 1831-38, and Dr Cumming's class, 1829-36, Edinburgh Central Library.
52　John McDonald was a first cousin of the Mackenzies.
53　Cameron, Journal, in *Brisbane River Valley*, p. 21.
54　Mort, letter, in *Brisbane River Valley*, p. 53.

55 Charles Archer to Julia Archer, 6 October 1845, 20 October 1845, in *Brisbane River Valley*, pp. 58-9.
56 Susanna Evans, *Historic Brisbane and its early artists*, (Brisbane: Boolarong, 1982), pp. 24-29.
57 Gregor, Journal, in *Brisbane River* Valley, p. 36 ; Archer, *Recollections, p.* 77.
58 Charles Archer to Kate Jorgensen, 11 April 1847, in *Brisbane River Valley,* p. 60; Charles Archer to Kate Jorgensen, 21 December 1845, in *Brisbane River Valley*, p.58.
59 For example, Charles Archer to William Archer, 23 November 1844, in *Brisbane River Valley*, pp. 84-6.
60 F.W. Leichhardt to R. Lind, 24 November 1843, in *Brisbane River Valley*, pp. 84-6.
61 Gregor, Journal, in *Brisbane River Valley*, p. 41.
62 Charles Archer, letter, 22 November 1844, in *Brisbane River Valley*, p. 84.
63 Ibid., p. 86.
64 Lang, *Cooksland*, p. 121.
65 Gregor, Journal, in *Brisbane River Valley*, pp. 38-9.
66 Lang, *Cooksland*, p. 144.
67 Mary McConnel, *Memories of days long gone by*, in *BRV*, p. 89.
68 Evan Mackenzie and Sarah Anne Parks, marriage, 1 August 1845, marriage register, vol. 94, no 89, NSW Registrar-General; Duncan Waterson, *Biographical register of the Queensland Parliament, 1860-1929*, (Canberra: Australian National University Press, 1972), p. 7.
69 J. O. Balfour, *A sketch of New South Wales*, (London: Smith Elder, 1845), p. 77; Elizabeth Windschuttle, comp. *Women, class and history: feminist perspectives of Australia 1788-1978*, (Sydney: Fontana, 1980), pp. 39,43.
70 Hiliary Joan Davies, Elite women of nineteenth century south-east Queensland: their role, independence, status and power within the family, MA thesis, University of Queensland, 1996.
71 *SMH*, 22 August 1843, in *BTN*, p. 26; Leichhardt to Nicholson, 6 February 1844, in *Brisbane River Valley*, p. 50.
72 Petrie, *Reminiscences*, p. 283; Leichhardt, 6 February 1844, in *Brisbane River Valley*. p. 50; Lang, *Cooksland*, pp. 186-7.
73 Russell, *The genesis of Queensland*, p. 393.
74 Leichhardt to Nicholson, 6 February 1844, in *Brisbane River Valley*, p. 50.
75 Thomas Archer to William Archer, 22 March 1846, in *Brisbane River Valley*, p. 133.
76 Gregor, Journal, in *Brisbane River Valley*, p. 41.
77 *SMH*, 27 August 1844, in *BTN*, p. 61; *Brisbane Courier*, 16 September 1869.
78 *SMH*, 13 June 1844, in *BTN*, pp. 55-7; *MBC*, 27 May 1848, p. 2.
79 Reet A. and Maxwell L. Howell, *The genesis of sport in Queensland: from the Dreamtime to Federation*, (St Lucia, UQP, 1992), p. 75.
80 *SMH*, 20 May 1844, in *BTN*, pp. 50-1.
81 *Brisbane Courier*, 16 September 1869.

82 *SMH*, 7 May 1845, in *BTN* pp. 94-5.
83 Dowse, Diary, 28 May 1846.
84 J.J. Knight, *In the early days: history and incident of pioneer Queensland*, (Brisbane: Sapsford, 1895), p. 167.
85 *MBC*, 29 May 1847, p. 2.
86 Dowse, Diary, 25 May 1847.
87 *MBC*, 9 June 1849, pp. 2,3.
88 Howell and Howell, *Genesis of sport in Queensland*, p. 77.
89 Ibid, p. 20.
90 *MBC*, 26 December 1846, p. 3.
91 *SMH*, 14 January 1846, in *BTN*, p. 123.
92 *SMH*, 28 December 1844, in *BTN, p.* 77.
93 *SMH*, 14 January 1846, in *BTN*, p. 122.
94 *MBC*, 19 January 1848, p. 2.
95 *MBC*, 23 November 1848, p. 3; 30 December 1848, p. 3.
96 *MBC*, 15 August 1847, p. 2.
97 *MBC*, 30 September 1848, p. 3.
98 *MBC*, 1 May 1847, p. 1.
99 *MBC*, 29 May 1847, p. 3.
100 John Gregor, Report to the Society for the Propagation of the Gospel in Foreign Parts, 22 May 1846.
101 Evan Mackenzie to Colonial Secretary, 19 January 1843, 43/49, Petition for a Court of Quarter Sessions, Colonial Secretary's in-letters from Moreton Bay.
102 George Wise to Colonial Secretary, 9 November 1842, Colonial Secretary's In-letters from Moreton Bay.
103 *SMH*, 22 February 1843, in *BTN*, p. 10; *SMH*, 12 December 1843, p. 3.
104 Connors, 'Drinking, folly and whoring by night', p. 498.
105 *MBC*, 11 December 1847, p. 3.
106 *MBC*, 27 June 1846, p. 2; 10 October 1846, p. 2; 17 October 1846, p. 2; 22 January 1847, p. 3;
10 April 1847, p. 3; 11 March 1848, p. 3.
107 *MBC*, 20 January 1850, p. 3.
108 *MBC*, 24 January 1857, p. 3; Mackenzie-Smith, 'Moreton Bay Scots', pp. 500-1.
109 Russell, *Genesis of Queensland*, p. 395; *MBC*, 2 March 1848, p. 3, 1 April 1848 p. 2, 22 July 1848, p. 2; Rosamond Siemon, *The Mayne inheritance*, (St Lucia: University of Queensland Press, 1997), p. 100.
110 *MBC*, 20 May 1848, p. 3.
111 *MBC*, 11 August 1848, p. 3.
112 Smout, *A century of the Scottish people*, p. 135; Sturma, *Vice in a vicious society*, p. 158; *MBC*, 4 July 1846, p. 2; 27 April 1847, p. 3; 1 May 1847, p. 2.
113 Russell, *Genesis of Queensland*, pp. 175, 337, 368; Archer, *Reminiscences*, p. 63.

114 Commissioner of Crown Lands to Colonial Secretary, 20 September 1842, Colonial Secretary's in-letters, Moreton Bay, (micro A2.12), JOL; *MBC*, 30 October 1847, p. 2.
115 Indenture Messrs North to John Smith, 1 November 1849, North family papers, in Marianne Eastgate, The North family, Dip. Family History thesis, Society of Australian Genealogists, Sydney, 1982, p. 44.
116 Gregor, Journal, in *Brisbane River Valley*, p. 42; Mort, letter, in *Brisbane River Valley*, p. 21; Cameron, Journal, in *Brisbane River Valley*, p. 21, Charles Archer to Julia Archer, 6 August 1845, in *Brisbane River Valley*, p. 59.
117 *MBC*, 18 August 1848, p. 1.
118 *MBC*, 16 September 1848, p. 4.
119 W.A. Duncan, Memoranda and literary journal, 1845-48, 1852-53, A2876, CY 161, Mitchell Library.
120 Lang, *Cooksland*, pp. 152, 162.
121 *Brisbane Courier*, extract from an 1872 edition in Thomas Dowse, Cutting book 1843-79, OM 79 688, JOL.
122 Patrick Leslie to William Leslie, 25 August 1846, Leslie family letters.
123 Anna Wickham to W.S. Macleay, 4 October 1847, A4304, 387-90, Mitchell Library.
124 Davies, Elite women of nineteenth century south-east Queensland, p. 198.
125 Eleanor Gordon and Esther Breitenbach, ed. *The world is ill-divided: women's work in Scotland in the nineteenth century and early twentieth centuries*, (Edinburgh: Edinburgh University Press, 1990), pp. 1-2.
126 Mort, Letter to mother, 28 January 1844, in *Brisbane River Valley*, p. 55.
127 Gregor, Report to Society for the Propagation of the Gospel [SPG], 22 May 1846.
128 Lang, *Cooksland*, p. 477.
129 Lang, *Cooksland*, p. 107.
130 Lang, pp. 478-9.
131 Lang, pp. 105-6.
132 Lang, pp. 481-2.
133 *SMH*, 23 December 1845, in *BTN*, p. 120.
134 Lang, *Cooksland*, pp. 105-6,
135 John Smith, baptism by J.C.S. Handt, 11 July 1841, 2156, vol: 25A, New South Wales Baptisms; Isabella Davidson, baptism by Christopher Eipper, 12 March 1843 at Durundur, handwritten statement; Eliza Jane Smith, baptism by John Gregor, 8 March 1845, 3165, vol: 30A, New South Wales Baptisms.
136 *MBC*, 5 September 1846, p. 3.
137 R. Gordon Balfour, *Presbyterianism in the colonies*, (Edinburgh: McNiven & Wallace, 1900), p. 164.
138 *MBC*, 25 March 1848, p. 2; 30 December 1848, p. 3.
139 *SMH*, 26 January, 1843, in *BTN*, p.8.
140 Keith Rayner, History of the Church of England in Queensland, PhD thesis, University of Queensland, 1962, p. 39.

141 *Cooksland*, pp. 475-6.
142 Gregor, Report to SPG.
143 Ibid.
144 *SMH*, 22 February 1843, in *BTN*, 9; Rayner, History of the Church of England, p.40.
145 James Demarr, *Adventures in Australia fifty years ago, being an emigrant's wanderings through the colonies of New South Wales and Queensland during the years 1839-1844*, (London: Swan Sonnenchien, 1893), p. 40.
146 Rayner, History of the Church of England, pp. 39-40.
147 *MBC*, 6 May 1848, p. 2.
148 *MBC*, 10 October 1846, p. 2.
149 *MBC*, 15 January 1848, p. 2.
150 *MBC*, 24 June 1848, p. 2.
151 *MBC*, 15 January 1848, p. 2; 10 June 1848, pp. 2,3.
152 Denis W. Martin, *The foundation of the Catholic Church in Queensland*, (Toowoomba: Church Archivists' Society, 1988), pp. 73-5.
153 Duncan, Autobiography, pp. 6-28.
154 Ronald Fogarty, *Catholic education in Australia 1806-1950*, vol. 1, (Melbourne: Melbourne University Press, 1957), p. 153; W.A. Duncan, Evidence to the Select Committee on Education, *NSWVP*, 1844, p. 23.
155 Brian Doyle, 'Australia's first Catholic newspaper editor', *The Advocate*, 9 January 1958, p. 13.
156 Duncan, Autobiography, p. 54.
157 Martin, *Foundation of the Catholic Church in Queensland*, p. 74.
158 W.A. Duncan, Evidence to the Select Committee on Education, *NSWVP*, 1844, pp.22-8.
159 *SMH*, 26 January 1843, in *BTN*, p. 8; *MBC*, 11 March 1848, p. 3.
160 Ezra Robert Wyeth, *Education in Queensland: a history of education in Queensland and in the Moreton Bay District of New South Wales*, (Melbourne, Australian Council for Educational Research, 1951), pp. 48-9.
161 *SMH*, 26 January 1843, in *BTN*, p. 8; *MBC*, 11 March 1848, pp. 3.
162 *MBC*, 4 December 1847, p. 2.
163 Gregor, Report to SPG.
164 *MBC*, 27 July 1847, p. 2
165 *MBC*, 14 October 1848, p. 3.
166 Duncan, Evidence to Select Committee, 1844, p. 26.
167 *MBC*, 3 June 1848, p. 2.
168 *SMH*, 22 February 1843, in *BTN*, p. 10.
169 *MBC*, 26 December 1846, 3; 24 April 1847, p. 3.
170 *MBC*, 3 July 1847, p. 3.
171 *MBC*, 4 July 1846, p. 3.
172 *MBC*, 29 June 1846, p. 3; 3 July, 1847, p. 3.
173 Duncan diary, 9 January 1856.

174 *SMH* 15 May 1848, p. 4; *MBC*, 3 June 1848, p. 2.
175 *MBC*, 11 November 1848, p. 3.
176 Baker, *Days of wrath*, p. 111.
177 Lang, *Cooksland*, p. 464.
178 Raymond Evans, 'The mowgi take mi-an-jin: race relations and the Moreton Bay penal settlement 1824-42', Rod Fisher, ed. *Brisbane: The Aboriginal presence 1824-1860*, Brisbane History Group Papers 11, (Brisbane: Brisbane History Group, 1992), p. 26; John Gregor, Reply to a circular letter from the Select Committee on Aborigines, *NSWVP*, 1846, p. 18; John Harris, *One blood - two hundred years of Aboriginal encounter with christianity: A story of hope*, (Albatross, 1990), p. 81.
179 Rod Fisher, 'From depredation to degradation: The Aboriginal experience at Moreton Bay 1842-60', in Rod Fisher, ed. *Brisbane: The Aboriginal presence*, pp. 25, 27, 46.
180 Henry Reynolds, 'The other side of the frontier: early Aboriginal reactions to pastoral settlement in Queensland and northern New South Wales, *Historical Studies*, 77 (1976), p. 60.
181 Denis Cryle, "Snakes in the grass": the press and race relations at Moreton Bay 1846-47', in Fisher, *Brisbane: The Aboriginal presence*, p. 69.
182 Gregor, Reply to circular, *NSWVP*, 1846, p. 17.
183 Demarr, *Adventures in Australia*, p. 224
184 Cryle, "Snakes in the grass", p. 69.
185 Payten, Duncan thesis, p. 242.
186 *MBC*, 6 March 1847, p. 3.
187 Duncan, Autobiography, p. 67.
188 Wickham told Duncan, ' ... the brutes, I would shoot them myself'. Duncan, Autobiography, p. 68.
189 *MBC*, 23 February 1847, p. 3.
190 Duncan, Autobiography, p. 68.
191 Colonial Secretary to Captain J.C. Wickham, Police Magistrate, Moreton Bay, 7 January 1847, Colonial Secretary's correspondence, AONSW; Payten, Thesis, p. 246, Duncan, Autobiography, p. 96.
192 Duncan, Autobiography, pp. 70-1.
193 *MBC*, 22 April 1847, p. 2; 5 February 1848, 3; 28 October 1848, p. 3.
194 *MBC,* 28 October 1848, p. 3.

CHAPTER 4

The Lang factor 1849-59

Although Lang generally stayed clear of the squatters when he visited Moreton Bay in November 1845, he experienced an unpleasant encounter with one of their more disrespectful members at South Brisbane. This incident left him with the same feelings of frustration and helplessness suffered by the respectable elements of Brisbane's community on the rare occasions when the squatters and their workers descended upon the settlement to 'let off steam'. Consequently Lang felt that his recent decision to withdraw his support for the squatters' cause in the colonial legislature was vindicated.[1] Such an affront to his dignity drove home the intensity of local resentment arising from the township's unwilling subservience to an elitist, self-centred group and the debased moral climate which it left in its wake. He avowed that public opinion would never permit such an affront to occur in Sydney. Thus he concluded that squatter power could only be subverted by the replication of similar, strong community insistence on moral standards at Moreton Bay.[2] This was uppermost in his mind as he formulated his vision for the future progress of the Moreton Bay District.

Lang laid out his blueprint for the development of the Northern Districts in the book titled *Cooksland in North-Eastern Australia: the future cotton field of Great Britain*, which he published immediately on disembarkation in England in early 1847. This widely circulated publication ensured that the target readership of parliamentarians, civil servants, evangelical clerics, cotton merchants, the dissenting press and the Protestant section of the British middle and working classes had the opportunity of becoming thoroughly familiar with the details of his unique plan. The substantial sales of this book were crucial to his overall propaganda campaign which centred around public meetings, letters to influential newspapers, submissions to key figures in industry, politics and bureaucracy. In sum, this campaign ensured that the capabilities and prospects of remote Moreton Bay were well-known. It was subsequently asserted that no other person promoted or publicised that region north of the 30th degree parallel as much as the energetic, persistent and uncompromising John Dunmore Lang.[3]

This crusade also revealed that old habits died hard. The questionable modus operandi he adopted in his early years as a Sydney cleric and replicated in other incidents was revealed in all its pathological determination. Not only was Lang willing 'to push his arguments to their most extreme limits', denounce opponents in outrageously vehement terms and adopt fraudulent strategies, but he was also careless with the facts and exhibited incorrigible financial mismanagement.

Moreover Lang was in the habit of proceeding with his plans, despite official rejection, in his deeply-held belief that divine providence would ultimately come to his rescue.[4]

The confrontational nature of Lang's Cooksland project, and his passionate belief in the dire necessity for its successful culmination for the benefit of his adopted 'homeland' predestined this project to be tainted by bitter acrimony. Lang's promotion provoked opposition from government administrators, division among his adherents and led to deprecation of his reputation. Nevertheless even the majority of the disappointed participants in his scheme, along with nonconformist elements of the British and Australian press, were prepared to overlook his dearth of business acumen, lack of adequate preparations and fraudulent dealings. Instead they focused on his energy, zeal, patriotism, advocacy for the operatives and the ultimate benefits his schemes conferred upon the colony in the face of government opposition. After all he 'was one of the first to see the need for systematic or organised immigration'.[5]

Moreover, Lang strove to gain land incentives for small capitalists and potential farmers. Under existing regulations they were virtually deterred from settling in Australia 'where they can become neither squatters nor freeholders, the squattages having all been taken up, and the price of freeholds placing them entirely out of the question'.[6] Cognisant of the fact that thousands of deterred settlers were migrating to the democratic United States where the land regulations encouraged farming, Lang mused in 1875 on his failure to re-write the immigration laws: 'Had I been permitted to carry out the principle of ensuring that reputable families of individuals be granted 16 acres of land for every 20 pounds they paid in passage money, I could have sent 20,000'.[7]

Lang's scheme was a direct challenge to the principles undergirding the existing bounty scheme which promoted pastoral investment at the expense of the fare-paying immigrants and agriculture.[8] Under existing, circumscribed immigration regulations, which were framed around the squatters' need for labour, the self-reliant middle class was at a distinct disadvantage. A polarised, plantation economy, the basis of a pastoral hegemony, was the most likely result. Lang was attempting to bring about a demographic revolution to augment the numbers of a stunted middle class. Having achieved this, he and his followers would then possess the ability to lay democratic foundations and foster moral regeneration.

Correspondence in 1850 from William Pettigrew, surveyor for Lang's Cooksland scheme, indicated that the new settlers took little time in identifying the bipolarised socio-political climate of Moreton Bay. They quickly recognised the plantation economy intent behind the squatters' pro-transportation labour policy:

> The aristocrats are of the opinion that they are born gentlemen and they shall continue so to all eternity by taking all lawful means to prevent people settling in this country that would oppose their ambitions. They mean to do this by gathering here all the blackguards Great Britain and Ireland produce, thereby

> reducing the labour ... to so low a state as prevents any person of small means from coming here to improve themselves. And as they have little fear of these slaves from ever accumulating so much capital as in business to oppose their views their course is therefore very clear.[9]

Although Lang experienced a 'rough ride' in the legislature at the hands of W.C. Wentworth and Deas Thomson over his handling of this venture, he was virtually the people's leader of the opposition. The *British Banner* readily acknowledged that 'Dr Lang, above all other men in the colony, was the antagonist of the Government, and incurred its deadliest hate, but obtained ample compensation in being the idol of the people. ... upon all occasions the Authorities found in him a potent and merciless adversary. He was alike terrible by tongue and pen - a power himself ...'.[10]

Lang's Cooksland scheme was indisputably provocative. Despite his proposal to destroy the basis of American slave labour and expand the district's economic base, it was racist, sectarian and a barely disguised threat to squatter power. Basically Lang proposed to initiate a steady flow of small capitalists, 'mere labourers', clergymen, medical practitioners and teachers of Protestant persuasion, preferably Scots, to the Moreton Bay District. There they would form discrete, respectable agricultural settlements. These potentially divisive enclaves were to be based on the cultivation of cotton, sugar and other products suitable for growth in the tropics. Each shipload would constitute a predetermined middle-class community which would occupy specially selected land on the flood plains of Moreton Bay's major rivers. Eventually, he expected cotton production to supplant pastoralism as the dominant industry. Moreton Bay would become the major supplier for the British textile industry - a blow to the cotton industry of the United States and slavery.[11] In addition the newly created middle class would 'provide a good example to the ... lower classes and help balance the growing power and influence of the ... squatters'.[12]

* * *

In 1849, between 500 and 600 of these God-fearing immigrants, personally selected by Lang, arrived virtually unheralded in three vessels at the unprepared Moreton Bay settlement. They were greeted on their arrival without expected government support and denied the land grants which Lang promised as the major incentive to join his venture. Moreover the colonial hosts at the point of disembarkation were disappointed with Lang's lack of communication and the arrogant assumptions underlying this omission. It had been fully expected that the inhabitants would have been prepared for the arrival of the *Fortitude* by communication via the *Artemesia*, the first ship to bring immigrants direct to Moreton Bay a few weeks earlier.[13] Instead, Lang merely sent letters for publication in the *Moreton Bay Courier* with each of his ships which followed. These missives introduced key arrivals such as the Baptist cleric Reverend Charles Stewart and surveyor William Pettigrew and solicited local help in receiving and settling the immigrants. In the final count, he had presumed to forward these newcomers without making any arrangements for their reception.

The arrival of the *Fortitude* induced an unexpected division in the ranks of Lang's Moreton Bay followers. Understandably John Richardson, whom Lang nominated as his Moreton Bay agent without prior consultation, refused to assume responsibility for these government rejectees, given the attendant high costs and lack of principle involved. Hence Lang's expectation that Richardson would 'take the deepest interest in the expedition' and would indicate appropriate land for division by the company's surveyor was not realised.[14] Wickham sought advice from the Colonial Secretary as he was at loss as to the nature of his official role in the dealing with the anomolous situation created by a private immigration scheme. To gain time until instructions were received from Sydney, he colluded with the Health Officer Dr David Ballow to quarantine the immigrants under canvas for two weeks at Moreton Island on the pretext of two typhus cases.[15]

Lang's immigrants had set sail with false expectations before the proposed land company was formed and in the face of government rejection of his scheme. In typical style, he was undeterred in flouting government regulations and ignoring official correspondence, expecting that exceptions would be made to the rules of the Colonial Land and Emigration Commission. Despite his desperate attempts to have the regulations waived, Lang could not budge the Colonial Office from strict adherence to policy. Following the orders of Earl Grey, the British bureaucrats refused to sanction bounties or land grants to persons who possessed the means to buy all or part of their passage. Those who had the financial wherewithal to become shareholders in the proposed company therefore stood no chance. Nevertheless Lang persisted in recruiting 'reputable and respectable families and individuals' with capital. They were attracted with the expectation of receiving free fares for their families and blocks of choice agricultural land on the Brisbane River; the area varying in proportion to the volume of their shareholding. Artisans and labourers, who paid for all or part of their passage, maintained that they were also entitled to smaller portions of land on disembarkation.[16]

Characteristically Lang would not conform to the rules that regulated immigration, ultimately resorting to deceit as he proceeded with his plan. The last-minute, desperate and fraudulent letter which he sent to Governor Fitzroy intimated that the British government had sanctioned the payment of bounties to immigrants on the first ship *Fortitude*. It cut no ice in Australia, only serving to damage his reputation beyond repair in both British and colonial government circles.[17]

Lang was quite correct in his assertion that the British government 'deliberately destroyed his great plan'.[18] The authorities rejected Lang's scheme of emigration out of hand. Suspecting personal profiteering, they had been assailed by his invective over time and tried to the limits of frustration by his evasive business style. Finally, his fatal mistake lay in persistent offering of crown land to his petit-bourgeois emigrants in direct contravention of official policy. Misleading the public by pretending that his non-existent negotiations with Grey were likely to result in a favourable reversal of policy, Lang continued to promote his scheme. Apart from land grants, the bounties which he sought were designed for government-approved immigrants from the highly sought-after labouring class who were unable to pay their own fares. Such concessions were unavailable to most of Lang's farmers, artisans and storekeepers who either paid above-average passage-money for the excellent conditions on the specially chartered ships or took out shares in his Port Phillip and Clarence River Colonisation Company.[19]

Following the debate on Lang's conduct in the Legislative Council on 20 August 1850, the House passed a resolution which would normally have destroyed the reputation of any person other than Lang. The colonial government had joined its imperial parent body in paving the way for criminal prosecution against Lang for obtaining money under false pretences:

> That the Rev. Dr Lang having been warned by competent authority that any emigrants sent out by him, contrary to the regulations in force for the conduct of immigration to these colonies, would not be entitled to any remissions in the purchase of land, he induced many persons, nevertheless, to pay him for their passage at rates above the current price, and to emigrate under the impression that they were entitled to land upon their arrival.[20]

Moral considerations aside, it must have been some small consolation to the battle-scarred Lang to realise that he had been ahead of his time when the newly-created Queensland government provided land orders to assisted immigrants some twelve years later.[21] In 1848 he had a good idea, but the inflexibility of immigration regulations and adverse official reactions to his belligerence, persistence and deviousness got in the way. Insistent on having the last word and confident that ends justify means, Lang explained away his rejection as 'hostility towards myself on the part of the Commissioners of Emigration in consequence of my having shown up their gross ignorance and presumption ... and also in consequence of my remonstrances and protests against the mode in which the funds of the Colony were expended for the promotion of Roman Catholic emigration'.[22]

Initially the *Moreton Bay Courier*, under Lang's adherent James Swan, was highly critical of the 'faulty detail', 'doubtful character', 'lack of prudent business arrangements' inherent in this undertaking. In fact, it was incredible that such an experienced colonist would embark on this radical experiment without consulting with the colonial government on proposed land grants. Moreover the *Courier* found it incomprehensible that this vocal agitator, who normally made full use of printed media for propaganda, failed to advise colonists of his plans and prepare for the reception of his immigrants in the sympathetic local journal.[23]

Once the turmoil accompanying this immigration fiasco had died down, local opinion began to focus on what Lang had achieved rather than what he had failed to do. With the opportunity to compare Lang's immigrants with their government counterparts who arrived ex *Artemesia* and via Sydney, it was concluded that the former were without question a superior class of people in demeanour, morals and business acumen.[24] Having settled willingly into the district and feeling that they were not deceived as to its qualities, they exerted a significant improvement on the morals and spirituality of society as well as stimulating its material progress.[25] One year after the first of his immigrants disembarked in Brisbane, it was maintained that Moreton Bay owed an everlasting debt to Lang whose motives were 'pure, disinterested and philanthropic'.[26] Because of his energy, zeal and unselfish services to that community, the *Courier* acknowledged that Britain could no longer claim to be ignorant of the location and capabilities of Moreton Bay.[27] Lang's altruism was also stressed. While regretting his well-meant indiscretions, his friends within the British evangelical press praised his indomitable spirit: 'We consider Dr Lang a great man and a great patriot ... He sees nothing but the colonies; he is utterly reckless in all personal considerations. Such a man shall never fail to command our esteem'.[28]

* * *

The antagonistic *Herald* opined that 'Cooksland, Cotton, Presbyterianism and Langism [were] the *summa bona*' of the northern venture, all of doubtful value to the colony. This view was apparently shared in Britain by those influential people he hoped to impress in the initial stage of his campaign in 1847, especially the Scottish people and the cotton magnates. Indeed Lang would have dearly loved to create at Moreton Bay a Scottish province based on the cultivation of cotton. In truth, he was sent 'home' chiefly by influential 'Scotch' on his quest for Protestantism, but his countrymen in Britain poured cold water on his scheme.[29] Furthermore, the prominent British cotton merchants had failed to give really serious consideration to the concept that Moreton Bay would develop the Empire's principal source of this raw material. At Glasgow and Manchester in 1848, Lang received a 'heartless reception'. The leading merchants looked upon the superior specimens of cotton grown at Moreton Bay as merely the products of hobby farming. Doubting that European labour could supplant slaves, they wished to see the products of extensive acres under cultivation before providing considered judgment. Even after developing a close relationship with Richard Cobden MP, the anti-slavery crusader, Lang was unable to convince the Select Committee on Negro Slavery in 1847, under the chairmanship of his lifelong friend John Bright. This powerful body doubted the 'practicability of growing either cotton or sugar by British free labour' in that part of the world designated Cooksland.[30]

Lang persisted as the Colonial Office's most constant irritant throughout the late 1840s. The ill-conceived parting shot he directed by open letter at Earl Grey, who was accused of 'haughty and contemptuous disregard [for] both the feelings and wishes of British colonists and colonial legislatures', ensured that he would never again receive an impartial hearing at the Colonial Office.[31] Wishing that letter had never been written let alone published, the *Moreton Bay Courier* fully realised the consequences of Lang's intemperate reactions to failure, predicting injury to his future undertakings.[32] On the other hand, the *London Atlas* was less diplomatic in its counter-attack in defence of the Secretary of State who sent Lang 'about his business'. The *Atlas* conceded that Lang's rabid reaction to Lord Grey's snub was to be expected from a 'red-hot Presbyterian of the colonial species'; the type which 'exhibits the most utter disregard for any feeling but their own; the most profound contempt of the ordinary rules of politeness and prudence; the most inflexible determination to hear no argument, and bear no opposition ...'.[33]

Yet it was such displays of persistent belligerence and indomitable vigor against government that enamoured the Australian and British nonconformists, especially those from the lower orders. This was vividly exemplified by the 2,000 people who gathered outside the legislature's chamber in Sydney to support Lang in the face of impeachment by the Legislative Council in late July 1850. His popular reception stood in contrast to the three loud groans which the mob directed to Wentworth, his most consistent detractor.[34] Moreover a meeting of his immigrants in Ipswich passed a motion of confidence which was later repeated at Brisbane following his incarceration for libel in Melbourne. On this occasion, not only did the electors of the County of Stanley resolve to retain his services as their member in the Legislative Assembly, but they petitioned, on the motion of James Swan, to demand his release. Seconding that resolution, James Spence, the Petrie foreman declared, 'Throughout all the dark times he was still a beacon to the working men throughout the colony'.[35] Lang himself intimated, without any indication of self doubt, that his popular image had in fact been enhanced in direct proportion to the ferocity of the establishment's attack upon his person:

> ... every effort to put me down has only tended to increase my influence throughout the colony and to enable me to attain a position that will enable me to speak with some authority in future at home, and to bid defiance to my adversaries of all kinds both here and in England.[36]

* * *

Lang deeply regretted that he was unsuccessful in enticing a myriad of Scots of Spence's 'superior character' to Moreton Bay. As a result of his strong support from the Scottish colonial urban community, it has been assumed since at least 1860 that the vast majority of Lang's immigrants hailed from his homeland.[37] In fact, about 58 or approximately ten percent of approximately 600 souls who disembarked from the *Fortitude*, *Chaseley* and *Lima* were Scots.[38] Lang had found a 'widespread indisposition to emigrate ... among the valuable classes of the [Scottish] community' as 'the subject was decidedly unpopular at home'.[39] His comments in *Cooksland* that his countrymen were traditionally loath to lend their efforts to projects based on high ideals, being more motivated by the prospects of making money, may have contributed to the remarkable Scottish reticence.[40] On the other hand, he may have felt his harsh appraisal was corroborated.

Having no lines of communication open with the Church of Scotland and being philosophically opposed to the non-voluntaryist approach of his preferred Free Church, Lang unsuccessfully sought help from an interested but financially fettered United Presbyterian Church - an amalgam of Scottish dissenting churches.[41] It was against such a background of Scottish rejection that Lang offered a free cabin passage aboard the *Fortitude* to Rev. Charles Stewart (and his sister), a Staffordshire Baptist pastor with considerable experience in Glasgow, to provide religious leadership to his cotton community.[42]

Lang's lectures throughout the length and breadth of Scotland reportedly drew large audiences, except at Edinburgh and Inverness where the halls were virtually empty. Few volunteer settlers were forthcoming. Even at Wick, where the curious apparently numbered 1,500 on one night and 2,000 on the following evening, not one person from the Caithness district was persuaded to emigrate to Moreton Bay under Lang's auspices. A similar paradoxical situation occurred at Aberdeen.[43] Furthermore his first newspaper campaign was ineffective and the limited reportage of his meetings and writings was barely sympathetic. The *Glasgow Herald* reflected that even if Lang's statements were to be trusted, his concept had 'a kind of Robinson Crusoe character of interest about it ... which Daniel Defoe would have been proud to imitate'. This was hardly the recommendation he sought.[44]

Cooksland, the vehicle for such ideas, sold well, but the basic objectives of his mission in Britain were unfulfilled. His proposal for linking the colonial production of cotton and sugar with the demise of slavery was quickly terminated at the parliamentary and industrial levels; his reception in Scotland was cool and his newspaper campaign produced few positive results. Similarly his grand plan to save Australia from descending into a 'province of the Popedom' by setting up Protestant provinces through immigration in the Northern Districts and Port Phillip received short shrift from Grey. Lord Grey's priority lay in alleviating the hunger and misery in Ireland rather than populating Moreton Bay with 'the decent and well-ordered population professing Presbyterianism'.[45]

This project was in danger of being abandoned by the end of 1847. At that time, Lang had not 'made a single step in advance'. However, providence, the final form of rescue in Lang's reckless campaigns, intervened on this occasion in the form of Rev. John Campbell. A Scottish soul-mate, Campbell was proprietor of the newly-established and widely circulated *British Banner*.[46] Under Campbell's leadership, this highly influential journal formed a newly-forged link in the strong and aggressive Dissenter newspaper chain which disseminated radical political thought and nonconformist zealotry throughout Britain.

Finding that regular articles in a national newspaper followed by public meetings and pamphlets was decidedly more effective than his former strategy in arousing interest in his cause, Lang entered a new phase in his recruitment drive. Between March 1848 and November 1849, he wrote detailed weekly letters to this journal which attracted a large, avid readership among the very classes he wished to influence - 'the religious public of the various Evangelical denominations in England, Scotland and Ireland'. According to Lang, the follow-up lectures arising from his popular newspaper articles were most successful in England. The editor and the predominantly English readers of the *Banner*, who were genuinely distressed at his return to Australia in November 1849, apparently could not get enough of his anti-Catholic diatribe. His involvement with the *British Banner* was truly the turning-point in his campaign.

According to Lang's evidence in support of his petition for financial recompense from the Queensland government in 1860, his popularity among the *British Banner* readership was 'the reason why so large a proportion of these immigrants were English nonconformists [and] there were very few Presbyterians among them'.[47] Contemptuously referred to as 'a mongrel mixture of every species of heterogeneous Protestantism' by the ever-hostile *Sydney Morning Herald*, the majority of Lang's party comprised an amalgam of respectable, middle-class Baptists and Congregationalists.[48] Most of these new settlers originated from southern England including 71% of the *Fortitude* and 57% of the *Chaseley*. Focusing on specific regions, one third of the settlers aboard the *Fortitude* hailed from Middlesex, in and around the London district.[49]

Not letting Scottish disinterest pass without some form of retribution, Lang used the columns of the *Banner* to mount a thinly disguised attack on his sceptical countrymen. Focusing on the patriotic sentiments expounded in Sir Walter Scott's jingoistic 'Home thoughts from abroad', Lang advised prospective settlers to leave their 'bastard sentiments' such as love of country at home (that very emotion which also prompted many to resist Lang's lure). Instead, they should be prepared to develop more pragmatic skills and open their minds if they wished to succeed as colonial settlers.[50] He could not easily forgive the Scots, religious and lay, who rejected this scheme in 1847 and 1849.

Nor did Scotland's attempts to assimilate Irish immigrants escape his wrath; the *British Banner* permitted him to give full vent to his anti-Catholic spleen. His homeland was accommodating successfully to the very same phenomenon of Irish influx which he had hoped his compatriots would labour to neutralise in the colony. Fired by his Australian apprehension, Lang warned that his homeland would eventually 'be overrun by a set of wretches, as decidedly inferior to the proper natives of Scotland in industry, honesty, truth and perseverance'. If inter-marriage was not quickly checked, 'the whole of Scotland would be leavened with Irish crime, Irish dirt, Irish disease and Irish degredation'.[51] Reverting to his mission for the colony, he appealed to the Protestants of England to emigrate in the face of Scottish indifference 'to erect another bulwark against the kingdom of the Anti-

Christ and to provide another grand centre of Scriptural Protestant influence'.[52] Single-minded to the end, a gathering of surviving immigrants from the *Fortitude* 50 years later was proud of the blow Lang struck for their version of 'religious liberty'.[53]

The *Sydney Morning Herald* hinted that Lang virtually had to persevere throughout the 1850s with the greener fields of Moreton Bay containing a large concentration of his adherents because his anti-Catholic invective received a hostile reception at the hands of the southern press, particularly the *Australasian Chronicle*.[54] Among other forms of intolerance towards Catholics and the Irish, Lang's *Question of Questions! or Is the Colony to be transformed into a Province of Popedom* was severely mauled by the *Chronicle's* editor William Duncan in 1841. Archbishop John Bede Polding, the Catholic archbishop, was proud of the role his champion played in ultimately ridding the Sydney press of such religious bigotry. Writing to Duncan following his attack on Lang, Polding stated, 'I am indeed glad the impertinent troublesome puppy has met with one who lays back and lays it on with such good will'.[55]

The Scottish-controlled *Moreton Bay Courier* of 1849 also condemned Lang's narrow views, regretting that such sentiments detracted from his valuable efforts which were anticipated to confer considerable benefits on Moreton Bay. A leading article in the *Courier*, entitled 'Thorough Protestant Immigration', commented on Lang's belated explanatory letter to the Moreton Bay community via the *Fortitude*. It argued that it was immaterial whether the future colonists believed in John Knox or the Pope; thoroughly useful and thoroughly honest settlers were more important to the nascent community than thoroughly Protestant or thoroughly Catholic immigrants.[56]

Thus the otherwise friendly and helpful welcome accorded to the unexpected arrivals at Moreton Bay was tempered by a warning that offensive religious bigotry was out of place in the Northern Districts. In a colony made up of all 'shades of Christian belief' as well as a handful of atheists, future plans for its development would only be acceptable if their architects stressed general cooperation and eradicated any notions of the retarding disease of sectarian division. Nevertheless, when stripped of its sectarianism, Lang's project, based on immigrants who were quickly recognised as prudent, confident, intelligent and industrious, was considered eminently feasible.[57]

* * *

Lang's new arrivals were naturally attracted to the urban inhabitants who were derived broadly from the same class and toiled at similar occupations. In addition, many were united by nonconformism. Further, a significant proportion were veterans of anti-establishment agitation in Britain, a movement which had spread to Sydney and was on the verge of emerging in Brisbane. Thus they were readily acceptable as valuable allies of the respectable urban proletariat and middle class. In common with Lang, many were Chartists and others had been involved in the anti-Corn Law movement. They were therefore familiar with the unfavourable press Australia received in radical British newspapers such as the *Northern Star*, arising from the socio-economic grip of the squatting monopoly, the lack of opportunity for farmers, the exploitation of labour and the unrepresentative legislature.[58] Hence 'Pastoral domination was to receive its first challenge in 1849 ...'.[59]

The English nonconformist liberals, totally committed to Lang's vision for Moreton Bay, joined with like-minded local residents such as English chemists Ambrose Eldridge and George Poole to mount a formidable urban opposition to the pastoralist hegemony and its inward-looking policies. Subsequently, these intelligent and assertive men attempted faithfully to put into practice Lang's theories on cotton farming, tropical horticulture, free labour, European immigration and separation from the Middle Districts. Their Scottish counterparts, who included David McConnel, Rev. Charles Stewart, John Richardson and Alexander Knowles, also played vital, but less prominent roles.[60] However, early departure from the colony, lack of aggression, political diplomacy and premature death among the Scots proved to be major inhibitors to the robust leadership required to effect substantial changes in political and economic conditions during the early 1850s.

The resident Scot who wielded the greatest power for the advancement of colonial liberalism, championed religious toleration, mounted an unwavering opposition to transportation and constantly supported Lang was James Swan, second proprietor of the *Moreton Bay Courier*. He was active in utilising both press and platform to mount an effective urban opposition against the squatters and heighten the effectiveness of the nonconformist challenge. As a personal friend of 'the Reverend Agitator', this strict Baptist did not hesitate to indicate the shortcomings of Lang's cavalier implementation of the Cooksland scheme. On the other hand, as a firm believer in his friend's ideals, Swan and his moral antithesis, the *Courier*'s iconoclastic English journalist William Wilkes, gave maximum support to Lang's initiatives. Wielding powerful pens, they supported and promoted Lang's crusades for more numerous and respectable immigration, separation of the northern district and the location of the northern boundary of the new colony. Between them, the dour Swan and the Bohemian Wilkes, actively ensured that Brisbane's influential journal 'remained a consistent medium of Lang influence' in the north.[61]

Nearly 800 immigrants from the government-sponsored *Artemesia* and Lang's three ships made a significant impact upon Northern Districts' population which numbered not more than 3,500 inhabitants at the end of 1848.[62] Immigration via those first four vessels which sailed directly to Moreton Bay from England accounted for half the increase of Moreton Bay's Scottish component from 124 in 1846 to 405 in 1851. Nevertheless that intake was unable to prevent the decrease in the Scottish proportion of the population from 10.3% to 8.5% in that same period.[63] Brisbane and its hinterland was a decidedly unpopular destination for proletarian Scots at that time.

Whereas the vast majority of the *Artemesia's* arrivals was quickly swallowed up by the inland stations, most of the higher quality and more financially buoyant Lang group settled in and around the two major settlements. Over 80 Langite men of mixed nationalities, mostly heads of families, located at Brisbane while 20 went to Ipswich. Bemused at the dichotomy between their avowed object of cultivating cotton and sugar on a wide scale and their substantial urban occupations, a contemporary correspondent asserted that the Langites were more akin to reapers than sowers.

Lang's campaign stressed that enterprising men with capital, whatever their occupational background, could readily adjust to farming. It also promoted the concept of self-contained settlements formed around this agricultural base. Thus it is not surprising that the full range of urban and rural occupations was represented within the three intakes. The bulk was drawn from the provident artisan elite, the middle and upper sections of Britain's respectable working class. While 24 experienced farmers composed the largest occupational group among the 180 males, seventeen carpenters and bricklayers were recruited to meet the construction needs of the farms and related settlements. In addition, the tailors, drapers, shoemakers, dressmakers, bakers and booksellers would have expected comfortable livelihoods in such communities and had no difficulty adapting to the existing townships when Lang's grand plan fell through. In fact, such small capitalists provided added services, created new demands and promoted the self-sufficiency of Brisbane and Ipswich with deleterious effects on long-established squatter control. Furthermore, the two engineers, an iron-founder and five blacksmith/wheelwrights heralded the genesis of a much-needed manufacturing sector which would reduce economic dependence on Sydney. The two doctors, two clergymen, one teacher and two governesses were included to ensure that religious, moral, intellectual and health needs within prospective agricultural settlements along the Brisbane River were met.

Lang proudly conveyed to readers of the *British Banner* the speed with which former successful English businessmen established themselves in the major townships. He highlighted their successes and was quick to point out the wider variety of services and skills they introduced to the district. Certainly these inordinately successful people provided choice and enrichment to the bare, essential fare of urban, colonial life. [64] A tangible indicator of this colonial success is reflected by the presence of seventeen Langites among the 142 men eligible to exercise the franchise at Brisbane in 1850 - just twelve months after the arrival of their first ship.[65]

This select body apparently had few serious adjustment problems once the majority accepted that it was not going to receive the land promised by Lang. Disappointed as they assuredly were, most held little resentment towards Lang. They believed his motives were pure, his concern for Australia was sincere and he was the victim of a plot between Grey and the New South Wales legislature to turn them against their leader.[66] Nearly half of the 85 males aboard the *Fortitude* had invested money in Lang's company, the amounts ranging from 20 pounds to 200 pounds, with commensurate land entitlements from 16 to 160 acres.

A handful of *Chaseley* passengers was ultimately deterred from prosecuting Lang by the necessity to return to England to mount such action. However, they had sufficiently long memories to mount a counter-action to Lang's petition for recompense to Queensland's Legislative Assembly in 1860 for his contribution to local immigration. Others like Pettigrew, who had even more reason to be aggrieved, tried to forget their betrayal and got on with improving their lot in the colony.[67] Late nineteenth century historian William Coote commented that it was most remarkable that in the main Lang 'maintained a good opinion and friendly relations'.[68] Altogether the Moreton Bay citizenry was remarkably forgiving.

The seemingly insensitive Lang was not without contrition. He eventually confided to Pettigrew:

> My regret at the disappointments and hardships that have been experienced by individuals, and particularly by yourself from the partial failure of our enterprise in the first instance, has been sincere and poignant; but I did all I could in the matter, and when I found I could do no more than I did, I could only wait for better times which I am confident are coming at last.[69]

* * *

Only when Lang sent his own land orders amounting to 850 pounds with the *Lima* immigrants did the government give Pettigrew permission to divide land at Moggill for farms in late 1849 for that group according to plan - twelve miles south-west from Brisbane and on the north side of the river.[70] In this vicinity, Scottish farmer William Broadfoot was among the six agriculturalists who attempted to fulfil Lang's dream by cautious and limited experiments in the cultivation of cotton.

Such farmers demonstrated clearly that cotton and sugar could be cultivated successfully by Europeans in the sub-tropics, but widespread farming ranked low on local priorities. Lang's vision for sugar really never made a start, the urban, back-yard clumps being merely items of curiosity; perhaps the legacy of advice left in early 1850 by a Sydney-bound, failed expert. This Scottish planter recommended that those occupying land should sow a few sugar cane plants.[71]

The initial, vigorous efforts of Thomas Bowden gradually petered out to ignominious failure after he unsuccessfully attempted to form the Moreton Bay Sugar Company. He was unable to attract sufficient shareholders in Brisbane and Sydney to promote the growth and manufacture of sugar in the north. An experienced superintendent from Sir Rose Price's estates (worked by 500 slaves) in Jamaica, Bowden occupied a central place alongside John Richardson, William Pettigrew, David McConnel and Rev. Charles Stewart in Lang's grand scheme.[72] Feeling let down by yet another key person, especially one who had received a free trip on the *Chaseley*, Lang blamed the collapse of his plans for a flourishing sugar industry on Bowden's extravagance and mismanagement. The *Moreton Bay Courier* was more charitable, indicating the disinclination of the residents, cash-flow problems and reticence to tackle the new as the major factors which hampered enthusiastic participation. [73] However, the support given by Duncan, McConnel, Richardson and Ballow, all keen horticulturalists, was sufficient to interest an adequate number of farmers or investors to prepare the proposed sites at Kangaroo Point and South Brisbane (Dutton Park) for cultivation.[74] Taking solace that his plans were achievable but ahead of time, Lang commented, 'The manufacture of sugar had consequently to be left in abeyance for 20 years thereafter'.[75]

Although evoking more enthusiasm and action than the sugar initiatives, the impetus that the Langites were expected to provide for cotton and agriculture was limited; efforts at cultivation never really advanced beyond project farming by a handful of prominent settlers. Capital needed for large-scale cultivation was severely limited. Even the necessity to produce fruit and vegetables for nutritional and survival purposes, in addition to the imperative of breaking dependence upon the Sydney profiteers for the colonial staple of flour, was insufficient spur to stir northerners on a large scale.[76]

As a result of local indifference and an irrational belief that wheat could not be grown in that climate, the Northern Districts were sending out over 36,000 pounds to Sydney to import 2,400 tons of flour. With insufficient produce to support a local mill, the north imported virtually all of its flour from the south. While the crops of wheat flourishing around the head stations in the interior and the 'splendid ears' produced at Moggill were proof of the district's potential, a dramatic increase was needed in the number of acres brought under cultivation. It was forecast that local supplies of wheat and vegetables would be insufficient in the face of a rapidly expanding population resulting from increased government immigration and northern adjustments to the gold discoveries. The stark reality was that attention to agriculture and horticulture was a matter of self-preservation, not to mention the need to staunch the outward flow of substantial capital which could be profitably retained for northern development.[77]

Prospective agriculturalists of lesser means were deterred from farming by the exorbitant price of land - an upset price of one pound per acre and the unrealistic 640-acre size of riverside blocks of Crown land auctioned quarterly.[78] Accordingly market gardening on smaller, urban blocks around Breakfast Creek, Bulimba Creek and South Brisbane produced the necessary high quality fruit, vegetables and flowers. Reflecting a change in land regulations which permitted farm land to be surveyed on application, the 1850s witnessed the sale of more affordable portions of country land for small-scale farming on the Milton reach, Toowong, Kedron Brook, Bald Hills, Cabbage Tree Creek, Yeerongpilly, Bulimba and around Ipswich in such localities as Normanby Plains.[79]

Much to Lang's satisfaction, David McConnel established a model farming community at Bulimba centred upon his 'Toogoolawah' mansion, selling and leasing land to 'tillers of the soil'. McConnel and ex-Scottish squatter Donald Coote, his successor at Bulimba, were praised for their efforts in raising crops of wheat. While the harvest of twelve acres for milling in the south or locally by miniature, hand-operated mills was insignificant in reality, its importance lay in debunking the myth that Moreton Bay was 'bad wheat country'.[80] Despite this clear message, it apparently fell on deaf ears. By the close of 1856, it had been reported that only 60 acres of wheat had been sown in the neighbourhood of Brisbane and a successful experiment with a Chilean strain had been undertaken at Booval, on the outskirts of Ipswich.[81] Even when the colony's first flour mill was founded in the vicinity of this township, it survived initially only by the importation of wheat from South Australia.[82]

Following disembarkation from the *Lima*, James Johnston took up land at Bulimba and obtained the position of gardener at McConnel's seat of 'Toogoolawah' which was noted for the high quality of its vegetables.[83] Money apparently being no object, the affluent McConnel had imported Scottish farm implements of the latest design and highest quality to guarantee the success of his agricultural and horticultural undertakings.

David Caldwell, Brisbane gardener and *Chaseley* immigrant from Midlothian, joined select company when he was elected an office bearer of the newly-formed Horticultural Society on 21 February 1853. Duncan and John Balfour, both experts on olives, led the committee which included the leading Scots: Richardson, McConnel, Swan, Richard Cannan and Knowles. Prominent non-Scottish gardeners included James Warner, who with Cannan, was widely acknowledged for the produce from his Kangaroo Point allotments.[84]

Most importantly, the Society hoped to overcome the failure to develop the capabilities of the district's natural resources. For a start, it was admitted that the state of agriculture by 1855 was deplorable. Lang's original manifesto rested on the optimal exploitation of the resources of the district by his immigrant farmers. The prevalence of the names of his followers within the membership list indicates their tacit commitment to this principle.[85]

The objectives of the society, besides encouraging 'the cultivation of useful plants in the district', included the introduction of 'desirable plants', the distribution of seeds and specimens to members, the communication of horticultural facts and eventually the establishment of a horticultural garden 'for the testing ... of imported plants'.[86] The latter aim was achieved in 1855 with the establishment of the Brisbane Botanical Gardens under the superintendence of the highly qualified Walter Hill. In establishing this new venture, he was ably supported by a management committee of three which was dominated by fellow-Scottish horticulturalists W.A. Duncan and R.R. Mackenzie.[87]

Born in Dumfries and a survivor of Frederick Strange's ill-fated natural history expedition to Percy Island in 1854, Hill had received his training as a botanist over a period of eleven years as a gardener at the Royal Botanical Gardens at Edinburgh and Kew.[88] Under his guidance, the Gardens 'gave a more scientific direction to the search for a tropic agricultural staple', persevering with sugarcane, promoting tropical fruit and preparing the way for cotton's resurgence in the 1860s.[89]

The Northern Districts' Agricultural and Pastoral Association, formed in February 1854 on squatter initiative to stimulate agriculture and grow cotton and sugar, was another stimulus to general agricultural production apart from Lang. Many Brisbane and Ipswich-based Scottish pastoralist sympathisers were prominent among its fifty members. Among the pastoralist members with interests in agriculture were Louis Hope, sixth son of the Earl of Hopetoun, and John Balfour who was then in partnership with George Forbes, son of his financial backer. Other past and current Scottish squatters included Donald Coutts, A.J. Henderson, Simon Scott and Robert Douglas, then a soap and candle manufacturer at Kangaroo Point. Brisbane publican George McAdam, George Street merchant John McCabe along with John McDonald, successor to George Thorne at the Queen's Arms in Ipswich, joined river-boat proprietor Thomas Boyland in supporting this district-minded innovation.[90]

The stimulus which this organisation gave to horticulture was apparent in perusal of the prize lists published following the society's annual exhibition held in January at the Brisbane School of Arts; there were many more keen part-time and commercial gardeners than the thirty who attended meetings. Robert Ramsay Mackenzie, fourth son of Sir George Steuart Mackenzie of Coul on the Black Isle and Brisbane-based squatter, acknowledged the work of his gardener at Bulimba in producing 'beautiful collections of flowers' by entering his exhibits in William Davidson's name. At the 1855 show J. Patience, another horticulturalist from the Black Isle but of humbler origins than Mackenzie, appropriately took out the prize for potatoes 'which were excellent for the season'. On that occasion South Brisbane butcher John Orr unexpectedly shared honours for grapes with the locally renowned Richard Cannan. In the previous year the Government Resident scooped the pool with his grapes, limes and quinces grown by his gardener Robert Lane at Newstead. Johnston produced the best carrots and Caldwell, after showing thirteen varieties of English melons, defeated Patience in the potato and cucumber sections.[91] The wheat and oats raised at Eldridge's riverside farm on the southwestern border of Brisbane, adjoining the estate of ex-*Fortitude* migrant and successful London businessman Robert Cribb, invariably took out the prizes in the cereal category.[92]

Meanwhile William Pettigrew, when not laying out allotments at Cleveland, establishing the boundaries of Brisbane River Valley runs or setting out farms at Moggill and Indooroopilly for James Warner, was engaged out of sight at Simpson's Woogaroo property as a privileged farm labourer. There he ploughed, sowed and harvested produce such as grapes, peaches, bananas, maize, oats, potatoes and onions - but never on a Sunday in accordance with his strict Calvinist beliefs.[93]

The Melbourne *Argus* noted at the end of 1849, nearly one year after the *Fortitude's* arrival, the predilection of Lang's immigrants towards unprofitable marketing gardening. This unexpected turn of events undermined Lang's expectations that they would found that branch of agriculture which would rival wool as export leader; 'Not one ... of the parties he has sent out has attempted to cultivate cotton'.[94] Almost seven years later, Robert Cribb stressed that Moreton Bay could never become a prosperous agricultural community until the district diversified its export commodities. In light of the failure of sugar along with the inconsequential production of wheat, its prospects were dependent upon fulfilling Lang's vision for cotton.[95]

It appeared that the cultivation of cotton in the 1850s was destined to follow the fate of sugar and wheat. This tenuous situation continued until 1861. At that time the change in land regulations encouraged large and small-scale farming and the deleterious consequences of the American War of Independence upon Lancashire's' supplies of raw cotton created an insatiable market. Thus the Moreton Bay District lacked that stimulus to embark on cotton cultivation on the scale undertaken by the Caboolture Cotton Company under the leadership of London-born Scot Robert Douglas and Langite William Hobbs in the sixties.[96]

Besides Lang's frequent encouragement through personal letters, the columns of the *Courier* and two visits in 1851 and 1856, the only other incentives to cultivation were distribution of free seeds of the Sea Island variety in 1851 by Sydney politician Stuart A. Donaldson MLC, and a small-scale competition conducted by the colonial government in 1853.[97] Never letting go of his vision of Moreton Bay as Britain's cotton colony, and having almost attained the status of a cult figure among the local Protestants, Lang was recognised as one 'who seems always to be thinking of us and acting for our benefit' - the antithesis of charges levelled against the colonial government.[98] Unfortunately, moral support, intervention in Britain and exhortation were not enough; pre-separation cotton production never emerged beyond the experimental stage.

Whereas numerous attempts around the town and in the interior to cultivate cotton had been unsuccessful, some limited results by Scottish agriculturalists provided reason for two English Langites to persevere. Foresaking the honour of being first in the field, squatter-oriented speculators including William Dorsey and George Leslie abandoned plans in April 1849 to form model farms to facilitate cotton production.[99] Two years were to elapse before Robert Douglas at Dunlop near Ipswich, Hobbs and Eldridge at North Brisbane, Poole at Moggill and David McConnel at Bulimba conducted successful experiments in cultivating that crop. Thereafter the field was virtually the preserve of the first three following McConnel's departure to Scotland and the premature death of Queen Street druggist G.F. Poole. The experiments were carried out on a small scale in 1851, Douglas producing half a ton from just over an acre (the district's first cotton export of 13 bags) and McConnel's half acre yielding 300 pounds.[100] The favourable reports from Manchester and Liverpool merchants on the samples sent from both crops concluded 'that Moreton Bay can produce very superior and truly beautiful cotton wool'. This was incentive enough for Poole to conduct experiments with various soils on twenty acres at Moggill and Eldridge to prepare half that area around Milton House in 1852.[101] No doubt, Poole's efforts in preparing the soil were given an added boost by Lachlan McLean's manufacture of a horse hoe similar to those used on progressive Scottish farms.[102]

By May 1853 the Government Resident was able to report to the Colonial Secretary that more than forty acres of land in the district were under cotton.[103] Following Lang's submission of samples to English authorities on his visit in 1851, there was every reason to be sanguine that cotton cultivation at Moreton Bay could be profitably undertaken. The secretary of the Manchester Chamber of Commerce believed that with energy and capital, 'cotton in Moreton Bay ... stands a better chance of success than any new industry of which I have heard or read'.[104]

With Lang's active encouragement, Scottish initiative and resilience contributed to improvements in the local milling of cotton and opening up of new settlement and land for extensive cultivation. Despite experimentation with seeds and soils, the major factor which held back the progress of a potential cotton industry was the difficulty of separating the seed from the cotton. It was all very well producing fine specimens of cotton, long in staple, beautiful in colour, but it had to be properly cleaned, a problem which pre-occupied the mechanical genius David Longlands.[105] Scottish shipping agent George Raff, a conservative from Forres who was poised to assume the mantle of Moreton Bay's cotton merchant, persevered in the face of government indifference to this problem. Accordingly he took up the government's suggestion and purchased an American gin. This machine, with improvements effected by Longlands, was demonstrated successfully to Lang during his visit in April 1857. So confident was Raff that Longlands had come up with the solution to that deterrent to extensive cotton culture, that he prepared several bales for export to England.[106]

Raff's future as cotton exporter was assured by mid-1859 when he distributed seed gratis to prospective planters and, acting on the instructions of Sir William Denison, the Police Magistrate permitted him to set up a gin 'of improved construction' sent by the Manchester Cotton Association. On the eve of separation, Moreton Bay, boosted by Hill's development of highly regarded specimens of long-stapled cotton at the Botanic Gardens, was poised to demonstrate to Manchester interests that it was indeed 'a cotton growing country ... wherein their surplus capital might be very profitably invested'.[107]

One of the most significant results of the Lang adherents' determination to promote the growth of cotton was the foundation of Cabbage Tree (Sandgate). This was accompanied by the prerequisite improvements effected in communication such as the repair of the Breakfast Creek Bridge, formation of a road between Sandgate and Brisbane and facilitation of communication with the Bay. Dismissed as a prospective quarantine station for the *Fortitude's* complement in 1849 and mooted by pro-urban, anti-squatter forces to rival Cleveland as the district's port, Sandgate was recommended to Lang during his visit in 1851 as possessing the ideal conditions for the growth of cotton.

In a letter to Pettigrew dated 8 December 1851, Lang intimated that Dr Hobbs was taking him to see the Cabbage Tree Creek neighbourhood which possessed an abundance of mud from creeks left dry from the tides, 'the best species of manure for cotton lands'. He reasoned that as the best cotton in America grew near the sea and salt mud appeared to be present at Cabbage Tree in inexhaustible quantities, that area might well contain 'land of the first quality'.[108] In a speedy reply Pettigrew agreed with that assessment, but took pains to indicate that Tighgam on Cabbage Tree Creek was but one of 'many fine patches of land along the coast of Moreton Bay'.[109]

Five months later, a party including John Richardson, George Raff and Robert Davidson visited the same location to determine the possibility of founding a village connected by road to Brisbane for the benefit of local trade and commerce.[110] Following petition to the Colonial Secretary, James Burnett mapped Sandgate which became the pet project of some businessmen who championed both Brisbane and Lang. Among those who successfully bid for Sandgate land on 10 November 1853, at the largest land sale held to that time in Brisbane, was a substantial Scottish contingent, mostly Langites, comprising David, John and Frederic McConnel, James Swan, J.H. Robertson, William Wilson and Alexander Knowles.

It was not until 1859 when the Aboriginal threat to European settlement was eliminated by Native Police action that Sandgate's development got underway. Dowse, a promoter of this locality, waxed lyrical about the economic benefits to settlers with adventurous spirits, especially those who were prepared to exploit the agricultural potential of the area.[111] Lang would have been heartened to read in mid-1859 that there were signs that the production of northern cotton could well develop beyond the experimental stage. No doubt encouraged by supplies of seed and the use of a more advanced gin available at Raff's, strenuous efforts were being made by 'enterprising individuals to carry out the growth of the cotton plant on an extensive scale' in the immediate neighbourhood of Sandgate. Two plantations totalling 700 acres, one of which was owned by Fortitude Valley publican William J. Loudon, were in the process of being cleared by twenty labourers.[112]

In the same year, an agricultural community was formed at Bald Hills which was known as 'the Scotch settlement'. Adjoining embryonic Sandgate, this settlement was founded by John and Margaret Stewart, the latter being the sister-in-law of Brisbane bootmaker Thomas Gray. They were accompanied by David, Charles and Jane Duncan who was to marry Stewart. All had been fellow passengers aboard the *Anne Milne* which brought the Mackenzie labour force to New South Wales. This extended family with connections to Mackenzie's Black Isle contingent formed one of the strong strands of the Scottish network with links to David McConnel of Cressbrook.

Deciding to relocate from the flood-prone Paterson River area in 1857, the Stewarts and Duncans were informed by Gray of the availability of good farm land on the outskirts of Brisbane in the vicinity of the South Pine. The *Moreton Bay Courier* welcomed them on 6 October of that year: 'three families from the Hunter, bringing with them three superior draught horses, settled ... on freeholds on the Bald Hills'. However, the Pine River Aborigines demonstrated their infamous hostility. Demonstrating the strength of the Scottish network, Gray's agitation to the Police Magistrate ensured that his kin were well protected by a detachment of the Native Police which was thereafter stationed at Sandgate. Assured of peace and security, this small settlement of Scots with leanings toward Lang eventually overcame considerable teething problems to become one of Brisbane's premier agricultural and dairy sources.[113]

* * *

Such attempts to be faithful to Lang's agricultural vision for Moreton Bay took place against a background of a major campaign for the separation of the Northern Districts from the Middle Districts of New South Wales. Commencing with a bitter wrangle between the squatters and Brisbanites when pastoralists embraced the British Government's proposal to reintroduce transportation, these opposing groups eventually buried their differences and formed an uneasy alliance to achieve their common objective of northern self-government. In the early stages when class conflict was at its height, Scottish settlers habitually aligned according to their socio-economic interests rather than ethnicity.

Intent on relieving pressure on its overcrowded gaols, the British government encouraged the labour-starved squatters to accept exiles as a condition for separation. The proposal was fiercely opposed by the southern legislature and Australian public opinion - even the largest pastoralists at Port Phillip were antagonistic. Many of Lang's immigrants, who had been primed by the radical elements of the British press before emigration, were able to confirm first-hand the media's warning that the squatters were the colonial equivalent of the embattled British landlords; they posed exactly the same threats to social and political justice.[114] Incited by the rhetoric of anti-transportationists, Lang and Parkes in Sydney and the *Moreton Bay Courier* in Brisbane, the political consciousness of the liberal, urban middle class of the north was aroused. Both radical and temperate factions of the proletariat united with middle-class liberals to mount a moral opposition to this major threat to democracy. Grey, ignoring the sensibilities of southern Australia and counting on the support of the northern squatters, revoked the abolition of transportation by an Order in Council during March 1849.[115]

Knowing that no significant clamour had been raised in the north and cognisant of southern opposition, a deputation of seven magistrates and stockholders from Moreton Bay waited upon Grey in London in the following September to exert direct pressure on an apparent ally. Led by Arthur Hodgson, this party included

Scottish squatters Walter Leslie, George Fairholme and Ross-based Sir Evan Mackenzie who also acted for his brother. Arguing that the Emigration Commission had announced its intention of not despatching emigrant ships direct to Brisbane and acknowledging the unpopularity of the district with immigrants who disembarked in Sydney, the large proprietors of stock petitioned for annual intakes of up to 600 exiles to arrive in Brisbane at times when the need for labour was at its height.[116]

While the *Sydney Morning Herald* fumed that this approach by the 'seven champions of convictism' was aimed to set the British government against the declared wishes of the Legislative Council and the vast majority of the Australian people, the *Moreton Bay Courier* regretted the lack of open consultation upon such a vital matter. This high-handed decision affected the welfare of all classes - not just those who had pecuniary interests and self-interest at stake.[117] The *Courier's* support of such democratic procedures was consistently rejected by stockholders who maintained that the control over land, animals and labour was the primary principle in determining those whose collective voice would direct the development of the district.

Neither Grey nor the northern squatters anticipated the adversarial power of the newly-created public opinion which had been aroused by the very 'new chum' immigrant settlers to whom the Secretary for State refused assistance six months earlier. For once, Lang was restrained when he recollected that the influence of his immigrants was 'felt pretty strongly during the anti-transportation conflict'.[118] Within a week of the arrival of 54 *Hashemy* exiles by the *Tamar* from Sydney on 20 June 1849, the *Fortitude* immigrants had petitioned the House of Commons. They objected strenuously to the deleterious effects on the moral tone of society, the diminished employment prospects of respectable labour and the tenuous future of free immigration which would follow. Applauding that public feeling and virtue had at last been aroused, the *Moreton Bay Courier* supported this form of resistance by the small group. They were unashamedly 'guided by their own sense of right' and 'unassisted by the older inhabitants of this place', to protest against the impending degrading threat to the district.[119] That public opinion which Lang wished to create to confront squatter power was a reality and thenceforth grew from strength to strength. H.S. Russell recollected that with the emergence of anti-squatter forces, 'the past and future broke out into strife in the districts of the north'.[120]

Beyond question, it came as a real shock to the advocates of transportation trying to elicit support on 13 November 1849 when the liberal element of Brisbane's society joined Lang's new settlers to defeat a resolution which requested equal numbers of free immigrants and exiles. Virtually amounting 'to an invitation to the Government to send these people here' irrespective of the wishes of the inhabitants, this resolution was rejected at Brisbane in late 1849 by 66 of the 70 men assembled who were mostly workers. As a result, long-standing liberal citizens joined Langites to form a committee to formulate resolutions for an anti-transportation meeting arranged for the end of the month. One third of the 18 committee members were Scots, including, David McConnel, Richardson, Swan and Stewart.[121] The district was clearly divided between transportationists and anti-transportationists, or specifically the squatters versus 'independent persons' and nearly all the workers in Brisbane.[122]

A meeting dominated by Scottish squatters including Magnus McLeod, David Forbes and William Leith Hay fired the first shot at their urban counterparts. On 2 January 1850 pastoralists at Warwick petitioned Grey to send annual supplies of exiles.[123] These 'representatives of the wealth and respectability' of the north then and there decided to 'rub salt into the wound', commissioning Dr Dorsey to convene a meeting at Ipswich on the 12 January to deal with Brisbane's oppositional petition.[124] Uninvited, but with a legal and moral right to be there to defend their resolutions, a large party of Brisbane supporters attended, swelling the gathering to 200. According to Russell, 'the meeting speedily became a perfect bear garden'.[125]

Unable to thwart democracy exerted by numbers, the squatters' ploy to relocate the meeting to confine it to squatters and employers also failed. At this alternative venue, which was packed by the recently arrived anti-squatter group and followers, Francis Bigge's resolution requesting an equal proportion of exiles and free immigrants was predictably defeated. In line with majority opinion, Stewart's amendment that the resumption of transportation would be injurious to the moral, social and political welfare of the colony passed comfortably.

Knowing full well that popular democracy would prevail over a minority assemblage of the socio-economic elite, the squatters gave vent to their rage. During the proceedings they personally attacked Stewart, denigrated free workers, declared 'war' on Brisbane and threatened to employ Chinese in preference to non-convict labour. 'Ipswich was the town to which the squatters looked, and to which they would bring their goods [and] would ship their produce at Cleveland Point', railed Patrick Leslie in supporting just one of Francis Bigge's' threats. Nevertheless, it was through Leslie's efforts that Stewart was allowed to speak to his amendment although the vicious interjections barely abated. Besides Ipswich-based Dr Henry Challinor, the English surgeon from the *Fortitude*, John Richardson and Anglo-Irish solicitor Robert Little supported Stewart's amendment. The latter's plea that the transportation issue should not set colonist against colonist fell on deaf ears in the pastoralists' camp.[126] This was the last occasion that Stewart participated as a speaker in a public protest meeting, confining his oratory thereafter to sermons delivered to a more captive audience.

In response to a petition of protest originating in Sydney and an anti-transportation address from the Legislative Council, Grey transmitted a despatch to Governor Sir Charles Fitzroy informing him that no more convicts would be sent to New South Wales. Furthermore, the *Bangalore* with its 292 exiles would be the last convict ship transmitted to Moreton Bay. As compensation for the 598 exiles transported (10% being Scots sentenced mainly for theft and assault in

Glasgow and Edinburgh), this ship would be closely followed by one containing an equal number of free persons.[127]

On learning six months later that Section 33 of the new Bill for the Better Government of the Australian Colonies gave the British government discretion to grant the boon of separation in response to a petition from inhabitants northward of the 30th degree of south latitude, elation was high at Moreton Bay. Forever loyal, but quick to indicate lack of sympathy with his religious prejudices, the *Courier* gave full credit to Lang's untiring efforts to increase Britain's appreciation of Moreton Bay's attributes. This was an important factor which contributed to the drafting of that vital clause.[128]

Predictably Lang accepted full credit, informing the *Courier's* readers that he proposed a clause identical to Section 33 when he wrote to the Colonial Office during early 1847. Nevertheless he advised the inhabitants of Moreton Bay that the time was not ripe; the population was too small at that juncture.[129] Egocentric to the end, Lang also attributed that contentious clause to the remedial effects which he ultimately exerted upon Grey. Lang conjectured that Grey possibly re-read to good effect his scathing, parting letter of 1849. Suitably chastened by the experience, Grey apparently re-directed his attention to the voluminous correspondence which Lang had directed to the Colonial Office. The result of this revision was the 'Magna Carta of Moreton Bay'.[130]

It was the colonial activities of Lang and other like-minded radicals rather than his constant stream of correspondence to London which provided the immediate motive for the insertion of Section 33. The strong southern liberal movement, Lang's Australian League, the Australian Anti-Transportation League and Parkes' oratory promoting republicanism and opposing anti-convictism, prompted the British authorities to defuse the threat posed to Empire by accelerating self government while granting the franchise to squatters.[131] Section 33 was obviously intended by the British government to placate the north as well as being a double-edged sword which would leave the way open for squatters to reintroduce convictism to Australia if that district fell into their hands. Pettigrew indicated that the settlers swiftly became aware of the damaging repercussions attendant to Grey's 'bribe'.[132] The colonial government, viewing the Northern Districts thereafter as a wild card which possessed the potential to undermine Australian stability, increased its antagonistic stance to northern society.

Although ensuring that Grey's offer of immediate separation with a modified transportation system in the unsettled areas was thwarted, the anti-transportationists were dissatisfied with the assurance that prisoners would not be sent to the colony again without the consent of the Legislative Council.[133] Indeed Grey had assured Hodgson that this stipulation could be but a paper tiger if the squatters' policies were adopted locally and the district successfully petitioned for separation.[134]

* * *

The distance of the New South Wales government from Moreton Bay and its neglect of the district's needs had convinced both the anti-transportationists and the squatters that separation was vital to the well-being of the district. However, a united campaign from the district was impossible until the squatters discarded their pro-transportation position. Reconciliation of interests lay in diffusing the demand for convict labour by inducing British and colonial authorities to direct a flow of respectable British labour in such quantities as to meet the needs of the pastoral industry and the district's development. Originating as attempts to fulfil the immigration objectives of their respective factions, direct, separate approaches in Britain in 1852 by Lang and Scottish squatters Hope and George Leslie were successful in achieving this object. They were no doubt assisted by the demographic changes and democratic influences arising from the discovery of gold in Victoria and most significantly Grey's loss of office in 1852.

Lang never passed up an opportunity of letting the inhabitants of the Moreton Bay District know that they owed him a debt for his immigrants of 1849 and for the official recognition of their right to eventual separation at the 30th parallel. In the process of doing so in mid 1851, he also cautioned the northern settlers to exercise their vote wisely in the election of their representatives to the Sydney legislature. With four votes in the chamber from the first parliamentary representatives domiciled in the district, Lang advised the electorate to redouble its efforts to gain their legislative and administrative independence. Indeed he felt the time was propitious, considering the impulse that the diggings would give to immigration. Not only would the frustrated squatters receive their labour, but the conditions were favourable for the creation of an agricultural population centred on the growth of cotton. Expecting that much of this labour flow would emanate from the impoverished Highlands and islands of Scotland, Lang welcomed the virtual disappearance of one major disincentive which had repelled the interest of such respectable people in the north. He proclaimed, 'The gold discovery has happily put an end to the transportation agitation in your district ...'.[135]

In typical style, Lang was acting precipitately. Only a fortnight before he penned that missive dated 8 June 1851, the squatters embarked on their last attempt to achieve separation at the 30th parallel with exiles. Having formed the Northern Districts Separation Society specifically to achieve this unaltered objective, a meeting of squatters at Brisbane resolved on the motion of Frederick Bigge and John Balfour that Colin Mackenzie and Louis Hope deliver a letter to this effect on behalf of the 'wealthy and influential inhabitants of the district' to Grey during their visit to Britain.

Within a year, following a further meeting, the Association had a change of heart. The squatters' mouthpiece, the *Moreton Bay Free Press*, declared that separation would not only produce labour for pastoral husbandry, but it would create agricultural enterprise centred around the growth of cotton. Furthermore a separate northern colony would draw capitalists, merchants and traders who had hitherto been deterred from settling. Predicting a confluence of all classes exhibiting an interest in the community, the editorial felt that separation was 'the only hope of resuscitation for the place'.[136] Realising that there would be no support from the colonial government, the advocates of northern separation addressed their efforts to Whitehall.

Convinced that its interests were not being served by the Sydney legislature, both Lang, on behalf of the urban forces, and the squatters delivered their petitions in person at Whitehall from 1852.[137] While acknowledging Lang's 'wild republican schemes' and poor standing with the British government, it was felt that he would accurately reflect the 'popular voice' to the Secretary of State and achieve positive results for the movement to establish a local government. On his visit north during late 1851, he gained widespread support following the adoption of his draft petition to the Queen for separation and his acceptance of the brief to entice a continuous stream of virtuous and industrious free immigration to the district - settlers of the same ilk as the arrivals of 1849.

With separation, free immigration and cotton cultivation to the fore, the meeting requested Lang to submit three resolutions passed at the meeting to the Secretary of State for the Colonies and the Manchester Chamber of Commerce. Attempting to use the gold-induced problems of population mobility and dearth of immigrants who wished to work the land as a lever, the meeting re-affirmed to the British government that Lang's rejected scheme was best for the colony's needs. It was asserted that fare-paying immigrants should receive the equivalent of their outlay in land. Swan was sanguine about the result. Lang, the perennial opportunist, chuckled that his colleagues in the legislature would view his actions on behalf of Moreton Bay as 'conspiracy and treason against the supremacy of New South Wales'.[138]

The petition was to become the model for several future memorials organised under Lang's influence in the district. It commenced by extolling the physical and climatic features of Cooksland, between the 30th parallel and the Tropic of Capricorn. After highlighting statistics related to population, stock and property, it listed the oft-repeated reasons for seeking a separate government from one remote in distance and attitude. Ignoring the claims of the dominant pastoral industry which bred suspicions of renewed transportation within government ranks, the document complained that Sydney-based legislature could not understand the needs of and was unwilling to adapt its management strategies to a region destined for tropical agriculture.[139]

Squatting and urban forces were by no means united; some pastoralists remained obdurate, reflecting the division within Scottish ranks. In one of the last expressions of pro-exile sentiments, Patrick Leslie provoked a literary duel with Lang in the *Sydney Morning Herald*. He protested that 'the Rev. Republican' was clearly misguided if he thought he was representing the majority of the northern squatters who had little confidence in him as a delegate, let alone the principles underlying the petition he was carrying to England. Mounting a predictably forceful defence, Lang contrasted his contributions to the district by sending nearly 600 free immigrants of 'the most unexceptionable character' and the positive effects they had on morals and religion with the squatters' attempt to degrade their adopted country as a repository for convicted criminals. In his usual bigoted manner, Pettigrew branded the latter as 'the blackguards of Great Britain ... the scum and filth of society'.[140]

While deciding to ignore Leslie's doomed infatuation with transportation, the *Moreton Bay Courier* similarly rejected Lang's inflammatory claims that his immigrants were solely responsible for defeating Brisbane's pro-convict clique and presented a more rational account. Attributing a smaller share to this achievement than Lang asserted, the *Courier* indicated that most were late in the fray. In fact, many held back and some openly joined the opposition. Led by a few persons who had no connection with Lang and backed by a determined press, the cause did not receive large numerical support from the 600 until it became a popular campaign.[141] Furthermore, Lang's suggestion that the squatters send their own delegates to England if they felt unrepresented by his efforts had in fact been put into train by their Brisbane meeting some six months previously.

Apparently Lang's exertions in Britain for a flow of immigration to Moreton Bay did not bear the same fruit as those of the squatters' representatives who were involved in a separate lobbying process. Although the Manchester authorities provided most favourable reports on Australian cotton, Lang's republicanism (which John Bright advised him to tone down) ensured that the Moreton Bay petition to the Colonial Office received scant consideration, despite an outward show of civility. The local fears that there may well be a heavy discount to Lang's advocacy in view of his low standing with the British government were confirmed. Although the Colonial Office personnel 'recognised him to be clever, they also judged him to be unscrupulous and worthy of no reliance'.[142] There must have been several among those whom Duncan dismissed derisively as 'the Lang mob', who questioned if his advocacy in Britain 'could ever be of much value to the district'.[143]

Lang and the squatter representatives, Louis Hope and George Leslie, were simultaneously petitioning Grey's successor Sir John Pakington in July 1852. A member of Lord Derby's ministry, Pakington was an implacable foe of transportation to New South Wales in any shape or form. This view was also shared by his successors, the Duke of Newcastle, Lord Aberdeen and Lord John Russell. They proceeded to discredit Grey's policies and 'naturally turned down Moreton Bay petitions' which continued to link separation with transportation.[144]

The Moreton Bay contingent of Hope and Leslie arrived in London to present a petition adopted at a meeting of squatters and urban allies on 17 May 1852 at Brisbane, which included fellow Scots George K.E. Fairholme, Robert Ramsay, Walter Gray, Dr Dorsey and R.R. Mackenzie. Leslie was well-briefed, having also been among the squatter deputation which waited on Sir Charles Fitzroy in Sydney before embarkation to represent the needs of Moreton Bay and to argue for direct immigration.[145] The delegation was authorised to protest against the assumed right of the Anti-Transportation League to interfere with the wishes of the inhabitants of the proposed new colony. Thus they argued that the introduction of exiles was the only way to deal with the threat posed by squatter-induced Chinese immigration.[146]

As a consequence of the change in government, the squatters' petition was destined to fail. Nevertheless Leslie and Hope eventually achieved significant gains in diverting a substantial flow of free immigration from Sydney to Moreton Bay. The emigration commissioners reacted favourably to the pair's account of the district's problems occasioned by the iniquitous immigration system practised in the colony. They presented a sound case, highlighting labour scarcity, high wages and the failure of stop-gap Chinese immigration. They also strengthened their argument by stressing the problems arising from the exodus of existing labour following the gold discoveries and drew attention to the large number of capital works at a standstill. Their achievement in acquiring immigrants for Moreton Bay at the rate of one ship-load per month was just the British extension of a successful campaign which was being waged on the colonial scene on the eve of Leslie's departure.

This approach was followed by a petition adopted at a pro-urban meeting at Brisbane on 4 March and subsequently printed in the *Sydney Morning Herald* and *Empire*. The committee, headed by John Richardson and including McConnel, complained of the great injustice done to the district. Up to September 1850, Moreton Bay had received not one immigrant from a prospective entitlement of 1,500 according to colonial revenue raised. The petitioners claimed that, rather than having their dire need for labour ignored by the Sydney-based government, one-fourth of the funds allocated to immigration should be spent north of the 30th parallel.[147] The *Moreton Bay Courier* played its part, protesting against the unjust system which allowed the expenditure of funds elsewhere in the colony which should have been ear-marked for Moreton Bay. In a self-congratulatory tone, the *Courier* marvelled at the resilience of the district which was surviving 'notwithstanding official neglect, and the damaging attractions of a neighbouring gold field'.[148]

The liberal concession granted to Leslie and Hope by Pakington of one immigrant ship per month to Moreton Bay applied only until the designated proportion of emigration was achieved. Thereafter, Fitzroy's will prevailed. H.H. Brown, Colonial Immigration Officer, convinced the Governor that Moreton Bay was indeed suffering severely from the want of 'every description of labour'. Accordingly Brown successfully recommended that a 'fair proportion' of immigrants be despatched direct to the district.[149] Dragging his feet every inch of the way, however, Brown was determined to restrict the number to six shipments per year in defiance of Wickham's recommendation of monthly intakes.[150] In contrast to the immigrants who disembarked before 1852, the subsequent arrivals were exactly the types required for the development of a pastoral district such as Moreton Bay.

***

From 1852 until 1859, 49 ships were sent to Moreton Bay; nearly 13,000 British and Irish immigrants arrived direct from English ports. Rather than meeting Fitzroy's target of six, only three or four ships were despatched yearly. The projected figure was reached only in 1853 and 1855 with six and eight ships arriving respectively.[151] The peak for Scottish immigration to Moreton Bay was achieved during 1855 when 664 or 20% of the New South Wales yearly intake disembarked at Brisbane.[152] Over 60% of the Scottish immigrants for that year travelled aboard the *Genghis Khan*, *John Davis* and the *William Miles*, the latter containing two-thirds Scots. This comparatively small number of Scots fell below the intake of German immigrants for the same period, an indication that the north was a second-best Scottish destination to the goldfields. The established middle district was far and away more preferable to the minority of the Scottish proletariat who chose the Antipodes in preference to the more popular Americas.

Altogether the identified 1,128 Scottish immigrants who arrived at Moreton Bay directly from England between December 1848 and December 1859 contributed significantly to the increase of nearly 2,000 in the Scottish component of the population in the Moreton Bay District from 1846 to early 1861.[153] Applying Earl Grey's theoretical estimate that a Scottish emigration quota of 10% would be demographically representative within the British total, it can readily be discerned that the percentage of 8.2% disembarking at Moreton Bay between 1848 and 1859 fell well below this projection. Nearly 3% below the Scottish proportion of British immigrants arriving in New South Wales from 1851 to 1860, this deficit reflected the general unpopularity of Moreton Bay as a destination compared with Sydney.[154]

Obviously pre-separation Moreton Bay with its penal stigma and frontier reputation was 'the end of the line' in Scottish opinion, holding limited attraction compared with the gold mining opportunities offered by Victoria and New South Wales. Between 1851 and 1856 the front page shipping and emigration advertisements in the *Inverness Courier* promoted Moreton Bay immigration on only one occasion. Although there were plenty of letters from the southern goldfields and articles on Port Phillip and Adelaide, the Moreton Bay District was entirely neglected by this popular Highland journal.[155] Thus it is hardly surprising that Scottish numbers from 1848 to 1859 were 325 fewer than the more aggressively recruited 1,584 direct German settlers who arrived after 1853.[156]

A significant 42.2% of the 1,128 adult immigrants hailed from the Highlands, mostly from Inverness and Ross and Cromarty. This was the region where the ramifications of the Industrial Revolution induced the most traumatic social and economic upheavals. The Lowlanders from the south-west comprised 23.3% - a large 18.3% from central Lowland areas such as Fifeshire, and a low 9.4% from the buoyant wool-producing south-east. A mere 5.5% from complacent Aberdeenshire saw the need to improve their lot in the antipodean northern outpost.

Focusing on the industrial and commercial belt, Lanarkshire (Glasgow) in the south-west area provided a large contingent amounting to 10% of the total, while 8% were derived from Midlothian (Edinburgh) in the central district.[157] Thus, as many Highlanders reached the shores of Moreton Bay as those from the industrialised Lowland areas. Confounding recent predictions, the disproportionate number of Highlanders attracted to the north contrasts starkly with the decided minority from that region landing at Sydney during the same period.[158]

The levels of literacy and degree of adherence to Presbyterianism were also markedly different from those derived from the total intake of Scots to Victoria and New South Wales. Defining literacy as the ability to read and write, a high rate of 96% adult literacy was revealed in the Moreton Bay sample. Attributing the cause to the high level of Highland immigration to Victoria, Prentis has determined that only 59% of Scottish immigrants to that colony in the 1850s were literate.[159] While Moreton Bay also featured a Highland majority, the significantly higher literacy levels of immigrants arriving there can be attributed to regional differences. Whereas Victoria received two-thirds of the 4,910 destitute and untutored Highland and Island Emigration Society refugees from the west of Scotland, none disembarked at Moreton Bay where the more sophisticated Invernessians predominated.[160]

Although 93.6% of the total Moreton Bay arrivals owned adherence to Presbyterianism, only 5% admitted to Free Church membership. In view of the large component from the Highlands, the region which embraced the Free Church, it is incongruous that this figure is so insignificant. Containing higher proportions of Episcopalians and Roman Catholics, 85% of Sydney-bound Scottish immigrants were Presbyterians 'of some description or other'.[161]

The gender ratio among the adults, specifically the unmarried component, indicates that Scottish single women did not find Moreton Bay to be a desirable colonial destination. The overall masculinity rate of 164 reflected this phenomenon, the 299 married couples having a neutral effect. The Scottish single male rate of 413 from the *William Miles*, the ship which disembarked the highest number of Scottish emigres in 1855, was even higher.[162] The significant disproportion of single males to females highlights the Colonial Land and Emigration Commission's perennial problem in balancing the numbers of male and female emigrants. Required by regulation to transmit equal numbers of single males and females, the Cormmission invariably met the shortfall in Scottish single females by recruiting a compensatory number of more adventurous and more desperate Irish females. Penal infamy, distance, protective attitudes and a buoyant labour market for domestic servants in Scotland were powerful disincentives to Scottish female emigration in the 1850s.[163]

Given the official bias in immigration selection, the predominance of labourers and domestic servants, together with other categories of semi-skilled and unskilled labour, such as sawyers, carters and ploughmen might be expected. This composite group, needed as servants in the burgeoning settlements and labourers for the pastoral industry, made up nearly 60% of the adult intake. The vast majority was from disoriented districts in the Eastern Highlands which were undergoing the process of social and cultural restructuring.[164]

It is highly unlikely that the Northern Districts received any significant numbers of poverty-stricken and desperate Scots such as those inhabiting the slums of the major cities or who were the victims of famine and the clearances in the Western Highlands and Islands. They were not the types of settlers Australia wanted.[165] Official obstacles such as the necessity to prove unbroken wage-earning history were put in place to exclude such potential encumbrances. From 1854 all adults were required to make payments towards their passages according to their level of skill and age before leaving Britain, the remainder to be paid in the colony in equal yearly instalments. Substantial additional expenses were also entailed in the mandatory purchase of prescribed items of clothing and other items of kit. Character references were further required to demonstrate the immigrants' sobriety, industry, moral character in addition to the requirement to demonstrate that they were 'in the habit of working for wages'.[166]

In examining Scottish emigration, Malcolm Gray concluded that the typical emigrant to Australia was 'a person of some means, independent in thought and action, capable of sustained effort, consciousness of purpose and personal force to gather funds'.[167] This description would almost certainly apply to the 127 skilled mechanics, dominated by 25 blacksmiths, 22 joiners, an equal number of bakers and 17 carpenters. Most predictably originated from Scotland's three largest cities - Glasgow, Edinburgh and Aberdeen. These bastions of lower middle-class respectability were the very politically aware and upwardly mobile emigrants who would join the forces of dissent in the colony against squatter pretensions. Although Russell Ward maintained that the Scottish workers and artisans exerted little influence upon working-class identity in the southern districts of Australia, many of these direct immigrants from Scotland's industrialised urban areas initiated, led and dictated the emergence of worker consciousness in Brisbane in the late 1850s.[168]

Despite George Leslie's application to send 700 Highland refugees per month in 1852, it is improbable that Moreton Bay received any substantial numbers of the destitute Scots who were the victims of famine and clearances in the north-west Scotland.[169] Coinciding with Leslie's overseas visit, the Highland and Islands Emigration Society was founded in 1852 to solve not only one of Scotland's major demographic catastrophies, but also to meet the desperate need for pastoral labour arising from a mass exodus to the newly-discovered Victorian goldfields. Leslie assured the Society that the Northern Districts were too far distant from the southern goldfields to lose a significant number of diggings-bound deserters.[170]

Forever vigilant to tap fresh sources of labour, Leslie came within sight of gaining for the north one ship load of the 5000 Highland immigrants who were either coerced or persuaded to leave their poverty-stricken and starvation-wracked native lands between 1852 and 1857.[171] Official records of the society confirm that the *Marmion* sailed from Liverpool during August 1852, bearing 240 such emigres from Iona, Mull and Ardnamurchan for Moreton Bay. Unfortunately, due to a clerical error, the ship deposited its human cargo at Portland Bay in Victoria, with proximity to the goldfields, where they were happy to remain.[172] Nevertheless the northern squatters may well have been relieved in ultimately missing out on the services of those wretched refugees whom British authorities claimed to be well suited to the rigors of pastoral labour. The contrary opinion prevailed in Victoria where Leslie's counterparts found them helpless and hopeless, ultimately despairing of their indolence, intransigence, clannishness and inability to speak English.[173]

* * *

On arriving back in the colony in August 1853, Louis Hope revealed that little was known about the district's critical dearth of labour in England, the impression being that there was a high retention rate among labourers because of distance from the goldfields. To overcome this injurious fallacy, to promote a large volume of emigration and to counteract the damaging representations from the Sydney government, Hope suggested that an agent be appointed in London to represent northern interests. The misinformation circulating in England along with obstructive reports from Sydney which constantly stressed the district's slow development, small population and financial unpreparedness undermined the claims for separation.[174] Even as late as 1856, Leslie, Bigge and Hodgson found it necessary to disabuse British authorities of the notion that transportation was still a viable option. On raising the issue for the last time, Secretary of State Labouchere was unceremoniously informed, 'there was now no division of opinion and that we are unanimous against the introduction on any terms'.[175]

Lang had been concentrating since April 1854 on the threats which Wentworth's Constitution Bill posed to the territorial claims of the imminent northern colony.[176] Incensed that the object of separation at the 30th degree parallel of latitude as designated by Grey was a lever to erect 'that insignificant depot into an entrepot for the convicts from the mother country', Wentworth was determined to put an end to such an unpalatable threat by inserting a special clause into the new constitution. Knowing full well that the transportation issue had been settled at the beginning of 1853, he proposed that the northern boundary of the new colony be extended to the 26th parallel - well to the north of Brisbane.[177]

Receiving the support of the three other parliamentary representatives, John Richardson presented a petition of protest without success to the Legislative Council, suffering 'insulting and unjustifiable language' in the process.[178] When the petition for separation at 30 degrees of latitude was presented, Russell sneered that his colleague's anticipated 'lion's retort' was reduced to 'but a purr'. Attorney General Plunkett also summarily dismissed 'Johnny' Richardson's sincere attempt, being impatient at concerted and persistent efforts to create a 'petty, paltry, insignificant state'. Nevertheless an earlier petition to the Queen protesting against the Sydney legislature's abrogation of power was successful; the colonial legislature was informed bluntly that it had no right to usurp the prerogative of the parliament and crown to determine boundaries of future colonies.[179]

Defeating Hodgson for the County of Stanley in a unique electoral tussle outside Brisbane's boundaries, Lang enjoyed no such sinecure as the establishment's darling. On taking up his seat on 18 September 1854, Lang immediately set about implementing the main planks of his platform which centred on separation and 'the organisation of requisite machinery for the introduction of a numerous, industrious and virtuous free immigrant population from the United Kingdom'.[180] He unsuccessfully moved in the House for an address to the Queen for the immediate separation of the Moreton Bay District according to the Australian Colonies Act of 1850. Patrick Leslie, possibly acting on biased personal feelings, was not among the seven voters who supported the motion.[181] The *Moreton Bay Courier* was at a loss to explain Lang's lack of support from his squatter-oriented colleagues in the legislature, suggesting that 'mere personal spleen' was the basis of their 'stupid opposition' which interfered with the performance of his duties for the district.[182]

Also on the outer with the likes of the Leslies was the pro-separationist Colin Mackenzie who lost the seat for the pastoral district of Clarence and Darling Downs to Clark Irving in 1856. Familiar with Irving's suppressed policy on separation, Lang condemned the electors' choice by open letter in the *Moreton Bay Courier*. Hardly assisted in the pastoral districts by Lang's interference, Mackenzie's lack of success was attributable to predicted low polling in the Clarence and his unexpected negligible vote from Warwick.[183] Furthermore, Mackenzie's overtures to the urban forces to form a united front to achieve separation would not have endeared him to electors in Leslie country at that juncture.[184] Probably out of spite, the Condamine voters ensured the election of a representative whose real interests lay south of their district. As Lang suspected, Irving was thenceforth active in both the legislature and his home-base at Grafton in undermining Moreton Bay's designs on territory north of the anticipated boundary at the 30th parallel.

Lang had invaluable support for his incessant demands for separation when Richardson re-entered the legislature, having successfully contested the election for the Borough of Stanley in April 1856. This urban-centred election was remarkable for the depth of bitter division which erupted within the district, particularly between Ipswich and Brisbane - a dysfunction seized upon by Sydney forces to further delay separation.[185] Whereas the *Moreton Bay Courier* attempted to put a dampener upon rising animosity during the campaign, the *North Australian* from Ipswich added fuel to the fire, especially targeting Richardson.

The *Courier* gave due credit to Richardson for his service to Stanley for nearly four sessions, stating that he had done more for the district than any other representative.[186] Arguing that he represented a select, narrow-minded element within Brisbane rather than the entire Northern Districts, the *North Australian* complained that persisting with 'this pocket-edition of human nature' precluded the election of men with talent, energy and independence of character such as the pastoralist Dr Dorsey. The editorial proceeded to claim that Richardson, who owed his position to his respectability rather than his mediocre legislative ability, was a threat to the future progress of the district.[187]

Despite these insults, Richardson mounted a well-conducted campaign in which the importance of pastoralism was promoted as secondary to agriculture. He was strongly backed by Brisbane's Scottish community including James Swan, George Edmonstone, William Cairncross, James Halcroe Robertson, Robert Davidson, Thomas Boyland, George McAdam, John Souter and former Mackenzie workers Thomas Gray, Lachlan McLean and Alexander McIntyre. This amalgam of middle-class and working-class activists joined forces with solicitor Daniel F. Roberts and Lang adherent Dr Hobbs to ensure Richardson's election.[188]

Richardson's nearest rival was conservative Ipswich solicitor Arthur Macalister who missed a seat at his political debut after attracting 45% of the vote at the less populous Ipswich and only 5% at Brisbane. Practising what was preached with regards to district union, the *Courier* praised Macalister's erudition, ability and oratory while regretting that there was not a place in the new parliament for a man of his talents. Magnanimously and accurately it predicted that this future premier of Queensland would eventually gain the deserved honour of being among 'the legislative founders of the yet to be important colony of Moreton Bay'.[189] To bring this situation about, Lang and Richardson combined to mount an unceasing and formidable onslaught within the New South Wales legislature and upon British authorities on behalf of all sectors of the Northern Districts.

Lang's visit to Moreton Bay in January 1856 resulted in a spate of petitions which he was only too willing to convey to England as the district's advocate.[190] Among Lang's petitions were one from each of Moreton Bay's major townships, another from his short-lived Moreton Bay Immigration and Land Company and a joint, well-argued submission in which he and Richardson provided the politician's slant. These northern members argued from experience that representation of the district in the Sydney legislature was a mockery and a delusion. In the legislature 'the best interests of the inhabitants are systematically compromised and sacrificed ... while every obstacle is tacitly thrown in the way of their expressive advancement'.[191] It was claimed once again that no more zealous, energetic, empathic and knowledgeable delegate for the district could be obtained to argue its case.

Lang's visit was a memorable occasion, one when squatters' representatives and urbanites combined their efforts for the benefit of the district's independence. Englishmen Hobbs, Eldridge, Challinor and Roberts rubbed shoulders with R.R. Mackenzie and Colin John Mackenzie in the committee to forward the objectives of the Brisbane meeting - a liaison which undoubtedly cost the latter a seat in the Legislative Council at the hands of his more intractable colleagues on the lower

Condamine.[192] By that stage, the Colonial Office had long realised that the separation movement was not driven by the squatters, but also had an urban, democratic flavour mainly provided by Brisbanites.[193]

The former contest between the squatters and the democratic will gave way to a concerted rebuttal of southern arguments against the expediency of separation, as contained in despatches from the Governor of New South Wales to the Secretary of State for the colony and in damaging articles printed in the *Sydney Morning Herald*. In his despatches of 1855 and 1856, Sir William Denison argued that separation was 'inexpedient and unwise', proposing municipal government as a substitute in a sparsely populated district dominated by a comparatively small number of squatters with little or no permanent interest in the area.[194]

Denison's unfavourable report had no sooner left Australia's shores than Secretary of State Labouchere rejected the Governor's former counsel which he viewed as unnecessarily prejudiced, pessimistic and antagonistic. He looked to the future of the Northern Districts, noted its potential, praised its progress and announced by despatch received in October 1856 that separation was inevitable - probably at the 30th degree of south latitude. It was only necessary to arrange the details and withstand one last rearguard action by Denison. The boundary issue thereafter became the major bone of contention and, mainly because of Lang's obsession with this issue, separation took another three years to achieve.[195]

***

Lang also appears to have overstated his role in achieving separation for the Northern Districts and underestimated the critical part played by the Scottish pastoralists in their successful direct negotiations with the Colonial Office. In fact the *Sydney Morning Herald*, forever ready to put Lang in his place, suggested in January 1856 that far from 'working on the fears of the authorities in Downing Street' to achieve separation, 'he did very little for Moreton Bay or any other part of the colony'.[196] Even the normally loyal *Moreton Bay Courier*, on announcing that the Imperial Government had decided upon separation, fully expected Lang 'to make it clear that the decision of the Government was owing entirely to some act of his own'. No doubt Lang did keep the quest steadily before the Home Government through press, platform and petition, but so did other sections of the vital separation movement at Moreton Bay whose 'strong and repeated representations' were more warmly received in London.[197]

Lang's most emphatic claim was that the British Government would not have considered separation if it had not been for the impact upon Earl Grey in 1847 of his well-received report on the agricultural potential of Moreton Bay and the desirability of fixing the future boundary at the 30th parallel.[198] Lang's fall from favour with Grey in 1849 would have ensured that a deputation of Northern District squatters in the same year, (including Hodgson, Fairholme, Walter Leslie and Evan Mackenzie) to obtain Exiles would have exercised more influence.[199] The decision of the British Government to reintroduce a form of transportation in the face of determined opposition from the New South Wales legislature and the receptivity of the powerful pastoralists to the proposal of separation with convicts were more likely to have determined Grey's decision to include a clause in the Imperial Act of 1850 which authorised the monarch to erect an independent colony north of the boundary suggested by Lang.[200] He may have made the first suggestion, but the final outcome was a product of the machinations arising from powerful, conflicting forces within imperial politics.

Colonial Office papers indicate that Lang's later representations for Moreton Bay in London were ineffective, so poor was his reputation in that department. He had burned his bridges with the parting vitriol directed to Earl Grey in 1849.[201] While the petitions he bore from Moreton Bay eight years later never proceeded beyond the senior clerk of the Australian department, it was the likes of Hodgson, Mackenzie, Hope, George Leslie and other well-connected pastoralists who gained favourable audiences with Henry Labouchere, Secretary of State for the Colonies. Having gained the ear of the British government, they successfully countered the opposition of Governor Denison and Colonial Secretary Thomson - once the department was convinced the squatters no longer harboured designs to reintroduce transportation. "No interest so represented [by Lang] would carry much weight or obtain much consideration'.[202]

Since 1855 Matthew Henry Marsh, English barrister, Legislative Councillor and New England pastoralist had been in London to press the separation cause for northern colonists. His effectiveness was increased following his election as member for Salisbury to the House of Commons where he promoted separation. At the Colonial Office he undermined the influence of Denison, lobbied effectively and gained the confidence of Labouchere as a northern Australian expert. According to Bruce Knox, who researched Colonial Office papers relating to separation, 'Marsh was largely responsible for Merivale's constant opinion that "separation is an unavoidable measure." '[203]

Marsh's detailed document which he was requested to prepare on Moreton Bay's case contained proposals which the Colonial Office readily accepted, although Deas Thomson in 1856 managed to undermine the recommendation that the future boundary be located at the 28th parallel. In mid 1858 the deputation including Colin Mackenzie, Patrick and George Leslie which Marsh presented to Sir E.B. Lytton was assured irrevocably that 'Separation must be and a Bill was to be introduced at the earliest possible period ...'.[204]

This news and more detail of future proceedings was conveyed to the district via the *Moreton Bay Courier* following the receipt of Marsh's letter to W.A. Duncan - the parliamentarian's 'correspondent in the district'. Marsh's thankful acknowledgement of Duncan's statistical information, knowledge and authority indicated the covert but important role which this unpopular customs official played in preparing detailed reports and arguments which swayed the influential at Westminster and Downing Street.[205] While Lang was approaching misrepresentation in exaggerating his role at the Colonial Office in achieving separation, the shadowy Duncan remained silent, ultimately to be criticised on leaving the district for his general, unwarranted interference. Whereas Lang's zeal on behalf of Moreton Bay was noisily acknowledged at the pioneers' dinner in 1869, special emphasis was directed to the achievements of Marsh.[206] Four years earlier he had been honoured in Brisbane at a testimonial dinner given by grateful Queenslanders who appreciated his crucial efforts on their behalf.[207]

While Duncan's unpopularity and clandestine involvement ensured that his contribution to the achievement of separation remained unheralded, Lang's dogged persistence with the border issue kept him in the public limelight. Popular or not, his refusal to accept a fait accompli pushed the northern parliamentary representatives beyond their tolerance level. Lang had journeyed to the Clarence and Richmond District in August 1856 to confront and persuade the householders at a large meeting at Grafton following the circulation of a letter from Irving which promoted the idea that this district's welfare would suffer immeasurably by detachment from the Middle Districts.[208] Irving's missive supported the designs of the Sydney government which was lobbying vigorously to have the boundary fixed at the 28th parallel instead of the 30th. Faced with the unpalatable prospect of losing 'some of the most wealthy and thriving towns' to New South Wales, the *Moreton Bay Courier* lauded Lang's personal attempt to convince those settlers of the advantages of union with the north. Yet again it was deemed that Moreton Bay was fortunate to have such a zealot agitating for its welfare.[209] And still, the time was not far away when even his most loyal northern colleagues cried, 'Enough'!

In a congratulatory letter to the inhabitants of Moreton Bay in late September 1857, Lang rejoiced that separation had been conceded at long last, albeit on 'terms which greatly neutralise the value of the boon and give a feeling of indignation...'. The boundary of the new colony, running west from Point Danger to the Diving Range may well have been the outcome sought by the Governor-General and most inhabitants of the Richmond-Clarence area, but it roused Lang's ire.[210] Although separation had been virtually achieved, it would not become a reality until the precise details, especially those of the unacceptable, proposed boundary at 28 degrees had been finalised. Thus, 1857 to 1859 were 'years of suspense, and not unfrequently tantalizing uncertainty'. Not only did Denison prolong the process by the tardiness of his replies to the Colonial Office, but Lang's intransigence and unremitting challenges to the unsympathetic British and colonial bureaucracy delayed speedy finalisation.[211]

A long series of petitions from politicians, public meetings and squatters from the Northern Districts requesting separation at the 30th parallel was counteracted by a sequence of counter-petitions from New England demanding retention within New South Wales. Public meetings at Brisbane and Ipswich continued throughout 1858 following the final decision to fix the southern boundary at Point Danger, culminating in a Lang-inspired petition containing 700 signatures.

Despite a public meeting held on 28 August 1858 which condemned Richardson and Hodgson as not representing the beliefs of their electorates, these northern members of the legislature rejected that application. Seeing no end to the action-reaction process in train, Richardson as Lang's foremost apologist, and Hodgson as his most active opponent, combined forces to prevent any further delays in the final promulgation of separation which would realistically follow Denison's formula.[212] As these legislators obviously had inside information on the inevitability of the outcome, they attempted to drag Lang away from kicking at a dead issue.

* * *

Within six months the members of Queensland's first Legislative Council were announced and Letters Patent, creating the colony of Queensland with Sir George Ferguson Bowen as first Governor, were granted by an Order in Council of 13 May 1859.[213] As a result of his prosperity and popularity among Brisbane citizens, Robert Cribb managed to combine effective representation on Brisbane's Council and the first Legislative Assembly which boasted no less than 42% Scots among its twenty-six members.[214] Predictably, Lang addressed an open letter to the colonists of Queensland telling them how they should conduct their affairs as an independent British colony. It was not unexpected that he also provided a lengthy overview of his allegedly dominant role in the attainment of that favourable result. Convinced of his infallible judgement, Lang did not doubt that the Clarence and Richmond districts would eventually be added to Queensland. He went so far as to predict they would even clamour for inclusion after experiencing the benefits which would accrue from direct road communication with the new capital - one of the first capital works which should be undertaken by the first government.[215]

One of the most urgent problems which the first Brisbane Town Council addressed at its inaugural meeting on 13 October 1859 was the settlement's inadequate and unhealthy water supply. Headed by Mayor John Petrie, a former student at Lang's Australian College in Sydney, the majority of the council of nine aldermen bore the distinct imprint of this querulous cleric or participated prominently in allied forms of radical, nonconformist religion.[216] However, the only Scottish member of the first Ipswich Municipal Council, which met for the first time on 12 April 1860 to confront the long-standing problem of roads and drains, was John Pettigrew, brother of the surveyor who was unable to carry out his brief for Lang's failed immigration company in 1849.[217]

In the final count, nationality was immaterial as Scots and English legislators along with the stray Irishman grasped responsible government with both hands and laboured cooperatively as Queenslanders to form a solidly-based colony. Duncan, safely ensconced in his coveted position in Sydney since April 1859, would have had no cause for worry about his fate at the hands of the 'Lang mob' whom he expected to control the legislature. Though they still exerted a strong presence, the Langites in no way were dominant in the new colony which they helped to create. So attenuated was their influence in the new legislature, that their champion had difficulty in persuading the designated committee of enquiry that he had in fact provided directly and unselfishly any important benefits worthy of financial recompense from the public purse to Moreton Bay over the previous decade - his importance as a social engineer, propagandist and motivator apparently did not count.[218] Having concluded that his immigration scheme of 1849 was a commercial and strictly sectarian effort tinged with some philanthrophy, the committee headed by liberal solicitor Charles Lilley rejected outright his claim for compensation for losses incurred. Nor did the counter-petition from some still-aggrieved *Chaseley* immigrants help his case. The new colony merely thanked him for his 'valuable and successful exertions' for bringing about the separation of Moreton Bay from New South Wales.[219] This was hardly just recompense for a man who maintained that separation was solely his idea and claimed to have persuaded an antagonistic British cabinet minister, whom he had once abused unmercifully, to sanctify his plans by act of parliament.[220]

The parliamentary committee confined itself to its frame of reference and in its verdict of a few paragraphs was not able to even scratch the surface of Lang's contribution to pre-separation Queensland. Unpopular with governments and bureaucrats, but basking in the role of the pugnacious and persistent voice of the respectable commoners, Lang created that promised public opinion which wrought a demographic, political and moral revolution in the Northern Districts from 1849. Leading from Sydney, Lang inspired his radical immigrants to join with long-suffering and intimidated Brisbanites to halt the squatters' drive to reintroduce transportation, establish a plantation economy and create a pastoral hegemony. By a combination of platform, pamphlets, press, petitions and the power of numbers, this avowed Chartist and republican introduced and maximised democratic procedures in the north to benefit the formerly subjugated populace. In this process, his efforts were assuredly given added impetus and clout by the support of Swan's *Moreton Bay Courier*.

Lang definitely had his share of failures. He never succeeded in founding an anti-Catholic colony; sugar production barely saw the light of day and cotton farming stayed at the experimental stage. However, it was mainly the colonial Scots along with a handful of energetic English businessmen, rather than his imports, who gave agriculture a start and formed new localities such as Sandgate and Bald Hills in the process. Although Lang did not recruit a significant number of his compatriots as immigrants, he attracted the Scottish liberal elements in the district to his cause to impede the might of the Scottish-led squattocracy. When the Scottish leadership of those intra-ethnic camps united for the good of the northern district, separation was ultimately achieved.

Lang was ahead of his time. Soon after the formation of Queensland, land grants were offered to all government immigrants; the vast squatting empires were broken up for agriculture; and cotton and sugar became important industries. Despite the lack of official recognition for his efforts, he remained the champion of Queensland's common people through his charismatic leadership and undeferential approach to the arrogant British and colonial establishments.

Lang's personal advances to the British government may have been treated with studied disdain, but his colonial leadership and agitation unleashed such a continuous force of northern protest upon Sydney and Whitehall that the Colonial Office finally bowed to the pressure of persistent reason. In 1869 Arthur Hodgson, who led the squatters' well-received and more successful approaches to the Secretaries of State, buried the hatchet, paying tribute to Lang's leadership and personal exertions for separation. Although Hodgson did not refer to Lang's hyperbolic and self-promotional claim that separation would not have occurred without his efforts, this successful pastoralist left no doubt that the 'reverend agitator's' efforts were significant and even crucial to the attainment of northern independence. A measure of his importance to contemporaries may be gauged by the prolonged cheering that accompanied Hodgson's pronouncement at the special gathering of pre-separation colonists under vice-regal patronage to celebrate their pioneering labours which founded the state of Queensland. Being on the ground floor of Queensland's development, the pre-fifty-niners were well placed to give credit where they felt it was due.[221]

ENDNOTES

1. Lang, *Cooksland*, p. 107.
2. Ibid.
3. Coote, *History of the colony of Queensland*, p. 94.
4. Lang, *Days of wrath*, pp. 32, 80, 104.
5. David S. Macmillan, *John Dunmore Lang*, (Melbourne: Melbourne University Press, 1962), p. 4.
6. *SMH*, 28 April 1849, p. 2.
7. John Dunmore Lang, *Narrative of the steps taken in promoting the separation of Queensland from New South Wales*, (Sydney: J.G. O'Connor, 1875), p. 13. This was no idle boast as the Queensland population quadrupled in eight years from 1859 when Premier Herbert adopted Lang's principle to grant 30 acres of land for every adult migrant landed, Ibid.
8. Cryle, *The press in colonial Queensland*, p. 26.
9. William Pettigrew to John Pettigrew, 1 December 1850, William Pettigrew Letters, RHSQ.
10. *British Banner*, 11 December 1852, p. 4.
11. Lang, *Cooksland*, pp. 174, 232-33.
12. Macmillan, *John Dunmore Lang*, p. 4.
13. *British Banner*, 12 July 1849, p. 489.
14. *SMH*, 9 February 1849, p.2; *British Banner*, 12 July 1849, p. 489.
15. *MBC*, 27 January 1849, p. 2.
16. *British Banner*, 20 September 1849, p. 649.
17. Earl Grey to Governor Sir Charles A. Fitzroy, Despatch No. 24, 15 December 1849, in *MBC*, 20 July 1850, p. 4.
18. Macmillan, *John Dunmore Lang*, p. 19.
19. Earl Grey, Despatch in *MBC*, 20 July 1850, p. 4; Lang, *Days of Wrath*, pp. 260-1.
20. *MBC*, 7 September 1850, p. 2.
21. Report, Select Committee on Immigration, *QVP*, 1860, p. 637.
22. J.D. Lang, Evidence taken on Dr Lang's petition, *QVP*, 1860, p. 1020.
23. *MBC*, 27 January 1849, p. 2; 13 October 1849, p. 2.
24. *MBC*, 6 December 1850, p. 1.
25. *MBC*, 28 July 1849, p. 2; 6 December 1850, p. 1.
26. *MBC*, 19 January 1850, p. 2.
27. *MBC*, 16 March 1850, p.2; 6 December 1850, p. 2.
28. *British Banner*, 4 August 1852 in *MBC*, 11 December 1852, p. 4.
29. Lang, Evidence, *QVP*, 1860, p. 1010.
30. John Dunmore Lang, *Narrative of the steps taken in promoting the separation of Queensland from New South Wales with notices on the founding and early history of the colony*, (Sydney: J.G. O'Connor, 1875), p. 5.
31. *British Banner*, 21 November 1849, p. 739.
32. *MBC*, 16 March 1850, p. 2.

33 *London Atlas*, 9 April 1850, in Russell, *Genesis of Queensland*, pp. 454 -5.
34 *MBC*, 7 August 1850, p. 2.
35 *MBC*, 30 August 1850, p.2; Ambrose Eldridge and Robert Cribb to J.D. Lang, 22 August 1855, Lang Papers, CY 2497, 81-2, Mitchell Library, Sydney; *MBC*, 11 August 1855, p. 2.
36 J.D. Lang to Pettigrew, 8 December 1851, Lang papers, Immigrants and ships sent to Moreton Bay, CY reel 1075, Mitchell Library, p.193.
37 Evidence, Lang's petition, *QVP*, 1860, p. 1011; Libby Connors and Bernadette Turner, ' "I cannot do any more": resistance, respectability and ruin - recapturing the Irish orphan girls in the Moreton Bay districts', in Trevor McClaughlin, ed. *Irish women in colonial Australia*, (St Leonards: Allen & Unwin, 1998), p. 107.
38 Passenger lists, arrivals at Moreton Bay 1848-55, micro Z598, Z599, QSA; John Mackenzie-Smith, 'Scottish immigrants to Moreton Bay 1841-59', in Rod Fisher and Jennifer Harrison, ed. *Brisbane: immigrants and industries*, BHG Papers No. 17 (in preparation). As no place of origin is available for immigrants arriving aboard the *Lima*, estimates of nationality do not permit precision. It is estimated that Lang's ships contained a little over 58 Scots - 18 males, 15 females and at least 28 children. Of the two Scottish families identified on the *Lima*, one consisted of 7 children and the number of children in the other was not specified.
39 J.D. Lang, *Narrative of proceedings in England, Scotland and Ireland during the years 1847, 1848 and 1849 with a view to originate an extensive and continuous immigration of a superior character from the United Kingdom into this territory*, (Sydney: D.L. Welch, 1850), p. 5.
40 Lang, *Cooksland*, pp. 478-9.
41 Baker, *Days of wrath*, pp. 250-1.
42 *British Banner*, 2 August 1848, p. 537.
43 *British Banner*, 29 August 1849, pp. 549-50.
44 *Glasgow Herald*, 21 June 1847, p. 2.
45 *London Atlas*, 9 April 1850.
46 Denis Cryle, *The press in colonial Queensland*, (St Lucia: University of Queensland Press, 1989), p. 26.
47 Lang, Evidence, *QVP*, 1860, p. 1001.
48 *SMH*, 6 March 1849, p. 2.
49 Passenger arrivals at Moreton Bay 1848-55, QSA. The records for the immigrants aboard the *Lima* do not indicate place of origin.
50 *British Banner*, 21 June 1848, p. 440.
51 *British Banner*, 24 May 1848, p. 377.
52 *British Banner*, 23 March 1848, p. 227.
53 *Brisbane Telegraph*, 3 May 1899; *Queenslander*, 13 May 1899, p. 878.
54 *SMH*, 22 January 1856, p. 3.
55 William Augustine Duncan, Autobiography, p. 13, CY 162, Mitchell Library.
56 *MBC*, 13 January 1849, p. 3.

57 *MBC*, 10 March 1849, p. 2.
58 Alan Beever, 'From a place of "horrible destitution" to a Paradise for the working class: the transformation of British working class attitudes to Australia 1841-51', *Labour History*, 40 (1981), p. 3.
59 Johnston, *Brisbane*, p. 145.
60 Knowles was the accountant for the Bank of New South Wales, before taking up auctioneering.
61 Cryle, *The press in colonial Queensland*, pp. 25, 26, 34. Although Wilkes is credited with being editor of the *Moreton Bay Courier*, the proprietor James Swan wrote every editorial until the end of January 1856. *MBC*, 19 January 1856, p. 2.
62 This estimate was calculated by adding the population of 2525 derived by the census of March 1846 to the 360 immigrant arrivals via Sydney between April 1846 and 15 December 1848. The number of immigrants who travelled overland is unknown. The immigrants who arrived per *Artemesia* on 16 December 1848 are regarded as 1849 arrivals as most would have taken some time to gain employment and settle into the district; Rod Fisher, 'The alien presence in early Brisbane, 1840-60', in Rod Fisher, ed. *Brisbane: Aboriginal, alien, ethnic*, Brisbane History Group Papers No. 5, (Brisbane: Brisbane History Group, 1987), p. 105.
63 New South Wales Immigration Agent, Passenger lists. Arrivals at Moreton Bay 1848-55, micro Z598, QSA; *MBC*, 4 July 1846, p. 2; 6 December 1851, p. 4.
64 *British Banner*, 10 October 1849, p. 645.
65 *MBC*, 11 May 1850, p. 3.
66 *Queenslander*, 13 May 1899, p. 879.
67 William Pettigrew to Rev. John Barclay, 11 October 1850, Pettigrew letters-miscellaneous, RHSQ.
68 Coote, *History of the colony of Queensland*, p. 103.
69 Lang to Pettigrew, 8 December 1851, Lang Papers, Immigrants and ships, p. 195.
70 Colonial secretary to William Pettigrew, 20 November 1849, Lang papers, Immigrants and ships sent to Moreton Bay, p. 161.
71 *MBC*, 2 March 1850, p. 2.
72 *MBC*, 2 June 1849, p. 2.
73 *MBC*, 28 July 1849, p. 3.
74 *MBC*, 2 June 1849, p. 2; 11 April 1857, p. 2.
75 Lang, *Narrative of the steps taken in promoting the separation of Queensland*, pp.7-8.
76 *MBC*, 14 June 1851, p. 3.
77 *MBC*, 14 June 1851, p. 3; 19 February 1853, p. 3
78 *MBC*, 17 November 1849, p.3. Fifteen blocks of 640 acres, mainly along the Logan River, were advertised for auction.
79 Land Regulations, *MBC*, 10 February 1849, p. 4.
80 *MBC*, 11 December 1852, p. 3; 5 November 1863, p. 3.
81 *MBC*, 17 May 1856, p.2; 1 November 1856, p. 2.
82 Coote, *History of the colony of Queensland*, p. 219.

83 *MBC*, 8 October 1853, p. 2.
84 James Balfour to Thomas Barker, 15 December 1841, Balfour-Barker correspondence; *MBC*, 26 February 1853, p. 2.
85 *MBC*, 19 February 1853, p. 3.
86 Ibid.
87 *MBC*, 21 July, 1855, p. 2.
88 J.H. Madden, 'Records of Queensland botanists', Paper read before the Australian Association for the Advancement of Science, (Brisbane: 1908), p. 377.
89 J. Farnfield, 'Cotton and the search for an agricultural staple in early Queensland', *Queensland Heritage*, 2 (1971), p. 22.
90 *MBC*, 18 February 1854, p. 1.
91 *ADB*, vol. 5, p. 171. *MBC*, 4 February 1854, p. 2; 13 January 1855, p. 2; 2 February 1856, p. 2.
92 *MBC*, 13 January 1855, p. 2; 2 February 1856, p. 2.
93 William Pettigrew, Diary, RHSQ.
94 *MBC*, 29 December 1849, p. 4.
95 *MBC*, 3 May 1856, p. 2.
96 Farnfield, 'Cotton and the search for an agricultural staple', p. 24; Stan Tutt, *Caboolture Country*, (Nambour: Caboolture Historical Society, 1973), pp. 20-21; *From spear and musket 1879-1979*, (Nambour: Caboolture Shire Council, 1979), p. 73.
97 *MBC*, 8 March 1851, p. 2.
98 *MBC*, 3 May 1856, p. 2.
99 *MBC*, 28 April 1849, p. 3.
100 *MBC*, 8 March 1851, p. 2; 5 April 1851, p. 2; 20 October 1851, p.2; 13 April 1852, p. 2; 23 April 1853, p. 3.
101 *MBC*, 21 February 1852, p. 3; 13 March 1852, p. 2; 3 July 1854, p. 2.
102 Johnston, *Brisbane*, p. 206.
103 Police Magistrate, Moreton Bay, to Colonial Secretary, 4 May 1853, 53/4718, Colonial Secretary's correspondence, Moreton Bay, AONSW.
104 Coote, *History of the colony of Queensland*, p. 134.
105 *MBC*, 23 April 1853, p. 3; 22 September 1853, p. 2.
106 *MBC*, 11 April 1857, p. 2.
107 *MBC*, 9 July 1859, p. 2; 12 December 1859, p. 2.
108 Lang to Pettigrew, 8 December 1851, Lang Papers, Immigrants and ships sent to Moreton Bay, pp. 199-200.
109 William Pettigrew to J.D. Lang, 13 December 1852, Lang Papers, Immigrants and ships sent to Moreton Bay, p. 56.
110 *MBC*, 12 June 1852, p. 3.
111 *MBC*, 9 January 1859, p. 3.
112 *MBC*, 25 July 1857, p. 2. The acreage under cultivation was probably 70 acres rather than 700, judging by the area of the site of one cotton plantation - the Sandgate Golf Club and sportsground. This was probably a typographical error.

113 Mackenzie-Smith, 'Moreton Bay Scots', p. 502; Barry Shaw, 'Bald Hills: from pioneers to pastoralists', in Rod Fisher and Barry Shaw ed. *Brisbane: people, places and progress*, Brisbane History Group Papers No. 14, (Brisbane: Brisbane History Group, 1995), pp. 19-23.
114 Beever, 'British working class attitudes to Australia 1841-51', p. 5.
115 Coote, *History of the colony of Queensland*, p. 106.
116 *MBC*, 23 April 1850, p. 1.
117 *SMH*, 11 April 1850, p. 3; *MBC*, 27 April 1850, p. 2.
118 Lang, *Narrative of the steps taken in the separation of Queensland*, p. 14.
119 *MBC*, 30 June 1849, p. 2.
120 Russell, *Genesis of Queensland*, p. 451.
121 *MBC*, 17 November, 1849, pp. 1, 3.
122 William Pettigrew to John Pettigrew, 14 January 1851, Pettigrew letters.
123 *MBC*, 12 January 1850, p. 3.
124 *MBC*, 14 January 1850, pp. 2, 3.
125 Russell, *Genesis of Queensland*, p. 451.
126 *MBC*, 14 January 1850, p. 3; 19 January 1850, p. 2.
127 Perry McIntyre, Convict pardons, tickets of leave, NSW 1810-75, (Sydney: W&F Pascoe, 1995), microfiche.; Scottish Record Office, 29 August 1994, personal correspondence; *MBC*, 27 April, 1850, p. 2.
128 *MBC*, 28 June 1850, p. 2;
129 *MBC*, 13 July 1850, p. 3.
130 Lang, *Narrative of the steps taken in promoting the separation of Queensland*, pp.9, 10.
131 Jan Kociumbas, *The Oxford history of Australia, Possessions, 1770-1860*, (Melbourne: Oxford University Press, 1995), pp. 298-300.
132 William Pettigrew to John Pettigrew, 14 January 1851, Pettigrew letters.
133 *MBC*, 31 August 1850, p. 2, 13 January, 1851, p. 2.
134 Grey to Hodgson, 30 October 1850 in *MBC*, 7 June 1851, p. 2.
135 *MBC*, 21 June 1851, p. 2.
136 *Moreton Bay Free Press [MBFP]*, 6 May 1852, p. 2.
137 *MBC*, 27 October 1851, p. 1
138 *MBC*, 29 November 1851, p. 2.
139 Bruce Knox, "Care is more important than haste": imperial policy and the creation of Queensland, 1856-59', *Historical Studies*, 17 (1976), p. 67.
140 William Pettigrew to John Pettigrew, 1 December 185, Pettigrew letters.
141 *MBC*, 3 January 1852, p. 4.
142 Baker, *Days of wrath*, p. 349.
143 *MBC*, 6 November 1851, p. 2; Duncan, Diary 1856, 4 January 1856, Mitchell Library, CY 164.
144 Bruce Knox, 'Moreton Bay separation: a problem of Imperial government 1825-56', *Historical Studies*, 14 (1971), p. 566.

145 G.F. Leslie to the Board of Commissioners of Colonial land Emigration, 19 July 1852, *British Parliamentary Papers*, 17, p. 72.
146 Russell, *Genesis of Queensland*, pp. 482-97; George Leslie left New South Wales on 10 March 1852; the petition would have been transmitted to his British address soon after the meeting of 17 May.
147 *MBC*, 13 March 1852, p. 3.
148 *MBC*, 13 March 1852, p. 2.
149 *MBC*, 17 July 1852, p. 2.
150 Brown to Fitzroy, 20 November 1852, *British Parliamentary Papers*, 19, p. 26; Police Magistrate, Brisbane, to Colonial Secretary, 15 December 1852, 19, p. 7.
151 Despatch from Earl Grey to Sir Charles A. Fitzroy, 15 December 1849, *MBC*, 20 July 1850, p. 4.
152 Fisher, 'The alien presence in early Brisbane', 1987, pp. 105-7; Passenger lists, Z598, Z599, QSA.
153 New South Wales Immigration Agent, Passenger lists to Moreton Bay directly from overseas, 1848-1859, micro Z 600, QSA; Jupp, *The Australian people*, Statistical volume, p. 10.
154 *MBC*, 20 July 1850, p. 4.
155 *Inverness Courier*, 1851-56; passenger lists for Moreton Bay 1848-59.
156 Fisher, 'The alien presence in Brisbane', p. 108.
157 See table, Direct adult Scottish immigration to Moreton Bay 1848-59, Appendix, p. 224.
158 Prentis, *Scots in Australia*, p. 75; Map: Mid-nineteenth century Scotland, Appendix, p. 225.
159 Prentis, *Scots in Australia*, p. 76.
160 Prentis, *Scots in Australia*, pp. 67-71.
161 Ibid, pp. 76-7.
162 Mackenzie-Smith, 'Scottish immigration to Moreton Bay'.
163 Deborah Oxley and Eric Richards, 'Convict women and assisted female immigrants compared', in Eric Richards, ed. *Visible women: female immigrants in colonial Australia*, Canberra: Australian National University, 1995, pp. 38-43.
164 Mackenzie-Smith, 'Scottish immigration to Moreton Bay'.
165 Eric Richards, 'The Highland Scots of South Australia', *Journal of the Historical Society of South Australia*, 4 (1978), pp. 55-9; 'The decline of St Kilda: demography, economy and migration,' *Scottish Economic and Social History*, 14 (1992), p. 147.
166 Her Majesty's Colonial and Emigration Commissioners, *Colonisation circular*, (London: Charles Knight, 1854), pp. 26-7.
167 Malcolm Gray, 'The course of Scottish emigration', in Tom M. Devine, ed. *Scottish emigration and Scottish society*, (Edinburgh: John Donald, 1992), p. 34.
168 Russell Ward, *The Australian legend*, (Melbourne: Melbourne University Press, 1970), pp. 46-7.

169 David S. Macmillan, 'Sir Charles Trevelyan and the Highland and Island Emigration Society, 1849-1859', *Royal Historical Society of Australia Journal*, 49, (1963), p. 175.
170 A.C.S. Balfour, Emigration from the Highlands and Western Isles of Scotland to Australia during the nineteenth century, M.Litt. thesis, University of Edinburgh, 1973, p. 114.
171 Ibid, Table VI, p. 131, compiled from List of immigrants, Her Majesty's Register House, Edinburgh.
172 Highlands and Islands Emigration Society, Letter book, 1852-55, HD 4/3, Scottish Record Office, Edinburgh.
173 Prentis, *The Scots in Australia*, pp. 70-3; Eric Richards, 'The Highland Scots of South Australia', pp. 55-9; 'St Kilda and Australia: emigrants at peril 1852-53', *The Scottish Historical Review*, 41, 1992, p. 147.
174 *MBC*, 13 August 1853, p. 2.
175 *MBC*, 11 October 1856, p. 2.
176 *MBC*, 11 April 1854, p. 3.
177 Coote, *History of the colony of Queensland*, p. 147. Grafton lies near 30 degrees latitude and Brisbane lies between the 27 and 28 degrees latitude. See the map, Suggested boundary between Queensland and New South Wales, Appendix, p. 228.
178 *MBC*, 19 May 1855, p. 2.
179 *MBC*, 24 December 1853, p. 2; Russell, *Genesis of Queensland*, pp. 499-500, 504.
180 *MBC*, 22 April 1856, p. 1.
181 Coote, *History of the colony of Queensland*, p. 159.
182 *MBC*, 19 September 1854, p. 2.
183 *MBC*, 1 February 1856, p. 3; 22 March 1856, p. 1; 26 April, 1856, p. 4.
184 *MBC*, 26 January 1856, p. 2.
185 *MBC*, 10 May 1856, p. 2.
186 *MBC*, 16 February 1856, p. 3.
187 *MBC*, 29 March 1856, p. 2.
188 *MBC*, 1 March 1856, p. 3.
189 *MBC*, 12 April 1856, p. 2
190 Coote, *History of the colony of Queensland*, p. 199.
191 Petition from Lang and Richardson, members of the Legislative Council of New South Wales in the district of Moreton Bay, 28 November 1856 in *Papers relative to the Separation of the Moreton Bay District from New South Wales and the establishment of a separate colony*, (London: George Eyre and William Spottiswoode for Her Majesty's Stationery Office, 1858), p. 8.
192 *MBC*, 19 January, 1856, p.2 ; 26 January 1856, p. 2; 16 February 1856, p. 2.
193 Bruce A. Knox, 'Moreton Bay separation', p. 570.
194 *MBC*, 18 October 1855, p. 2; 1 September 1856, p. 2.
195 Labouchere to Denison, 21 July 1856 in Knox, 'Moreton Bay separation', p. 377.
196 *SMH*, 22 January 1856, p. 3.

197 Labouchere, despatch to Denison, 21 July 1856, reproduced in *MBC*, 28 October 1856, p. 2; Knox, 'Moreton Bay separation', p. 576.
198 E. Hawes to J.D. Lang, undated, reproduced in *MBC*, 23 October 1847, p. 1.
199 *MBC*, 23 April 1850, p. 1.
200 *MBC*, 28 June 1850, p. 2; Lang, *Narrative of the steps taken in promoting the separation of Queensland from New South Wales*, p. 10.
201 *MBC*, 20 July 1850, p. 4.
202 Minute by Gordon Gardiner, senior clerk of the Australian department, Colonial Office, 27 November 1857, in Knox, 'Care is more important than haste', p. 67.
203 *Australian Dictionary of Biography*, vol. 5, p. 213.; Knox, 'Moreton Bay separation', p. 569.
204 *MBC*, 20 October 1858, p. 2.
205 Henry Marsh to Duncan, 31 July 1858, in *MBC*, 20 October 1858, p. 2.
206 *MBC*, 29 May 1869, p. 2.
207 *ADB*, vol. 5, p. 213.
208 Coote, *History of the colony of Queensland*, p. 194.
209 *MBC*, 1 August 1856, p. 2.
210 *MBC*, 26 September 1857, p. 4.
211 Coote, *History of the colony of Queensland*, p. 208.
212 John R. Laverty, Development of the town of Brisbane, 1823-59, BA thesis, University of Queensland, 1955, p. 27.
213 Eight of the twelve appointees were prominent Scots: J.C. Wickham, Louis Hope, R.R Mackenzie, J. McDougall, G. Raff, A. Macalister, J. Balfour and J. Douglas. Laverty, Development of Brisbane, p. 57; Coote, *History of the colony of Queensland*, p. 225.
214 Charles Arrowsmith Bernays, *Queensland politics during sixty (1859-1919) years*, (Brisbane: A.J. Cumming, 1920), pp. 7-16.
215 *MBC*, 27 December 1859, p. 3.
216 Gordon Greenwood and John Laverty, *Brisbane 1859-1959: a history of local government*, (Brisbane: Brisbane City Council, 1959), pp. 67-72, 81.
217 Leslie E. Slaughter, *Ipswich municipal centenary*, (Ipswich: Council of the city of Ipswich, 1960), pp. 21-4.
218 Dr Lang's petition. Progress report, Final report, Minutes of the proceedings of the committee on Dr Lang's petition, *QVP*, 1860, pp. 979-1039.
219 Final report from the select committee on Dr Lang's petition, *QVP*, 1860, p. 993.
220 Lang, Evidence to the committee on Dr Lang's petition, 24 July 1860, *QVP*, 1860, p. 1008
221 *Brisbane Courier*, 29 May 1869, p. 2.

Rev. John Dunmore Lang
(John Oxley Library)

Ship *Fortitude* which transported the first of Lang's immigrants to Moreton Bay, 1849
(*John Oxley Library*)

James Swan M.L.C.
(Queensland Newspapers)

William Pettigrew
(John Oxley Library)

Rev. Thomas Mowbray
(John Oxley Library)

John Richardson

John Petrie
(John Oxley Library)

William Street 1856 - United Evangelical Chapel and Commissariat Stores (Centre) - St John's Church of England at left (John Oxley Library)

Brisbane 1862 - Congregational church and first School of Arts at left of photo - Normal School under construction at centre (John Oxley Library)

South Brisbane 1862 - First Presbyterian church right background (John Oxley Library)

George Raff
(John Oxley Library)

Arthur Macalister
(John Oxley Library)

James Rendall   *John Scott*
Reproduced with the permission of the Queensland Education Department

Sir Robert Ramsay Mackenzie
(John Oxley Library)

United Evangelical chapel 1872, William Street
(John Oxley Library)

Ann and Albert Streets corner 1862 - Ann Street Presbyterian church left of photo - Wesleyan Chapel on right   (John Oxley Library)

Chapter 5
W.A. Duncan and material, moral Brisbane 1849-59

Brisbane developed as both the focus for anti-squatting forces and the religious and moral regeneration of the district. Within these movements Scottish leadership and factionalism were prominent. Urban development emerged as a parallel and contrasting form of socio-economic growth to the dependency which arose from squatter domination before 1849. The anti-liberal squatters withdrew to their stations as prosperity returned and a reliable supply of labour was assured. Their hegemonic aspirations had been dashed and their attempt to make Cleveland the regional port foiled, though they continued to favour Ipswich as their base for service, provisions and recreation. 'The majority held aloof from the new society that was being shaped so vociferously about them'.[1] By 1859 Brisbane had become a bustling commercial centre and the residents were confident that their town had finally claimed the status of the district's entrepot. Not only was the township well on the road to limited self-sufficiency within a pastoralist economy, but it also boasted a vibrant political, cultural and religious environment.

Between 1849 and 1859 Brisbane and Ipswich became the preferred destinations for a large proportion of the middle and working-class Scottish immigrants who were able to avoid station labour because they possessed the skills and/or funds in demand in these two towns. The highly moral, socially-fluid milieu, particularly in Brisbane, facilitated the achievement of upward mobility and respectability sought by the newly arrived immigrants. The optimum conditions for capital accumulation, acquisition of property, employment and cultural enrichment existed in the rapidly growing town with its churches, temperance society and excellent school of arts.[2]

Brisbane was a typical emergent liberal regional centre, increasingly dominated by a middle class which sought wealth and success in business. Such prosperity was achieved by the pursuit of individualism, exercise of personal effort and government encouragement of free-enterprise. Having successfully challenged squatter privilege and aligned with the colonial equivalent of Scotland's labour aristocracy, the middle-class nonconformist faction sought democratisation of society and the removal of inequality. In this process, they had to contend with the resistance of that section of their peers advocating maintenance of the status quo within society, limitations on the spread of democratic influences and formation of a new privileged group based on education, wealth and property. This was the source of much of the dissension within the northern middle class.

In this turbulent environment, supposedly neutral government officials such as William Augustine Duncan were occasionally embroiled, often unintentionally. More often, it was by design.

Duncan emerged from self-imposed isolation in the late 1840s, having stepped aside from his official role; he felt he had something worthwhile to contribute. He had first-hand experience in both Britain and Sydney of the moral and cultural problems which were besetting Brisbane in the midst of the turmoil associated with the anti-transportation and separation campaigns. Girded with his unshakeable convictions, he also wanted to make Brisbane a moral, religious and better-educated community - possibly a reflection of the Scotland of his youth. Because of his superior intellect, his powerful position and the respect which he commanded within the highest civil and government circles, he was assured of attention. His leadership record in Sydney in tackling the same humanistic problems which were currently besetting Brisbane and the surrounding district should have accorded him a prominent place in the district's affairs.

The politically conservative Duncan encountered constant conflict with those of a more radical disposition such as the Langites who promoted democracy in all spheres of community life. His lack of charisma, unpopularity and failure to achieve publicly approved goals and strategies ensured that his leadership in civil affairs was not always effective. Like Evan Mackenzie before him, Duncan clearly identified problems and outlined effective remedial strategies; but he was ultimately obstructed in putting many of them into effect by local jealousies and limitations of his own personality. The leading businessmen in Brisbane would never have forgotten his high-handed decisions regarding the location of the customs house and his initial advocacy of Cleveland over Brisbane as a district port. Although his rigid personality and high intellect often got in the way of his good intentions, Duncan, as a meddler, motivator and mediator exerted significant influence in the north. He played a prominent role in effecting within Brisbane those high moral and cultural improvements which were readily recognised and extolled by Sir George Ferguson Bowen and Rev. George Wight as newcomers to Moreton Bay in the late 1850s.

Duncan's evident mistrust of democracy, along with his defensive reactions when it appeared to emerge within his sphere of influence, possibly contributed to his unfulfilled potential in a township which was regarded at Ipswich and in the interior as a hotbed of Chartism. He certainly did not have that sizeable following among the working-class or middle-class Scots that the unequally uncompromising Lang enjoyed. His level of support in Brisbane contrasted starkly with his popularity in Sydney in 1840 when he was accorded a public dinner and presented with a suitably inscribed gold medal by the operatives who regarded him as their champion. However, his arrival at Moreton Bay six years later marked the beginning of his social conservatism and therefore alienation from the proletariat whom he had grown to mistrust.[3]

While some failed, the majority of Scottish settlers at Moreton Bay who laboured outside the select pastoralist circles succeeded disproportionately, rising to the highest levels in politics, administration and business. In particular, the Scottish members of the proletariat were inordinately successful in creating their own security and prosperity. The values, attitudes and behaviours instilled into them by their national societal institutions led them to seek fiscal goals, religious redemption, middle-class respectability and to eschew intimate political involvement. This also provided impetus to the quest for moral and cultural advancement within a highly materialistic society. In contrast, many of the squatters were officially criticised for their preoccupation with making money and demonstrating 'no possible interest in the colony'. Their general lack of attachment to the country had not only resulted in the opposition of the colonial government to northern separation, but also fostered societal malaise.[4]

John Balfour was typical of the pastoralists who succeeded in accumulating capital, but contributing little to the moral and cultural betterment of colonial society. Nevertheless he was the model of respectability in his own behaviour. William Pettigrew, the epitome of Calvinist self-righteousness, admired Balfour's hard-won success. Casting aside his anti-squatter stance in 1851, he marvelled at Balfour's struggle from initial debt to current affluence. Stressing that Balfour gained his prosperity by dint of the Calvinist qualities of industry, prudence and frugality, Pettigrew neither begrudged him the 1,000 pounds per annum profit he was then reaping nor his impending visit to Britain after twelve years of unremitting toil.[5] On the other hand he poured contempt on Lord Ivory's son at Eskdale. Having recently parted company with David Graham who took up Tambourine before returning to Scotland, James Ivory let his standards drop - a reflection of his apparent failure. He was living in a dwelling that would not be regarded as fit for a pigsty in Scotland, 'one of the most miserable houses in the district'.[6] Ivory offended the standards of middle-class respectability. At nearby Cressbrook, however, David McConnel was one of a minority of squatters who combined profitable pastoralism with significant contributions to the development of the morality, religion and education of the wider rural and urban societies.

Among the prosperous proletariat, those who fulfilled their mission of respectability, property ownership, employee status and upward social mobility while contributing to cultural and moral improvements were Thomas Gray, bootmaker, Alexander Noble, baker, and George Edmonstone, butcher and town councillor. Arriving as a labourer and dying a grazier, Black Isle immigrant John Smith was possibly the most remarkable example of socio-economic mobility in the pre-separation era. With his wife Isabella Davidson, he established on Joseph North's property the strategically located and much needed Wivenhoe Inn which put an end to sly-grog trading outside Ipswich and established respectability in the area.[7] A friend of John Pettigrew and Robert Cribb, both Langites, Smith changed his allegiance from the squatter camp to the urban liberals in the quest for social justice.[8]

Conservative Ipswich solicitor Arthur Macalister, who represented the Smiths' squatter opponents, quickly established himself within local social, commercial and political life from 1850. A strong leader of cultural, educational and religious developments within Ipswich, Macalister was a shining example of a professional with a strongly developed social conscience who was also eminently successful in business and politics.[9]

William Pettigrew, the proprietor of Brisbane's first and most prosperous steam sawmill from 1853, was arguably the town's most successful, religiously-driven businessman with concern for the community. In common with most Scottish settlers he arrived at Moreton Bay, not with the intention of gaining riches, but merely to 'make an independent living'.[10] Calvinistically thorough in preparation, planning and execution, Pettigrew could not be anything but successful in his undertakings. Beset by many problems, which involved malfunctioning machinery, flooding, quarrels with his brother John, dissolution of partnership with engineer James Breckenridge and arson, the resilient Pettigrew persevered with the assistance of his half-brother John McKergow to create a profitable enterprise.[11]

A staunch upholder of nonconformist religion and intimately involved in associated educational provision, Pettigrew practised inflexible moral standards according to Presbyterian dogma. Not unexpectedly, this preciously respectable Langite exceeded his business ambitions and, within the limits of his rigidly moral framework, did his best to ameliorate Brisbane society. He possibly exemplified the stereotypical characteristics of the successful Scottish colonial.

In common with the legendary Scottish character traits which forged successful enterprise, Pettigrew was foresightful and shrewd. He provided the highly-sought, milled timber to afford shelter for the large increase in population arising from the upsurge in immigration from Britain in 1852. Like his squatter compatriots he saw the advantage of employing dependable, industrious Scottish labour and facilitated chain migration by relatives and friends, as well as sponsoring recommended countrymen. Although he generally advised such people to emigrate, he encouraged them to reach their own decisions after providing information on colonial conditions, including employment prospects and living costs. While he realistically informed colonial aspirants that most would be destined for employment in pastoralism, he gave ready encouragement to men with more specialised skills and experience needed by him and the district.[12]

* * *

The conditions at Moreton Bay for immigration from Scotland were favourable after the first flush of the gold mania started to wear off and optimistic letters from 'new chums' were published in the local Scottish newspapers which enjoyed wide circulation among a highly educated populace. For instance, the *Inverness Courier* printed a letter from a northern emigrant which not only assured Highlanders of the high regard in which they were held in the colony, but also guaranteed them well-paid employment arising from the shortage of labour.[13] A Lochaber emigre indicated that Australian employers considered Highlanders to 'have few equals' arising from their desirable worker qualities such as perseverance, prudence and endurance.[14] With the knowledge that 'Highlanders stand high 'and are the most respected [and] sought after' and 'Labour! labour! labour!' is the cry here', a former Fort William resident entreated his kinfolk to take advantage of the government immigration scheme to create a more secure life where 'the remuneration is much better, the living far superior, and the climate much more agreeable'.[15]

In the more radical, industrialised south-west, the climate for immigration to the antipodes was also favourable. The democratic spirit that pervaded the entire colony following the influx of assertive immigrants to the southern goldfields, the ensuing decision to grant responsible government, full employment and high wages induced Scotland's *Northern Star* to proclaim Australia as a working-man's paradise. In regions such as Moreton Bay, Chartism was on the ascent and privilege on the decrease. Agricultural labourers and urban workers, faced with pauperism and begrudging assistance from parish boards in Scotland, were encouraged to emigrate to such temptation-free and gold-free areas as Moreton Bay. Conditions there were deemed ideal to achieve, through frugality and industry, socio-economic goals which were beyond reach in their homeland.[16] Although differing in terms of scale, the middle-class oriented Scottish workers were driven just as intensely towards the goal of private capital formation as their squatter compatriots. Calvinism was the handmaiden of capitalism. Labour was a calling which was regarded as an economic means to a spiritual end.[17]

The vast majority of the Scots who arrived as immigrants between 1848 and 1859 worked anonymously at wage-paid labour, unheralded by advertisement, keeping clear of court lists and not coming to notice for newsworthy achievements. Most disappeared into the interior as bush labour while some unknown, single women occupied the advertised positions as milliners, domestics, laundresses, cooks and governesses principally in the towns. A handful of men, such as William Macdonald who built the first steam and flour mills at Ipswich for Joseph Fleming, received scant one sentence recognition in the press. A similar number, including educator John Scott and future mayor of Brisbane John McMaster, left their indelible marks on Queensland's history. However, most of the Scottish immigrants, numbering around 1,130, performed the jobs basic to the district's development.

With levels of 96% literacy and 94% adherence to Presbyterianism (Church of Scotland and the Free Church), Scottish immigrants possessed those middle-class values which would augment religious morality in the district and boost the demand for efficient educational provision. Enhancing their quest for self-improvement, they exemplified those work habits inculcated by Calvinism which would ensure immediate employment.[18] As products of the cohort of Kirk and parish school system, which encouraged acceptance of the status quo in Scotland, most would be primarily concerned with bettering their station in life and being minimally involved in colonial politics.[19]

Although it took until 1859 for determined signs of working-class unity to emerge, a small number from among these Scottish immigrant workers from Glasgow, Ayr and Perth assumed leadership roles in this movement.[20] Comprising little more than 10% of the total population of the Northern Districts, cliques and individuals within the largely non-political Scottish component contributed as much to maintaining the status quo as challenging it. Among the activists, they exerted a disproportionate influence in relation to their statistical inferiority.

Sir George Ferguson Bowen observed superficially that Moreton Bay was a religiously nonconformist, class-oriented society in which Scots aligned with English according to their socio-economic status and interests. Although it was a community in which the boundary between middle and working classes was fluid and could be readily breached by the acquisition of sufficient capital and property, hierarchy based on exclusive cliques and factions within cliques, was strictly enforced.[21] The pursuit of property was common to all classes, reflecting a liberal ethos in which the 'triumph of the individual and the free play of self-interest' reigned supreme. Scottish Calvinists, especially the 'hard-headed' set of 'Scotch merchants and manufacturers', settled easily into this situation where it was possible to rise by 'industry and careful habits'.[22] The Scottish workers of moderate means welcomed the chance to earn good wages and save to improve their lot in life in a society where want and poverty were unknown.

Sydney interests considered that the progress of northern society had been retarded by such relentless individualism, the influence of which was just as deleterious as factionalism. While the squatter-urban rift, Brisbane-Ipswich rivalry and North Brisbane-South Brisbane competition were well documented, the southern press added the dimensions of individual selfishness, inter-class contention and overall societal turmoil to explain the lack of cohesion in Moreton Bay's community. The *Sydney Morning Herald*, in countering the northern assertion that the government systematically neglected and even obstructed its development, argued that the fault lay within the divisive, acquisitive and unenterprising nature of Moreton Bay society. In turn, this anti-development spirit could be attributed to party interest, political contention, a 'contemptible history of local squabbles' and motives of self-interest. In fact, it was claimed, 'the normal condition of the Moreton Bay community is one of internal strife'.[23] Ironically, Brisbane's Sub-Collector of Customs, William A. Duncan, identified the same phenomenon as a blight upon Sydney's community in the early 1840s, remarking that materialism dominated colonial life to the detriment of public spirit. The problem was in fact a stultifying and divisive influence throughout the entire colony, not one merely confined to Brisbane.[24] The various factions within the Scottish sector of the population contributed significantly to this dissension and strife.

Alexander McIntyre's continuous harassment of his HRSNCo. riverside neighbours at South Brisbane, ostensibly in the name of cupidity, springs to mind as a prime example of Scottish involvement in this northern dysfunction. His aggression and petulance not only severely curtailed the company's plans for northern expansion, but also undermined South Brisbane's plans to become Moreton Bay's shipping centre.[25] Conversely, individuals such as Andrew Petrie and Arthur Macalister continually agitated to improve navigability of the Brisbane and Bremer rivers for the benefit of the entire Northern Districts. Even when community support was aroused by public meetings and memorials, such important public works were delayed by lack of finance, official investigations, reports and obstruction within the legislature.[26]

The *Moreton Bay Free Press*, with some reason to be proud of the industry, cooperation and enthusiasm of Ipswich citizens, observed that self-centred pursuit of material gain was just as important as 'party wrangling' in contributing to local discord and general improvements. After all, sugar production had failed, cotton cultivation was still experimental, agriculture was negligible and industrialisation was fixated at the level of processing primary produce, partly because of lack of community cooperation and self-seeking, individual insularity.

Individuals may well have demonstrated 'energy, effort and enterprise against all odds' to forge struggling or successful businesses - and there was a large number of pre-industrial Scots such as Thomas Gray, William Pettigrew, Alexander Cameron and James Campbell who were prosperous in this sector - but their efforts were destined to be modest and severely constrained before separation.[27] Until the population increased dramatically, perhaps by the discovery of gold, or the district attracted the long-awaited substantial capitalists, it was necessary for the aspiring industrialists to look beyond their own destinies and gain the support of a community which lacked a wider vision and the will to work together. It was lamented:

> The blighting spirit of selfishness is carried into everything. It checks individual effort; it throws a damper on enterprise; it freezes up whatever sociality of feeling which may exist; it hampers trade, it tends to encourage the government in its course of systematic neglect ... .[28]

So frustrated were Brisbane's operatives in early 1856 at the ineffectiveness of the agitation and the failure of John Richardson's persistent efforts to gain funds for much-needed local improvements, that they organised their own memorial. They had little faith in their 'betters'. In too many cases, the resolutions of public meetings were not followed up and applications for funds were not forthcoming or deadlines were missed. An important outcome of this early display of working-class consciousness under the Scottish leadership of James Swan and James Spence was the plea for 'united action and cordial cooperation' to overcome local apathy and government indifference.[29] Pastoralist energy and enterprise aside, it was apparent that individual materialism was stultifying district unity. Although the divisive and materialistic Scots of all ranks were significant contributors to this malaise, it was the initiative of their compatriots with advanced social consciousness which attempted to rectify the situation.

Referring more to the political and cultural scene than economic development, William Coote identified the source of 'the contemptible history of local squabbles' as the radical elements within the middle class.[30] The machinations of Pettigrew, Swan and their English associates dramatically changed and complicated the local political situation of 1850. By the introduction of radicalism into the expanded middle class and the formation of an alliance with the Scottish-led working class, a collision course with the opposing interests of the urban allies of Moreton Bay's 'born to rule aristocrats' was inevitable.

Several of those with radical beliefs were emigrants from the south-west of Scotland where the less violent form of Chartism flourished and trade unionism was nascent. Predisposed to identify privilege and injustice from their Scottish experience and incited by republican advocates like Lang and Parkes in the colony, James Spence, James Johnston, John Scott, John Murray, William Geddes and William Murdoch played secondary roles to middle-class agitators until local working-class consciousness broke through in 1859.

Apart from Swan, who faithfully supported liberalism and nonconformist morality as avidly as he opposed the revival of transportation, the Scottish radical leadership was transient. Fiery Stewart, moderate McConnel and responsible Richardson left the district, ambitious Pettigrew entered the fray late and the promising Knowles died prematurely. Subsequently, Lang's English imports took the lion's share of the initiative in the campaign for increased democratic practice and justice within Brisbane's institutions.

* * *

The establishment in Scotland had done its best by legal and informal means to create a docile proletariat without political pretensions. In addition to the overriding effort to create a new life in a new land, this social opiate within the Scottish cultural baggage may explain the relative lack of assertion by the Scottish proletariat at Moreton Bay before 1859. Anticipating that popular democracy sought by the Chartists and trade unionists would inevitably lead to excessive change, Lord Cockburn ensured that the Scottish Reform Act of 1832 kept power in the hands of an upper middle class which was sympathetic to the maintenance of aristocratic and landowner power.[31] In common with other members of the Scottish establishment, Cockburn feared that, although the 'opinions of the great majority of the lower orders here are safe and constitutional', mechanics and radicals would eventually learn their strength and abuse it. It was with a sense of relief that Cockburn noted that the law-abiding common Scots had not resorted to violence as 'the Scotch are bad mobbers'. Not used to large public meetings of protest and 'not allowed to express their opinions regularly along with their superiors', their inexperience provoked violence on the rare occasions when they were aroused. Almost as bad as revolution was the prospect of democracy 'when the House shall be returned by mere population'.[32]

With social control exerted by various social, political, religious, educational and cultural agencies in Scotland, it is not surprising that Paisley's impoverished weavers perceived their plight as a community problem. They were incapable of seeing their employers as class enemies whose management policies destroyed their livelihoods. Convinced of the inter-relatedness of class interests purveyed by the same propaganda of their colonial masters, immigrants from the harsh Scottish economic system were only released from this ideological bondage by the influences of urban radicalism and mateship of post-1851 Australia. Brisbane workers were well aware of the trade union agitation occurring in Sydney in 1856 under the leadership of Henry Parkes to institute the eight hour day - eventually achieved at Petrie's firm in 1860.

In the mid-1850s, such workers as James Spence were fully conscious that they made up the majority of the population and possessed the potential to exert political power. It was just a matter of time before their class interests were represented in the legislature of their adopted land by those who shared the same values and beliefs.[33] Integrating easily into colonial society and being comparatively well-educated, they were attracted by the democratic fervour and saw the benefits of submitting temporarily to middle-class liberal leadership. Others, probably the majority, ignored the currents of change, and accepted the situation in which they found themselves. Making full use of the desirable personality traits and habits developed at home, they got on with the task of self-improvement.

In 1859 Scottish-led Brisbane workers had reached the stage of development where they clearly defined their class enemies and acted decisively upon such sentiments. Colonial representatives of the Scottish establishment, such as absentee squatters Thomas Coutts from British banking circles and Ross aristocrat R.R. Mackenzie, were not popular with the urban operatives. Possessing long memories, the working class full remembered squatter supression and threats to their livelihood during the district-wide conflict centred upon the threatened importation of cheap labour. They were adamantly opposed to the leadership pretensions of such pastoralists who retired to the town where they enjoyed the profits from expropriated rural labour - facilitated by a biased magistracy and unjust legislation.

Emboldened by new-found assertion under Scottish leadership, the workers mounted a successful protest against Mackenzie's appointment to lead the welcoming party for Queensland's first Governor. A forceful letter of complaint published in the *Moreton Bay Courier* during September 1859, probably written by Perth cartwright John Murray, influenced Mackenzie's decision to withdraw.[34] Class conflict was out in the open for the first time. While foreshadowing a separate working-class demonstration of welcome, the missive suggested that appropriate symbols of squatter exploitation be displayed during Mackenzie's mission - a reflection of pastoral labour's bitter relationship with the squatters. While admitting Mackenzie was 'not a bad fellow for a squatter', the correspondent nevertheless condemned the choice of a pastoralist to represent the people of the new colony. Giving pride of place to the infamous Masters and Servants' Act, he also recommended that the new Governor be familiarised with the armoury of devices by which pastoralists exploited workers to reap their fortunes.

> Let a squatter magistrate follow with the scale of justice unequally balanced in his hand .... Let a poor shepherd follow him with handcuffs on and labelled, "disobedience of orders", "insolence", "misconduct", "lost sheep", "forfeiture of wages", "imprisonment" etc. A squatter's agent might follow with an imaginary list of articles never supplied to a shepherd, but for which he is expected to pay long figures. ... we do not fear the squatters, but we do not wish to honour them.[35]

Unlike the workers' unsuccessful, bread and butter protest to the Government Resident concerning the preferential employment of German labour to repair Brisbane's streets two years earlier, this campaign was based on class and racial antipathy.[36] Yet there was no hint of any intentions to overthrow the capitalist system in which they lived and worked. Although the workers were well organised, they were no threat to the prevailing system. Bereft of many skilled artisans with middle-class pretensions, they had not reached that advanced stage of consciousness which demanded the creation of a new social order.

Worker vitriol extended to Spence who had been invited to join the official organising committee to welcome the Governor, in the company of a cross-section of Brisbane's elite and prosperous middle class. Stung by the implication that he was a class traitor, Spence exchanged membership from that select body for leadership in the separate working men's demonstration. Having briefly associated with Judge Alfred Lutwyche, Daniel Roberts, Robert Douglas, George Raff, Andrew Petrie, James Swan and R.R. Mackenzie, Spence joined humbler Scottish comrades such as John Murray, James Gledhill, William Murdoch, John McKenzie and William Geddes at the proletarian steering body which met in John Scott's schoolroom.[37] This affirmation of worker solidarity probably contributed to the failure of the middle-class initiated Queensland Liberal Association, formed two months previously in Fortitude Valley.[38]

One quarter of the 170 subscribers to the working-class demonstration fund were Scots, many from Glasgow and nearby Ayr.[39] The large, scarf-clad working-class deputation sporting distinctive trade badges and preceded by a band, stood proudly before Governor Bowen as Murray delivered its welcome. Sensing community disunity, the Governor's reply was curt, didactic and deflating, intended to reprimand the operatives and disabuse them of their presumption. Denying that there was such a separate class in a society in which all citizens were indeed workers, Bowen resorted to the increasingly discredited hoary palliative used by the Scottish establishment and their colonial representatives which stressed the inter-relation of the interests of all sectors of society. He harangued, 'Capital is powerless without labour, and labour is unprofitable without the aid of capital'.[40]

Notwithstanding such rear-guard efforts by entrenched interests to deflate working-class consciousness, the patrician Governor and his allies were warned in the final days of 1859 that 'the struggle between classes was inevitable and should be prepared for'. It was proclaimed that the economic interests of employers and employees were in fact hostile to one another.[41]

* * *

To reinforce conservatism and curb the emergence of such radicalism in those aspects of colonial life which came under his sphere of influence, Duncan did his utmost as Brisbane's leading bureaucrat and member of the established power clique. Forever vigilant against abuse of privilege and rashness of popular power, he took it upon himself to act as arbiter while administering Brisbane's Customs and the School of Arts.[42] This stance was congruent with his defence of the 1856 New South Wales constitution and his attack on colonial democratic forces from the platform of the latter. Duncan's arguments for maintenance of the status quo were loudly lauded by the government and civil establishment both in Australia and Britain. Whereas William Charles Wentworth's proposal to establish a 'bunyip aristocracy' was popularly mocked, Duncan defended the dilution of this component in the form of a nominated upper house within a constitution which approximated the British safeguards of just government - monarchy, lords and commons.[43]

Duncan's experience with the Scottish aristocracy predisposed him to reserve a prominent role for this ancient British institution within his brand of political philosophy. He was intensely proud of the close relationship he and his father enjoyed with Sir Charles Forbes, proprietor of the Aberdeenshire estate in which his family possessed a rare perpetual tenancy. In addition, he personally escorted the youthful Scottish aristocrats Lord Henry Scott and Lord Schonberg on some pleasurable and some forgettable excursions, during their visit with their tutor Rev. Henry Stobart to Moreton Bay in 1853.[44] Despite Duncan's high regard for members of this privileged class in Britain, he placed great faith in the thinking section of the traditional middle class in determining the colony's future. Invariably he was especially wary of the Langites, the advocates of popular democracy.

Duncan upheld the claims of those with superior birth, intelligence, education, enterprise and talent to assume a dominant role in colonial government. On the other hand he despised the socially-divisive Langite Chartists, the ascendant liberals, the uninformed plebians and most of the upstart squattocracy alike. Content to march to the beat of a different drum, this Scottish isolate did not even appear to have been particularly impressed by those Scots in Brisbane, such as Richard Cannan, Robert Douglas and Thomas Boyland, who supported the status quo.

Duncan's bureaucratic decisions, most of which had direct impact on individual prosperity, locality progress and district trade, had a divisive effect on the community, especially within Brisbane. Not since the short stay of the cavalier Evan Mackenzie were the actions of one influential man so critical to the development of Moreton Bay. By a mixture of iconoclastic and brave deeds he offended most of the settlers, alienated the squatters, struck a blow against racism and attempted to alter the dynamics of business and commerce within Brisbane.

Swan levelled severe criticism against Duncan's high-handedness based on incontrovertible 'private opinion' in overriding the sound judgement of local interests based on long experience. While recognising the right of officials to make recommendations affecting their departments, Swan questioned decisions based on 'the superior right of government officers to sit in judgement upon matters affecting public convenience, or upon some fancied superiority of intelligence' and treating local wisdom with contempt. [45] This supposed politically-neutral bureaucrat was in fact a compulsive meddler in local affairs - despite his avowed intention in 1846 to remain aloof. [46]

The two public meetings called in December 1859 to agitate for Brisbane's incorporation as a municipality enabled Duncan's adversaries to level charges of duplicity against him. On the basis of seniority as a government official and his experience in establishing Sydney's municipal government, Duncan was elected to chair the first gathering which resolved to petition the Governor-General for incorporation of Brisbane. While these meetings brought to the surface the 'Kilkenny cat feeling' existing between Duncan and Robert Cribb, they created a temporary alliance between the working class and conservative forces to ensure that the object of the petition was achieved.

Cribb, who argued that a municipality was premature in the light of impending separation, was opposed by Duncan and a solid group of supporters including Mackenzie, Raff and Pettigrew. During the second rowdy meeting, the working class, represented by Spence and Murray, ensured Brisbane's application by providing guarded support for Duncan's clique. Although they suspected the commitment of that elitist group to the long-term future of Brisbane, these representatives of labour emphasised their aspirations were intimately connected with the town's future. Hence it was in class interests to ensure Brisbane's incorporation, even if it meant rare class collaboration. While applauding the outcome, The *Moreton Bay Courier's* editorial of 12 April 1859 placed no faith in those who were prominent in bringing it about. It declared openly: 'We don't want such men as Duncan, Raff and Mackenzie'. Instead, unqualified support was given to men of the quality of the soundly-defeated but unbowed Cribb and others whose 'hearts [were] tied to the town' as the future political representatives.[47]

Well before this, probably since the middle of the decade, Duncan had been clandestinely charting his course to the pinnacle of the colonial public service in Sydney. He had no intention of committing himself to Moreton Bay's future as a permanent resident. With an eye on Colonel John G.N. Gibbes' position in Sydney as Collector of Customs, he brought himself to the favourable attention of the southern cabal. On hearing gossip of Gibbes' imminent retirement, Duncan immediately commenced treading the corridors of power. He sent a welcoming letter to the Deas Thomsons on their return from an overseas trip, ingratiated himself with Moreton Bay's visiting Judge Milford and lobbied leading legislator Stuart Alexander Donaldson. Furthermore he ensured that his widely acclaimed paper defending Wentworth's new constitution was placed in the hands of such powerful officials as Chief Justice Alfred Stephen, as Judge Therry, the Colonial Secretary, the Attorney General and the Governor. Waiting patiently in the wings, he saw out his time 'when not engaged in official duties in library, music room and garden, varied by just as much visiting as the forms of society require'.[48]

Duncan's abiding interest in culture was not confined to self-gratification and community neglect. He may have been regarded as a temporary Brisbanite, but he played a significant role in transforming its rough and ready image. Plotting a course parallel to that of the equally important radical dissenters, this leading Catholic layman was intensely involved in coaxing the cultural awakening of the north. Brisbane, the 'hotbed of Chartism', was transformed by gifted individuals like Duncan and the incompatible democratic forces into a decent, law-abiding society.

* * *

In common with Duncan in 1846, Lang found the Moreton Bay District some six months earlier to be more demoralised and irreligious than any other in New South Wales.[49] With an element of truth, Lang ascribed this moral transformation of the population by 1859 to the influence of his God-fearing immigrants - a verdict echoed by Congregational minister George Wight. According to Wight, the orderly, church-going population met the moral standards found in most parts of Scotland.[50] In contrast to the established settlers, the Lang imports and their like-minded cohorts had been motivated to look beyond the mere pursuit of material wealth, deeming it their mission to enlighten and improve the uncivilised community in which they found themselves.

Lang's imports themselves were not immodest in pressing such catalytic claims. They definitely were different from the frontiersmen in dress, manners and morals. George Holt, nearly a centenarian in 1923, claimed to the *Brisbane Courier*: 'The Lang people completely revolutionised society in Brisbane and Ipswich'. Their common garb, consisting of 'long-faced black hats, frock coats and gloves', contrasted starkly with the colonials' dress of cabbage-tree hats, blue dungaree shirts and moleskins, reflecting overtly a set of differing values and providing a portent of inevitable clash of interests.[51] In all events, the *Moreton Bay Courier*, which under Swan's proprietorship reflected sympathy with the stance adopted by Lang's arrivals, challenged Brisbane's nonconformists to seize the opportunity offered by impending separation to create a new civilisation in the north, to further disseminate humanising influences. An editorial in the early months of 1856 foreshadowed success arising from a considered attempt to implant a liberal humanistic community based on 'moral principle enshrined by christian purity'.[52]

To bring about such a virtuous society it was necessary to modify the values and expectations of those who comprised the operative and labouring sections of the community. Concurrently with the moral restrictions imposed by evangelical religion, a two-pronged attack was mounted upon drunkenness and pub culture - the two major contributors towards immorality and crime among the lower orders. From 1849 regulations governing the operation of hotels were strictly enforced, steps were taken to stultify the all-pervasive sly-grog trade and the establishment of temperance and total abstinence societies was encouraged.

Generally the establishments conducted by the large contingent of Scottish publicans were exemplars of respectability. John Smith's Wivenhoe Inn was lauded for that quality by the McConnels, praised for the high standard of its hospitality by Dowse, Pettigrew and Bartley and welcomed by the authorities as a counter-influence to the trade in illicit grog.[53] Other former Kilcoy pioneers who gravitated toward the hotel trade were Donald Davidson and John McDonald in Ipswich and Alexander McIntyre, a late entrant, at South Brisbane. George McAdam, originally one of the Leslies' retinue, conducted the Sovereign in Queen Street before turning to storekeeping, while John Souter took over John McCabe's Commercial at South Brisbane in 1855.[54]

Following the strict implementation of the New Publican's Act in 1849, McIntyre was brought to trial on one occasion for allowing music to be played on his premises and Souter was prosecuted for opening on a Sunday. Apart from those indiscretions, the Scottish-run hotels were in the main orderly, McCabe's being singled out as a model establishment.[55] In fact Souter went rather overboard to meet the lighting regulations, totally illuminating his building with gas - the first in Brisbane.[56] As a result of strict adherence to regulations by such reputable publicans and the growth of the local temperance movement, there was only one case of drunkenness in Brisbane for the last week in September 1857.[57] This commendable statistic had dire consequences for the hitherto profitable nightwatchman service which had been conducted by James Macalister since September 1849 - no doubt arising in part from the excesses of the *Hashemy* exiles who had been unloaded upon Brisbane earlier in that year.[58]

The total abstinence movement - an omnipresent, female-driven crusade in hard-drinking Scotland - was revived locally in 1854 following five years of inactivity.[59] Apparently the district's renowned drinking reputation was getting further out of hand and swift remedial action was needed. Boosted by the nonconformist clerics Stewart and Sinclair with support from Wickham, the association eventually flourished among members of the working class, particularly when popular leaders Spence and Johnston became involved. Between them they exerted considerable influence to ensure that working men heeded Thomas Dowse's appeal to give up dram drinking and thereby 'stop the flood of intemperance sweeping through these beautiful districts'.[60]

James Johnston, a future member of the Legislative Assembly, advanced the anti-liquor crusade and assisted in establishing the Brisbane Total Abstinence Society's credentials by writing a series of forceful letters to the *Moreton Bay Courier*. Therein he deplored the widespread drunkenness arising from the trade of hotels which remained open on polling day for the seat of the County of Stanley in April 1856.[61] It would appear that this dour *Lima* immigrant together with Glaswegian James Spence became significant influences in the reformation of Brisbane's popular drinking habits. Spence was able to announce with pride at the temperance meeting on 13 May 1859 that 'Drinking habits are getting into bad odor with the workmen of Brisbane...'. He cited the unremitting toil of the crew constructing the new gaol as a shining example of the moral revolution associated with the rise of temperance. Spence reported: 'There has not been one case of drunkenness before the Bench in which any workman at the gaol was the offender'.[62] This was indeed a victory for respectability, the common view holding that immorality and crime supposedly originated within the labouring section of the community.[63]

The likes of Spence, Johnston and Pettigrew did their best to implement Lang's plans for the moral improvement of northern society, placing great faith in the assertion of the tenets and institutions of Scottish Presbyterianism. The diary and correspondence homeward from Pettigrew reveal the central place in the lives of the Scottish common folk of Presbyterian Calvinism. The dour Pettigrew was continually aware that his every action needed to be acceptable to God if he expected to be among the chosen few to be saved. As one who was grateful to God for each day of his life, Pettigrew periodically goaded himself to show even more faith and vigilance 'in this heavenward journey' for 'every idle word a man shall speak he shall give account thereof in the day of judgment'. Even toothache was viewed as divine retribution occasioned by sin and interpreted as a warning to redirect the sinner on the straight and narrow path.[64]

Pettigrew was devoted to his calling, whether he was surveying allotments at Cleveland Point or keeping up an exhausting work-schedule among Dr Simpson's gardens, fields and herds at Woogaroo. Never a moment was idly wasted nor money spent heedlessly. He accounted for every halfpenny spent on dire necessities. In fact Pettigrew was so frugal that he was able to lend money to his employer. His only forms of recreation were short walks, attending public meetings and lectures at the School of Arts.[65]

The behavioural deviations of others rarely escaped Pettigrew's humourless scrutiny. His propensity for minding the morals of others even led one promiscuous couple of fellow-workers at Woogaroo to set up false sexual assignations to trick him into his indignant fulminations. A committed Langite, Pettigrew had little time for the squatters 'humbugging' about their runs to Simpson, carrying on 'vile conversations' and 'punishing' bottles of 'Colonial wine'.[66] Having made the acquaintance of virtually every Moreton Bay squatter, his only positive comments on members of that caste were reserved for John Balfour. He admired this arch-squatter from the Brisbane Valley for his financial acumen and success.[67]

Pettigrew revealed himself as the exemplar of morality, being severely judgemental towards those who did not live up to his exacting standards. He held the Sabbath dear, reserving most of his self-righteous reproaches for those who travelled, drank, frolicked, did business or worked on this day of rest and religion. He invariably read the Bible, the Confession of Faith, history, collections of sermons and other religious publications. Even after walking around a paddock with Simpson one Sunday he reproached himself for sinning. Being on the Brisbane River midway between Ipswich and Brisbane, he nevertheless felt at ease journeying by steamer on the Sabbath to the Evangelical church at North Brisbane and the Presbyterian church on the opposite side of the river.

Apparently varying the amount he placed in the collection plate according to the quality of the sermon, Pettigrew scrutinised severely the sincerity, spirit and communication skills of the officiating ministers. On one occasion he deemed that Stewart excelled, demonstrating 'more of the gospel & power thereof than before & less of himself'. Because of its divisive effect on the nonconformist congregation and the destruction of Lang's ecumenical plans, Pettigrew initially rejected the Free Church formed at South Brisbane. On the one occasion he visited the Church of England chapel, he found the order of service incomprehensible. To the Roman Catholics he demonstrated the anticipated antipathy and bigotry of a Calvinist dissenter.[68]

* * *

Such was the type of Scot who was successful in the colonies and upon whom Lang relied. Lang hoped that individuals of this stamp would provide more support to his religious plans for this colony than he received at home. Ostracised by the Church of Scotland and the Free Church, unable to entice one Presbyterian cleric and attracting less than anticipated support from the Scottish people, Lang planned to assert nonconformism in the district by importing an amalgam of Presbyterians such as Pettigrew, Congregationalists and Baptists. In doing so, Lang tapped into and hopefully wished to harness in the antipodes the dissenting forces of democratic consciousness among 'the British middle and social orders [who] were abandoning the Established churches' in droves for nonconformism and social radicalism.[69] He was thoroughly familiar with ecumenical cross-border links being forged by Scottish and English evangelicals through shared educational initiatives, social reform agendas, radical protest, temperance associations and interchange of ministers.

Lang would have been well aware that the puritanism accompanying such proletarian alienation in Scotland encouraged 'religious expressions of social protest' within middle and lower class cultures. He anticipated that 'the will of an urban majority' engineered by his immigration scheme would produce a change in Moreton Bay's sinful culture.[70] Mindful of the impossibility of establishing Presbyterian predominance, Lang decided to formalise an evangelical union to provide religious and moral leadership within Brisbane. Whereas he was familiar with the first Evangelical Alliance created at London in 1846, Rev. Charles Stewart's experience with its equivalent body in Birmingham ensured that he 'grasped [the] ideal of evangelical unity even more consistently than his mentor'.[71]

During the planning phase and for a short time after arrival, doctrinal problems appeared to be of little consequence in Lang's bold move in establishing a unique composite which promoted its scriptural commonality under Stewart, a Scottish Baptist minister. Putting aside the contentious practice of adult baptism, which eventually assumed some significance in contributing to the demise of his creation, Lang saw no practical barriers to realising the establishment of such an 'Evangelical Alliance' in Moreton Bay.[72] Regardless of Stewart's training, preaching, devotion and pastoral strength, the 'crotchety' Presbyterians within this 'broad and scriptually based church' would never be contented until they were shepherded by a 'thoroughly Presbyterian minister'. Thus Stewart soon found himself waging a 'desperate war' against devotees of the Westminster Confession of Faith.[73]

Lang's prediction that the Presbyterians would defer to the views and opinions of the other sects to secure unanimity was totally unfounded. Scottish nationalism and the hold which the Kirk exerted on the Scottish psyche proved to be major impediments. It appears that Scots were willing to align according to class and assimilate socially in the quest for material prosperity and democratic progress, but in matters of theology they were inflexibly attached to one religion and one religion only - even if it meant choosing between the established and evangelical versions. Cliff Cumming's analysis of Scottish Presbyterianism at Port Phillip is equally applicable to the north, especially to the failure of Lang's ecumenical model:

> The Scots Presbyterians not only maintained their distinctiveness, but were encouraged by their home Church of Scotland to do so. While they found it expedient, on occasions, to form an alliance with other Protestant groups within the community, they never sought to do this at the expense of their own national or regional identity'.[74]

The defection of the Scottish Presbyterians in December 1849 from the United Presbyterian Church before it was restructured as the United Evangelical Church began the process of disintegration which was completed with Stewart's resignation in late 1854. Initially satisfied that the United Presbyterian Church formed under Stewart's leadership would follow the worship and doctrine of the evangelical Presbyterian Church, eleven Scots led by David McConnel dissented from the Evangelical Alliance which aimed to unite all sects within its congregation. Upholding the Westminster Confession of Faith as basic to their Scottish religion, not willing to embrace any other principles and realising the unfavourable repercussions of Lang's failure to attract Scots in any significant numbers, the uncompromising Presbyterians realised that they were a minority within this church. William Pettigrew commented to the Reverend John Bradley in a letter homewards: 'It was understood all along to be a Presbyterian church but recent arrivals had augmented the number of independents, baptists etc so that they conjointly had a majority and swamped the Presbyterian interest'.[75]

By the decision to establish a separate Presbyterian church at a meeting held at the Reverend Thomas Mowbray's residence at Kangaroo Point on 12 December 1849, the intransigent Scots provided additional fodder for Sydney's anti-separation propaganda.[76] The early split within the nonconformist community reinforced the southern argument that Moreton Bay was indeed a disunited community. This was yet more evidence of the intra-township conflicts which arose from the relentless pursuit of party interests.

Whereas the Baptist Swan and the Congregationalist Richardson remained with the parent body as trustees of the United Evangelical Church, Gray, McLean, McIntyre, Cairncross, McAdam, McNaught, McConnel, Edmonstone, McKergow and George Raff formed the committee for the Presbyterian church which affiliated with the Synod of Eastern Australia.[77] Considering Brisbane's formative radical nonconformist ethos, the Highland background of the first three men and McConnel's family connections, it is not unexpected that the new church was associated with the Free Church rather than the conservative Church of Scotland. Mowbray's participation was limited by his indifferent health and initial adherence to the Synod of Australia's neutrality toward the Scottish religious factions. However, he conducted occasional services following the periodical bouts of illness among a succession of Presbyterian clerics who came to the north partly to convalesce. Credited as being Brisbane's first Presbyterian minister, he also had filled the void of infant baptism created by the dictates of Stewart's Baptist faith. He subsequently lent a helping hand to the Reverends Walter McLeod, Alex. Sinclair and Thomas Bell when illness impeded the fulfilment of their pastoral duties.[78]

Before the ministry centred on the new church at South Brisbane was taken up in August 1851 by McConnel's brother-in-law and Free Churchman, the Reverend Walter Ross McLeod, Lang attempted to change Brisbane's affiliation to his newly established Synod of New South Wales - a recently-formed, third, gratuitous division within the colonial Presbyterian church. Lang was incensed not only by the northern visit of the Reverend A. Salmon, Moderator of the Synod of Eastern Australia, who expounded Free Church principles to large Scottish audiences, but by the initial appointment of the Reverend John Tait to the Brisbane position. Never forgetting the Synod of Australia's preference for Tait over him for the position of Moderator in October 1841, Lang proposed a London-born Mr Lodge from his faction as the much-needed, 'thoroughly Presbyterian minister at Moreton Bay'. The subsequent rejection of Lang's counsel indicates that his motivational

210

and reformist influences among the partisan Moreton Bay Scots over matters religious were far less effective than those arising from his socio-political agenda.[79]

This alignment with the Free Church demonstrated blatant disregard for the wishes of the established Church of Scotland which attempted to export the Disruption to Australia. The rejection of the uncomfortable neutrality towards the two forms of the Scottish church decreed by the Synod of Australia and the destruction of Lang's dream exacerbated the cracks in the social and religious edifice of local and colonial society.[80] Importantly, the tenacious attachment of Moreton Bay Scots to the evangelical form of their national religious institution in the face of opposition from the establishment in Scotland and within Australia 'testified to the fact that whatever the geographical horizons of the emigrants, their mental horizons remained emphatically Scottish'.[81]

However, when McConnel reported to Salmon in late 1849 that there were some divisions among the local Presbyterians, he indicated that Scottish religious disunity arose as much from their Scottish background as local differences.[82] Pettigrew, who swallowed his pride to become a member of the South Brisbane committee three years later, wrote home to his clerical friend Barclay in October 1850 that he originally intended to have no part in the Moreton Bay's Free church. Apparently remaining true to Lang's principles which deplored the dependence of the clergy upon state support, he was also critical of the lack of accountability for the manner in which those funds were spent. His disjointed style of writing reflected perversity rather than lucid argument. Allied in Scotland to the United Presbyterian church, the third body emerging from the Disruption of 1843, the normally Kirk-centred Pettigrew also expressed his opposition to Brisbane's Free church in terms of the sectarianism it fostered. Like Lang, he was evidently disappointed at the role taken by the South Brisbane model in initiating the disintegration of a bold religious innovation to unify Brisbane's evangelical sects.[83]

During McLeod's incumbency which lasted less than a year, the minister conducted services on both sides of the river, the North Brisbane site being the Court House.[84] In the course of Sinclair's term of four years, the manse was established on church property at Ann Street - a portent of the impending decline of southside Grey Street as the principal place of worship.[85] By 1857 a split between the South and North Brisbane congregations was evident, exacerbated by Sinclair's replacement - another Free churchman, the fiery Reverend Charles Ogg. Pettigrew recalled: 'He began quarrelling at first with one and then another'.[86] When the new church was built at Ann Street by Joshua Jeays, an irremediable rift between South Brisbanites and their pastor and antagonism between the two congregations became clearly manifest. Badger as he might, Ogg could not persuade the South Brisbanites to worship across the river. The Reverend Alexander Hay reported, 'The contention was so sharp between the two parts of the congregation, that they parted asunder one from the other'. Although South Brisbane Presbyterians retained ownership of their church, they were left without 'a settled pastor' until mid 1864.[87]

Mowbray, while commenting on Oggs' unsatisfactory report on the state of the Brisbane Presbyterian community in 1857, implored his fellow parishioners to 'cultivate a better spirit and suppress any little differences which might arise among them'.[88] Lang's ensuing comments on the division of the national church into three synods in a letter to the *Moreton Bay Courier* were equally applicable to the Brisbane situation where the emergence of three congregations was impending. Referring to the plans of the Stewart's successor, the Reverend Thomas Bell, to form a congregation loosely affiliated with the United Presbyterian Church at Creek Street, Lang enveighed, 'Now, it must be evident to all of us that these divisions destroy the unity of effort so necessary to the prosperity of any religion today'.[89]

Not one to give up without a fight, Lang travelled to Brisbane to buy the William Street property containing the United Evangelical Church for Presbyterians such as Andrew Petrie who followed the anti-state stance of the Synod of New South Wales. Looking to the national scene on the eve of separation, Lang interfered in Brisbane's Presbyterian affairs again. In yet another letter to the *Moreton Bay Courier*, the third in three months, he advocated that the local Presbyterian church distance itself from the Scottish and New South Wales organisations and take control of its own affairs.[90] Political separation should be accompanied by religious independence.

Although he was consistent in his argument that the differences between the two Moreton Bay congregations should be overcome in the name of local unity, he sowed the seeds of further dissent. Not only did he object to the formation of yet another congregation under Bell at Creek Street, but he disapproved of the proposal to call it the United Presbyterian Church. Amid Lang's accustomed financial mismanagement in dispersing the sale money to the three churches within the evangelical alliance, Bell's congregation refused the opportunity to take over the William Street church, especially with the self-appointed Lang as one of the five trustees. Furthermore, in defiance of Lang's advice, the short-lived United Presbyterian Church intended to forge links with the Scottish parent body.[91] Originally appointed by Lang to succeed Stewart, the dying Bell became a Gregor-like pariah in his eyes when the newly-formed church thereafter broke away from the Synod of New South Wales. Lang's plans to gain a foothold in Brisbane for his Synod, which eschewed state connections, were dashed by this defection.

The United Presbyterian church, incorporating Congregationalists who sought a home after Stewart resigned and the United Evangelical Church was disbanded, survived for less than a year. Following Bell's sudden death in 1859, members of his congregation either dispersed or joined the Independents. The Creek Street property was then offered to the Reverend George Wight who had arrived from Scotland with the mission of forming Brisbane's first Congregational church.[92]

Despite the apparent chauvinism of the Presbyterian Church, ecumenical cooperation among the nonconformist churches was still flourishing. As each dissenting denomination established its own church, the support given by other sects was plainly evident by the presence of leading nonconformist ministers in planning meetings, provision of facilities, participation in inaugural ceremonies, preaching and unselfish gestures such as the Creek Street gift.[93] Sinclair played a leading role in the establishment of Brisbane's Baptist congregation in which Swan and Spence were among the leading laymen. In February 1859 John Petrie built its neat stone chapel which allegedly resembled the Cathedral of Pisa.[94]

It was only by a team effort from Rev. Charles Stewart, Dr Henry Challinor and Thomas Welsby, fellow *Fortitude* immigrants, that the evangelical alliance survived for a few years at Ipswich. No doubt contributing to his deterioration in health, Stewart attempted to keep Lang's vision alive after being let down by those recruited to take charge of the other urban component of the Protestant union at Ipswich. Joseph Clift, preacher from the *Fortitude* and the Reverend Thomas Kingsford of the *Chaseley* proved to be more hindrance than help. The former quickly abandoned his post to head southwards and the latter stayed two years and forsook Lang's brief, opting for the role of a Presbyterian minister, unconnected with the alliance. After removing to the Darling Downs, Kingsford was replaced in 1853 by Scottish cleric Rev. Dr Walter Lambie Nelson who founded Presbyterianism according to the established church on a firm footing in Ipswich. After a brief union with the Baptists, the Congregationalists struck out to form their own church under Rev. Edward Griffith. Thus the dissolution of the Protestant alliance in Ipswich was well ahead of the corresponding decline in Brisbane.[95]

The United Evangelical Church, the Scottish-led vehicle of early Protestantism in Moreton Bay was disbanded by yet another demonstration of local factionalism and disunity. Conceived by Lang's fertile and bigoted mind, its short existence was due to the indefatigable efforts of his faithful servant Charles Stewart. Although Stewart was unable to prevent the Presbyterian defection, he managed to retain a large portion of the remainder as long as his health held. Stewart, as a 'valiant servant of Christ', is remembered in nonconformist circles as one who 'succeeded in creating a beachead for evangelical Protestantism of the Reformed ... variety against the strong tides of infidelity, Puseyism and Popery'.[96] Although such sentiments were rejected by the lay founder of the Baptist religion in Queensland, the moral revolution which this Protestant band wrought upon Moreton Bay society is undisputed.

* * *

On the other side of the religious fence, Duncan and Wickham exerted lay leadership roles in the Roman Catholic and Anglican churches respectively. A staunch Anglican, Wickham supported the succession of Church of England incumbents from the hapless Gregor to the assertive Reverend Henry Offley Irwin. It was predictable that the incumbency of the latter, whose brief was to tighten internal discipline and re-establish the authority of the Bishop of Newcastle over a lay-dominated parish, would be controversial. Supporting Irwin and Bishop

William Tyrrell in a range of issues which were interpreted locally as introducing Puseyism into the church, Wickham, with the backing of both English and Scottish parishioners, provided the strength to implement such controversial measures. Scottish representation among those who supported Irwin's most divisive decision to introduce a collection into the service included John Innes, J. Leith Hay, Robert Davidson and William Cairncross, a former adherent to Presbyterianism and founder of its South Brisbane church. Threatening to walk out of church on the conclusion of the sermon with Police Magistrate William A. Brown were Scottish Episcopalians Mackenzie and Douglas. They mounted a fierce opposition to this controversial innovation.[97] Inclined towards Low Church theology rather than the threatening High Church variety, these prominent Scots had long left the home country before the Oxford Movement made a foray into the Episcopalian religion which was the preserve of many of the Scottish elite and their camp followers.

Duncan was a long-standing opponent of the colonial Church of England as an obstacle to religious equality within a plural society, battling to have the status of the Catholic primate recognised as equivalent within the Church of England. He challenged the Church of England's establishment claims and its opposition to a Catholic Episcopal See in Sydney.[98] With the Anglican authorities he waged a pamphlet war, systematically dismantled their theological arguments and even attacked the very validity of their religious orders.[99] Furthermore, his hard-hitting editorials in the *Australasian Chronicle* resulted in a diminution of anti-Catholic prejudice and misrepresentation within colonial newspapers.[100]

Still harbouring dislike for the divisive influence of Irish Catholicism and having turned against Polding's Benedictine-based style of administration, this champion of colonial Catholicism arrived in the north with combative experience in yet another critical area relevant to northern moral development. Confining his northern activism to voluminous, anti-Benedictine correspondence as "Icolmkill" and other noms de plume in the *Freeman's Journal*, Duncan otherwise stayed aloof from local religious contention. Instead he provided lay leadership within a church void of fellow Scots.[101] He closely cooperated with the Reverend James Hanly, his parish priest, to found the second largest and most active religious congregation in Brisbane. Devoting much of his spare time to church activities, Duncan worked tirelessly to obtain property for a church, supervised the building of St Stephen's chapel in 1850, enriched worship by his musical skills and exerted a management role over the parish school.[102]

* * *

Duncan well knew that the Scottish educational aim was to provide universal schooling for children, despite its far from perfect mid-nineteenth century record with female literacy in many Highland areas and within the industrial centres. Nevertheless English political leaders admired Scotland's success in creating 'commons' which 'were considered to be the most enlightened people of [that] rank in Europe'.[103] In supporting popular education, the moral guardians adopted two differing philosophical stances. Whereas the supporters of the status quo advocated the use of society's religious, educational and cultural institutions to ensure social control and ideological conformity, the radical nonconformist elements viewed such organs as enriching and liberating agents.[104]

Needless to say, the prominent educational proponents and reformers in the Moreton Bay District had been conditioned by their British experience. At that time the Scottish educational system maintained its reputation for producing the highest levels of mass literacy in Europe. The report of the Scottish education commission of 1868 attributed the disproportionate success of 'Scotch skilled labourers and Scotsman of business everywhere' to its superior grass-roots education. Reflecting the political slant, W.E. Gladstone even ascribed Scotland's transformation from economic and social backwardness to the widespread availability of quality education within the nation.[105]

Lord Henry Cockburn, an architect of the Scottish Reform Act of 1832, made no secret of the social control intent behind this strong educational tradition. Writing in his journal in 1843, this bastion of the Scottish establishment revealed that church and school along with other social agencies were designed to inculcate subservience. Cockburn intimated that these institutions aimed 'to reconcile the poor man to his condition, by explaining its necessity and uses, by showing how happiness may be extracted out of it, and how the individual may rise above it, while the moral and personal duties of education, temperance, pecuniary prudence, affection, domestic order, a taste for intellectual culture, and the habit of decorous recreation are shown to be all within their reach ...'.[106]

Such mass education was therefore designed to ensure social stability in a near-revolutionary atmosphere by creating an industrious, obedient and relatively docile labour force. In addition, plebian conformity was generally ensured by producing a proletariat inculcated with non-threatening middle-class values, 'the thoughts and behaviour ... harmonious with the moral presumptions and economic interests of their social and economic superiors'.[107] However, the ruling-class reactionaries were taking a risk in the creation of a highly-educated work-force which could possibly use its knowledge for subversive purposes. Such operatives were basically equipped with the intellectual wherewithal to take aboard counter-ideology spread by radical compatriots and those of other parts of Britain from which they had hitherto been geographically insulated. The conditions in the fluid, radical and Anglo-Celtic melting-pot at Moreton Bay were ideal for the emergence of this conflict.

According to contemporary thought expressed in the *Moreton Bay Courier*, the major threat to the well-being of the northern society lay in illiteracy rather than the revolutionary potential of the educated. About 20% of adults and probably more than twice that proportion of children within the northern population were unable to read.[108] It was asserted that ignorance was the parent of crime. According to this simplistic theory, it therefore followed that the incidence of criminality decreased in proportion to knowledge acquired. According to such reasoning it was imperative to establish a general system of education instead of the defective system currently being administered by the churches.[109] In particular there was a real fear of the impact which the ignorance of female servants - potential mothers of children and wives of mechanics and labourers - would have upon the future generation if the educational deficiencies remained unremediated.[110] It was confidently asserted that 'Education, like Vaccination and Innoculation, is necessary for the health and welfare of the community'.[111]

Duncan had probably been trained in the Irish National system which was being promoted by the government as the basis for the school system throughout the colony. He had long held that the failure to create a viable system for the unique needs of Australia lay with the Anglican and pastoral elites.[112] This charge could scarcely apply to Darling Downs squatters whose National school innovations at Warwick and Drayton were well ahead of those at Brisbane and Ipswich. Still, he never shifted in his position regarding the divisive and unproductive nature of schools conducted by the uncompromising Church of England and his beloved Roman Catholic Church.[113]

Widely read in educational theory and practice and familiar with current trends, Duncan's evidence to the Legislative Council's Select Committee on Education in 1844 detailed his criticisms of the current practice in New South Wales and provided a blueprint for improvement.[114] He predictably reiterated these views six years later at the Brisbane School of Arts when he delivered his widely-acclaimed lecture supporting the National system of education.[115] In fairness, the Reverend J. Wallace, Brisbane's Church of England incumbent, was given equal time and as much space as was needed in the *Moreton Bay Courier* to mount a formidable but unconvincing defence of the besieged system. This Scottish-owned newspaper was scarcely sympathetic to Wallace's arguments, preferring a system where 'people [were] cultivated in intellect but deficient in theology, to a population of clergy-ridden innocents'.[116]

In that lecture which 'attracted considerable attention in Sydney' and set him apart as one of Australia's leading educational reformers, Duncan proclaimed without equivocation:

> Children of all denominations should be educated together, receiving a good moral and intellectual education, together with as much instruction in Christianity as not to interfere with the controversial tenets of each denomination.[117]

As one of three members of the local board to supervise Roman Catholic education within Brisbane, Duncan saw no conflict with his church by advocating the National system. He dealt with and dismissed this concern in his Brisbane lecture, noting that the Catholic Church contained bishops who were among the most ardent advocates for National education as well some of the strongest opponents.[118]

Duncan's ideas differed in only one respect from those of George Rusden of Sydney, agent for the National Board, as outlined in his promotional meetings in Brisbane and Ipswich in May 1850. Speaking to his Brisbane meeting comprising a 'respectable and highly intelligent' audience and chaired by Duncan in the presence of the visiting Attorney-General J. Plunkett, Rusden provided details of the National system and the mechanism to establish its schools. Diplomatically he claimed to imply no attack on the denominational system, although he went to extreme lengths to stress the absurdity and impracticability of sharing Brisbane's educational grant among four denominations instead of funding one secular school. Like Duncan he was particularly critical of employing an excessive number of teachers in districts favouring the inefficient denominational system when one teacher would suffice.[119] Casting aside tact for unpalatable truth, Duncan characteristically mounted a strong attack on the social divisiveness and 'the unprofitable waste of labour' fostered by the denominational system which employed mainly untrained and incompetent teachers on paltry pay.[120]

A persistent advocate for the uniform training of teachers in a Normal school before practising in any system, Duncan argued that good teachers who produced good results would only be forthcoming when adequate remuneration was paid. Supported by the nonconformist clergy, the liberals and the *Moreton Bay Courier*, Duncan's plea for better quality teachers working within a system free from sectarian prejudice propagated by too many of the 'old soldier and sailor class' was well received in principle by the community.[121]

Land for national schools was purchased after this initial burst of energy on both sides of the river, but eight years elapsed before interest was re-activated.[122] The North Brisbane community under Duncan, Mackenzie, Raff and Pettigrew eventually raised a relatively insignificant sum for the government grant to build a school and provide a trained teacher.[123] The *Moreton Bay Courier* claimed that, inertia aside, the opposition of the Anglican and Roman Catholic clergy had been successful in obstructing the emergence of Brisbane's first National school; they were identified as 'the principal obstacles in the way of a general plan of education being introduced'.[124]

On the other hand, all of Brisbane's nonconformist clergy, including the Scottish leaders of the Presbyterian and Congregational churches, supported the National cause at the meeting held in August 1859. At this gathering at Raff's warehouse, the Congregationalist Wight, who delivered yet another lecture on the National system at the School of Arts in August 1859, was joined by the Presbyterians Ogg and Mowbray.[125] Ogg supported the National schools staffed by suitable teachers because he considered it to be the best educational vehicle to 'allay prejudices and sectarian feelings among the population'.[126]

Besides Duncan, the most prominent educator in Brisbane was the well-qualified and highly effective John Scott. Instructing at St Andrew's House on the corner of Ann and Creek streets, Scott was the principal educator of the children of Brisbane's Scottish community, claiming the patronage of the township's various Presbyterian congregations.[127] Half-yearly examinations of his pupils by the Reverend Charles Ogg in the presence of the parents revealed such high standards compared with other private schools in the town that the Scottish community regarded Scott as a rare and valuable acquisition.[128] His wide acclaim was testimony to the validity of Duncan's assertion that the best trained and best paid teachers achieve the best results. In line with Lang's principle of voluntaryism, Scott's Presbyterian school was not affiliated with the denominational system, preferring to rely on parental fees.[129]

Scott's high reputation throughout Brisbane ensured that his flourishing St Andrew's school was patronised by children from all denominations and nationalities in addition to its Scottish majority. The *Courier* gloated: 'It cannot but be a matter of congratulations to this community that a teacher of Mr Scott's high standing and respectability at home should have settled in this part of the colony, when such teachers are in so much demand in the old country, and temptations for them to "come over and help us" are so few'.[130]

In addition to his prominence in local educational circles, Scott was among the leading militants of the nonconformist, liberal section of Brisbane's population which often dictated the agenda of political and moral progress. His activity in supporting the fledgling working-class movement, the emergence of liberalism and teacher unionism distinguished him as one of Moreton Bay's most valuable immigrants.[131] As the brother-in-law of *Lima* immigrant James Johnston, Scott arrived from 'Red Clydeside' in 1852 with other members of his wife's family. He had been persuaded by Johnston to settle in a new district in which a pedagogue of his talents was very much needed and sound financial remuneration was assured. Subscribing to the Confession of Faith, trained at Scotland's foremost institutions, excelling within his profession and with a family and personal background of radical agitation, Scott became an important catalyst for proletarian assertion in Brisbane.

Scott's nonconformist, radical credentials were as impeccable as his professional qualifications. Trained as a teacher at the Old Normal School at Glasgow and the Madras College at St Andrews, Scott had been employed for thirteen years in Scotland, principally at Dundee and Crail.[132] In common with Duncan, Scott was an advocate of a modified form of the Bell and Lancaster monitorial system which was criticised widely by the English establishment when introduced in the first decade of the nineteenth century.[133] The reactionaries claimed that this teaching method and form of classroom organisation would render the labouring classes fractious and reactionary instead of accepting subordination.[134] Scott's training at the Old Normal School, supported by the reform-oriented Glasgow Education Society, stressed that education was a major vehicle for the worker's moral, financial and social elevation.[135]

Because of his involvement within the Denominational system, Scott was overlooked for the headmastership of Brisbane's National school which opened at Adelaide Street in April 1860. James Rendall, a fellow Scot with an impeccable background in the National system and one of the few with competence to rival Scott's, was appointed head teacher. Scott's well-deserved reputation throughout Brisbane ensured that he was appointed as assistant.[136] Thereafter the Board of General Education under the chairmanship of R.R. Mackenzie, dictated Queensland's educational policy. John Gerard Anderson as under-secretary and David Ewart as general inspector, two arrogant and autocratic Scottish administrators, oversaw the daily functioning of schools. With Scots occupying the principal political, departmental and teaching positions, the foundations of Queensland education were securely but inflexibly laid along the lines of the system acquired in their homeland.[137]

* * *

The formation of the Brisbane School of Arts and Sciences in September 1849 was also motivated by the desire of Lang's immigrants to recreate in Moreton Bay the cultural institutions which were integral to their lives in Britain and to improve working-class morality.[138] By the time the Langites and government immigrants left Britain, the Glaswegian model upon which such institutions were based had been significantly modified. Although Mechanics Institutes still provided lectures, libraries and literacy training for workers, they had developed into social and cultural centres for the middle class and the ambitious sector of the upper working class.[139]

Despite the ban on religious and political topics within the Brisbane School of Arts, the predominance within its membership of middle-class radicals with democratic intent ensured that it became on occasion a potent source of social disharmony. With Duncan as the long-serving president over a society with a membership comprising a conservative minority and a Langite majority, the stage was set for political controversy. Consequently party divisions, personal animosity and in-house hostility dominated the early years of this educational facility - a far cry from the benevolent ideals of the creators of these Scottish institutions in the late eighteenth century.

As elsewhere in Britain and Australia, the Brisbane School of Arts was lacking in working-class subscribers. The membership was dominated by Lang's followers. Of the eighty foundation members, twenty-three were Lang immigrants and a further sixteen members such as Andrew Petrie, Swan and Spence were associated with this radical group. These nonconformist businessmen, skilled tradesmen and professionals were constantly in the forefront of the district's political, economic and cultural life, virtually determining the local development program. Thus it was inevitable that the wider conflict in Brisbane's political life between dissenting radicals and rear guard conservatives would be played out in miniature within this institution.

The Scottish presence was also strong among office bearers and subscribers. While 50% of the first committee and 30% of the foundation members were Scots,

W.A. Duncan as president and John Innes as secretary provided leadership throughout most of the 1850s. In the early stages Swan, Ballow, Richardson and John Petrie also played leading roles in the institution's decision making as committee members.[140] Unappealing lectures, expensive subscriptions and long working hours were major deterrents to a larger working-class membership, irrespective of national origins.[141] The apparently apathetic workers were preoccupied with survival, material advancement and fleeting pleasures.

In the foundation year there is no indication whatsoever of working-class Scots among the active membership of the School of Arts. Apart from Spence, who occupied a supervisory position at Petries in the 1850s, the only visible members with working-class backgrounds were McLean, Gray and McIntyre who were at that stage property owners, voters, employers of labour and prominent churchmen.[142]

Basically the Brisbane School of Arts of the 1850s was a middle-class institution with a large Scottish and Langite membership. Apart from Duncan, Innes and Swan, who were leaders in the institution's affairs, other Scottish members of the institution were active principally as users of the well-stocked library, members of the audience at lectures and voters at meetings. There was also a good representation of Scots, particularly ministers of religion, among the lecturers. Knowles, Duncan, Stewart, Buchanan, Wight, Ogg and Scott attracted large audiences on subjects ranging from phrenology by the first to a discourse on moral and intellectual benefits of education from the last. When Duncan spoke from the School of Arts platform, his carefully-crafted arguments on educational and the constitutional issues reverberated throughout the colony; even his lecture on the cultivation of the olive tree marked him as an expert.[143]

The large library, the only public facility in Brisbane, encompassed a wide range of interesting topics. In fact much of the collection had been donated from Duncan's own extensive library. The reading room also contained Scottish periodicals including *Edinburgh Review*, *North British Review* and *Fraser's magazine* to keep the Scots abreast with home events.[144] Under Duncan's surveillance, this library enjoyed a reputation by 1854, 'equal, if not superior to any similar Establishment of the kind in the colony'.[145]

The dynamics within this institution 'exemplified the hostilities and divisions of colonial society'.[146] Such conflicts were mainly confined to power struggles between liberals and conservatives. They were usually activated by extreme changes to programs, rules or procedures which were either perceived as elitist or Chartist. Such altercations were fully reported with bias by the liberal *Moreton Bay Courier* and the reactionary *Moreton Bay Free Press*. Frequent eruptions and consistent 'needling', characteristic of the on-going conflict between Duncan and Robert Cribb, compounded and exacerbated the explosive political situation. Duncan, caught between the two forces as president, attempted to adopt the role of mediator though he was quick to intervene when his own firmly-held principles were affronted. Faced with the frequent prospect of being out-voted by Cribb and his associates, Duncan registered his protest on occasion by threatening to withdraw his highly valued leadership.

In a society with a strong radical, reforming influence among its members, Duncan was required in the early stages to counter criticisms held in influential circles that the institution was a covert vehicle for 'the diffusion of republicanism'.[147] In defending the School of Arts against the *Moreton Bay Courier*'s alleged misreporting of the political intent of the debating program, Duncan gave reassurance that as an officer of the government he would never countenance presiding over any society which reeked of Chartism. In a rage he turned on the editor and committee member James Swan who would have been thoroughly familiar with political undercurrents within the membership. Attempting to prevent the early demise of this fledgling establishment, Duncan claimed that the *Courier*, with similar socio-political views as the majority of institute's members, was bent on subversion. Immediately Swan refuted Duncan's charges, stating that the *Courier* only wished the institute prosperity. However, he gave notice that the *Moreton Bay Courier* under his proprietorship would continue to uphold the inalienable right of citizens and newspapers to discuss all subjects important to community welfare - irrespective of Duncan's 'rash and totally unwarranted' reactions.[148]

In January 1853, open friction erupted between the radical and the conservative elements of the institution when attempts were made to remove the ballot and increase the annual membership fee.[149] While the first issue would predictably raise the ire and resistance of those with Chartist convictions, the success of the latter move was a further disincentive to future working-class involvement. The reactionary *Moreton Bay Free Press* also entered the fray, extolling this attempted resurgence of conservatism which was attacking a basic principle of the Charter.[150] In a futile attempt to gain control over the institution which was on the brink of being 'debased into a Chartist debating club' and a 'hotbed of radicalism', the reactionaries were ultimately unsuccessful in effecting the critical changes to the constitution 'to render the institution aristocratic [and] keep out the working man'.[151] The compromise to have a lesser fee for working men was scornfully rejected. It was clear that the School of Arts was on the brink of being constitutionally socially-divided - 'twenty shillings gentility and ten shillings vulgarity'.[152]

In the campaign which was fought out over eight months and in which various combinations of fee structures were proposed and defeated, W.M. Smith, Robert Little, William Kent, Daniel Roberts and Henry Buckley were ably opposed by Scottish liberals James Spence, John Innes and Alexander Raff who joined forces with English Langites Dr William Hobbs, George Poole and the irrepressible Robert Cribb. John Richardson, dismissing notions of aristocratic dominance, supported the subscription increase as he was convinced of the validity of the committee's argument that ensuing improvements in run-down society facilities would lead to increased working-class participation.[153]

Duncan, believing the increased subscription might be beneficial to the institution, behaved with 'candid and impartial conduct' before resigning because of the dissension, antagonism and party division. Moreover he was dismayed and angry that his preferred options did not gain the required two-thirds majority when put to the ballot. Cribb's continuous 'needling' over the constitutional legitimacy of a supposed application for a governmental grant of 100 pounds did not help matters either.[154] Duncan had failed to fulfil his self-appointed role as a safeguard against the assertion of plebian power.

Duncan's withdrawal from the society to which he was deeply committed was destined to be temporary. In 1856 he once more assumed the reins of an institution 'which remained in the hands of urban middle class, public-spirited men who valued education' and operated within a community which then was according urban liberalism a greater measure of respectability.[155] When Duncan delivered his last presidential report on 14 April 1859, supported by a committee including Innes, Scott, Pettigrew, Raff, Wight and John Petrie, he left the Brisbane School of Arts in a strong position. There were 268 members on the books, 3,444 volumes on the shelves and a strong lecture program was drawing large audiences.

Although Duncan failed in fulfilling his self-appointed role as a buffer against the assertion of radical power in this situation, he maintained the School of Arts in a healthy state. Never emerging as a threat to the township's political stability as feared by Brisbane's conservative elements, the School of Arts under Duncan's guidance became the acknowledged social and cultural centre of Brisbane. This vibrant, urban vehicle of adult education stood in stark contrast to its politically embattled Ipswich equivalent which was attempting its third start at the time of Duncan's graceful departure.

From the start of proceedings in July 1850, the initiative of Lang immigrants under the leadership of Dr Henry Challinor, the *Fortitude* surgeon, was met with suspicion and overt opposition by the dominant squatting forces and their town-based allies. By that time, the radical reputation of the Brisbane institute and other mechanics institutes had exacerbated the predisposition of Ipswich's numerous and influential conservative elements to fear the revolutionary outcomes of popular education, especially the variety which originated from the proletarian body. Disapproved of and unsupported by the pastoral sector and weakened by financial instability, the Ipswich Literary Institute was disbanded in the following year despite Challinor's impassioned attempts to assure them of the non-political nature of the new enterprise.[156]

The Scottish-led conservative sector of Ipswich then attempted to fill this educational void by establishing the Ipswich Subscription Library and Reading Room under the strict surveillance of a specially selected committee. The anti-liberal actions which were subsequently undertaken by conservative Scots such as the president Colonel Charles Gray (also Police Magistrate), storekeeper Francis A. Forbes and solicitor Arthur Macalister ensured that it never attracted a healthy membership. They went to excess in attempting to ensure the 'respectability' of this second educational body. The expulsion of a well-educated Langite for criticising the police office by the highly unpopular Gray and Macalister's success in raising the subscription rate by 100% made membership of this institute an unpopular, if not impossible, option for the workers and tradesmen of Ipswich.[157]

Learning from the deleterious effects of the suspicion, mistakes and bickering which had held back the cultural climate of Ipswich for nearly a decade, and fuelled by inter-township rivalry, squatter and liberal interests pooled their resources to establish the Ipswich Mechanics School of Arts in 1858. This joint effort aimed to provide 'classes, lectures and wholesome amusement' for the working classes. Taking a prominent part in its establishment, Benjamin Cribb, a fervent and fiery Langite and legislator, emphasised the need for a community centre as well as a medium for the benefit of working-class edification. This new spirit of cooperation for social unity was marked by the donation of the entire collection from the Subscription Library and Reading Room to the new institute and halving of the membership fees.[158] Nevertheless the Ipswich establishment was a decade behind its flourishing Brisbane counterpart which had taken initiatives to progress beyond its literary and debating focus to encompass the performing arts within its cultural aegis.[159]

* * *

After two previous attempts over eight years to form a musical society with School of Arts assistance and Duncan's commitment, the Brisbane Choral Society was secure enough to embark upon its first concert under the baton of the multi-talented Englishman Silvester Diggles.[160] Duncan, undoubtedly the driving force behind Brisbane's musical development, was 'a lover of music and a believer in its capabilities to elevate, instruct and amuse the people'. As an extension of this passion he was deeply involved in fostering community appreciation and participation in music. Before a local demand became apparent, Duncan contributed to the birth of musical activity in Brisbane at St Stephen's where he was choirmaster and harmonium player.[161] Each week, from a room in his home especially set aside for his musical activities, Duncan arranged choral and liturgical scores for Sunday Mass.[162] Labouring against the distraction caused by the southern gold mania, his first attempt in 1851 to mould Brisbane's estimated twenty-five musical instrumentalists and sixteen vocal performers into a performing arts company was unsuccessful. After an initial burst of energy under his presidency, the Moreton Bay Amateur Musical Society failed to progress beyond the rehearsal stage - so typical of the 'Brisbane malaise' which ensured the demise of other enthusiastically-received, local projects.[163] Five years later, an attempt by the committee of the School of Arts under the management of Duncan and Innes to form a choral society led by Diggles similarly resulted in disappointment.[164]

The enthusiasm shown by Brisbane's music lovers in October 1852 and April 1853 to the over-subscribed lecture/demonstrations at the School of Arts and the subsequent, successful independent performance arising from that series augured well for the future of musical concerts by local artists in Brisbane.[165] Furthermore, the enthusiastic reception accorded to visiting professional artists such as Flora Harris, Sydney-based cantatrice, appeared to support this prediction.

However, theatre, like the School of Arts, became the preserve of the middle class and the elite of Brisbane society. Disdained by the *Moreton Bay Free Press* as 'the shillingless unwashed', the working class was even unable to afford the usual entrance fees to School of Arts functions.[166] Theatre-going and musical performances became another basis of class division within the district. Working-class Scots and Irish no doubt fulfilled their musical needs with spontaneous ceilidhs centred around ballads, traditional dances, fiddles, pipes and drums.[167]

Duncan appeared to be the promoter of visits by performing artists to Brisbane, especially Scottish entertainers such as Flora Harris. The performance of this Scottish soprano on a tour in 1854 surpassed 'anything of the kind before attempted in Brisbane ...'.[168] Apparently representing the School of Arts, Duncan and William Craies led a deputation to present the professional female singer with a purse of 25 sovereigns after her final performance.[169] As a result of further entrepreneurial initiative emanating from the School of Arts' organising committee, which included Duncan, Craies and Mackenzie, Miss Harris re-appeared in the north in January 1855 as a valued member of the company of Miska Hauser (the 'modern Paganini').[170] During the final item in each concert of his series, Hauser played 'Scotch airs' which proved to have universal appeal with Moreton Bay audiences.[171]

Aware of the concentration of Scots at Moreton Bay and the popularity of traditional Scottish songs among the wider community, many of the visiting entertainers included Scottish numbers in their repertoire. However, it was not until Scottish baritone J.R. Black performed in Brisbane and Ipswich over a four month period some five years later that the music-loving community was treated to a substantial fare of Scottish ballads. Reflecting the widespread appreciation of Scotland's bard, his Nicht wi' Burns, which featured 'My love is like a red. red rose', 'Come under my plaidie', 'Scots wa hae' and 'Duncan Gray' was well-received by Sir George and Lady Bowen as well as 'the strong muster of Mr Black's countrymen'.[172] As a final gesture to the town which took him to its heart, he performed with the Brisbane Choral Society which had developed into 'an efficient musical company' since their first public performance in May 1859. On that occasion, 'Natives of the land of Burns' led the company into the finale, 'Auld Lang Syne', the chorus being taken merrily up by the general choir.[173]

On the eve of his departure for Sydney, Duncan would have felt that the positive public reaction to this triumph finally demonstrated acknowledgement of his good works for the local community. He would have been singularly proud to have received the tribute directed to those who had 'taken an interest in bringing the members of the Choral Society to their present state of proficiency ...'.[174] Just when his northern service had reached its completion, he found that music gained him a moment of that popular acceptance that he had always unconsciously sought within the former cultural desert.

* * *

Through the promotion of a Scottish baritone who exploited the appeal of Robert Burns, Brisbane music came of age. Given the general popularity of performances featuring Burns' work, it was possible that wider exploitation of his attraction could have positive effects on the morale and harmony of Brisbane's divided community. Allowing for the fact that Lowlander Robert Burns did not enjoy universal reverence throughout Scotland, especially in some parts of the Highlands, it appears that his ballads created a unifying effect on middle-class audiences at public functions in Brisbane. Cognisant of the fact that the Scots assimilated with ease into Moreton Bay society, it might be conjectured that the centenary birthday celebration of 'Britain's other Bard' could promote cohesion and goodwill in Brisbane's Anglo-Celtic community for one night at least. The *Moreton Bay Courier*, while concurring that such an occasion would permit all men to 'shake hands in fellowship', gave a prominent role to Burns' radical influence, declaring that he 'first opened up to the minds of the middle and lower classes the mighty powers of poetry to enliven and educate'.[175]

Despite a relatively low price of five shillings for soiree, fruit and wine, the first reported proceedings at North Brisbane in 1859 attracted a disappointing gathering of fifty persons. The report by the local press indicated a minimal Scottish flavour, although only a few of the 'great many' speeches and songs were perfunctorily listed. Under the chairmanship of English liberal Charles Lilley, the toasts to the Queen, the Governor-General, the British Constitution as well as the musical program featuring "God save the Queen', 'Rule Britannia' and 'Rouse brothers rouse' appeared to inject a distinct Sassenach atmosphere into the function. While the Scottish community may have withdrawn its support from this near-alien celebration, the selective reporting of the *Moreton Bay Courier* indicated that Scottish working-class Lowlanders James Fenwick, John Murray and William Murray played minor roles. It would appear that this attempt on 25 January 1859 to unite Brisbane's British community around a Scottish hero who 'touched the universal mind' met with limited success.[176]

The more formal celebration in 1860 was reportedly better organised and attended, attracting the cream of Brisbane's society, including a host of government and civil officials under vice-regal patronage. In addition to Sir George and Lady Bowen, the Colonial Secretary Robert Herbert and Chief Justice Cockle formed the majority of the official party. Although John Murray delivered a creditable oration to Burns, the Governor's polished speech on 'the common ploughman [with] most uncommon genius' and the inevitable reference to 'Green grow the rushes O!' in his response to the usual toast to the ladies drew prolonged applause. Pettigrew's toast to the town corporation completed this celebration which clearly had been hijacked by officialdom and politicians.[177]

Working-class sentiments expressed by wearers of 'the hodden grey' would normally have been relevant on Burns night, but were out of place in this heavily

Anglicised and elitist gathering. Such opinions were tactfully delayed until the official party had retired. Away from official scrutiny, William Murdoch was permitted to express hopes and aspirations for the democratisation and expansion of the School of Arts. Although Duncan had long been an advocate for working-class access to libraries, he would not have been receptive to working-class control over the institute, even in the face of middle-class inertia.[178] Murdoch hoped 'that the institution ... might become like those of Manchester, Liverpool and Oxford - possessed of free libraries and open to the public without subscription. ... If the wealthy men would not use their efforts to place the institution in such a state, then let the working men ... do it themselves ...'.[179] The only speech on that occasion reflecting Burns' true sentiments was accorded inferior status.

On that same evening, across the river at McIntyre's hotel, the alternative celebration was being played out in a more spontaneous manner befitting this anniversary. Receiving scant space in the local paper, the colourful and boisterous function was rated high in the culinary department. The piece de resistance was two large haggis which not only 'reflected great credit on the worthy host, [but] ... would have warmed the heart of Burns himself...'. After John Souter eloquently proposed the toast to Burns, which was drunk in silence, the company 'enjoyed themselves to their hearts content'.[180]

No doubt the riverside gathering contained many of McIntyre's Scottish friends who were pioneers of the district - well-documented Highland pipers, tipplers, dancers, songsters and revellers. These men and women were familiar with that era when capital and labour were indeed interrelated. Many as Highlanders maintained their distinct identity and independence. As a result of working alongside their equally inexperienced employers in the pioneering era, they knew full well that 'the rank is but the guinea stamp' and could separate the 'birkies' from the men of worth. Rejecting the celebration on the north side which had been taken over by prominent English late-arrivals, the less distinguished but more chauvinistic members of the Scottish community arranged their own function on ethnic and class lines. The south bank revellers knew how such a Scottish event should be kept. There is no doubt where the true Burns celebration was held. Consistent with all major issues arising at Moreton Bay, the Scots identified where their interests lay and aligned with their socio-economic class.

* * *

By 1859, emergent middle-class liberalism and new-found working-class militancy had combined to ensure that Queensland's major town was distinguished by its democratic flavour, radical image and high moral tone. Lang's English nonconformists joined south-west Scottish artisans to bring about this revitalised state of affairs. Brisbane owed its nonconformist flavour, working-class sobriety, National education and a democratic School of Arts, as well as its divided nature, to this temporary alliance. Indeed the non-denominational education system only became a reality after the Scottish nonconformist clergy added support to the brilliant, but ineffective advocacy of the unpopular Duncan. Lang's plan for a united evangelical religion may have failed due to Scottish Presbyterian dissent, but his vision of a just, respectable Moreton Bay became a reality due to the amicable religious partnership which emerged. With the critical support of Swan's *Moreton Bay Courier*, the negative influence of the Scottish-led pastoralists within Brisbane had been diluted and their conservative urban allies were constantly challenged.

Despite Duncan's success as a Catholic layman, his competence as an administrator, his courageous defence of social justice and his patronising attempts to enculturate Brisbane, he was a failure as a leader. The charismatic Lang, who selected, introduced and encouraged the right mix of immigrants to follow his vision, made a much greater impact upon the improvement of Moreton Bay society, even from afar. It is significant that Lang was regarded by government and bureaucracy as an arch enemy, while the obverse was Duncan's case. One identified with non-elitist northern sentiments and aspirations, while the heart of the other was still within the Sydney establishment. In common with others of their ethnic group, these two formidable Scots also aligned according to their socio-economic interests.

Although Lang harboured other ideas, there was no discernible Scottish position towards the events which moulded the material, moral and cultural development of Moreton Bay between 1849 and 1859. Scottish representatives were as active within the Langite middle-class forces which challenged the status quo as they were among the conservatives who fought to maintain it. Gravitating socially, economically and politically to relevant class and intra-class factions, they not only exerted positive influences upon the district's economic and ethical progress, but contributed to the disunity within it.

Regardless of class, Moreton Bay provided the ideal socially-fluid environment for the majority of the individualist Scots to improve their lot in life. However, the Scottish psyche, oriented towards middle-class values, was equally concerned with religious and cultural development as with the relentless pursuit of capital.

Individual Scots, especially Duncan, Swan and Lang were at the forefront of the moral, religious and cultural awakening which was readily apparent to eminent newcomers at the turn of the decade. Whereas Lang's plans for a united Protestant front were short-lived and Duncan's selective displays of leadership lacked the capacity to arouse community action, Swan kept up a relentless newspaper campaign to explain, defend and promote liberal ideals which formed the basis of democracy in the reinvented north.

While R.R. Mackenzie and Arthur Macalister were ascendant stars on the brink of brilliant parliamentary careers, the laurels for initiating many of the significant apolitical achievements in pre-separation Moreton Bay rested upon a brilliant but socially isolated Customs officer who was on the verge of creating a distinguished record in education, religion, public administration and the arts. It was a pity that Duncan apparently regarded his northern service as doing time in a cultural desert and his over-refined reasoning led to some critical decisions that were insensitive and on occasion insulting. Even if he did make more enemies than friends through his intransigent and idiosyncratic views and he never received due respect for his extensive experience and substantial achievements, he did his best to leave Brisbane a better place than he found it.

Indeed such commitment to local development according to strongly-held vision was the common feature of many individuals who fostered the district's progress. Such clear-sighted leaders exerted more Scottish influence on the Moreton Bay District than the combined efforts of their moral, conformist and self-seeking compatriots who had confined their energy to their calling. Yet this apparent acquiesence and aloofness should not be confused with submissiveness as was discovered in the Highlands by economic innovators and advocates of religious patronage. Class, economics and politics may have divided the Scots, but those who attempted to diminish or dilute their national religion could expect to feel the full force of this formidable minority group whose leaders had a record of prominence within the power structure of both developing and well established colonial societies.

ENDNOTES

1. Ken Buckley and Ted Wheelwright, *No paradise for workers: capitalism and the common people of Australia 1788-1914*, (Melbourne: Oxford University Press, 1992), p. 110.
2. Allan A. Morrison, 'Colonial society 1860-1890', *Queensland Heritage*, 1 (1976), pp. 21-3.
3. Duncan, Autobiography, p. 40.
4. B.A. Knox, 'Moreton Bay separation', p. 575.
5. William Pettigrew to John Pettigrew, 2 March 1851, p. 25, Pettigrew letters: miscellaneous, typescript, RHSQ.
6. William Pettigrew, Diary, 1849-53, 9 February 1851, 8 May 1851.
7. *MBC*, 29 June 1850, p. 4; 14 August 1850, p. 3; 22 February 1852, p. 3.
8. *North Australian*, 10 July, 1860, p.2; *NSWVP*, 1859-60, vol. 1, p. 73.
9. Paul Wilson, The political career of The Honourable Arthur Macalister, C.M.G. BA thesis, University of Queensland, 1969, p. 10; *MBC*, 3 August 1850, p. 3; 11 December 1852, p. 3; 2 July 1853, p. 2.
10. William Pettigrew to John Pettigrew, 15 November 1852, p. 18; Sir John Pakington to Sir C.A. Fitzroy, despatch, 18 July 1852, *British Parliamentary Papers, Papers relating to emigration to the Australian colonies 1852-53, Colonies Australia* 17, p.66.
11. William Pettigrew to Adam Pettigrew, 11 December 1853, p. 47; *MBC*, 20 May 1854, p. 3.
12. William Pettigrew to Adam Pettigrew, 17 June 1851, p. 2.
13. *Inverness Courier*, 27 January 1853, p. 3.
14. *Inverness Courier*, 16 October 1851, p. 6.
15. *Inverness Courier*, 27 January 1853, p. 3.
16. Beever, 'British working class attitudes to Australia 1841-51', pp. 11-13.
17. Max Weber, *The Protestant ethic and the spirit of Capitalism*, reprint, (London: Routledge, 1992), p. 27.
18. Mackenzie-Smith, 'Scottish immigrants to Moreton Bay 1841-59'.
19. Houston, *Scottish literacy and Scottish identity*, p. 221.
20. *MBC*, 17 December 1859, p. 3; 23 December 1859, p. 3.
21. Thorpe, *Colonial Queensland*, p. 139.
22. Bowen to Newcastle, 6 February 1860, Governor's despatches to the Secretary of State, vol. 1, pp. 76-7, GOV/22, QSA.
23. *SMH*, 29 March 1859, p. 3.
24. Payten, Duncan thesis, p. 138.
25. John James Knight, *In the early days: history and incident in pioneer Queensland*, (Brisbane: Sapsford, 1895), pp. 118-19.
26. Knox, ' Moreton Bay separation', p. 573.
27. Rod Fisher, 'Against all odds: early industrial enterprise in Brisbane 1840-60', *Journal of the Royal Australian Historical Society*, 76 (1990), pp. 104-6.

28 *MBFP*, 20 July 1858, p. 2.
29 *MBC*, 8 March 1856, p. 2.
30 Coote, *History of the colony of Queensland*, p. 234.
31 Cockburn, *Journal*, vol 2, p. 272.
32 Ibid.
33 *MBC*, 13 December 1856, p. 2.
34 *MBC*, 25 September 1859, p. 2.
35 *MBC*, 28 November 1859, p. 2.
36 *SMH*, 15 June 1857, p. 3; 29 June 1857, p. 5.
37 *MBC*, 23 November 1859, p. 2.
38 *SMH*, 11 October 1859, p. 6.
39 *MBC*, 23 November 1859, p. 2; 22 December 1859, p. 3.
40 *MBC*, 13 December 1859, p. 3.
41 *MBC*, 27 December 1859, p. 3.
42 James T. Cleary, The North Brisbane School of Arts 1848-99, BA Hons. thesis, University of Queensland, pp. 52-3.
43 William Augustine Duncan, *A plea for the New South Wales Constitution*, (Sydney: Waugh & Cox, 1856), pp. 13-17; *MBC*, 23 June 1856, p. 2
44 Duncan, Diary, pp. 76-79; Henry Stobart to his mother, 20 and 21 July 1853, pp. 14-16. Letters of Henry Stobart MA, giving an account of his voyage from England to Australia, his travels in New South Wales to Moreton Bay ... covering the period October 1852 to April 1856, FM4/2129, AJCP reel M467, Mitchell Library.
45 *MBC*, 3 March 1849, p. 3.
46 *MBC*, 4 May 1859, p. 2.
47 *MBC*, 12 April 1859, p. 2.
48 Duncan, Autobiography, p. 74; W.A. Duncan to Stuart Alexander Donaldson, 28 June 1856, Duncan Papers, Mitchell Library, CY 774, pp. 155-9.
49 Lang, *Cooksland*, p. 477; *Narrative taken on the steps of promoting the separation of Queensland from New South Wales*, p. 14.
50 George Wight, *Queensland the field for British labour and enterprise and the source of England's cotton supply*, (London: G. Street, 1862), p. 152.
51 *Brisbane Courier*, 24 November 1923.
52 *MBC*, 29 February 1856, p. 2.
53 Mary McConnel, *Memories of days long gone by, by the wife of an Australian pioneer*, (London: Private Printing, 1905) in *Brisbane River Valley*, p. 90 ; Dowse diary, 31 October 1851; Pettigrew diary, 16 August 1850, 15 May 1851; Nehemiah Bartley, *Opals and agates; or scenes under the Southern Cross and Maghelans: being memories of fifty years in Australia and Polynesia*, (Brisbane: Gordon & Gotch, 1892), pp. 99-100.
54 Norris, *Brisbane hotels and publicans index*, pp. 18, 23, 24.
55 *MBC*, 23 March 1849, p. 3; 15 December 1849, p. 4; 10 September 1859, p. 2; 17 October 1857. p. 2

56 *SMH*, 4 August 1857, p. 10
57 *MBC*, 3 October 1857, p. 2.
58 *MBC*, 22 September 1849, p. 3.
59 *MBC*, 12 May 1849, p.3; 3 June 1854, p. 2.
60 *MBC*, 17 July 1854, p. 2.
61 *MBC*, 19 April 1856, p. 2; 10 May 1856, p. 2; 17 May 1856, p. 3; 24 May, 1856, p.2.
62 *MBC*, 18 May 1859, p. 2.
63 Lang, *Cooksland*, p. 479; William Pettigrew to Hugh Hunter, 22 October 1849, William Pettigrew, Letters, miscellaneous, RHSQ.
64 Pettigrew, Diary, 22 September 1850, 11 January 1852; 5 June 1852; Pettigrew to Rev. John Barclay, 11 October 1850; Pettigrew to Hugh Hunter, 18 July 1852, Pettigrew letters, miscellaneous.
65 Pettigrew, Diary, 5 November 1849; 6 November 1852.
66 Ibid, 12 September 1851, 19 January 1851, 16 April 1851.
67 Pettigrew to John Pettigrew, 2 March 1851, Pettigrew letters.
68 Pettigrew, Diary, 12 August 1849, 9 September 1849, 30 September 1849, 23 December 1850; Pettigrew to Rev. John Barclay, 11 October 1850.
69 Callum Brown, 'Protest in the pews: interpreting Presbyterianism and society in fracture during the economic revolution', in T.M. Devine, ed. *Conflict and stability in Scottish society 1799-1850*, (Edinburgh: John Donald, 1990), p. 101.
70 Ibid, p. 100.
71 Parker, "Strange bedfellows", p. 16.
72 *British Banner*, p.p. 536-7.
73 Parker, "Strange bedfellows", p. 14.
74 Cumming, 'Covenant and identity', p. 203.
75 William Pettigrew to Rev. John Barclay, 11 October 1850, p. 16, Pettigrew letters, miscellaneous.
76 *MBC*, 8 December 1849, p. 2; 15 December 1849, p. 3.
77 Memos about [the] Presbyterian Church Brisbane, p.1, Pettigrew Papers, RHSQ.
78 R. Gordon Balfour, *Presbyterianism in the colonies with special reference to the principles and influence of the Free Church of Scotland*, (Edinburgh: Macniven & Wallace, 1900), p. 165.
79 *MBC*, 4 May 1850, p. 1; 16 August 1851, p. 3.
80 Barbara C. Murison, 'The Disruption and the colonies of Scottish settlement', in Stewart J. Brown and Michael Fry ed. *Scotland in the age of the Disruption*, (Edinburgh: Edinburgh University Press, 1993, p. 147.
81 Ibid.
82 David McConnel to Rev. A. Salmon, 17 December 1849, Memos about [the] Presbyterian Church, p. 2.
83 William Pettigrew to Rev. John Barclay, 11 October 1850, pp. 14-15, Pettigrew letters.

84 Alexander Hay, *Jubilee memorial of the Presbyterian Church of Queensland 1849-99*, (Brisbane: Alex. Muir, 1900), p. 9.
85 Ibid, p. 10.
86 Balfour, *Presbyterianism in the colonies*, p. 166.
87 Hay, *Jubilee memorial of the Presbyterian Church of Queensland*, p. 11.
88 *MBC*, 10 January 1857, p. 2.
89 *MBC*, 21 March 1857, p. 2.
90 *MBC*, 11 April 1857, p. 2.
91 Parker, 'Strange bedfellows', pp. 31-3.
92 Ibid, p. 16; George Wight, *Congregational independency: its introduction into Queensland*, (Brisbane: Gordon & Gotch 1887), p. 151.
93 *MBC*, 3 March 1855, p. 2; 8 September 1855, p. 2 ; 14 May 1859, p.3; 4 June 1859, p. 3.
94 *MBC*, 5 February 1859, p. 2.
95 Parker, "Strange bedfellows", pp. 9-11.
96 Ibid, p. 35.
97 Rayner, The history of the Church of England in Queensland, pp. 49, 76-9; *SMH*, 20 March 1855, p. 3; *MBC*, 10 March 1855, p. 2; 31 March 1855, p. 2; 14 April 1855, p. 2; 4 August 1855, p. 2.
98 Duncan, Autobiography, pp. 40-1; *Australasian Chronicle*, 5 May 1840, p. 2; 31 October 1840, p. 2.
99 William Augustine Duncan, *A letter to the Lord Bishop of Australia containing remarks upon his Lordship's protest against the metropolitan and Episcopal Jurisdiction of his grace the Archbishop of Sydney*, (Sydney: G.&C. Morely, 1843).
100 *Australasian Chronicle*, 4 August 1840, p. 2.
101 *The Freeman's Journal*, 20 June 1857, p. 9; 4 July 1857, p. 9.
102 Denis W. Martin, *The foundation of the Catholic Church in Queensland*, (Toowoomba: Church Archivists' Society, 1988), pp. 73-7.
103 R.A. Houston, *Scottish literacy and the Scottish identity: illiteracy and society in Scotland and northern England 1600-1800*, (London: Cambridge University Press, 1985), p. 3.
104 Ibid, p. 221.
105 Ibid, pp. 6, 214.
106 Cockburn, *Journal*, p. 85.
107 Houston, p. 224.
108 Analysis of 1851 census, *MBC*, 6 December 1851, p. 2. Because the child literacy figures were embedded within the 21 and under-age category, it was impossible to calculate figures accurately for children between 6 and 14 years of age.
109 *MBC*, 20 May 1850, p. 3.
110 *MBC*, 24 April 1853, pp. 2, 3.
111 *MBC*, 23 June 1856, p. 2.
112 Payten, Duncan thesis, p. 138.

113 Ezra R. Wyeth, *Education in Queensland: a history of education in Queensland and in the Moreton Bay District of New South Wales*, (Melbourne, Australian Council for Educational Research, 1951), pp. 50-69.

114 W.A. Duncan, Evidence to the select committee on education, 2 July 1844, *NSWVP*, 1844, pp. 22-8.

115 W.A. Duncan, *Lecture on National Education*, (Brisbane: James Swan, 1851).

116 *MBC*, 20 July 1850, p. 3.

117 Duncan, *Lecture on National Education*, p. 7.

118 Duncan, *Lecture on National Education*, p. 14.

119 *MBC*, 20 May 1850, p. 3.

120 Duncan. *Lecture on National Education*, pp. 12-13.

121 *MBC*, 23 June 1855, p. 2.

122 *MBC*, 24 April 1853, pp. 2, 3.

123 *MBC*, 18 August 1858, p. 2.

124 *MBC*, 23 June 1855, p. 2; 13 December 1856, p. 2.

125 *MBC*, 13 August 1859, p. 2.

126 Reverend Charles Ogg, Evidence before the select committee on the Board of General Education, 1 July 1861, *QVP*, 1861, p. 41.

127 *MBC*, 31 December 1853, p. 3; 12 January 1856, p. 4; 6 August 1859, p. 2.

128 *MBC*, 24 December 1853, p. 2; 5 July 1856, p. 2; 27 December 1856, p.2; 27 June 1856, p. 2.

129 Ogg, Evidence, p. 36.

130 *MBC*, 5 July 1856, p. 2.

131 Andrew Spaull and Martin Sullivan, *A history of the Queensland Teachers' Union*, (Sydney: Allen & Unwin, 1989), p. 334.

132 June T. Hunter, personal correspondence with author, 2 October 1996; John Scott, personal record, Register of teachers employed 1860-1876, Board of National Education, Queensland, EDB/ 01-2, QSA.

133 Duncan, Evidence, p. 27; *MBC*, 31 December 1853, p. 3.

134 H.C. Barnard, *A short history of English education from 1760 to 1944*, (London: University of London Press, 1958), p. 65.

135 Marjorie Cruickshank, *A history of the training of teachers in Scotland*, (London: University of London Press, 1970), p. 42.

136 Greg Logan, 'Rendall of the Normal School: Brisbane's first state school teacher, 1860-73', in Greg Logan and Tom Watson, ed. *Soldiers of the service: some early Queensland educators and their schools*, (Brisbane: History of Queensland Education Society, 1992), pp. 39-41.

137 Logan and Watson, *Soldiers of the service*, pp. 21-33.

138 James T. Cleary, The North Brisbane School of Arts 1849-1899, BA thesis, University of Queensland, 1967, pp. vi, 7; *MBC*, 29 September 1849, p. 3.

139 Thomas Kelly, *George Birkbeck: pioneer of adult education*, (Liverpool: Liverpool University Press, 1957), p. 56; John Thomas Lea, *The history and development of the Mechanics' Institutions*, (Oldham: Research in Librarianship, 1968), pp. 3, 10, 11; Barnard, *History of English education*, p. 107. Kociumbas, *The Oxford history of Australia*, pp. 217-21; Map Brisbane ca 1850s, Appendix, p. 227.

140 *Rules and regulations for the government of the Brisbane School of Arts and Sciences*, (Brisbane: 1849), p. 7.

141 Lea, *The history and development of the mechanics' institutes*, p. 7.

142 *Rules and regulations, Brisbane School of Arts*, 1849, p. 7.

143 *MBC*, 1 December 1849, p. 3; 24 August 1850, p. 2; 11 October 1851, p.3 ; 25 October 1851, p. 2; 18 November 1851, p. 3; 15 May 1852, p. 2; 2 June 1852, p. 3; 20 July 1853, p. 3; 17 November 1855, p. 2; 16 July 1859, p. 2.

144 Cleary, Brisbane School of Arts thesis, p. 86.

145 *MBC*, 13 January 1855, p. 3.

146 Cleary, Brisbane School of Arts thesis, pp. xii, 45

147 *MBC*, 6 October 1849, p. 3

148 *MBC*, 13 October 1849, p. 2.

149 Cleary, Brisbane School of Arts thesis, pp. 54-65.

150 Ibid. p. 57; *MBFP*, 25 January 1853, p. 3.

151 Ibid.

152 *MBC*, 29 January 1853, p. 2.

153 MBC, 12 January 1853, p. 3.

154 *MBC*, 17 September 1853, p. 2.

155 Cleary, Brisbane School of Arts thesis, p. 68.

156 *MBC*, 3 August 1850, p. 3.

157 *MBC*, 27 December 1854, p. 3.

158 *MBC*, 14 August 1858, p. 3.

159 Cleary, Brisbane School of Arts thesis, pp. 45-51.

160 *MBC*, 16 April 1859, p. 2; Warren Bebbington, ed. *The Oxford companion to Australian music*, (Melbourne: Oxford University Press, 1997).

161 *MBC*, 1 January 1859, p. 2; Martin, *The foundations of the Catholic church in Queensland*, p. 99-100.

162 Duncan, *Diary*, 17, 18, 20, 21 March 1856.

163 *MBC*, 10 May 1851, p. 2; 14 June 1851, p. 3.

164 *MBC*, 26 April 1856, p. 2; 3 May 1856, p. 3.

165 *MBC*, 30 October 1852, p. 2; 29 January 1853, p. 3; 30 April 1853, p. 3.

166 *MBFP*, 2 November 1852, p. 2.

167 *MBC*, 7 May 1859, p. 2.

168 *MBC*, 25 November 1854, p. 2.

169 *MBC*, 9 December 1854, p. 2.

170 *MBC*, 27 January 1855, p. 2

171 *MBC*, 17 March 1855, p. 3.

172 *MBC*, 26 June 1860, p. 2; 19 July 1860, p. 2.

173 *MBC*, 18 September 1860, p. 3; 14 May 1859, p.2; 7 May 1859, p. 2.
174 *MBC*, 7 May 1859, p. 2.
175 *MBC*, 19 January 1859, p. 3.
176 *MBC*, 29 January 1859, p. 2.
177 *MBC*, 28 January 1860, p. 2.
178 Payten, Duncan thesis, p. 143.
179 *MBC*, 28 January 1860, p. 2.
180 Ibid.

Chapter 6

The Scottish presence 1841-59

Governor George Bowen was probably well briefed in England during 1859 about the future colony over which he would exercise vice-regal powers. He was no doubt aware that prosperous, moral Brisbane and its flourishing hinterland, in which successful pastoralists reportedly led the life of Virginian planters, were incompatible socially and politically.[1] Although the new colony's economy was highly dependent on wool and Brisbane's claim to entrepot status had been unequivocally established, a disharmonious relationship existed between the urban and rural capitalists who controlled the production and export components within this vital industry's infrastructure.

The deep gulf scarcely hid the fact that a bloodless revolution had occurred during most part of the preceding decade. A substantial influx of radical, nonconformist, urban immigrants, the very people whom squatters sought to curtail numerically, prevented the establishment of a plantation economy and pastoral hegemony. Power shifted from the bush to the town. The squatter oligarchy was replaced by incipient democracy. Unlocking the land and closer settlement were imminent, heralding the advent of a more civilised interior. The threat to the European proletariat by convict labour, the basis of squatter autocracy, was removed by imperial legislation while the influx of free immigrants swelled the workers' ranks. Competition from cheap Asian labour receded as the squatters came to realise that they would have to build a more expensive labour component into their strategic planning. Meanwhile the inflow of free immigrants had transformed Brisbane from a rough frontier society into the very model of middle-class morality.

It was Scottish planning that laid the foundations of pastoral autocracy and it was Scottish initiative in marshalling opposing urban forces which brought its demise. In addition, it was Scottish idealism emanating from urban society which provided leadership to that movement for cultural and moral reform which gave Brisbane a reputation for respectability in the 1850s. Not only did Scottish pastoralists produce 'remarkable economic achievements' in the face of almost overwhelming vicissitude, but they were at the forefront of the separation movement.[2] For much of the period, they also constituted most of the local government officials and magistrates who ensured the district ran on an even keel, peer group bias aside. At a humbler level, the Scottish proletarian settlers amongst others, provided the backbone and sinew for colonisation.[3] Indeed, this numerically under-represented ethnic minority group was inordinately successful at Moreton Bay.

It is within this milieu of socio-political turmoil, a classic example of class conflict, that this study has focused on the role of Scottish settlers in the development of the Moreton Bay District. Predictably, the task of evaluating the Scottish contribution has been difficult.[4] The settlers from this enterprising nation contained the full range of many diverse elements of Scottish society and were clearly divided by regional differences. Moreover, aspiring colonists from other nations, especially the nonconformists, were driven by the same thrift, industry, frugality, piety and persistence.[5] In fact, the Protestant work ethic was a common characteristic to those upwardly-mobile immigrants who strove to better their condition in a more socially open and fluid environment than their homelands offered. Materialism, devotion to calling and individual virtue, Calvinist precepts shared with others in the British and German evangelical fraternity, were also the indelible hallmarks of Scottish Presbyterianism.[6]

Furthermore the Scots assimilated easily, especially the increasingly Anglicised Lowlanders, forming few enduring ethnic concentrations. Possibly the less refined, less compliant and culturally-proud Highlanders, especially the Gaelic speakers, continued to remain as distinctive ethnic entities, resisting as long as possible the strong colonial forces of uniformity. The Anglicised Lowlanders were more accommodating. Further, the Scottish leadership, often with experiential and employment backgrounds in England and Europe, adapted readily to conditional integration within the English-oriented colonial structures.

The frontier character of colonial society was a substantial impediment to the establishment and maintenance of a Scottish community. Although they put their national assertiveness on hold on the frontier in the name of survival, the Scots had no intention of subjugating their national identity to English homogenisation. Conversely, when close settlement was made possible and systematic immigration swelled their ranks, the Scots were in the optimum situation to proclaim their distinctiveness by stronger affiliation with their unique religion and its superior educational provision.

Despite some doubts expressed by academics such as Duncan Waterson about the relationship of Calvinism with Scottish economic success, others like Malcolm Prentis concluded that Presbyterianism was undoubtedly a significant vehicle for Scottish culture, identity and achievement.[7] The validity of this assertion was vividly illustrated by the strong back-lash against evangelical amalgamation when Scots found their religion in danger of being diluted and swamped by other numerically superior nonconformist sects in Lang's short-lived religious experiment in Brisbane. As the Scottish character was too intricately embedded within Presbyterianism, any assault on this religion was repelled vigorously. In Brisbane, such a perceived affront ultimately resulted in the dissolution of Lang's ecumenical dream and the formation of an unadulterated, Scottish-centered, evangelical variety of the national institution. The relative anonymity of most of the instigators of this move and their subsequent decisive actions provided a salutary lesson; Scottish willingness to cooperate to achieve specific community goals should never be equated with passivity and subservience.

It has been consistently asserted that Scots, no matter how humble, never entertained the notion of subverting their national character or concealing their distinctiveness.[8] 'While they found it expedient, on occasions, to form an alliance with other Protestant groups within the community, they never sought to do this at the expense of their own national or religious identity'.[9] The failure of Brisbane's attempt to form an ecumenical Protestant church, building on nonconformist interaction in Britain and doctrinal parallels, serves to emphasise that the Scots would not tolerate attempts to interfere with that vehicle of their national psyche which was as distinctive and inseparable as their inimitable regional accents. Hence Lang's attempt to induce migrants from his homeland to eschew other forms of 'bastard [national] sentimentalism' in favour of the values of colonial pragmatism was ultimately doomed to failure.[10] The Scottish colonists adapted their national heritage to the peculiar demands of a novel society and in turn helped shape the character of the emergent urban community. But they had no plans to become anonymities; they never supressed their national consciousness despite the similarities they shared with colonists from other nations. Their clannishness and the strong network throughout the region not only facilitated their material success, but provided that social and emotional support which maintained their Scottishness.

* * *

In the main, this investigation has focused on the prominent Scots who were at the vanguard of significant events related to the development of Moreton Bay. While acknowledging that most of the well-connected could only but succeed and prosper, it also emphasises the role played by the proletarian Scots in developing the district. In reaction to recent criticism emanating from Scottish historians relating to selective reporting on the Scottish contribution to colonisation, the occasional Scottish failure is highlighted in addition to the hitherto neglected achievements of the humble, 'invisible Scots'.[11]

Several prominent Scots were only partially unsuccessful in attaining their goals at Moreton Bay. Evan Mackenzie, though his colonial career was punctuated with a string of successful and district-saving achievements, failed in his ultimate goal of forging a direct trade route to London, as his Scottish and colonial support system collapsed.[12] The Reverend John Gregor, rejected by his Brisbane parishioners as an unsuitable pastor, entered the annals of Australian Anglican history as 'a second rate man placed in a position where only a first rate man could have succeeded'.[13] Lang, a cruel critic of Gregor, was singularly unsuccessful in interesting his compatriots, the British cotton merchants and the Colonial Office, in his Cooksland scheme.[14] W.A. Duncan was temporarily ruined emotionally and financially by the southern squatters after publishing several newspaper articles supporting Gipps' unpopular land regulations.[15] Among the northern squatters, James Ivory's 'pigsty' living conditions at his station homestead in 1851 reflected a rare example of Scottish inability to forge a prosperous pastoral run after nearly a decade.[16] In addition, John Balfour and Robert Graham lost heavily following their failure to supplant Brisbane and establish Cleveland Point as the shipping port for the Northern Districts.[17] At the district, colonial and Westminster levels, the Scottish-led squatters failed in their campaign to re-introduce transportation, thereby ringing the death knell to their designs of establishing a bipolarised plantation society.

Nevertheless most failures were only temporary set-backs. With typical Scottish perseverance and grit, many regrouped, took stock and progressed to other colonial ventures which were outstandingly successful. When all was said and done, the Scottish squatters were only as good as their labour force which was often made up of their humbler compatriots. To date, there has been no investigation into the qualities which ensured the high reputation which the Scottish workers enjoyed throughout the district.

The analysis of passenger lists of direct immigrants between 1848 and 1859 determined the group profile of those people who provided much-needed pastoral labour.[18] In addition, an examination of two bundles of surviving proletarian writing has provided an insight into the value system of the ordinary 'Scots on the make'.[19] Further, a longitudinal study of a discrete group of Highlanders has been compiled to reveal their colourful, colonial biographies, 'warts and all'. Reported fully elsewhere, the Moreton Bay fortunes of the Black Isle contingent, which constituted the labour force on the Kilcoy run in the early forties, correlates with the results of other forms of research in terms of age, education, piety, Presbyterianism, occupations and deference.[20]

Unlike the immigration profile for the whole of New South Wales between 1849 and 1859, the new arrivals contained a large proportion of Highlanders, over 40%. Mainly destined to labour on the pastoral runs in the interior, they proved to have less impact on Moreton Bay's socio-political agenda during this period than immigrants from the radical south-western and central areas of Scotland. In all, nearly 25% of the immigrants were derived from that industrial and commercial belt embracing Lanarkshire and Midlothian, the cradle of Scottish working-class assertiveness, trade unionism and Chartism.[21] Over 100 politically-aware mechanics and artisans, the most skilful of whom were destined for urban employment, emigrated from these districts. Whether they were politically passive like the majority or within the ranks of the minority of activists, they were the types of immigrants which Moreton Bay wanted. Immigration regulations ensured that prospective colonists were employable, respectable and possessed some financial means. However, Moreton Bay's convict taint was of more influence in causing the relative dearth of Scottish single women among the total migrant intake from that country than the worthiness of compatriot emigres.[22]

Many remained invisible or anonymous, principally in the interior, and would make their mark as community leaders in and around the small settlements which grew up after the squatters' land was finally broken up into farm lots from 1861. It was more likely that the fortunes of immigrant children such as photographer

Thomas Matheson, bushranger James McPherson and Esk shire chairman Alexander Smith would bring their respectable and well-established parents into prominence.[23]

The foundation labour force at Kilcoy, which made up the first specially imported Scottish pastoral labour component in the Moreton Bay District, reveals a similar but more spectacular pattern of colonial success. Exemplifying the same characteristics as the later immigrants, which supposedly set Scots apart as disproportionately successful settlers, this Highland group was remarkable for the unusual speed of its social and economic ascent after serving their rural contracts. They made the most of distinct advantages of being on the ground floor of urban development and took full advantage of their influential contacts within the Scottish northern network. The rapid attainment of employer status, property ownership and franchise qualifications by many of this non-deferential body nevertheless demonstrated that the fluid environment of the Moreton Bay District provided optimum conditions for the achievement of the main immigrant goal of socio-economic self-improvement.

This close-knit Black Isle contingent is also noteworthy for its dramatic change in allegiance from the squatter camp to that of the Langites as more of their peers with radical views arrived and pastoralist hegemony alienated the urban forces. By the mid 1850s, these upstart Scottish petit bourgeois employers possessed the financial ability to challenge the more arrogant and exploitative of the Northern District's socio-economic elite. With the aid of prominent Langites such as Robert Cribb, some legal challenges were mounted to counter ominous signs of British class distinction and privilege by temporary speculators in a new homeland with its promise of a new order. Such action was a clear, assertive, democratic message to the squattocracy who had formed their arbitrary and exploitative attitudes towards labour through the bias of the Masters and Servants' regulations and the partiality of magistrates.

With such grassroots opposition to the 'intelligence and capital' of the district, Mackenzie's plantation economy had no prospects of flourishing.[24] As well as being disappointed at this group's disaffection from the squatting party, Mackenzie would have disapproved of the upward social mobility of its unskilled members. Considering it morally repugnant for 'mere labourers' to own property, he overestimated the extent of social control and underestimated the efficacy of the Protestant work ethic which the alliance of church and school fostered among the Scottish proletariat. Nevertheless Presbyterian Calvinism was certainly a driving force in their lives. Gregor noted their respectability, attention and piety at Kilcoy as early as 1843.[25] The centrality of Presbyterianism to their psyche was evident when many of their number in Brisbane joined David McConnel to form a Free Church. The Scots refused to be a subordinate unit within a proposed hybrid evangelical church even if it was close to Lang's heart.[26]

Historical research of immigrants' records, newspaper reports and observations of contemporaries has consistently isolated Presbyterianism as the framework upon which disproportionate Scottish success was built. The inner thoughts contained within two surviving sets of proletarian papers have provided details of the overriding impact it had on everyday life. The parental letters of Mount Brisbane employee Andrew Watherston demonstrate the anguish felt when the steadying influence of the Kirk was absent in godless areas such as the Brisbane River Valley. In his rude but caring style, Watherston senior beseeched his son to maintain unwavering faith by Bible study and warned him about the dangers of drink and profaning the Sabbath. Every action and every thought was to be acceptable to God.[27]

The same precepts for salvation are evident in greater detail in William Pettigrew's diary and correspondence homeward. If Pettigrew was typical of the successful Scottish colonial, there is no doubt that adherence to the religious precepts of Scottish Calvinism permeated daily life and produced the Scottish stereotype.[28] Strict adherence to the doctrines of predestination, divine intervention, Sabbatarianism and temperance led not only to an uncompromising work ethic, independence, thrift and irreproachable respectability, but also to bigotry, meanness, gravity, self-righteousness and intransigence. This creed also produced many of the self-seeking individuals who thrived in Brisbane's nonconformist, capitalist climate of the late 1850s, distinguished by high morality, societal contention, pursuit of profits, acquisition of property and self-interest. It would appear that Calvinism was indeed the counterpoint of capitalism as claimed by Weber.

* * *

This form of capitalism sanctioned by nonconformism was closely associated with the moral revitalisation and economic growth of Brisbane. However, it differed in intensity from that practised in the interior. With its roots in Scotland's economic rationalisation of agriculture and driven by Scottish industrialists and accountants, the type of capital accumulation developed by the pioneer squatters on the unpoliced frontier left numerous human casualties in its wake. According to the opinion of late twentieth century Scottish historians, dispossession of the Aborigines was more violent than the Highland Clearances, and the exploitation of non-Scottish colonial labour apparently rivalled that within the industrial concentrations in Scotland. Edinburgh-based capitalists financed and exercised close surveillance over the Scottish vanguard which occupied the Moreton Bay District. On the spot, a Highland capitalist ensured the area's survival while planning for squatter oligarchy. However, from 1849 a Glaswegian-influenced concord of the petite bourgeoisie and workers contributed significantly to undoing the damage done by pastoral capitalism to morality, social justice and nascent democracy in Brisbane. Ultimately, these antagonistic forces combined to achieve political and economic independence from their common southern foe which had been perceived as a perverse, retarding influence on northern progress.

Jim Hewitson, a Scottish journalist who has written many articles on Scotland's mysterious and romantic past for popular journals with world-wide circulation, is familiar with pastoral expansion in northern Australia. He has detected a definite Highland influence in the first decade of free settlement at Moreton Bay. This was especially evident in the manner in which Aboriginal resistance was dealt with.[29] It was also reflected in early urban development. Evan Mackenzie, as local leader, injected traditional Highland ruthlessness, intrigue, feuding and paternalism into his antipodean career as a squatter and a merchant. By sound planning and vigorous execution, he replicated in the colony his father's role of successful merchant, important steam company shareholder and estate proprietor. He quickly established a profitable run, operated a remunerative trading business, owned the only industrial enterprise and controlled Brisbane's exports by 1844. Although he exerted influence over most of Brisbane's key servicing, hospitality and legal facilities through Highland patronage, his attempt to establish Brisbane as an estate town similar to his father's Munlochy failed because of his over-developed propensity for Highland treachery.

Not content to be the de facto leader of the district, Mackenzie over-reached himself in attempting to re-create the equivalent of an aristocratic Highland elite from pastoralist ranks. An increasingly egalitarian colonial society resisted this plantation concept which was also based on squatter control of the labour market, similar to the practice on the Kilcoy estate. In setting up a rival shipping port at Kangaroo Point, creating a tariff war with his steam company employers and attempting to eliminate them altogether from northern trade, his grand designs were ultimately thwarted by alienating the colony's powerful Scottish financial and bureaucratic establishment. While Mackenzie and the Moreton Bay District, especially Brisbane, benefited from Mackenzie's Highland heritage, its excesses led to his colonial demise.

There was a definite Glaswegian flavour to the process of dismantling Mackenzie's plans for a squatter hegemony and the creation of a radical, moral Brisbane during the 1850s. The distinctive features of nonconformism, the Free Church, provident societies, the School of Arts, St Andrew's school, the temperance league, worker assertion and Chartism all had their origins in and around the Clyde. The radical traditions of Glasgow, the font of Scottish Chartism, infant trade unionism, mass riots, protests and strikes, were transplanted to Moreton Bay by the more militant immigrants who joined ranks with middle-class liberals.[30] Although a core of English radicals was prominent among those who laboured to fulfil the vision of Lang, their democratic victories were assured by the support from numerous workers, largely Scots. Moreover, the closely associated liberal humanist climate fostered by the *Moreton Bay Courier* had its source in James Swan who was the mouthpiece of Lang. Both hailed from the Clyde district.[31]

The Reverend Thomas Chalmers, who led dissident Scottish clerics from the Church of Scotland to form the Free Church in 1843, was Lang's mentor and spiritual advisor when he was studying theology at Glasgow University. Of a more conservative persuasion than Lang, whose democratic and republican notions were fuelled by his American experience, Chalmers was noted for the positive steps he took to overcome the debasing influence of industrialism upon his Glaswegian parish of Tron - a campaign he wished to extend to reform the rest of Scotland. In common with Lang's plans for Moreton Bay, he aimed to 'ruralise' the depraved areas by the influence of the church, school and the example of the respectable middle class.[32]

Unlike the democratic idealism which drove Lang's quest to restore community values, Chalmers' concern for Glaswegian workers was devoid of understanding of their aspirations and dismissive of their means of assertion. Stressing the responsibility of the individual to progress by thrift, sobriety and self-help, Chalmers upheld the doctrine of divine hierarchy while deploring trade unionism, democracy and radical agitation. Little wonder that Lang was regarded as the champion of the church-going masses at Brisbane and Chalmers' policy ultimately estranged and alienated their urban counterparts in Scotland. Whereas Lang questioned successfully the existing social framework and attempted to alter the distribution of property and power, a reluctant Chalmers clung to the inequalities of the old order.[33] Nevertheless it was significant that the Free Church, the one formed in reaction to the exercise of entrenched elitist power, was established as the first Presbyterian church in Moreton Bay. In this district, the major nonconformist political agenda focused on suppressing the emergence of the pastoralists as such a powerful and privileged group.

Glaswegian Scots were well represented among the proletarian sector which struggled for democracy and working-class rights. Typically, they were nonconformist, Chartist-oriented, teetotal, well-educated and active in worker affairs - the products of their reformist class in the radical Clydeside society.[34] James Johnston became Brisbane's first president of the Band of Hope with its origins in the Scottish Temperance League founded in Glasgow by the evangelical publisher William Collins.[35] His brother-in-law, John Scott, was Brisbane's foremost educator, having been trained in the monitorial-based methods at the Glasgow Normal School and St Andrew's. In common with Johnston, Scott was foremost in encouraging the working men's movement in Brisbane led by Glaswegians James Spence and William Geddes. He was a pioneer of trade unionism in Brisbane, rising to the presidency of the Queensland Teachers' Union in 1890.[36] The strength of Brisbane's Chartism, a British political movement of moral force originating in Glasgow, is reflected in the fact that the Queensland foundation parliament went within a whisker of being the first in the world to incorporate those democratic principles. Nevertheless, agitation of local, Chartist-inspired radicals for social reform was most effective. In 1858 an agreement between labour represented by Spence and the management under John Petrie resulted in an eight-hour working day being instituted at Petries'- the same year in which the stonemasons formed Queensland's first union.[37]

In addition the Brisbane School of Arts and Sciences, founded and dominated by Lang's immigrants, was based on the prevailing model of Mechanics Institutes in Glasgow and London. Virtually functioning as middle-class recreational centres, these institutes had long forsaken their original roles to technically and scientifically educate working-class artisans as practised at Birkbeck's seminal Glasgow Mechanics' Institution in the early nineteenth century.[38] In Brisbane this institute earned the reputation as a stronghold of Chartism following the frequent intra middle-class clashes in which democratic reformers did battle with Duncan-led conservatives.

* * *

Mackenzie, Lang and Duncan, the Scots who cast the most influence over the development of the pre-separation Moreton Bay District, had clearly articulated their visions for the type of society which should be engineered according to their socio-political beliefs. While Lang was instrumental through his immigrants in bringing down Mackenzie's plans for elitist social control, Duncan through his official position facilitated the trading arrangements which would have met with the approval of Brisbane's foremost booster. In addition, he privately enriched the township's cultural and religious life by following his aesthetic interests.

The visions of Lang and Duncan reflected their Scottish backgrounds as agriculturalists in farming communities, while Mackenzie's model was derived from the elitist perceptions inherent in estate management. The plans of the former pair, based on the promotion of agriculture to facilitate the free immigrant's desire for self-advancement, were antithetical to the squatters' designs for an oligarchic social structure. The infant district gave promise of a new democratic society and a better order - a small man's frontier with a prospect of comfortable independence.[39] Squatter attempts to transpose the class inequalities of landowner-dominated Scotland to the colony not only contributed to a breakdown in religion, morality and order, but were also a disincentive to respectable, plebian immigration. The studied indifference of the temporary Scottish pastoralists to the obverse of the highly moral rural climate of their homeland is indicative of the unscrupulous practice of Scottish capitalism derided recently by Scottish historians. Therefore planned immigration and land reform were prerequisites to diminish the influence of 'the barbarism of the pastoral industry' and elevate the civilising agencies.[40]

Whereas Lang and Duncan had every intention of spreading agriculture throughout the interior, Evan Mackenzie only paid lip-service to the acknowledged need for pastoralism to admit limited farming. On paper, Mackenzie supported a restricted and selective system of farming around grazing properties in the name of civilisation. However, he and his ilk did their utmost to inhibit the emergence of close settlement and agriculture. In common with Lang, Duncan advocated planned immigration and land reform to diminish the pastoralists' influence. It was Lang's anti-Catholic and anti-Irish bigotry, a long-standing characteristic of many Scottish and English Protestants, which ensured that these like-minded, pro-agricultural strategists would never form a united anti-pastoral alliance. Even the highly influential James Swan, a fierce supporter of Lang's immigration and agricultural policies, was repelled by the prospect of religiously-based divisions which could be fostered by his former mentor's respectable migrants. Nevertheless he realised only too well that they offered the best prospects of leading Moreton Bay's moral and political revitalisation.

The religious intolerance of Lang aside, these three Scottish leaders were men ahead of their time. Mackenzie's dream of Brisbane as an international trading port, collecting its own customs' dues with shipping links direct to Britain was realised within two years of his departure from the north. In the early sixties, the greater part of Lang's economic plans had been fulfilled. The squatters' land was opened to free selection, sugar production became firmly established and cotton was grown successfully and extensively around Caboolture - although not on a scale to rival production in the USA. Furthermore, from 1860 each immigrant to Queensland was entitled to a land order - fulfilment of the very principle which Lang had belligerently advocated to an unsympathetic Colonial Office between 1847 and 1849.[41] The conservative and generally aloof Duncan must have had a sense of deja vu as pre-separation Queensland came to grips with anti-transportation, National education, teacher recruitment, working-class assertion and cultural extension - battles which he had fought and won as 'champion of the operatives' in Sydney in the thirties and early forties.

Each displayed forceful personalities which not only ensured that their message was clearly received but probably also contributed to their propensity to make bitter enemies. The aristocratic, urbane Mackenzie initially managed to unify the various elements of northern society in the name of district survival. However, his ruthless and under-hand manoeuvres against the southern merchant establishment and his success in establishing Kangaroo Point to the detriment of other Brisbane interests caused widespread astonishment and rancour.[42] His apparently cavalier and generally popular image effectively disguised his ability to discharge extreme forms of aggression when cornered. Hailing from the Highland aristocracy in which subterfuge, feuding and assassination were legend, the rebellious Mackenzie relentlessly targeted those who obstructed his grand designs. Neither the powerful nor the marginalised of society was spared from his effectively disguised viciousness. Accordingly, he sabotaged the HRSNCo's northern trade, undermined established North and South Brisbane businessmen and was a scourge of the Aborigines in the interior.[43]

Whereas Mackenzie, Lang and Duncan subscribed to the doctrine of Terra Nullius, they were less than unanimous in the manner in which Australia's indigenes were dispossessed. They especially differed in their reactions to the northern conspiracy of silence which prevented instances of Aboriginal abuse and other contentious issues reaching the authorities. In comparison with Mackenzie, whose name is inextricably associated with Aboriginal suppression in a manner more brutal than that experienced in the Highland Clearances, Lang and Duncan were in the forefront of those Scots who defended Aboriginal rights. By their separate, benevolent actions they were instrumental in rending the curtain of silence drawn around the district. Having disclosed the Kilcoy poisonings to the Governor of New South Wales and initiated inquiry into white vigilantism in Brisbane, Lang and Duncan respectively ensured that northern settlers would no longer be able to randomly attack Aborigines without facing legal consequences. Both of these Scots, in the name of human justice, put aside personal concerns of safety and social acceptance to make significant inroads into what had become an entrenched malignancy in northern culture.

The vindictive Lang's pugnacity was legend. However, his habitual deception through half-truths and propensity for fraud, together with an abusive tongue and pen, detracted from his acknowledged abilities and considerable achievements - particularly having an alienating effect upon the Sydney legislature and press. Duncan's hyper-conscientious personality was described as belligerent, sarcastic, tactlessly independent, outspoken and unyielding, especially towards those who opposed his uncompromising decisions.[44] Such aggressive intransigence earned him a cold farewell from the *Moreton Bay Courier* which grudgingly acknowledged his dedicated leadership at the School of Arts. The fact that he was one of the most significant middle-class leaders of the new lower class political forces of the 1840s cut little ice in Brisbane which was going through a similar stage of radical assertion. He was judged at Moreton Bay not on his past leadership, but on his current irritable, self-seeking conservatism and a long-standing reputation of being a sycophant of the adversarial southern government.[45]

This derisive label could hardly be applied to the rebellious Mackenzie with his propensity to ignore and subvert. Nor was it attributable to a decidedly unsubmissive Lang who stood toe to toe with the likes of Wentworth in the legislature to competently and faithfully press northern claims.[46] So tenacious and unremitting was Lang's advocacy for a boundary advantageous to the new Queensland that it was necessary for the other northern representatives in the legislature to undermine his efforts as he was delaying the finalisation of separation.[47]

At length Mackenzie was recognised by Lang for his far-sighted actions within Brisbane and venerated by Dowse for his district-saving enterprise. He was also remembered for his eloquent and optimistic vision for Moreton Bay development articulated at a dinner for Leichhardt, but was wrongly accused of poisoning Aborigines at Kilcoy.[48] This misdirected charge ensured that his positive contributions to the foundation of the Moreton Bay community were erased from Queensland's history for nearly 150 years.

D.W.A. Baker, has competently analysed Lang's personality and behaviour in his extensively researched and incisive biography of that intimidating initiator of the Australian republican movement. Baker assessed that Lang was a stirrer, propagandist and public motivator rather than a creative politician. The consummate manipulator of press, pamphlets, platform and public opinion, 'He had many ideas, but few political or creative achievements'.[49] The Queensland political establishment of 1860 concurred. Doubting the altruism of his immigration fiasco of 1849, it gave only tentative acknowledgement to his role in achieving separation from New South Wales.[50] His charisma and popular leadership, however, were largely unrecognised.

Further, scant regard was paid to the inspiration he provided to aggrieved northerners, his labours within the legislature and his success in tempering squatter social and political control by substantially increasing the middle class by his one northern foray into respectable immigration. Nevertheless grudging recognition was accorded to this group which exerted a positive moral influence upon the tone of Moreton Bay society. Indeed the activities of these radical, anti-squatter, middle-class colonists, encouraged from afar by Lang and goaded by Brisbane's radical newspaper, exerted similar democratic effects on the Northern Districts as did the forces unleashed by discovery of gold in the southern states. Little wonder that the British and colonial establishments regarded Lang as an agent provocateur.

Henry Parkes, a fellow republican and one not given to rash judgements, lauded Lang's 'services for immigration', his bold advocacy for the political rights and liberties of the colonies, his altruism for the public good and the quality of his performance in the Legislative Council. Parkes concluded, 'We look in vain for his equal'.[51] Vance Palmer, the celebrated author, declared, 'He stimulated people to think for themselves, speak their full minds openly [and] stand upright on their own feet. Even more than Parkes ... , he was an image of the stubborn democracy he had done so much to build'.[52] Consequently, Lang was both popular hero and scourge of politicians and bureaucrats.

Whereas the positive and negative influences of the pre-eminent Scots had been widely acknowledged, the equally unspectacular toil of the Scottish proletariat has received scant recognition. The ordinary Scots at Moreton Bay between 1841 and 1849, however, were a small minority group, never representing much more than a tenth of the population. Yet their presence was strong in terms of visibility, power and influence. Comprising 60% of squatters, a large proportion of magistrates and nearly all senior government officials until the mid-fifties, the Scots were heavily represented in the leadership ranks - including that of the small military detachment.

Equally important, a Scot controlled the most influential and widely circulated newspaper in the district. In the period between 1848 and separation year, the Scot who espoused liberal-humanitarian ideals and supported the forces of democratic radicalism was James Swan, proprietor of one of the two significant newspapers. In addition to being significant within the driving force to establish culture and improve morality in the district, two well-qualified Scots conducted the best schools in Brisbane. Not only was a Scot president of the Brisbane School of Arts, but the majority of the committee and membership was composed of men from this national minority group. Scotsmen were also foremost among the leadership which moulded working-class consciousness and identity which was belatedly engineered during separation year.

Entrenched in the northern power structure, the dominant Scots never entertained the creation of a xenophobic enclave at Moreton Bay. The history of Scottish participation and disproportionate success in other colonies within the empire indicated that narrow ethnocentrism was not the traditional Scottish style. In common with their more humble compatriots, the Scottish leaders worked for the benefit of all colonists bent on self-improvement within the frontier society. As in other districts, Moreton Bay Scots assimilated easily, formed few durable ethnic concentrations and thrived without fanfare in a highly materialistic, competitive and ultimately moral society - grist for the mill of Calvinist-reared, aspiring capitalists.

These observations relating to the visible Scottish presence should not be interpreted to indicate unity of purpose among that ethnic group. In fact they reflect the extent of those divisions which were a characteristic of the Moreton Bay community. In common with the majority of northern colonists, most Scottish settlers, ranging from predominantly temporary squatters to the universally permanent proletariat, were self-seeking in the hope of accumulating status, capital and property.

It is unwise to generalise about a single Scottish position on any colonial issue. In matters of class and district development, Scots invariably locked horns as proponents and opponents. In the main, Scottish settlers transferred their class and humanitarian allegiance to the colonial situation, finding companionship and support in the appropriate local group. Hence highly moral issues such as the treatment of Moreton Bay's indigenes attracted significant numbers of Scottish colonists to the philanthropic group which advocated protection, justice and dignity.

Moreton Bay became a classic arena for class conflict and Scots aligned according to their economic and social affiliations within laissez-faire capitalism to protect their interests. In fact, on all issues fought in the district - economic, political or cultural - Scots could be found, often as leaders, taking up opposing positions. It was indeed ironical that Scottish religion, education and character could only emerge in the interior when the power base of the Scottish pastoralists was substantially eroded. Their aspirations for socio-political ascendancy, obstruction to moral influence in the bush and influence on urban immorality divided northern society and therefore the Scottish ethnic group.

However, it was a few visionary insurgents within elite ranks who determined the direction in which pre-separation Queensland progressed from pastoral ascendancy via the transportation threat to achievement of colonial status. Credit has been accorded to three disparate Scots - a rebellious aristocrat, a belligerent clergyman and a churlish government official - for masterminding, operationalising and overseeing a large part of the unique course of social, political and economic development in this rebellious and divided northern region. Constantly pushing back the boundaries and living on the edge, these innovators were alienated in various degrees from once-valued, formative and controlling institutions in Scotland. Two of them carried this mutinous attitude into their colonial careers. Sharing a dislike of authority and determined to have their own way, it was not unremarkable that Mackenzie and Lang were also out of step with and contemptuous towards the colonial establishment and its obstructive regulations. Inexorably they came to lock horns with the legislature in Sydney and the Scottish-led bureaucratic and mercantile machines.

Mackenzie earned his official disapprobation through 'Highland treachery'; by stealth, deception and betrayal of those who had trusted him because of his suave manner, his aristocratic background and his highly-placed contacts. Lang's underachievement can be largely attributed to his belligerent behaviour towards key legislators and administrators as to be expected from a thwarted Scottish evangelical zealot who feared God only. By his offensive tongue and vindictive pen, Lang alienated those within the power structure who possessed the influence and clout to realise his radical schemes. It is claimed that his achievements would have matched those of Parkes in education and Robertson in land reform, 'had his intense inner drive not been inextricably compounded with an irresistible impulse to hurt those who showed opposition or were merely lukewarm towards his designs'.[53] Undoubtedly, he was a true patriot, but hardly a statesman or diplomat.

On the other hand, William Duncan, the temporarily-exiled third agent of change, while pursuing his own interests (much to Brisbane's benefit), curried favour with the British and Australian authorities. Grateful for such a formidable ally at the cutting edge of colonial progress, they readily rewarded him for his superior talents, courage and long-standing loyalty. Although possessing the same inscrutability as Mackenzie and capapable of Lang's pugnacity, the inflexible, politically-sophisticated Duncan fully realised the ultimate impotence of mere public demonstration without access to those who wielded societal power. Thus he was canny enough to exploit to its utmost the potential of 'treading the corridors of power' and building compatible relationships with significant establishment figures in government and administration.

Yet, the resistance of Mackenzie and Lang to Sydney-based imperious rule had helped unite in spirit and resolve the majority of colonists from all British nationalities in the north. It was this manifestation of popular dissent which provided the impetus for the popular movement seeking independence from southern control. Ultimately, it was the charisma, common touch, credible plans and local chauvinism of these two opinion leaders, rather than their evident Scottishness, which earned them that popular following which fuelled the drive for economic prosperity and statehood. Only when these conditions had been attained by the 1860s was the influence of the primitive, frontier society diluted and the dominion of respectability enhanced. Rather than being achieved by the intensity of mass discontent and protest, this regional renewal resulted primarily from the diplomatic conduct of those who gained access to the newly-receptive

British policy makers and the early initiatives of the infant colonial legislature which opened up the land. Aided by a liberal immigration scheme, with a decided Lang flavour, it then became possible for an influx of Scottish immigrants to concentrate in the townships to establish the institutional forms of Scottishness such as churches, schools, lodges and societies. Once formed, they acted as ethnic rallying points, vehicles for revitalisation of a temporarily-muted national character, foci for the intricate networks and initiating agents for newly-arrived settlers.

* * *

James Swan, the fair-minded, liberal and rational editor of the *Moreton Bay Courier*, approached the above triumvirate in significance at Moreton Bay. However, Swan, like the Petries and Pettigrew, was more parochial in effort and clout during this period. On the other hand, Mackenzie, Lang and Duncan saw the 'big picture', differing from Swan in the lengths to which they would go and the power structures they would fearlessly confront to fulfil their visions. Acting within the confines of the Northern Districts, Swan responsibly utilised the power of the press to assist in creating a humane, liberal and respectable local society. He acted as a restraining but nevertheless powerful influence on the Moreton Bay community, especially attempting to restrict the excesses of over-zealous leadership. In the process, he encouraged tolerance, equality and assertion among the respectable citizenry. Besides cutting Lang down to size for bigotry, but nevertheless focusing appropriately on the undoubted, positive features of the Cooksland scheme, Swan also exercised responsible control over the *Moreton Bay Courier* to defend the freedom of the press against the threats of the likes of the officious Duncan. His editorials and policy were invariably directed towards bettering the position of all settlers in the pioneering society, regardless of religious creed, political alignment or socio-economic status. Therein he provided an unremitting appraisal of the district's development and its developers while promoting the principles of religious freedom, political liberalism and social justice. Consistent with this philosophical approach, Swan's stance against the re-introduction of transportation and his role as an important champion of separation ensured him a foremost place among the founding fathers of northern democracy.

* * *

While 'anonymity' and 'invisibility' may infer active but unacknowledged participation within the community, there is no suggestion that it entailed denial of Scottishness. Furthermore, lack of prominence should never be equated with inactivity. Scots never fitted blandly and unnoticed as homogenised units into an English-dominated society. The Scots were never guilty of 'becoming an indistinguishable group blending ... into the colonial background contributing nothing to shaping their new surroundings'.[54] They never attempted to hide the readily-recognisable aspects of their national character in the name of assimilation. Even on the frontier where they cooperated readily with persons of other nationalities, the Scottish proletariat was singled out by employers for their work attitudes which were widely regarded in colonial circles as unique to their ethnic group.

The Scottish settlers fully appreciated that their muted Scottishness could not be fully reinvigorated until the district developed sufficiently for the Presbyterian church to flourish. Accordingly, they and their home-based anxious parents eagerly anticipated the critical renaissance accompanying the establishment of the district's first Kirk. With the arrival of such vehicles of Scottish culture and identity, their unique values, practices and behaviours were reinforced by their religious and secular collective.[55]

Full Scottishness was never eradicated, but merely attenuated until conditions were appropriate for national consciousness to be given institutional form. Even the extreme conditions in isolated Moreton Bay, remote from established Scottish influence, could not eradicate the national distinctiveness and identity which had been developed throughout their formative years by the church-school nexus. So strong was the influence of the Kirk, even non-churchgoers reflected its values.

The all-pervasive link with Scottish Presbyterianism transcended geographical distance as well as presence in the pews. The 'Church Connection' was not only critical to the maintenance of Scottish identity, but it provided its expatriates with characteristics which led to their disproportionate success in the major fields of colonial endeavour. Girded by the self-assurance of being 'God's chosen people' and fortified by harsh, Calvinist self-discipline, they were well-equipped to prosper and exert positive moral and fiscal influences within any society in which they chose to settle. Congruent with the Scottish experience in other capitalist colonies within the British Empire, and alcohol aside, the majority did not succumb to the immoral influences that accompanied frontierism. Divided by region, class and politics on most societal issues, they were nevertheless united in affinity to Scotland and its value system. Consequently the respectable and prosperous society at Moreton Bay observed by Governor Bowen was largely attributable to that Scottish Protestant ethic.

As leaders or toilers, the vast majority of Scottish settlers proved to be the backbone of both rural and urban enterprise in their adopted country. Free of British aristocratic suppression and demonstrating the same ease of assimilation which distinguished their adaptability in other parts of Australia, the Scots took every advantage of the relatively level playing field at Moreton Bay which followed the opening of the land after separation. In Queensland the Scots manifested those recognisable and ethnic characteristics which emanated from their religious and historical background. Although there was a privileged minority who still fought for the status quo, the sizeable liberal element sought through their single-minded determination to create the ideal society they so desired for their homeland. The Scottish contribution to the establishment of a colony espousing democratic principles and practices was, considering their small number, immeasurable.

ENDNOTES

1. S. Lane-Poole, *Thirty years of colonial government*, (London: 1889), p. 128.
2. Gordon Greenwood, ed. *Australia: A social and political history*, (Sydney: Angus and Robertson, 1955), p. 47.
3. Eric Richards, *That land of exiles: Scots in Australia*, (Edinburgh: HMSO, 1988), p. 12.
4. Ibid, p. 10.
5. Waterson, *Squatter, selector and storekeeper*, p. 136; Eric Richards, 'Varieties of Scottish emigration in the nineteenth century', *Historical Studies*, 21 (1985), p. 484.
6. Callum G. Brown, 'Protest in the pews: interpreting Presbyterianism and society in fracture during the Scottish economic revolution', in T.M. Devine, ed. *Conflict and stability in Scottish society 1700-1850*, (Edinburgh: John Donald, 1990), p.90.
7. Prentis, *The Scots in Australia*, p. 219.
8. Richards, *That land of exiles*, p. 38.
9. Cumming, 'Covenant and identity', p. 203.
10. *British Banner*, 21 June 1848, p. 440.
11. Donnachie, 'The making of "Scots on the make"', p. 135.
12. The Mackenzie referred to throughout this chapter is Evan Mackenzie.
13. Keith Rayner, History of the Church of England in Queensland, p. 40.
14. Lang, *Cooksland*, p. 475.
15. Duncan, Autobiography, p. 59.
16. William Pettigrew, Diary, 8 May 1851.
17. Dushen Salecich, "Brisbane, Ipswich or Cleveland: the capital question at Moreton Bay 1842-59', in Rod Fisher, ed. *Brisbane: people, places and pageantry*, Brisbane History Group, Papers No 6., (Brisbane: BHG, 1987), pp. 83-6.
18. John Mackenzie-Smith, 'Scottish immigrants to Moreton Bay 1841-59', BHG Papers No. 17, in press.
19. William Pettigrew, Letters, RHSQ; Andrew Watherston correspondence, Gareth Gillott, Ipswich.
20. J. Mackenzie-Smith, 'Moreton Bay Scots 1841-95: a Black Isle contingent', pp. 493-514.
21. See map mid-nineteenth century Scotland after Harrison and Prentis, Appendix, p. 225.
22. Mackenzie-Smith, 'Scottish immigrants to Moreton Bay 1849-59'.
23. Kerr, *Confidence and tradition*, p. 237.
24. Mackenzie-Smith, 'Moreton Bay Scots: a Black Isle contingent'.
25. Gregor, 'Missionary Journal', in *Brisbane River Valley 1841-50*, p. 37.
26. David McConnel to Rev. A. Salmon, 10 May 1850, Pettigrew Papers, RHSQ.
27. Andrew Watherston Snr to Andrew Watherston, 31 January 1854, 31 May 1854, Watherson letters.

28 Pettigrew diary, 12 August 1849, 9 September 1849, 30 September 1849, 23 December 1850; Pettigrew to Rev. John Barclay, 11 October 1850.
29 Hewitson, *Far off in sunlit places*, p. 176.
30 Alex Watson, 'Chartism in Glasgow', in Asa Briggs, ed. *Chartist Studies*, (London: Macmillan, 1959), p. 262.
31 Melvin Williams, *Cameos of Baptist men in nineteenth century Queensland*, (Brisbane: Baptist Historical Society of Queensland, 1995), p. 6.
32 Donald Macleod, 'Thomas Chalmers and pauperism', in Stewart J. Brown and Michael Fry, ed. *Scotland in the age of the Disruption*, (Edinburgh: Edinburgh University Press, 1993), p. 63.
33 John F. McCaffery, 'Thomas Chalmers and social change', *Scottish Historical Review*, 60 (1981), p. 37.
34 Ipswich solicitor Arthur Macalister, hailing from Glasgow, was an exception.
35 Smout, *A century of the Scottish people*, p. 140.
36 Spaull and Sullivan, *A history of the Queensland Teachers' Union*, p. 334.
37 Dornan and Cryle, *The Petrie family*, p. 121.
38 Lea, *The history and development of the Mechanics Institutes*, p. 4.
39 Payten, Duncan thesis, p. 135.
40 Ibid, p. 105.
41 Lang, *Narrative of steps taken in promoting the separation of Queensland*, p. 10.
42 John Mackenzie-Smith, ' The foundations of Kangaroo Point 1843-46', in Rod Fisher, ed. *Brisbane: people, places and pageantry*, Brisbane History Group Papers No. 6, (Brisbane: BHG, 1987), pp. 98-101.
43 John Mackenzie-Smith, 'Evan Mackenzie of Kilcoy and the foundation of Brisbane 1841-45', Ibid, p. 24.
44 Payten, Duncan thesis, pp. 186, 199, 225.
45 Ibid, pp. 134, 196.
46 *MBC*, 10 May 1856, p. 2.
47 Laverty, Development of the town of Brisbane, p. 210.
48 Mackenzie-Smith, *Brisbane's forgotten founder*, p. 75.
49 D.W.A. Baker, 'Republican: John Dunmore Lang', in Eric Fry, ed. *Rebels and radicals*, (Sydney: George Allen & Unwin, 1983), p. 83.
50 Charles A. Bernays, *Queensland politics during sixty (1859-1919) years*, (Brisbane: A.J. Cumming, 1920), p. 22.
51 *MBC*, 30 June 1855, p. 3.
52 Vance Palmer, 'The nonconformist: John Dunmore Lang', in Bill Wannan, ed. *The heather in the south: a Scottish-Australian entertainment*, (Sydney: Lansdowne, 1966), p. 84.
53 *ADB*, vol. 1, p. 83.
54 Cumming, 'Covenant and identity', p. 202.
55 Cumming, 'Scottish identity in an Australian colony', pp. 26, 38.

SELECT BIBLIOGRAPHY

REFERENCE WORKS: BOOKS

Eastgate, Marianne. *A name directory of the Moreton Bay Region of New South Wales, 1850-51, 1852-53, 1854-55.* Brisbane: Queensland Family History Society, 1984, 1985.

Eastgate, Marianne. *A guide to the pre-separation population index to the Moreton Bay Region 1824-1859 together with a short history of the region.* Brisbane: Queensland Family History Society, 1990.

Gibbney, H.J. and Smith Ann G. (comp.) *A biographical register 1788-1839. Notes from the name index of the Australian dictionary of biography. 2 vols.* Canberra: Australian National University, 1987.

Harrison, Jennifer. *Guide to the microform collection of the State Library of Queensland.* Second edition. Brisbane: Library Board of Queensland, 1990.

Johnston, W.Ross and Zerner, Margaret. *Guide to the history of Queensland.* Brisbane: Library Board of Queensland, 1985.

Jupp, James (ed.) *The Australian people: an encyclopaedia of the nation, its people and their origins.* North Ryde: Angus & Robertson, 1988.

McIntyre, Perry. *Convict pardons, tickets of leave, NSW 1810-75.* Sydney: W & F Pascoe, 1995 (microfiche)..

Pugh, Theophilus. *Pugh's Moreton Bay Almanac for the year 1859.* Brisbane: T.P. Pugh, 1859.

Queensland State Archives. *Index to pastoral holdings and lessees 1842-1859.* Brisbane.

Ritchie, John (gen. ed). *Australian dictionary of biography.* 12 vols. Melbourne: Melbourne University Press, 1966-1991.

The topographical, statistical, and historical gazetteer of Scotland. 2 vols. Glasgow: A. Fullerton, 1842.

Waterson, D.B. *Biographical register of the Queensland Parliament 1860-1929.* Canberra: Australian National University Press, 1972

MANUSCRIPTS:
Archives Authority of New South Wales, Sydney:

Colonial Secretary, New South Wales, Register of letters received 1854-5. AO Reel 2580.

Colonial Secretary's correspondence 1841-45. 4/2539.2, 4/2581.2, 4/2618.1, 4/2656.2, 4/2696.2.

Surveyor-General. Letters received from surveyors. James Charles Burnett, 1 January 1848 to 21 July 1854. (AO Reel 3055). 2/1516.

Castle Fraser, Aberdeenshire:
Kilcoy estate papers:

Names of tenants and crofters on the estate of Sir Colin Mackenzie of Kilcoy Bart. who paid rents since 13 November 1838 (to 8 June 1839).

List of payments made by tenants and crofters to amount of rent crop 1838 and preceding (Dec. 1839 to Jan. 1840).

Fryer Library, University of Queensland:
Hon. Louis Hope. Journals (A.J.C.P. M 980). micro 7433.

Lang, Dr John Dunmore. Papers re Moreton Bay immigrants 1848-9. micro. 7924

McConnel, A.J. Old times at Cressbrook and Durundur, 89/207

Gareth Gillott, Ipswich:
Watherston letters.

Guildhall Library, London:
Baring Brothers and Company Limited correspondence. Documents 1844-8 concerning Moreton Bay, including letters of Charles and James Balfour and Evan Mackenzie, HC6/4/2 (JOL micro M 1974).

John Oxley Library, Brisbane:
Archer brothers. Durundur diary 1843-4, OM 79-17/1.

Archer brothers. Some letters mainly from Australia, written home between 1833 and 1855, by the brothers Archer, late of Gracemere, Queensland (London: 1933). Typescript. OM 79-72.

Campbell, John. The early settlement of Queensland and other articles. Typescript. OM 90/105.

Colonial Secretary, in-letters from Moreton Bay, 1840-1859. micro A2.10 to A2.42

Dowse, Thomas. Recollections and reminiscences 1828-1878; letters regarding finance 1856-8; Cutting book 1846-79. MSS. OM 79-688.

Dowse, Thomas. Diary 1844-1853, OM 84/31.
994.303 gre.

Leslie family letters 1834-1862. Typescript. OM 71-43.

Mitchell Library, Sydney:
Lang, Dr John Dunmore. Moreton Bay immigrants 1848-9 (micro CY 1075). A 1390.

Lang, Dr John Dunmore. Queensland Separation papers 1848-78. Papers re the cultivation of cotton and sugar 1848-69 (micro CY 2497). A 2241.

Duncan, William Augustine. Papers 1854-56 (micro CY 161). A 2876-2879.

Monash University Library, Melbourne:
Lang, Dr John Dunmore. Letters in *The British Banner*. Typescript. M RARE PAN 994.403 L269.

Queensland State Archives, Brisbane:
Board of National Education, Queensland. Register of teachers employed 1860-1876. EDB/ 01-2.

Government Resident's correspondence book 1853-4. micro Z1496.

Government Resident's correspondence book 1855-6. micro Z1497.

Governor's despatches to the Secretary of State, vol. 1, 1860, GOV/22.

New South Wales Immigration Agent. Passenger Lists. Arrivals at Moreton Bay. 1848-1855. micro Z598.

New South Wales Immigrant Agent. Passenger lists. Arrivals at Moreton Bay 1855-1859. micro Z599.

New South Wales Immigration Agent. Passenger lists to Moreton Bay directly from overseas 1848-1859. micro Z600

Royal Historical Society of Queensland, Brisbane:
Pettigrew, William. Diary, 1849-1853.

Pettigrew, William. Letters, 1849-1863.

Society of Australian Genealogists, Sydney:
Barker Thomas. The Balfour correspondence 1840-44.

PRIMARY SOURCES: BOOKS

Archer, Thomas. *Recollections of a rambling life*. Yokohama: Japan Gazette, 1897.

Balfour, J.O. *A sketch of New South Wales*. London: Smith Elder, 1845.

Banks, Mary. *Memories of pioneer days in Queensland*. London: Heath Cranton, 1931.

Bartley, Nehemiah. *Australian pioneers and reminiscences 1849-1894*. Brisbane: Gordon and Gotch, 1896.

Bartley, Nehemiah. *Opals and agates; or scenes under the Southern Cross and Maghelans: being memories of fifty years in Australia and Polynesia*. Brisbane: Gordon and Gotch, 1892.

Campbell, John. *The early settlement of Queensland and other articles which are printed in "The raid of the Aborigines" by the late William Wilkes*. Ipswich: Ipswich Observer, 1875.

Cockburn, Henry. *Journal of Henry Cockburn, being a continuation of the memorials of his time 1831-1854*. 2 vols. Edinburgh: Edmonston and Douglas, 1874.

Coote, William. *History of the colony of Queensland from 1770 to the close of the year 1881 in two volumes. Volume 1: from the year 1770 to the separation of the district from New South Wales and its constitution as a separate colony in December 1859*. Brisbane: Thorne, 1882.

Ford, G (ed). *Irish University Press series of British Parliamentary Papers. Papers relating to emigration to the Australian colonies 1852-53. Colonies Australia 17*. Shannon: Irish University Press, 1969.

Gregor, John. *The church in Australia, Part II, two journals of missionary tours in the districts of Maneroo and Moreton Bay, New South Wales in 1843*. London: The Society for the Propagation of the Gospel, 1846.

Hodgson, Christopher Pemberton. *Reminiscences of Australia, with hints of the squatters life*. London: Wright, 1846.

Lang, John Dunmore. *Cooksland in north-eastern Australia: the future cotton field of Great Britain: its characteristics and capabilities for European colonisation, with a disputation on the origin, manners, customs of the Aborigines*. London: Longmans, Brown, Green and Longmans, 1847.

Lang, John Dunmore. *Narrative of proceedings in England, Scotland and Ireland during the years 1847, 1848 and 1849 with a view to originate an extensive and continuous immigration of a superior character from the United Kingdom to this territory*. Sydney: D.L.Walsh, 1850.

Lang, John Dunmore. *Narrative of steps taken in promoting the separation of Queensland from N.S. Wales with notices of the founding and early history of the colony.* Sydney: J.G. O'Connor, 1875.

McConnel, Mary. *Memories of days long gone by/by the wife of an Australian pioneer.* London: Private Printing, 1905.

Mackellar, Duncan. *The Australian emigrant's manual, or, a few practical observations and directions for the guidance of emigrants proceeding to that part of the colony.* 2nd ed. Edinburgh: John Fletcher, 1839.

Mackenzie-Smith, John (comp). *Brisbane River Valley 1841-50: pioneer observations and reminiscences.* Sources No 5. Brisbane: Brisbane History Group, 1991.

Mackenzie-Smith, John (comp). *Brisbane Town News from the Sydney Morning Herald 1842-46.* Sources No 3. Brisbane: Brisbane History Group, 1989.

Petrie, Constance Campbell. *Tom Petrie's reminiscences of early Queensland.* 2nd ed. Sydney: Angus and Robertson, 1932.

Russell, Henry Stuart. *The genesis of Queensland: an account of the first exploring journals to and over the Darling Downs: the earliest days of occupation; social life; station seeking; the course of discovery, northward; and a resume of the causes which led to the separation from New South Wales.* Sydney: Turner and Henderson, 1888.

Somers, Robert. *Letters from the Highlands* (after the great potato famine 1848). Originally printed 1848. Inverness: Melvin Press, 1985.

The Simpson letterbook. Transcribed by Gerry Langevad. *Cultural and historical records of Queensland No 1.* St Lucia: Department of Anthropology and Sociology, 1979.

Waugh, David .L. *Three years of practical experience of a settler in New South Wales being extracts from letters to his friends in Edinburgh from 1834 to 1837. With a preface by the editor, and an appendix containing notes and information for all classes of intending emigrants from the latest authorities and public documents.* Fourth edition with a map. Edinburgh: John Johnston, 1838.

SECONDARY SOURCES: BOOKS

Baker, Donald W.A. *Days of wrath: a life of John Dunmore Lang.* Melbourne: Melbourne University Press, 1985.

Briggs, Asa. *Chartist studies.* London: Macmillan, 1959.

Buckley, Ken and Ted Wheelwright. *No paradise for workers: capitalism and the common people in Australia 1788-1914.* Melbourne: Oxford University Press, 1992.

Cage, R.A. (ed). *The Scots abroad: labour, capital, enterprise 1750-1914*. London: Croom Helm, 1985.

Connell, R.W. and Irving, T.H. *Class structure in Australian history: documents, narrative and argument*. Melbourne: Longman Cheshire, 1980.

Cryle, Denis. *The press in colonial Queensland: a social and political history*. St Lucia, University of Queensland Press, 1989.

Cumming, Cliff. *Port Phillip Presbyterians: the continuing Scottish connection*. London: Australian Studies Centre, Institute of Commonwealth of Studies, University of London, 1988.

Devine, Tom. M. ed. *Conflict and stability in Scottish society 1700-1850. Proceedings of the Scottish Historical Studies seminar, University of Strathclyde, 1988-89*. Edinburgh: John Donald, 1990.

Devine, Tom .M. ed. *Scottish emigration and Scottish society. Proceedings of the Scottish Historical Studies seminar, University of Strathclyde, 1990-91*. Edinburgh: John Donald, 1992.

Dornan, Dimity and Cryle, Denis. *The Petrie family: building colonial Brisbane*. St Lucia: University of Queensland Press, 1992.

Drummond, Andrew L. and Bulloch, James. *The Church in Victorian Scotland 1843-1874*. Edinburgh: The Saint Andrew Press, 1975.

Fisher, Rod. (ed). *Brisbane: the Aboriginal presence 1824-1860*. Brisbane History Group Papers No. 11. Brisbane: Brisbane History Group, 1992.

Fisher, Rod. (ed). *Brisbane : people, places and pageantry*. Brisbane History Group Papers No. 6. Brisbane: Brisbane History Group, 1987.

French, Maurice. *Conflict on the Condamine: Aborigines and the European invasion*. Toowoomba: USQ, 1991.

Greenwood, Gordon and Laverty, John. *Brisbane 1850-1959: a history of local government*. Brisbane: Brisbane City Council, 1959.

Harper, Marjory. *Emigration from North-East Scotland. Volume I. Winning exiles*. Aberdeen: Aberdeen University Press, 1988.

Hewitson, Jim. *Far off in sunlit places: stories of the Scots in Australia and New Zealand*. Carlton South: Melbourne University Press, 1988.

Houston, R.A. *Scottish literacy and the Scottish identity: illiteracy and society in Scotland and northern England 1600-1800*. London: Cambridge University Press, 1985.

Howell, Reet A. and Maxwell L. Howell. *The genesis of sport in Queensland.* St Lucia: University of Queensland Press, 1992.

Johnston, W. Ross. *Brisbane: the first thirty years.* Brisbane: Boolarong, 1988.

Kerr, Ruth. *Confidence and tradition: a history of Esk Shire.* Esk: Council of the Shire of Esk, 1988.

Kiddle, Margaret. *Men of yesterday: a social history of the Western District of Victoria 1830-1890.* Melbourne: Melbourne University Press, 1961.

Levitt, Ian and Smout, Christopher. *The state of the Scottish working class in 1843: a statistical and spatial enquiry based on the data from the Poor Law Commission Report of 1843.* Edinburgh: Scottish Academic Press, 1979.

Logan, Greg and Watson,Tom (eds). *Soldiers of the service: some early Queensland educators and their schools.* Brisbane: History of Queensland Education Society, 1992.

Mackenzie-Smith, John. *Brisbane's forgotten founder : Sir Evan Mackenzie of Kilcoy 1816-1883.* Brisbane: Brisbane History Group, 1993.

Macmillan, David S. *Scotland and Australia 1788-1850 : emigration, commerce and investment.* London: Oxford University Press, 1967.

Martin, Denis. *The foundation of the Catholic Church in Queensland.* Toowoomba: Church Archivists' Society, 1988.

Murphy, Denis, Roger Joyce, and Margaret Cribb (eds). *The premiers of Queensland.* Revised edition. St Lucia: University of Queensland Press, 1990.

Prentis, Malcolm D. *The Scots in Australia: a study of New South Wales, Victoria and Queensland 1788-1900.* Sydney: Sydney University Press, 1983.

Reynolds, Henry. *The other side of the frontier: Aboriginal resistance to the European invasion of Australia.* Harmondsworth: Penguin, 1982.

Richards, Eric (ed.) *Poor Australian immigrants in the nineteenth century. Visible immigrants; two.* Canberra: Australian National University, 1991.

Richards, Eric et al. *That land of exiles : Scots in Australia.* Edinburgh, HMSO, 1988.

Richards, Eric (ed.) *Female immigrants in colonial Australia. Visible Immigrants four.* Canberra: Australian National University, 1995.

Roe, Michael. *Quest for authority in eastern Australia 1835-1851.* Melbourne: Melbourne University Press, 1965.

Saunders, Kay. *Workers in bondage: the origins and bases of unfree labour in Queensland 1824-1916.* St Lucia: University of Queensland Press, 1982.

Smout, T.C. *A century of the Scottish people 1830-1930.* London: William Collins, 1987.

Sturma, Michael. *Vice in a vicious society: crime and convicts in mid-nineteenth century New South Wales.* St Lucia: University of Queensland Press, 1983.

Tynan, Patrick J. *Duramboi: the story of Jem Davis of Glasgow (1808?-1889).* Brisbane: Church Archivists' Press, 1997.

Ward, Russell. *The Australian legend.* Melbourne: Melbourne University Press. 1965.

Weber, Max. *The protestant ethic and the spirit of capitalism.* London: Unwin University Books, 1930.

Wilson, Alexander. *The Chartist movement in Scotland.* Manchester: Manchester University Press, 1970.

Wyeth, Ezra Robert. *Education in Queensland: a history of education in Queensland and in the Moreton Bay District of New South Wales.* Melbourne: Australian Council for Educational Research, 1951.

SECONDARY SOURCES: ARTICLES
Connors, Libby. " 'Drinking, whoring and folly by night' : law and order in the 1840s." *Journal of the Royal Historical Society of Queensland,* 15 (1995) 497-499.

Cumming, Cliff. *"Covenant and identity: Scots Presbyterians at Port Phillip, 1838-51".* The Journal of Religious History, 16 (1990) 202-16.

Cumming, Cliff. "Scottish national identity in an Australian colony". *The Scottish Historical Review,* 62 (1993) 22-38.

Fisher, Rod. "David Canon McConnel's second 'bump of hope': Bulimba House and farm 1849-53". Rod Fisher (ed.) *Brisbane: people, places and pageantry.* Brisbane History Group papers No. 6 (1987) 29-44.

Fisher, Rod. "Against all odds: early industrial enterprise in Brisbane 1840-60". *Journal of the Royal Australian Historical Society,* 76 (1990) 102-23.

Jay, L.J. " Pioneer settlement on the Darling Downs: a Scottish contribution to Australian colonisation". *Scottish Geographical Magazine,* 7 (1957) 36-45.

Kerr, Ruth. "Construction of Pettigrew's sawmill close by the Commissariat Store in 1853". *Journal of the Royal Historical Society of Queensland,* 14 (1990) 177-9.

Knox, Bruce A. "Moreton Bay separation: a problem of Imperial government". *Historical Studies*, 14 (1971) 561-78.

Knox, Bruce A. " '... care is more important than haste' : imperial policy on the creation of Queensland, 1856-9". *Historical Studies*, 17 (1976) 64-83.

Mackenzie-Smith, John. "Kilcoy, the first six months: Sir Evan Mackenzie's albatross". *Journal of the Royal Historical Society of Queensland*, 13 (1989) 429-44.

Mackenzie-Smith, John. "Moreton Bay Scots 1841-95: a Black Isle contingent". *Journal of the Royal Historical Society of Queensland*, 16 (1998), 493-514.

Mackenzie-Smith, John. "Rev. John Gregor - like a lamb to the slaughter". *Journal of the Royal Historical Society of Queensland*, 14 (1992) 517-28.

Morrison, Allan. "Colonial society 1860-1890". *Queensland Heritage*, 1 (1966) 21- 30.

Parker, David. "Rev. Charles Stewart, Brisbane's first Baptist minister and the United Evangelical Church". *Journal of the Royal Historical Society of Queensland*, 16 (1998) 525-41.

Reynolds, Henry and Loos, Noel. "Aboriginal resistance in Queensland". *Australian Journal of Politics and History*, 22 (1976) 214-26.

Richards, Eric. "Varieties of Scottish emigration in the nineteenth century". *Historical Studies*, 21 (1986) 473-494.

Stewart, Jean. "The Brisbane career of John Richardson". *Armidale and District Historical Society Journal*, 36 (1993) 1-17.

THESES:
Balfour, Roderick. Emigration from the Highlands and Western Isles of Scotland to Australia during the nineteenth century. M Litt. thesis, University of Edinburgh, 1973.

Cleary, James T. The North Brisbane School of Arts 1849-99. BA thesis, University of Queensland, 1967.

Collyer, Angela. The process of settlement: land occupation and usage in Boonah 1842-1870s. MA thesis, University of Queensland, 1991.

Cumming, Clifford. Vision and Covenant: Scots in religion, education and politics in Port Phillip 1838 - 1851. PhD thesis, Deakin University, 1988.

Laverty, John R. Development of the town of Brisbane, 1823-59. BA thesis, University of Queensland, 1955.

Payten, Margaret. William Augustine Duncan 1811-85: a biography of a colonial reformer. MA thesis, University of New South Wales, 1965.

Rayner, Keith. History of the Church of England in Queensland. PhD thesis, University of Queensland, 1962.

McPheat, W. Scott. John Dunmore Lang: with special reference to his activities in Queensland. MA thesis, University of Queensland, undated.

Waller, Ken. G.T. The letters of the Leslie brothers in Australia, 1834-54. BA thesis, University of Queensland, 1956.

Wilson, Paul D. The political career of The Honourable Arthur Macalister, C.M.G. BA thesis, University of Queensland, 1969.

APPENDIX

Direct adult Scottish immigration to Moreton Bay 1848-59

	18-48	18-49	18-50	18-51	18-52	18-53	18-54	18-55	18-56	18-57	18-58	18-59	Total
Highlands	8	10	1		20	48	62	216	11	30	32	39	*447*
N. Lowlands							1	3	1	2		3	*10*
Cen. Lowlands	8	6			1	31	41	58		22	31	13	*211*
S-E Lowlands		9			3	24	9	33	1	15	7	4	*105*
S-W Lowlands	37	6	2		8	30	35	74	18	25	19	9	*263*
N-E Lowlands					4	13	8	22		8	1	6	*62*
Total	53	31	3	0	36	146	156	406	31	102	90	74	*1128*

Source: Passenger lists to Moreton Bay directly from overseas 1848-59, New South Wales Immigration Agent, Z600, QSA.

MAPS

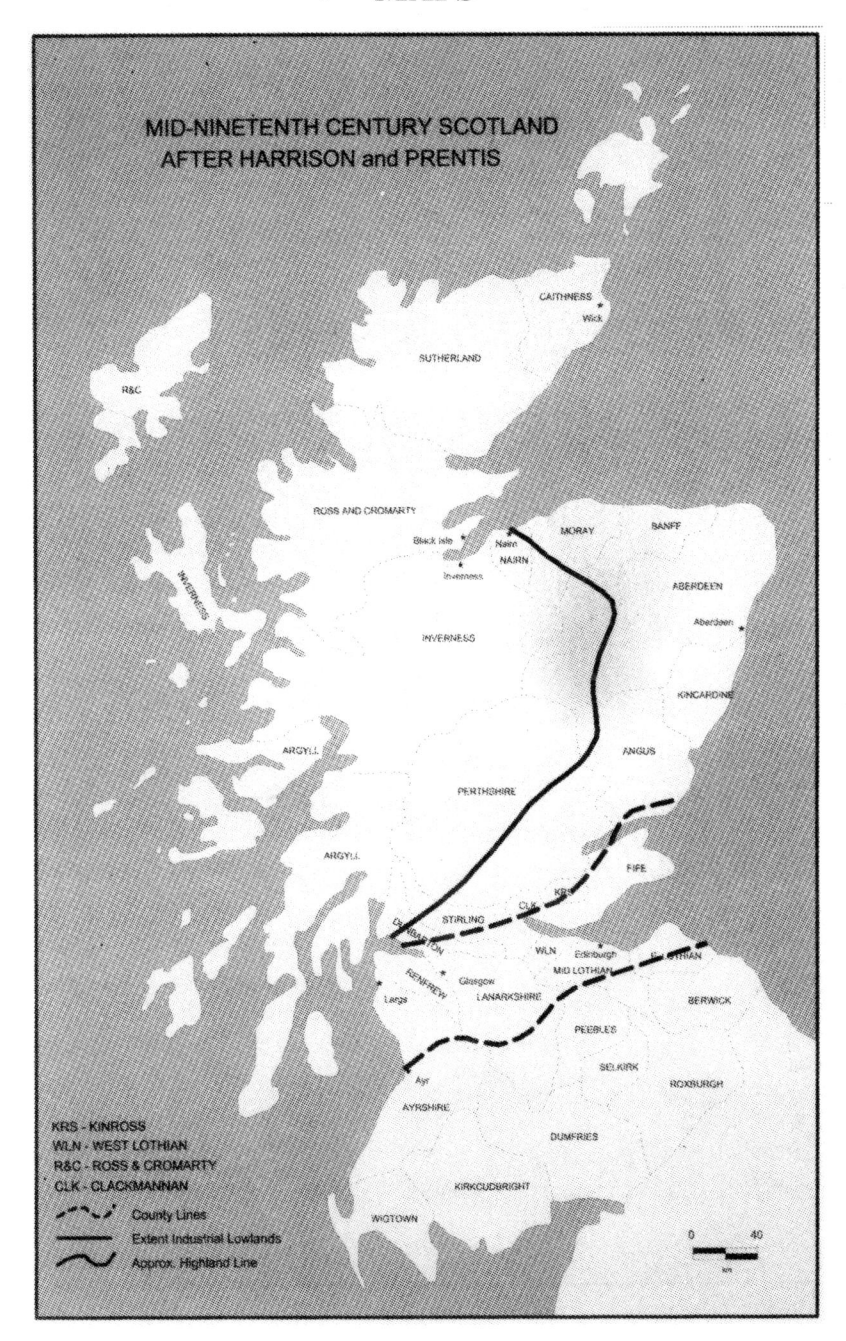

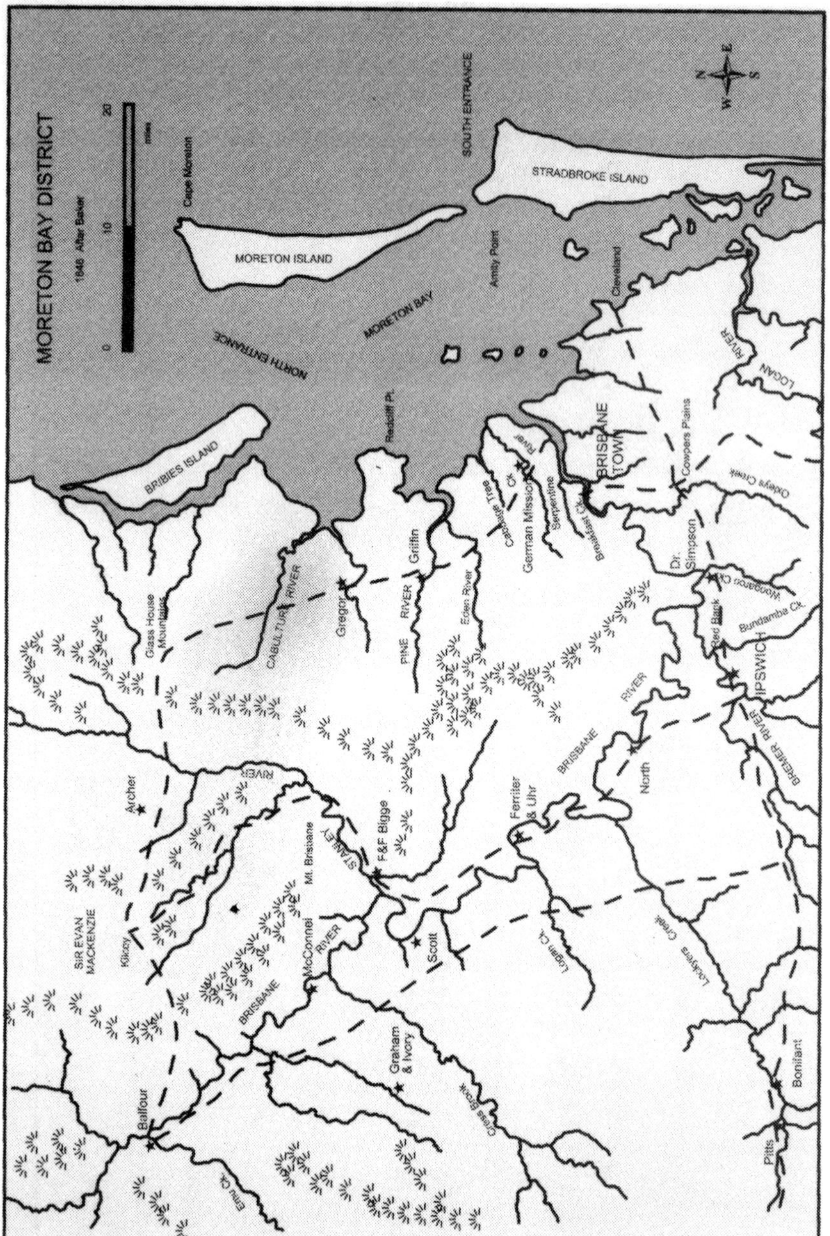
MORETON BAY DISTRICT
1846 After Baker
0
10
20
miles
Cape Moreton
MORETON ISLAND
SOUTH ENTRANCE
STRADBROKE ISLAND
NORTH ENTRANCE
MORETON BAY
Amity Point
Cleveland
BRIBIES ISLAND
Redcliff Pt.
BRISBANE TOWN
Cowpers Plains
LOGAN
RIVER
Oxley's Creek
German Mission
Serpentine
Breakfast Ck.
Cabbage Tree Ck.
River
Dr. Simpson
Red Bank
Bundamba Ck.
IPSWICH
BREMER RIVER
Glass House Mountains
CABULTURE RIVER
Gregor
PINE RIVER
Griffin
Eden River
BRISBANE RIVER
North
Ferriter & Uhr
RIVER
Archer
F&F Bigge
STANLEY
Mt. Brisbane
SIR EVAN MACKENZIE
Kilcoy
McConnel
RIVER
BRISBANE
Scott
Logan Ck.
Lockyers Creek
Graham & Ivory
Balfour
Emu Ck.
Bonifant
Pitts

1841-59

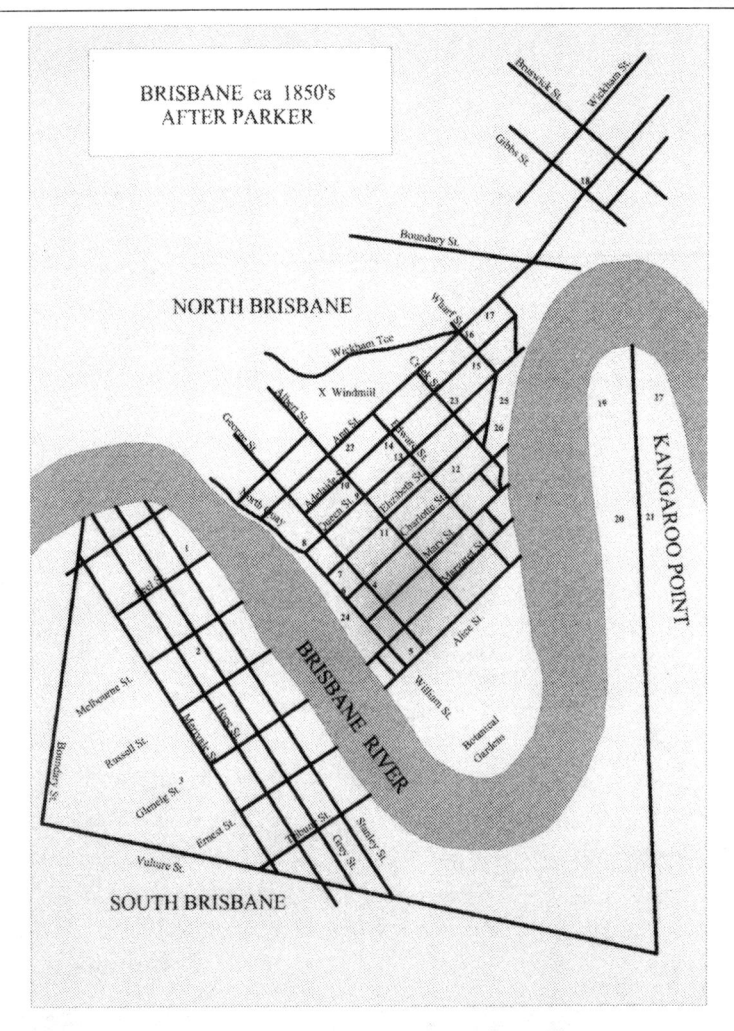

BRISBANE ca 1850's AFTER PARKER

1. Rev. C. Stewart's first lodgings (?)
2. Presbyterian Church (1st)
3. Park Presbyterian Church
4. Moreton Bay Courier
5. Rev. C. Stewart's Land
6. United Evangelic Chapel
7. St. John's Anglican Church
8. Anglican Church
9. Court House
10. Wesleyan Chapel (1st & 2nd)
11. Roman Catholic Chapel (1st) (approx. site)
12. St. Stephens Roman Catholic Church
13. School of Arts
14. United Presbyterian Church (Bell)
15. Wharf St. Baptist Church
16. Wharf St. Congregational Church
17. Dr. Hobbs' House
18. Jireh Baptist Church (site)
19. Petrie's Store (former B.D. Works)
20. Wesleyan Church
21. Anglican Church
22. Ann St. Presbyterian Church
23. Petrie's Residence
24. Commissariat Stores
25. Customs House
26. Richardson & Raff's Store
27. Soap & Candle Factory (former B.D. Works)

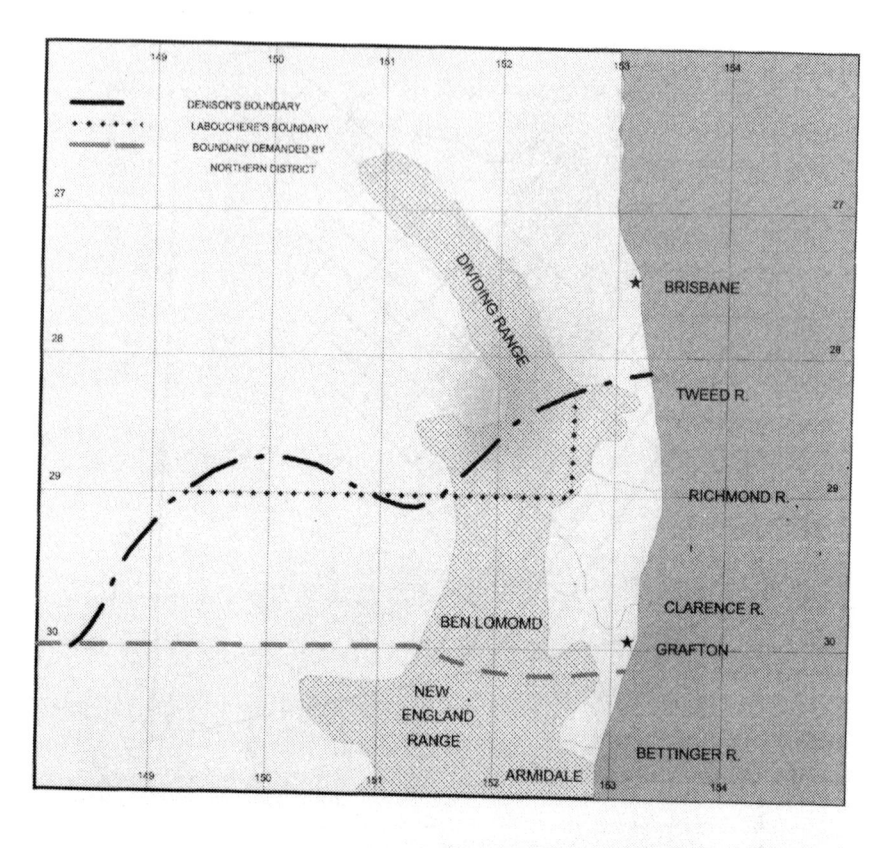

Suggested Boundary Between Queensland and New South Wales.

INDEX

A

Abberton 5,11
Abbott, Carl 76
Aberdeen 3,18,19-24,39,53,62,120,142, 164
 Lord 160
Aberdeenshire 47,162
Aborigines 95,103,109,110,116,123-25, 134,154,242,247
Academy, Ediburgh 102
Act, Australian Colonies 166
 Imperial 169
 Masters & Servants xi,29,112,202
 New Publican's 206
 Scottish Reform 200,215
Adams, Thomas 50,59
Adelaide 162
Aikman, Hugh 8
Alpin, Henry 67
Amoy 31
Anderson, John Gerard 219
 Mary 9
Anne Milne 25,27,153
Archer, Charles 21,27,30,38,40,83,102, 129,130,132
 David 11,12,20,30,38,102,106
 John 6,11,19,35,38
 Julia 129,130,132
 Thomas 11-14,27,30,37,40,83,96, 102,106,113,128,129
 William 12,35,37,38,40,48,129,130
 Brothers x,12,18,94,95,101,103
Archives, Brisbane Anglican xiv
 Queensland State x
Ardnamurchan 165
Argus 150
Armidale 4
Artemesia 32,137,140,145,146

Assembly, Legislative 171,207
 Queensland's Legislative 147
Association, Australian Pastoral 16
 Indian Labour 30,31
 Manchester Cotton 152
 Moreton Bay District 61,106,119
 Moreton Bay Pastoral 15,54,60,61, 63
 N.D. Agricultural & Pastoral 150
 Queensland Liberal 202
 Southern Pastoral 60
Attorney-General 21,165,217,205
Australasian Chronicle 19,71,114,120, 144,214,232,
Australian Dictionary of Biography 181, 254
Ayr 198,202

B

Baker, Donald viii,ix,xii,41,129,134,175, 178,247,254
Bald Hills 53,148,153,154,172,178
Balfour, A.C.S. 180
 Charles 10,35,60,74,77,78,106
 James x,1,2,4,9,11-14,22,25,27, 34-37,38,40,43,60,62,74,76,77, 97,98,129,177
 John 4-8,10,17-19,23,30,34,37-39, 48,63,65,77,129,130,149,150,158, 181,195,208,240
 R.G. 232
 Robert James 97
 Roderick 36,132,231
 Brothers 3,13,24,56-58,102,114
Ballow, Dr David 32,48,49,59,119,123, 138,148,220
Band of Hope 244
Bangalore 156
Bank, Baring Brothers 6,7,60,61,77,78

Banks, Mary McLeod 37
Baptists 100,143,208,213
Barclay, Rev. John 176,,211,231
Barker, Thomas x,10,13,24,34,35-37,39,
 40,60,74,76,77,97,98,129,177
 William 8,29
Bay, Portland 165
Beau Desert 8,20
Bell Rev. Thomas 212,210
Benton Hall 11
Berkshire 25,26,50
Berlin 124
Bigge, Francis Edward 5,11
 Francis Thomas 5,11,156,165
 Frederick W. 39,158
 Judge John Thomas 11
 Thomas Hanway 11
Bigges Brothers ,102,106
Bill, Constitution 165
Binstead, Arthur 109
Birbeck 245
Birmingham 209
Bishop of Newcastle 213
Black, J.R. 224
Black Isle 9,10,25,26,51,52,111,118,123,
 150,153,195,240,241
Blackett, Thomas 119
Board of General Education 219
Boonah 8
Boorstin, Daniel 53,76
Booval 149
Borough of Stanley 166
Bow, David 50,62,68,113
Bowden, Thomas 147,148
Bowen, Lady 225
 Sir George Ferguson 171,194,198,
 202,225,229,252,237
Boyd, Benjamin 8,15,60,61
Boyland, John 66,118
 Thomas 150,167,203
Bradley, Rev. John 210

Breckenridge, James 196
Bridge, Breakfast Creek 152
Bright, John 140
Brisbane viii-x,4-6,8,28,33,43-48,54,56,
 61,58-60,62,63,64,69,70,72,73,
 100,106,107,110,111,112,116,118,
 121-3,126,127,141,146,147,150,
 153-56,166,170,182,188,201,203,
 205,208,216,240
Brisbane Courier 35,76,130,132,181,205
Brisbane, Sir Thomas 34,35,56,81
Britain 5,7,60,61,63,95,96,100,114,117,
 158,194,195
British Banner 137,142,143,146,174-76,
 231,253
Broadfoot, William 147
Bromelton 8
Brook, Kedron 119,148
Broughton, Bishop W.G. 118-20
Brown, H.H. 161,179
 Stewart J. 231
 William A. 214
Buchanan 220
Buckley, Henry 221
 Ken 229
Bulimba 148-151
Buntin, David 119
Burnett, James 48,62,63,78,125,126,153
Burns, Robert 224,225,226

C

Caboolture 246
Cairncross, William 50,167,210,214
Caldwell, David 149
Caledonian 50,62
Calvinism viii,x,31,97,116,197,238,241,
 242
Calvinists 108
Camden 115

Cameron, Alexander 199
  Charles 10,21,23
  Donald Charles 10,21,38,74,102,
    114,129
  John 8,10
Campbell, Captain Alymer 65,66
  James 199
  John 'Tinker' 4,28,35,49,50,53,54,
    55,59,62,65,77,86,106,109,111,113
  Rev. John 142
  Robert 8
Cannan, Dr Richard 50,59,108 109,115,
  118,149,150,203
Challinor, Dr Henry 156,167,213,222
Chambers, Captain 66
Chalmers, Rev, Thomas 116,243,244
Chapel, United Evangelical 192
  St Stephen's 214,223
Chaseley 141,143,147-49,172,213
Church, Anglican 121
  First St John's C.of E. 91
  of England 47,49,98,122,127,208,
    214,216
  of Scotland 118,142,208,243
  Presbyterian viii,95
  St John's 105
  St Stephen's R.C. 1868 91
Church, United Evangelical 210,213
  United Presbyterian 142,209,211,
    212
Clan, Giggabarah 23
  Ningy Ningy 103
  Turrbal 124-26
Cleary, James T. 230,233,234
Cleveland 54,58,63,65,68-70,107,150,
  152,193,194
  Point 45,49,63,64,68,72,156,207,240
Clough, Monica xii,xv
Club, Australian 106
  Moreton Bay Jockey 107
  Moreton Bay Racing 106,107

Cobden, Richard MP 140
Cockburn, Lord Henry 200,215,230,232
Cockle, Chief Justice 225
Coley, Captain John 20,21,38,76
Colinton x,5,7,10,18,19,24,25,27,28,97,
  99,102
Collector of Customs 205
College, Australian 100,171
  Madras 218
Collins, William 244
Colonial Observer 39
Colonial Office 140,141,158,160,168-70,
  173,239,246
  Secretary 69,111,138,152,153,169,
    205,225
Commerce, Manchester Chamber of 159
Commercial 206
Commission, Colonial Land &
  Emigration 138,163
  Emigration 155
Committee on Education 216
  Select on Negro Slavery 140
Company, Australian Agricultural 3
  Caboolture Cotton 151
  Hunter River Steam Navigation 44,
    53,
  58,59,66,68,199,246
  Moreton Bay Immigration &
    Land 167
  Moreton Bay Sugar 147
  Port Phillip & Clarence R.
    Colonisation 139
Congregationalists 143,208,212,213
Connel, R.W. xiii,129
Coochin Coochin 8
Cooksland 32,136,137,140,142,145,
  159,174
Cooper, Joan xiv
Coorparoo 124
Coote,William ix,xii,30,38,40,147,174,
  176,178,180,181,200,,230

271

Council, Brisbane Town 171
　Ipswich Municipal 171
　Legislative 31,139,141,155-57,
　　165,167,171,216,248
County of Stanley 141,166,207
Court, Police Magistrate's 108
Coutts, Donald 8,10,30,150
　John 8
　Thomas 49,66,201
Cowper's Plains 107
Craies, William 224
Crail 218
Creek, Breakfast 148
　Bulimba 148
　Cabbage Tree 148,153
　Cressbrook 103
　Myall 19
Cressbrook 12,14,17,18,20,102,104,113,
　153,195
Cribb, Benjamin 223
　Robert 150,151,171195,204,220-22,
　241
Croft, George 110
Cromarty 162
Crow's Nest 12
Cryle, Denis 35,75,76,134,174,175,254
Cumming, Cliff 209,231,253
Customs House 68-70,92

D

Dalton, Francis 12
Darling Downs x,xii,1,3,7,12,19,22,27,28,
　30,45,50,52,64,65,6796,98,101,105,
　107,119,166,213,216
Davidson, Donald 52,99,206
　Isabella 26,40,195
　John 27,52
　Robert 51,108,153,167,214
　William 150
Davis, James 23,52,86,110,119
Denison, Sir William 152,168-71,180
Derby, Lord 160

Devine, T.M. 78,129
Diggles, Silvester 223
District, Caithness 142
　Lockyer 10
　Moreton Bay viii,ix,xi,1,7,9,14,16,
　　27,33,36,43,57,73,93,94,96,99,104,
　　105,127,135,137,151,158,162,166,
　　205,215,228,241,242,243,245
　New England 3,4,12
　Richmond 170,171
Donaldson & Dawes 13
　Stuart Alexander 151,205
Donnachie, Ian 2,34,44,55,74,253
Dorsey, Dr William McTaggart 48,49,
　65,109,122,123,151,156,160,157,
D'Orsey, Rev. Alex. 123
Douglas, J. 181
　Robert 59,150,151,202,214,203
Dowse Thomas x,54-56,58,63,65,77,78,
　93,105-09,128,131,153,206,247
Drayton 107,216
Dugandan 8
Duke of Newcastle 160
Duke of York 125
Dumfries 11,149
Duncan, Charles 153,154
　Jane 153,154
　William Augustine x,15-19,37,38,
　　45,46,48,64,68-70,72,79,89,93,
　　114,119-23,125,126,127,128,
　　132-34,144,148,149,153,154,160,
　　169-71,175,178,181,194,203,204,
　　206,213,214,216-24,226,227,229,
　　230,232,233-35,245-47,250,251,
　　253
Duncan's Weekly Register 16
Dundee 3,218
Dunlop 151
Duramboi 23,110
Durundwr 6,11,12,14,19-21,52,27,63,84,
　99,102
Dutton Park 148

272

E

Edinburgh viii,x,1,3,9-14,23,60,104,142, 149,157,163,164
Edinburgh Courant 114
Edinburgh Review 220
Edmonstone, George 50,111,167,195,210
    Mr & Mrs George 118
Education, Select Committee on 120
Edwards, John 36
Eldridge, Ambrose 145,150-52,167
Eliza Kincaird 62
Empire 161
Esk 113,241
Eskdale 11,23,28,195
Estate, Belmaduthy 25,26
    Kilcoy 77,243
    Rosehaugh 26
Evans, Raymond 38,134
Ewart, David 219
Experiment 66

F

Fairholme, George K.E. 102,155,160,168
Falconer's Plains 4
Fassifern 8
Fenwick, James 225
Fifeshire 162
Fisher, Rod x,xv,75,134,178,179,229, 254
Fitzpatrick, Constable William 119
    Chief Constable 111
Fitzroy, Governor Sir Charles 156,160-62, 179,229
Fleming, Joseph 197
Forbes, David 156
    Francis A. 222
    George 5,10,13,34,37,56,77,97, 129,150
    Sir Charles 203
    Sir William 129
Forres 152
Fortitude 137,138,141-44,146,150,152, 155,156,184,213,222

Fraser, Barbara 27
    Lexie 112
    Thomas 27,52,111
    William 39,52,111,112
    Brothers 111,112,114
Fraser's Magazine 220
Free Church 163,208,210,211,241,243, 244
Freeman's Journal 214
Friell, Philip 30
Fund, Moreton Bay Labour 28
Fyfe, William 8,112

G

Gap, Cunningham's 29
Gardens, Brisbane Botanical 149,152
    Royal Botanical 149
Geddes, William 200,202,244
Genghis Khan 162
Germany 100,101
Gibbes, Colonel John 68,205
Gilchrist & Alexander 13
Gipps, Sir George 10,14-16,18,19,60,61, 63,71,239
Gladstone, W.E. 70,215
Glasgow viii,3,112,123,140,142,157,163, 164,198,202,218,243-45,
Glasgow Herald 142,175
Gledhill, James 202
Glen Innes 4
Glen Nevis 10
Glenelg, Lord 9,36
Gorman, Lt Owen 113
Governor-General 170,204
Grafton 166,170
Graham, Andrew 50,113,119
    David 11,102,106,195
    Dugald 8
    & Ivory 23,28
    Professor 9
    Robert 28,40,48,49,60,61,63,66,68, 99,240

Gray, Colonel Charles 222,223
   George 52
   Malcolm 164,179
   Mr & Mrs Thomas 118
Gray, Thomas 27,53,68,108,109,153,154, 167,195,199,210,220
   Walter 160,65,66,122
Greenwood, Gordon 181
Gregor, Andrew 8,20,59,124
   Rev. John x,23,27,39,40,47,49,74, 86,98,99,102,103,106,108,110, 114-16,118,121,123,124,129, 130-34,212,213,239,241,253,
Grey, Earl 29,138,139,142,154-58,160, 162,165,168,169,174,178
Grieve, Walter xiv,5,99
Griffin, Francis 7
   George 7,103,104
   John 7
   Mrs Janet 7,104
Griffith, Rev. Edward 213
Guyra 4

H

Handt, J.C.S. 132
Hanly, Rev. James J. 119,126,214
Harp of Erin 50
Harrington, William 110
Harris, Flora 224
Hashemy 155,206
Hauser, Miska 224
Hawes, E. 181
Hawk 66
Hay, Alexander 232
   J. Leith 214
   Rev. Alexander 211
   William Leith 156
Head, Cabbage Tree 63
Henderson, A.J. 150
Herbert, Robert 225
Hewitson, Jim 34,38,39,243,254
Highlander's Arms 50

Hill, Walter 149
HMS Beagle 62
HMS Bramble 62
HMS Rattlesnake 63
Hobbs, Dr William 151,153,167,221
Hodgson, Arthur 94,96,128,154,157, 165,166,168,169,171,173,178
   Christopher Pemberton 3,5,14, 20,34,35,38
Holt, George 205
Hope, Hon. Louis 90,150,158,160,161, 169,181
Hopetoun, Earl of 150
Hotel, Bow's 106,113
   Brisbane 113
   Red Cow 52
   Victoria 107,107
   Woogaroo 67
House of Commons 155,169
   St Andrew's 217,218
Hunter, George 8

I

Iggo, Betty 36
Independence, American War of 151
Indooroopilly 150
Industrial Revolution viii,2
Inn, Bush 108
   Wivenhoe 113,195,206
Innes, John 220-22
Institute, Ipswich Literary 222
   Mechanics 245
Inverell 4
Inverness 9,27,53,142,162,163
Inverness Courier 25,39,77,114,162,179, 196,229
Iona 165
Ipswich viii,7,8,43,45,48,52,63-65,67,68, 72,73,93,107,109,110,113,116,117, 121-23,141,146,148-51,156,166, 167,170,181,193,195,197,205,206, 208,213,216

Irving, Clark 166
Irwin, Rev. Henry O. 213
Island, Moreton 61,138
Ivory, James 11,99,102,106,195,239
    Lord 9,195

J

Jay, L.J. 34
Jeays, Joshua 211
Jenny Lind 66
John Davis 162
John 5
Johnston, James 66,149,200,206,207,218, 244
    W. Ross ix,xii,xiv,53,74,76,176,177
Joyner, Isabella 7

K

Kangaroo Point 46,49-51,54,55,58,59,62, 63,66,69,108-10,111-13,148,149, 150,210,243,246
Kelly, Thomas 234
Kent, William 221
Kew 149
Kiddle, Margaret 95,96,101,128
Kilcoy 6,9-11,18,19,21-24,25,26-28,39, 48,52,55,56,57,60,98,99,102,206, 241,240,247,
    Baronetcy of 60
    Castle 39
Kilner, H. 123
King, Captain 3
    William Francis 110
Kingsford, Rev. Thomas 213
Knight, John James 131,229
Knockhill 11
Knowles, Alexander 145,149,153,176, 200,220
Knox, Bruce 169,178-81,229

L

Labourchere, Henry 165,168,180,181
Laidley 8
Lanarkshire 163,240
Lancashire 151
Lane, John 29
    Robert 115,150
Lang, Dr John Dunmore ix,x,6,15,16,18, 22,31,32,38,39,41,46,50,51,55,63, 64,71-74,76,94,100,103,116,-18, 120,123,124,126,127,129,130, 132-45,147,148,150,151,153-55, 157-60,165-77,178,180,181,183, 200,205,208-13,218,219,222,227, 230,231,238,239,241,243,244,245, 246-48,250,251,253,254,
Langholm 11
Laverty, John R. xv,74,181,254
Le Breton, George 69,79,119
League, Anti-Transportation 161
    Australia 157
    Australian Anti-Transportation 157
    Scottish Temperance 244
Leichhardt, Ludwig x,20,24,38,39,61,98, 99,101,103-06,128-30,247
Leith 3
Leslie, Corporal 123
    George 19,29,34,38,40,122,129, 151,158,160,164,165,169
    G. F. 179
    Kate 115
Leslie, Patrick 4,30,34,40,61,78,83,97,98, 106,108,115,119,128,129,132,156, 159,160,161,166,169,171
    Thomas 34
    Walter 156,168
    William 27,40,97,98,128,129,132
    Brothers x,19,46,64,106
Library, Ipswich Subscription 222
Lilley, Charles 172,225
Lima 141,147,149,207,218
Lind, R. 130

Little Benton 11
  George 50,51,122
  Ipswich 48,52,65
  Robert 156,221
Liverpool 57,151,165,226
  Plains 3,4,13
Lodge, Mr 210
London 9,55,57,62,209,245
London Atlas 141,175
Londonderry 65
Long Pocket 65
Longlands, David 152
Lord, Edward 48,59
Loudon, William J. 153
Lowe, Robert 15
Lutherans 100
Lutwyche, Judge Alfred 202
Lyon, Arthur Sydney 31,114,125
Lytton, Sir E.B. 169

M

M.D.Hunter & Co. 13,56
Macalister, Arthur 167,181,190,196,199, 223,227,229,254
  James 111,126,206
Macarthur, Anna 64,115
  Hannibal Hawkins 115
  William 115
Macdonald, C.L. 8
  John 22
  William 197
Mackellar, Duncan 2,34
Mackenzie, Colin 9,10,21,22,30,48,65, 102,104,158,166,167,169
  Evan x,xiv,5-10,14,15,19,21,22, 25-28,30,33-38,44,45,48-56,57-59, 60-63,65,66,70,72-74,76,78,102, 104,106-08,111,113,130,131,168, 169,194,204,239,241,243,245-47, 250,251,253
  Sir Colin 9,10,25,26,29,36,57,60
  Sir Evan 82,155

Mackenzie, Sir George Steuart 150
  Sir Robert Ramsay 149,150,160, 167,181,191,201,202,214,217,219, 224,227
  Brothers 21,24,98,118
Mackenzie-Smith, John xii,xiii,34,36,38, 40,74,75,78,175,178,179,229,253, 254
MacLaughlin, Donald 8
Macleay, Alexander 10
  W.S. 132
MacLeod, Donald 254
MacMillan, David S. ix,174,180
Macquarie, Governor Lachlan 11
Maitland 4
Manchester viii,9,12,140,151,152,160,226
Marmion 165
Marsh, Matthew Henry 169,170,181
Mary Ann 66
Matheson, John 26
  Thomas 241
Matong 10
McAdam, George 118,150,167,206,210
McCabe, John 50,113,150,206
  Mr & Mrs John 118
McConnel, David viii,8,9,12,17,26,48, 102-04,106,122,123,145,147-49, 151,153,156,195,200,209,231, 241,253
  David & Mary 87
  Frederick 12,17,48,153
  John 12,17,20,25,27,30,48,104, 106,153,161,210,211
  Mary 130,230
  Brothers 95,102,206
McDonald, Alexander 29,83
  George 3
  John 102,129,150,181,206
McGarvie, Rev. John 112
McIntyre, Alexander 26,51,53,59,68,108, 167,199,206,210,220,226
  Donald 4

1841-59

McIntyre, Mr & Mrs Alex 118
    Mr & Mrs John 118
    Perry 178
McKay, David 52
McKenzie, Donald 102
    John 202
McKergow, John 196,210
McLean, Lachlan 68,51,111,152,167,210, 220
    Mr & Mrs Lachlan 118
McLeod, Magnus 156
    Mary 104
    Rev. Walter Ross 210,211
McMaster, John 197
McNaught, David 49,210
McNicol, Daniel 52
McPherson, James 241
Melbourne 141
Melcolm 8
Middlesex 143
Midlothian 149,163,240
Milford, Judge 205
Milton 148
Mission, German 39,116,123
Mitchell, Sir Thomas 9,36,59
Mocatta 23
Moggill 147,148,150-152
Montefiore & Graham 49,66
Montefiore, Jacob 49
Moogerah 8
Moreton Bay Courier x,27-29,31,33,38, 40,41,49,67,74-76,78,79,93,99,110, 112,113,114,118,121,125,126,128, 129,131-34,137,139-41,144,148, 151,154,155,157,160,161,166-70 172,174-81,201,204,205,207,212, 215-18,220,221,225-35,243,247, 252,254
Moreton Bay Free Press 158,178,199, 220,224,230
Morrison, Allan A. ix,xii,229

Mort, Henry 14,17,38,102,114,116,129, 132
Mort, Thomas Sutcliffe 59
Mount Beerwah 6
    Brisbane 7,11,242
    Esk 11,102,103
    Flinders 8
    Kilcoy 21,23
Mountains, Bunya Bunya 103
    Glasshouses viii
Mowbray, Rev. Thomas 49,118,186,210, 212,217
Mull 165
Munlochy 52,57,243
Munro, Mr 122
Murdoch, William 200,202,226
Murray, John 200-02,204,225
    William 225

N

Nairn 26
Nelson, Rev.Dr Walter L. 213
New England 170
New Farm 48,107,108
New South Wales ix,1,3,8,12,16,25,26,30, 46,71,96,120,122,156,158-60,162, 163,168,169,170,172,203,205,240, 247,248
Newcastle 11
Newstead House 48,85,108115,119,150
Nimrod 32
Noble, Alexander 195
Normanby Plains 8,148
North Australian 166,167,229
North Brisbane 46,58,63,67-69,107,109, 113,117,121,151,198,208,211,217, 225
North British Review 220
North, Joseph 195
Northern Star 145,197
Northumberland 11,22

O

Officer, Colonial Immigration 161
  Government Medical 48
Ogg, Rev. Charles 211,212,217,218,220, 233
Ord, William 11
Order, Benedictine 119,120
Order in Council 154,171
Orr, Ebenezer 50
  Edward 109
Orr, John 50,150
Oxford 226
Oxford Movement 214
O'Reilly, Philip 59

P

Pakington, Sir John 160,161,229
Palmer, Vance 248,254
Pamby Pamby 23
Parker, Rev. Dr David xiv,xv,231,232
Parkes, Henry 71,79,93,128,154,157,200, 201,248,250
  Sarah Anna 65,130
Parramatta 119
Patience, J. 150
Payten, Margaret 17,37,38,71,74,79,134, 229,232,254
Pearce, James Canning 12,49,66
Peebles 11,25
Perry, F.A. 43
Perth 198,201
Petrie, Andrew 6,23,49,52-54,58,59, 62-64,66,68,72,88,106,108,130,199, 202,212
  Constance Campbell 35
  John 49,59,66,109,186,201,213, 220,222,244
  Mary 6
  Mayor John 171
  Walter 109
  Brothers 113,251
Petrie Bight 68

Pettigrew, Adam 231
  John 171,174,178,195,196,207, 208,211,217,222,225,229,231
  William x,136,138,147,150153,157, 160,174,176,178,186,195,196,199, 200,204,206,210,229,231,242,251, 253,254
Piper, Captain 52
Pisa, Cathedral of 213
Plunkett, James 21,165,217
Point, Amity 109
  Danger 170
  Walmsley 108
Polding, Archbishop John Bede 18,38, 120,144,214
Poole, George F. 145,151,152,221
Port Essington 61,106
  Phillip 154,162,209
Prentis, Malcolm 128,163,179,180,238, 253
Presbyterian Church 49
Presbyterianism viii,31,32,72,100,116, 118,127,140,142,163,197,207,213, 214,238,240,241
Presbyterians 116-18

Q

Queenslander 176
Queen's Arms 150

R

Raff, Alexander 221
  George 70,152,153,181,190,202, 204,210,217,222
Range, Conondale viii,21
  D'Aguilar 7,67
  Great Dividing viii,1,170
Raven 66
Rayner, Rev, Dr Keith 119,132,133,232, 253
Red Clydesdale 218
Redbank 66

Regatta, Brisbane 109
Reid, James 49,66
Rendall, James 190,218
Revolution, Industrial 162
Reynolds, Henry 38,134
Richards, Eric xiv,179,253
Richardson, John 28,51,68-70,72,73,123,
    127,138,145,147-49,153,156,161,
    165-67,171,180186,199,200,220,
    221,210
Riddell, Campbell 60
River, Albert 8
    Boonah 7
    Bremer 10,65,199
    Brisbane viii,6,12,43,52,62,64,67,
    105,107,138,199,208
    Burnett 30,52,113
    Caboolture viii,8
    Clarence 4,98,166,170,171
    Clyde 243
    Condamine 4,166,168
    Dumaresq 4
    Esk 11
    Gwydir 4
    Hunter 154
    Logan 7,8,45
    Mary 21
    North Pine 45
    Paterson 154
    Pine 7,8,20,103,115,124
    South Pine 154
Roberts, Daniel F. 167,202,221
Robertson, James H. 23,153,167,250
    William Halco 50,123
Robinson, Dr William xiv
    Joseph Phelps 8,20,21,38
Roe, Michael 96,100,128,129
Rosebrook 8
Rosewood 10
Ross 162
Rowland, Robert 119
Roxburgh 11,22

Rusden, George 217
Russell, Henry Stuart ix,xii,23,35,39,98,
    106,113,129-31,155,165,178,179
    Lord John 160

S

Salmon, Rev. A. 210,211
Sandeman, Gordon 30
Sandgate 152-54,172
Sassenachs 22
Saunders, Kay 18,38,39
Schmidt, Rev. William 22,124
Schonberg, Lord 203
School, Brisbane National 218
    Glasgow Normal 244
    of Arts, Brisbane 150,203,216,217,
    219-24,243,245,247
    of Arts, Ipswich Mechanical 223
    St Andrew's 243
    Sydney Grammar 123
Scott, Alexander 9,11
    Caroline 11
    David 50,123
    Francis 16
    Gideon 11,30,119
    John 197,200,202,217,218,219,220,
    222,244
    Lord Henry 203
    Simon 11,12,150
    Walter 11,12
    Brothers 104
Secretary of State 29,141,155,159,165,
    168,169,173,229
    Colonial 126
Seventeen Mile Rocks 66
Shamrock 22
Shannon, Mary 20
Shaw, Barry xv,178
Sheehan, Michael 119
Simpson, Commissioner 20,22,150
    Dr Stephen 38,207

Sinclair, Rev. Alex 36,40,205,210,211, 213
   G. 23
Smith, Alexander 26,27,52,53,241
   Isabella 27,113
   John 26,27,40,53,57,113,132,195, 206
   Mr & Mrs John 118
   W.M. 221
Smout, T.C. 128,131,254,262
Society, Baptist Historical x
   Brisbane Choral 223,224
   Brisbane Total Abstinence 207
   for Propagation of the Gospel 97, 121
   Glasgow Education 218
   Highlands & Islands Emigration 163,164
   Horticultural 149
   Moreton Bay Amateur Musical 223
   Northern Districts Separation 158
   Royal of Ediburgh 4
Somers 52,76
Souter, John 167,206,226
South Brisbane 46,49,52,58,59,63,66,68, 69,108-11,113,114,117,135,148, 150,186,189,198,199,206,208,210, 211,214
Sovereign 50,63,66,109,206
Spence, James 141,199,200,201,202,204, 206,207,213,220,221,244
St Andrews 218
Stanley, Captain Owen 63,69,79,70
   Lord 15
Stephen, Chief Justice Alfred 2-5
Stevenson, Robert Louis viii
Stewart, John 26,51,76,79,111,118,153, 154,156,200,208,220
   Margaret 153,154
   Rev, Charles 138,142,145,147,206, 209,212,213
Stirling Castle 6,100

Stobart, Rev. Henry 203
Strange, Frederick 149
Street, Adelaide 218
   Ann 211,217
   Creek 212,213,217
   Downing 168,169
   Eagle 70
   Edward 51
   Grey 50,211
   George 50,52,150
   Queen 48-51,59,69,70,107,151,206
   Russell 48
   William 187,212
Streets, Ann & Albert 192
Stuart, William 118
Sturma 128,129
Sutherland, James 51
Swan, James 31,46,49,126,127,139,141, 145,149,153,156,159,167,172,185, 199,200,202,204,210,213,220,221, 227,243,246,248,251
   Mr & Mrs James 118
Sydney 5,11,13,15,18,22,28,29,31,44,47, 49,54,55,58,68,70,71,73,93,100, 104,106,112-14,117,135,140,147, 148,154,155,159-61,171,173,194, 214,217,246
Sydney Gazette 40,114
Sydney Morning Herald ix,x,40,54,61, 74-78,93,114,117,121,128,130-34, 140,143,144,,155,159,161,168,174, 178,181,198,229-31
Synod of Australia 210,211
   of Eastern Australia 210
   of New South Wales 210,212

T

Tabragalba 8
Tait, Rev. John 210
Tamar 155
Tamarookum 8
Tambourine 8,195

Tarampa 10
Tarome 8
Taromeo 11
Taylor, Rev. R. 49,117,118
Telamon 8
Tent Hill 30
Tenterfield 4
Terra Nullius 3,18,246
The Advocate 128,133
The Freeman's Journal 232
Therry, Judge 205
Thomson, Edward Deas 3,17,18,60,69,
    137,169,205
Thorne, George 38,65,74-76,150
Tighgam 153
Toogoolawah 148,149
Toorbul Point 63,64
Toowong 148
Tropic of Capricorn 159
Tyrell, Bishop William 119,214

U

Ullathorne, Rev. Dr William 120
Union, Queensland Teachers' 244
University, Glasgow 243
    of Ediburgh 11,12,102
    of Queensland xiv

V

Valley, Brisbane River x,1,7-9,11,13,18,
    20,24,45,49,52,56,67,99,101,103,
    106,108,119,150,208,242
    Fortitude 202
    Hunter 8
    Lockyer 8,67
Victoria 50,62,162,163-65

W

Walker, Edward 12
    James 12
    Thomas 12
    William 12
Wallace, Rev. J. 216

Wallerowang 12
Ward, Russell xii,164,180
Warner, James 59,149,150
Warra Warra 30
Warthill 97
Warwick 107,156,166,216
Waterson, Duncan xii,238,253
Watherston, Andrew xiv,242,253
Watson, Alex 254
Waugh, David 24,34
Weber, Max viii,xii,229
Weekly Register 71
Wentworth, W.C. 137,141,165,203,205,
    247
Wesleyans 100
West Maitland 120
Westminster 169
Wharf, Queen's 70
Wheelwright, Ted 229
Whitehall 159,173
Whiteside 7,104
Wick 142
Wickham, Anna 115,132
    Captain J.C. 23,45,48,58,59,62-64,
    69,70,86,111,118,119,125,126,134,
    138,161,181,206,213,214
Wide Bay 21
Wight, Rev. George 194,205,213,217,220,
    222,230,
Wilkes, William Charles 126,145
William Miles 162,163
William Walker & Co 13
Williams, John 52
Wilson, John Ker 22.39
    Robert 8
    William 8,59,153
Wise, George 111,131
Woogaroo 150,207
Wright, Alexander 50,62,113

Y

Yeerongpilly 148
York's Hollow 124
Yule, Lieutenant 62,63

Z

Zion's Hill 117,123